# ENVIRONMENT, POPULATION AND HUMAN SETTLEMENTS OF SUNDARBAN DELTA

## About the Author

**Dr. Anuradha Banerjee** has presented a holistic approach to the study of human settlements in the less studied Sundarban Delta. She has used a blend of theoretical and empirical information, as well as the latest analytical methods.

Dr. Banerjee has graduated with honours in Geography from Lady Brabourne College, Calcutta University. She has also to her credit a Master of Arts degree in Geography, followed by a Master of Philosophy from Jawaharlal Nehru University, New Delhi. A research fellow of the Council of Scientific and Industrial Research during 1988-1993, she had also been awarded with a Doctor of Philosophy from JNU. She belongs to the fraternity of Social Scientists, the thrust of her research being Population and Human Settlements. Her research line also includes Human Ecology, Environment, Resource Studies, Social Development, Women and Child Development and Participatory Research. She has worked in the project "Impact of Sea Level Rise Due to Green House Effect—West Bengal and Orissa Coasts" sponsored by Department of Environment and Forests, Government of India during 1991-1992. She has also been associated in various capacities with voluntary organisations. She is a life member of Institute of Landscape, Ecology and Ekistics, Calcutta; Indian Association for the Study of Population, and The Geographical Society of India.

At present the author is working as a consultant in the Human Resource Development area of the National Council of Applied Economic Research, New Delhi.

# ENVIRONMENT, POPULATION AND HUMAN SETTLEMENTS OF SUNDARBAN DELTA

ANURADHA BANERJEE

CONCEPT PUBLISHING COMPANY, NEW DELHI-110059

ISBN 81-7022-739-9.

First Published 1998



*Published and Printed by*
Ashok Kumar Mittal
**Concept Publishing Company**
A/15-16, Commercial Block, Mohan Garden
New Delhi 110059 (India)

Phones: 5648039, 5649024
Fax: 091-(11)-5648053

*DEDICATED*
*TO*
*THE MEMORY OF MY MOTHER*
*PROF. MAYA BANERJEE*

# FOREWORD

The deltaic West Bengal or Sundarbans is one of the least studied areas of the country. It is a difficult terrain with lesser influence of civilization, settlement and development; and it also attracted lesser attention of the academicians. Hence, the attempt made by Dr. Anuradha Banerjee is unique and commendable. Since this area is less explored and the official records are scanty, the observations have to be made based on fieldwork as well.

For geographers or environmental scientists, the Sundarban is unique. It is a challenge for them. The present study of human settlements in extremely interesting because it deals with human adjustments in partly stable and partly unstable environmental conditions. The Indian part of the Sundarbans falls in the South 24-Parganas district of West Bengal. There are several physical and human factors, which have influenced the present status of human settlements. The *Imperial Gazetteer* noted in 1908 that 'the process of land making has not yet ceased and where morasses and swamps, now gradually filling up, abound'. The wild animals of the area, including tigers, crocodiles and snakes were dangerous to human habitation. Further, the region was also infested with pirates which caused depopulation. Rennell's map of Lower Bengal (1772) shows this area as depopulated by the Maghs (pirates). Frequent cyclones have also come in the way of permanent settlements. Nevertheless, some areas were reclaimed and brought under cultivation by the coolies from the neighbouring districts of undivided Bengal. However, some areas were transformed to reserved or protected forests. Later these areas became tiger reserves, world heritage sites and biosphere reserves. The Sundarbans are claimed to be the largest estuarine forests in the world.

The imperial powers had to pass through the Sundarbans to reach their destinations or footholds in India. Some of these were

Calcutta, Hugli, Bandel and Chandannagar. From the 18th century the importance of Calcutta grew. This city in the north was connected with this region by all possible means, e.g. roads, railhead and canals. Due to such development, several outposts of civilization grew up in this inhospitable area. Some of these settlements are now in Bangladesh. The revenue history clearly reveals the initial difficulties in having settlements here. The region has a vast network of creeks and channels forming islands of different shapes and sizes.

The selection of the study area is important, as it is full of varieties in terms of location in relation to Calcutta metropolis, environment and economy. Unfortunately, it took so long to undertake a systematic study on human settlements. This volume should help in filling the void. For this investigation the author has used all possible sources, which includes census reports, district gazetteers, official reports, topographical maps and the NATMO publications. This was supported by extensive fieldwork based on questionnaires. A detailed household survey was designed with sample strength of about 400 covering 36 villages well spread over active and stable Delta. Quantitative and cartographic techniques have been judiciously used to process the data and to present the findings as well.

While going through the volume, one gets an impression of appropriate and latest approaches taken for the analysis of human settlements. These approaches are comparative regional, genetic or evolutionary, deductive, theoretical, quantitative and inductive. The whole work is divided into several chapters. The research design has been developed after reviewing the literature on the subject. The study contains details on physical and natural environment by providing the conventional background information on geology, geomorphology, climatology, ecology and the like. The most important aspect of this analysis is how these factors have been responsible for shaping the population and settlements of the Delta

The following part of the study deals with the population profile. It also includes the important aspects related to population such as density, distribution, composition etc. Here aim is to analyze the differences in population characteristics in different geo-ecological sub-regions as base for human settlements. The interesting aspect is the analysis of the different elements of the composition of population such as sex ratio, literacy, scheduled castes and tribes, and working population. All these characteristics have been supported with the help of tables and diagrams.

The important part of the study is about various aspects of settlements such as evolution, urban and rural, type and pattern, spacing, dispersion, and hierarchical arrangements. Here, in addition to maps and tables, mathematical analysis and photographs have been used in order to provide comprehensive picture of the settlements. The overshadowing influence of Calcutta as a major hindrance in the way of development has been highlighted.

A part of the study had to be based on intensive and extensive fieldwork due to lack of supplementary information. These aspects are related to the inter-regional patterns of human settlements which is based on surveyed villages spread well over the district. Out of 2,151 villages, 200 villages (100 from Active Delta and 100 from Stable Delta) were taken for detailed studies, which is a good sample size. It contains detail analysis based on age and location patterns, natural resource base and environmental constraints, human resource base, land use, functional classification, housing, basic amenities, rural infrastructure, trade connection and interaction, rural art and crafts, plans and proposals, quality of human settlements and the like.

This intensive study also contains the analysis of some aspects of population and human settlements of the deltaic West Bengal at a micro-level with the help of questionnaires from 400 households spread over 36 villages. It has all the usual details for studying the composition of population such as age and sex, marital status, economic profile, religion, caste, language, literacy, family assets, family planning and health care. The interesting part of the analysis is that it is based on the sub-regions of the Stable and Active Delta.

The last part contains some recommendations for human settlements. Here the author has pleaded for "sustainable human settlements" and has put forward 14 points for improvement. Some of these suggestions are important because they deal with the peculiar problems of the concerned district such as proximity to Calcutta, cyclones, forests and wild life. In order to make the work complete, there are appendices and bibliography as well.

Judging as a whole, the book is an excellent exposition to the understanding of a lesser region of the country. It is an original contribution to the literature of Environment Population and Human Settlements of the Sundarban Delta. The author has brought many new facts and analyzed their inter-relationships. The entire work bears the evidence of the author's capacity for critical examination and judgement of the delicate physical-human relationship.

26th January, 1998

**Dr. Prithvish Nag**
Director, NATMO
President, INCA & IASLIC

# PREFACE

With bountiful natural resources, the Sundarbans constitute one of the most fragile environmental zones of the country representing a delicate balance between man and nature. The region provides a unique case where land evolution and human occupancy is proceeding hand in hand. The innumerable creeks and islands, deltaic estuaries, mangrove forests, wild life varieties, tidal complicacies shaping the daily lifestyle, frequent visits of natural catastrophes; all provide a maze to the environmental and social scientist.

The aim of this study is to provide a systematic and all comprehensive view of this challenging, maritime country, the peculiar components of the natural environment, the population resources and how these in turn have shaped the various components and pattern of human settlements. The study is supportive of an intensive fieldwork covering even the end limit of human habitation in the margin of the Biosphere Reserve of the Sundarban forests. The inter-regional human settlement pattern is based on 200 surveyed villages equally distributed over the active and stable portions of the Delta. The in-depth household characteristics have been based on a survey of 400 households. The quality of human settlements as well as the quality of life has been also ascertained. Based on these realities certain recommendations aiming at sustainable human settlements have also been forwarded.

The interest for this area stemmed up during my M.Phil. research, "Natural and Human Resources of the Coastal Districts of India: A Geographical Analysis". At a later date, I had been working for a project, "Impact of Sea Level Rise Due to Green House Effect—West Bengal and Orissa Coasts" sponsored by the Department of Environment and Forests, Government of India. Further my geographical excursions to the Sundarbans gave me a visual exposure to the prevailing state of human settlements and environmental constraints, in these parts.

This work has been based on research of the Sundarbans for my doctoral thesis. The work is a mixture of literature and personal field experience, and combines various analytical tools for data interpretation. It has been written for individual researchers, educational and research organisations, non-governmental organisations, voluntary organisations, religious and charitable organisations, and also for the environment and social scientists and planners.

It gives me greatest pleasure to thank all my well wishers who have contributed in various capacities to this work. I wish to extend my immense gratitude and respect to my supervisor, Professor Sudesh Nangia, Chairperson, Centre for the Study of Regional Development, School of Social Sciences, Jawaharlal Nehru University, New Delhi; for her constant help and meticulous guidance during my research. Prof. M.K. Premi, Prof. Amitava Kundu, Prof. Aslam Mahmood and all my teachers at CSRD, JNU, have also provided me constant encouragement and inspiration. I acknowledge the Council of Scientific and Industrial Research (CSIR), for providing me the financial support through junior and senior research fellowships.

I owe my sincere regards to Dr. Prithvish Nag, Director, National Atlas and Thematic Mapping Organisation (NATMO) Government of India, for his valuable suggestions, help at various stages to the successful completion of my work. I was also encouraged by Dr. B. K. Roy, Retd. Deputy Director General, Census of India, and Retd. Director NATMO, GOI, for undertaking this work. At various stages of my field visits to the South 24-Parganas, I was immensely benefited by Sri G.N. Saha, Joint Director, Sri Manas Kumar Maity, Scientific Officer, and Dr. N.D. Bhattacharya, Retd. Deputy Director NATMO, GOI.

I express my sincere regards to Dr. Sudhansu Sekhar Sarkar, Head Master, Rajat Jubilee High School, Sadhupur, the end point of human habitation in the Sundarbans, who helped me to survey the interior Sundarbans, including the widow village, where nearly all the menfolk have lost their lives due to tiger attacks. In Sagar Island, I was guided by Sri Ashutosh Jana, LIC agent who introduced me to Kakdwip and Fraserganj, the caretaker of the youth hostel, and the ground engineer of Beguakhali Light House, due to whom a panoramic view of Sagar Island was possible. My knowledge of the severed islands like Khasimara, Ghoramara, which face severe erosion, was also possible due to them. Besides my deep appreciation goes to the local people all over the Delta, for their cooperation.

During my fieldwork, I received enormous assistance from different gram panchayats, Sub Divisional Officer Diamond Harbour; gram sevikas, and local leaders of Sonarpur and Rajarhat. In Mathurapur, Sri Jimut Bahan Chowdhury (NATMO), provided me guidance. Further, I acknowledge the cartographic assistance provided to me by Sri Ashok Kumar Mitra, Research Assistant, NATMO.

I am greately inspired by Prof D.B. Gupta, Retd. Head of Dept. Population Research Centre, Institute of Economic Growth, Delhi University, and Senior Consultant NCAER. I also wish to express my deep appreciation to be associated with NCAER, I express my regards to Dr. Rakesh Mohan (Director General) and to Mr. P. K. Krishnaswami (Registrar and Secretary) and to all my colleagues at the NCAER.

I owe endless debt to my father, Dr. R.K. Banerjee, Retd. Joint Director, NATMO, GOI, whose tremendous contribution to the art of map making, Aerial Photographs, Earth Science and Geography has constantly provided colour to my work.

I extend my heartfelt appreciation to my husband Sri Jay Prakash for his spontaneous support to my research work. I acknowledge all the sacrifices undergone by family members during my involvement with this book. The inspiration provided by little Twisha, my daughter, acted as a catalyst to all my efforts.

This book is the outcome of the endeavour of my mother, Late Prof. Maya Banerjee, Head of Department of Geography, Lady Brabourne College, Calcutta University. Her dream of myself undergoing the assignment successfully was shattered suddenly by her untimely demise. Her constant flavour of the subject, love, inspiration, guidance and immense sacrifice has blossomed through my text. Her shower of blessings and touch, live within me as an inseparable part of my life. I dedicate this book to her loving memory.

New Delhi,
Date 10.2.1998 ANURADHA BANERJEE

# CONTENTS

## 3. POPULATION PROFILE



## 4. SETTLEMENT PATTERN

## 6. A MICRO LEVEL ANALYSIS OF POPULATION AND HUMAN SETTLEMENTS

## 7. SUMMARY AND CONCLUSIONS

# LIST OF TABLES

# LIST OF MAPS AND FIGURES

# LIST OF PLATES

# 1

# INTRODUCTION

## 1.1 DEFINITIONS

Human Settlements present some of the most dynamic and challenging issues before us. For a long time it has been recognised that there is a very close inter-relationship between man, his environment and his habitat. The study of man and his visual imprints upon the physical landscape in the process of occupancy has been the core of interest of the Geographers for ages. With researches intensifying and broadening into the space and time phenomena, however, the study of Population and Human Settlements have become the focus of all related disciplines; that has transcended it to a very complex, all inclusive and existing new concept.

The most significant theoretical framework of Human Settlements was developed in recent years by Doxiadis through *Ekistics*, the Science of Human Settlements[1] popularly known as the 'Ekistic School of Greece'. The concept of Human Settlements incorporates two major dimensions: Geographic and Population, where the sequential stages begin with 'Man' and end with the concept of the 'Universal City'. In 1976, during the Conference on Human Settlements in Vancouver, a *global recognition* was given to the holistic concept of Human Settlements. Doxiadis in his book titled, *Action for Human Settlements* put forward the definition 'Human Settlements are territorial arrangements made by Anthropos/Man himself'.[2] Doxiadis's definition was given a new shape later in 1987 by Alexander B. Leman, who proposed a second definition, 'Human Settlements are spatial/operational arrangements made by humans within certain scales, in order to support life and to pursue their aspirations, goals and targets'.[3] The terms spatial/operational aims to include fully all the aspects pertaining to Human Settlements in an interlocking and integrative way; because it denotes the practical, non-static, continuously changing aspects of the spatial arrangements made by human beings. The definition also tends to impart the fact that Human Settlements do have many similarities with natural, biological entities; and Human Settlements do mutually interact with the natural systems (eco-systems) within which they are made, and within whose constraints they must operate. Yet another definition put forward at the UN Conference of 1976 defines Human Settlements as 'the totality of human community-whether city, town or village-with all the social, material, organisational, spiritual and cultural elements that sustain it'.[4] The dynamism of Human Settlements in the spatio-temporal context provide useful tools for analysing the 'sequence of change in the cultural landscape'.[5]

## 1.2 THE REGION

The Sundarban Delta of West Bengal in the South 24-Parganas District is quite unique in its own way. It forms the western part of the largest and Active Delta of the world,[6] the Ganga Brahmaputra Delta, with its estuarine system, an intricate coast line, clusters of smaller deltas, innumerable islands, criss-crossed by numerous distributaries, provide a great diversity in the eco-system. It is a low flat country, which would be completely submerged if the sea level rose by only a few metres.

The region presents a highly productive environment, supporting a variety of economic activities, based on agriculture, fishery and forestry. However, 'the littoral fringe of West Bengal is economically backward area. The soil is young in the sense that it is being freshly laid to form numerous deltaic islands'.[7] Many constraints lead to this backwardness. But on the other hand the rich potential of natural resources has understandably attracted migration of people to this area. Human Settlements have come up and some of the forestlands have been converted into Human Settlements.

It is known that 'Pattern of Human Settlements vary significantly according to complex and interrelated Historical, Geographic, Cultural, Political, Economic and Demographic factors'.[8] The peculiar components of natural environment or the local ecosystems have given rise to variations in population densities and have attributed distinctive types and characters to the Human Settlements here. The much-forested littoral fringe of the deltaic estuary is known as the Sundarbans. This was surveyed and delineated as a Special Forest

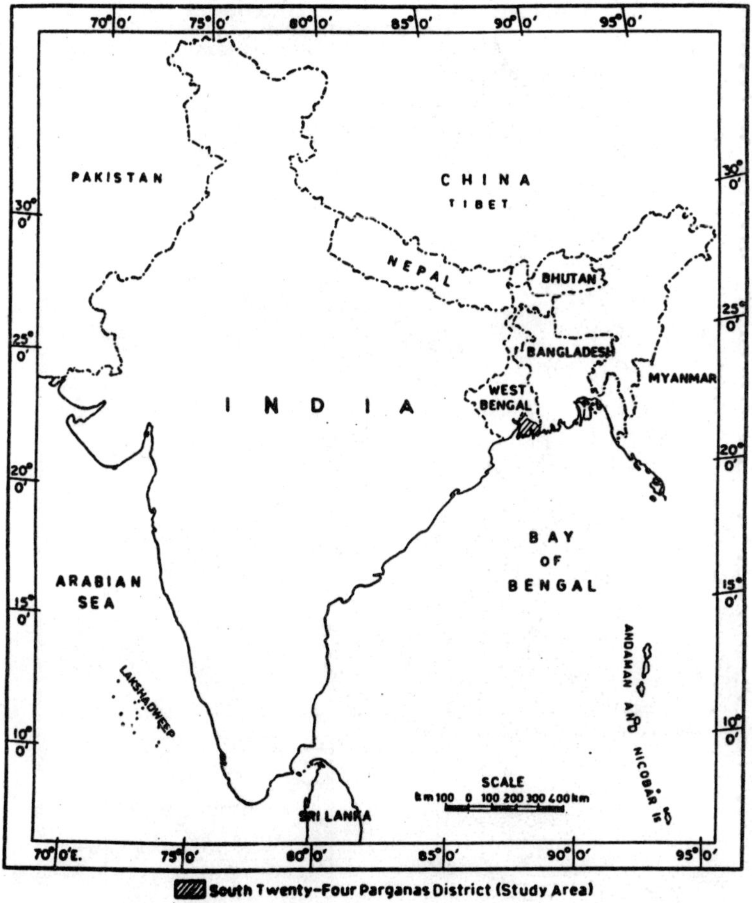


**MAP 1.1** : Location of South 24-Parganas District in India

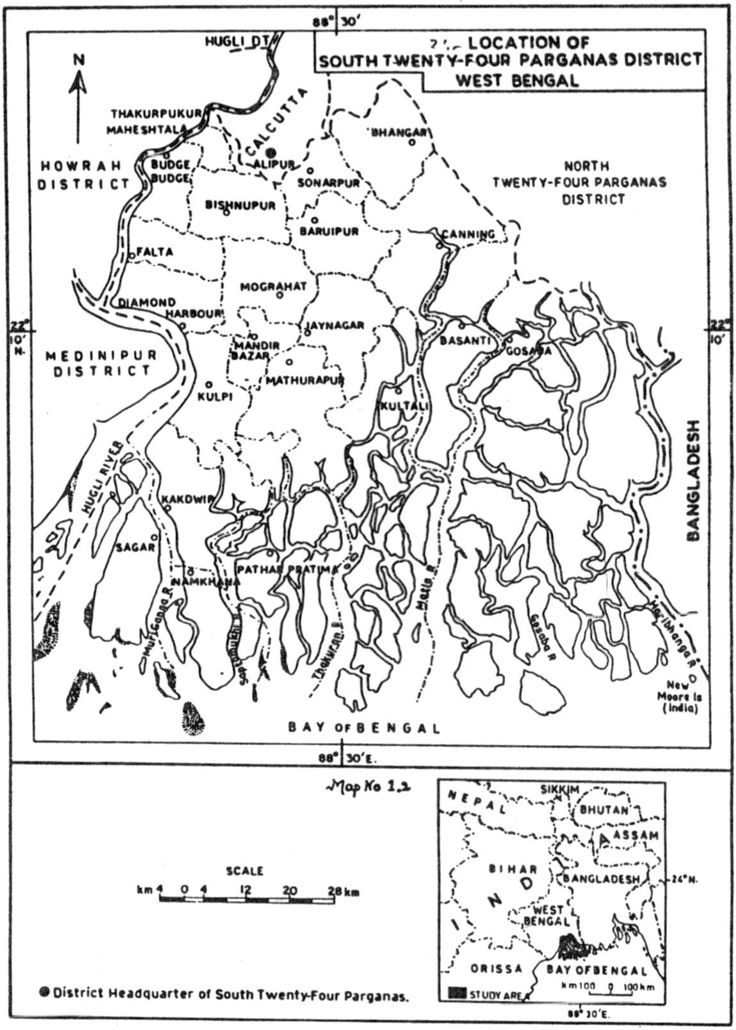


**MAP 1.2** : Location of South 24-Parganas District in West Bengal

Cover by Mr. Dampier and Lt. Hodges during 1829 to 1830. This at present encompasses approximately an area of 10,000 sq. km. in India.

The Sundarban Delta once extended far into the interior, even as far as Job Charnock's famous 'mid-day halt', which led to the foundation of Calcutta. However, the present limit of the Sundarban Forests is actually a modification of the of the Dampier and Hodges Line, adjusted according to the administrative boundaries of the police stations or blocks. Out of the 22 blocks of the deltaic South Twenty Four Parganas district, 8 blocks fall within the Dampier and Hodges Line of actual forest cover. This region comprises of a network of tidal channels, river creeks and islands, the land being still under formation. Unfortunately, before the normal delta building process could proceed further, human beings started interfering with the natural environment. In this premature stage of land formation, the normal geomorphic processes proved to be totally incompatible with the prospect of Human Settlements. Since priority and immediacy prevailed over futuristic desires, nature had to be tamed, environment changed and ecology disrupted, to meet the requirements of this human habitation.

In the Sundarban Delta one would envisage a changing set of environmental factors as one proceeds from the coast towards the interior. The littoral margin is constrained by environmental hazards of rigorous salinity, severe soil erosion, furies of storms and cyclones, tidal bores, periodic inundations as well as by the menace of wild animals. The forested part of the Sundarbans is usually uninhabited in marked contrast to the western, northern, and even the north-eastern parts. Fishing and collection of forest produce are typical primary activities in the littoral parts in contrast to monoculture of rice in the interior Sundarbans.

The Stable Delta incorporating 14 blocks lies to the north of the Active Delta with its fertile alluvium soil and more favourable physical and cultural environment influencing the Human Settlement pattern, the most dominating influence being exerted by the highly industrialised and commercial belt of the Calcutta District. Therefore with increasing distance from the coast, Human Settlements undergo a change in not only type, spatial distribution and density, but also in land utilisation, economy, and interaction among settlements, so much so that a marked contrast arises within the Stable and Active portions of the Delta.

Coastal communities being open to the outside influence have developed over the ages a marked identity and a distinctive culture. But in the Sundarban Delta, certain frictional drag on the society, especially in the littoral portions constitute additional problems to the existing physical constraints. There exists illiteracy and ignorance about the more effective and remunerative methods of production from land and aquatic sources. Additional problems like non-availability of better labour saving productive equipment and accessories for individual artisan folks, dearth of amenities and infrastructural facilities, like roads, suitable communication links, storage godowns, easily accessible markets, landing sites, coupled with inadequate financial support in proper time, lack of awareness about community participation and sustainability among cultivators and fishermen; and all these put together have rendered them easy pawns for exploitation by money-lenders, businessmen and landlords.

Hence the book illustrates the inter-relationships between Environment, Population and Human Settlements, in different portions of the Delta, in order to build-up a clear perspective of the problems and constraints in ensuring a sustained socio-economic development of human beings in their different environmental set-ups and human settlement systems.

## 1.3 OBJECTIVES

The major objectives pursued in this study, are related to the contrasting character between the Stable Delta to the north and the Active Delta to the south. The district of South 24-Parganas is a rich resource based region. By dimensions of area and population, again it is indeed a large region. However, without massive efforts of mobilising all available resources, no appreciable changes in the region can be achieved. So as a first step, an understanding of certain basic issues becomes inevitable.

1. To appraise scientifically the environmental/geo-ecological factors, natural constraints and hazards and other physical parameters that give rise to variations in the meso and micro regions of the study area, as base for Human Settlements.

2. To identify the areas of differential population density and distribution, population composition and the areas of rapid changes in population growth, and to appraise the causes thereof.
3. To evaluate scientifically the changing, underlying forces and various environmental factors responsible for the variations in form, type, density, spatial distribution, concentration and geo-ecological patterning of settlements as well as their changes from the littoral to the interior.
4. To portray the micro-regional contrasts of the study area, the natural and human resource base attributing to the various settlement types of the region in relation to the problems and prospects of the settlements, and thereby workout the hierarchical system of settlements.
5. To probe into the regional development plans initiated for the development of the problem regions and to find the constraints regarding their implementation.
6. To trace out the demographic and socio-economic profile of the household members and their rural to rural and rural to urban interactions among settlements leading to their developmental process and scale of amenities available.
7. Finally, to summarise all the observations made during the course of study and the net results thereof.

## 1.4 HYPOTHESES

The hypotheses that were tested during the course of the study entail :

1. The population size and density of population, together with the changes in density increases from the coastal margin towards the interior.
2. The growth rate of population reveals faster changes from the littoral towards the interior.
3. The urban areas by contrast reveal strikingly high population densities and higher growth rates than the rural counterparts.
4. The areal and population density size of the settlements tend to have an inverse relationship in the deltaic zone; for instance, the population density size of the Human Settlements closer to the coast is smaller, but the areal size larger; and reciprocal will hold true as one proceeds towards the interior.

5. Agglomerated and compact type of settlements tend to increase towards the Calcutta Region in the North, this in contrast gives rise to dispersed and isolated forms towards the littoral.
6. Again the spacing of settlements (inter settlement distances) tend to fall as one moves from the coast towards the interior.
7. Considering the homogeneity of landscape, the deltaic settlements rather have a tendency towards uniform, random distribution rather than complete clustering.
8. The type of economic activities are more of a primary base in the littoral than in the interior.
9. The intensity of landuse increases with increasing distance from the coast (expressed by the availability of a greater amount of fallow land and cultivable wastes near the coast).
10. The proportion of non-agricultural landuse tend to increase from the coast towards the interior indicating a variation in the nature and types of economic activities from the coast towards the interior.
11. Interaction among settlements and its frequency is more intense towards the interior than near the coast.
12. Quality of Human Settlements as well as Quality of Housing is poor near the coastal zone and away from it, a better quality may be discernable.

## 1.5 DATA COLLECTION

The study entails the collection of both secondary and primary level data to analyse the settlement pattern of the Sundarban Delta.

### Secondary Data

Secondary Data have been collected to gather information regarding the geographical and ecological base within which the Human Settlements of the region operate or face constraints, their population characteristics and the pattern of settlements of the region, both rural and urban. They have been procured from the Census of India Volumes, Final Population Totals, West Bengal District Census Handbook of 1981, series 23 Part XIII-A and Part XIII-B, of South 24-Parganas (Village and Townwise Primary Census Abstract and Village and Town Directories). The 1991 data has been drawn from unpublished district census floppies of South Twenty Four Parganas.

Other sources include "Statistical Abstract of West Bengal 1978, Census of India - District Handbook of 24-Parganas; West Bengal" by Asok Mitra 1951, Government of West Bengal Press, Alipore; "An Account of Land Management in West Bengal 1870 to 1950, Census of India 1951" by Asok Mitra, West Bengal Government Press, Alipore; "A Statisatical Abstract of South Twenty Four Parganas" by W.W. Hunter; "Regional Divisions of India - A Cartographic Analysis" Series I Vol XXII West Bengal, Census of India by B.K. Roy and Vijoy S. Verma; District Gazetteers of 24-Parganas; Project Report on Sundarban Development prepared by the Sundarban Development Board (Government of West Bengal in Collaboration with the Ministry of Agriculture and Irrigation, Government of India, July 1979; Census Volumes on Urban Population, 1991, and finally the Topographical Sheets by the Survey of India (1965) pertaining to South Twenty Four Parganas and documents of the National Atlas and Thematic Mapping Organisation, Ministry of Science and Technology, Government of India. The topographical sheets of the Survey of India were published in 1973. 11 such sheets bearing the numbers of 79 B/2, B/6, B/10, B/12, B/16; 79 C/2, C/5, C/9, C/13, C/14 and 79 G/1 have been referred to.The census period chosen for such data include both 1981 and 1991, in order to probe also into the temporal differences.

### Primary Data

To strengthen, support and develop the secondary data base, primary data have been collected from extensive sample surveys of the villages and households of South 24-Parganas during 1992 based on various criteria.

## 1.6 LOCATION

Lying in close juxtaposition with the conurbation of Calcutta, the Hugli-Matla estuary (a part of the Ganga- Brahmaputra Delta) is the study area. Administratively it comprises of the district of South 24-Parganas and presents a marked contrast from the immediate littoral of the Bay of Bengal in the South to the highly industrialized, commercialised and urbanised boundary of Calcutta District in the North; the International Boundary of Bangladesh in the East from the River Hugli (separating Medinipur District) in the West; extending from 21° 31' and 22° 40' North latitudes, 88° 05' and 89° 06' East Longitudes. It covers a total area of 6388 sq.km and supports a total population of 5.8 million in 1991. The district comprises the last or is the outlying district among the 17 districts of the State, and consist of 2151 rural settlements or villages (1991) and 42 urban centres or towns spread over 22 Blocks of 1991 (Police Stations of 1981), of which 8 comprise the famous Tidal Mangrove forested, wildlife infested and much challenging Sundarban Forests of the southern littoral bounded by the Dampier Hodges line and having a separate identity of its own.

## 1.7 SAMPLE SURVEY DESIGN

Based on certain geographical and ecological parameters, the study area has been compartmented into Meso and Micro regions for a detailed insight. The samples for survey have been selected with a view to have a coverage of each geo-ecological subregion.

First of all it becomes imperative to state that two sets of survey work has been conducted. The first set involves a detailed village survey covering 200 villages all over the district, selected at a stratified random basis with 100 villages from the Stable Delta of the Hugli in the North and 100 villages from the Active Delta of the Sundarbans in the South.

In the next stage a detailed household survey has been designed with a sample strength of 400 covering the households of 36 villages, 18 villages from the Stable delta and 18 villages from the Active delta. The regional distribution has been selected with population proportions in mind.

## 1.8 THE QUESTIONNAIRES

The questionnaires used for the collection of the primary data used for a micro-level insight into the region has been prepared at two levels.

I. At the village level, and

II. At the household level.

### I. The Village Survey Questionnaire

The village study questionnaires have been framed such that every detail at the village level (200 villages) can be observed minutely through certain major sections and subsections. They provide information regarding :

1. Origin, age and location of the villages;
2. The natural resource base and environmental constraints;
3. Type, pattern and distribution of the villages including their site and situation;
4. Population resource base of the villages;
5. Housing and basic amenities;
6. Economic activities of the villagers;
7. Education, medical, credit, marketing and communication facilities;
8. Village arts and crafts;
9. Government plans for the area; and
10. The trade connections.

**II. The Household Study Questionnaire**

A separate set of questionnaires have been framed for survey work of the 400 households and families with an aim to trace the family characteristics of individual households.The broad heads include:

1. Locational characteristics, number of members, religion, caste, language spoken, age, sex, marital status and literacy level.
2. The next section deals in detail with the employment characteristics followed by
3. Pattern of migration of the households;
4. Family assets;
5. Housing and other amenities;
6. Level of personal hygiene;
7. Family interaction pattern;
8. Mortality, health, family planning and care of the mother and child;
9. Environmental hazards and consequences; and
10. Lastly the social environment faced by the individual families.

## 1.9 METHODOLOGY AND CARTOGRAPHIC TECHNIQUES

The study incorporates different methods and cartographic techniques used for data compilation, data analysis and data representation through various statistical, qualitative, quantitative and cartographic techniques.

### A. Qualitative Methods

As a first step towards a regional analysis, a qualitative regional approach has been used to identify the geo-ecological regions and subregions and their respective settlement pattern, by analysing the relevant topographical sheets published by the Survey of India.

### B. Quantitative and Statistical Methods

The various statistical methods used include the calculation of simple percentages, ratios, growth rates, frequency distribution, and measures of central tendency.

The quantitative methods used for settlement analysis are related to the methods of identifying the spacing of settlements; their degree of dispersion, through nearest neighbour analysis; size-clustering, and size classification of all the rural settlements by frequency distribution followed by certain statistical methods as rank size rule, coefficient of determination, correlation and regression analysis, tests of significance to study the spatial change of settlements have also been used.

Computers have been used at various stages of work specially during the compilation of village and household information by using the LOTUS for data compilation and SPSS for data processing. In addition, a theoretical model of villages was developed based on selected development indicators and a hierarchy of settlements based on development indicators is thus identified.

Finally the interaction pattern, and frequency of interaction between the families and the villages have been calculated.

### C. Cartographic and Mapping Techniques

At the first instance, the base map of the region has been prepared by compiling all the 22 Blocks by bringing them at par to one scale and then by fitting them to the district boundary, the sources of information being the District Census Handbooks, Survey of India topographical sheets and Census Cartographic Analysis of West Bengal.

Certain maps showing distributional pattern of settlements have been made directly from the Survey of India topographical sheets of Scale 1 : 50,000, utilising the conventional symbols.

Most of the thematic maps have been made by using choropleths, after arranging data through the range method.

Statistical diagrams like graphs, bars, pie diagrams and the pyramids have been used to present certain data.

**D. Approach**

In order to study the Population and Human Settlements of the Sundarban Delta in South-24 Parganas, over space and time the following approaches have been followed:

(i) By considering the region as an aggregate whole,

(ii) Comparative regional approach or studying the characteristics of population and settlements in the various geo-ecological subregions,

(iii) Genetic or evolutional approach involving the study of the histogenesis of settlements,

(iv) Deductive, theoretical and quantitative approach, where certain statistical methods have been used to study the population and settlement pattern from secondary data base. This has been done at two levels viz. at the regional level (geo-ecological) and also at the block level, and

(v) Finally, an Inductive approach has been used through case studies again at two levels viz. the village and at the household level, to study the Environment, Population and Settlements of the area.

## 1.10 ORGANISATION OF CHAPTERS

The study aims to portray the characteristics, distribution, attributes and interlinkages of settlement patterns basically in the light of man - environment interaction and is divided into the following seven chapters:

**Chapter 1** is the *INTRODUCTION* which deals with the statement of the problem, objectives, hypotheses, data base, the study area, the sample survey, the questionnaires, methodology and cartographic techniques, approach to the study, organisation of chapters, a review of relevant literature and references.

**Chapter 2** *NATURAL ENVIRONMENT* provides a brief background to the Geology, Tectonicity, Evolutionary History, Geomorphology, Fluvial characteristics, Climatology, Pedology and Bio-

Geography. Further based on all these parameters certain Geographical and Ecological regions have been identified, which have been used in the text as regions to understand Population and Human Settlements.

**Chapter 3** *POPULATION PROFILE* contains an analysis of the spatial distribution, density, composition and growth of population (1981-1991). Each of these topics carry further subdivisions like the composition of population has been studied in the light of Demographic composition, Social and Economic composition. The aim is primarily to analyse the differences in population characteristics in the different geo-ecological subregions as base for Human Settlements.

**Chapter 4** *SETTLEMENT PATTERN* covers the study of the origin of settlements, rural and urban, and the spatial changes in settlement patterns. Each of the sub-sections carry further divisions. For example Rural settlement patterns have been analysed in the light of (a) site and locational factors, (b) pattern of settlements and (c) spatial distribution through spatial and dispersion analysis and village-size distribution. The Urban settlements too of the region has been studied in the light of evolution and growth, spatial distribution, urban primacy and rank size rule.

**Chapter 5** and **6** basically comprise of case studies.

**Chapter 5** is titled as *INTER-REGIONAL PATTERN OF POPULATION AND HUMAN SETTLEMENTS.* This chapter contains information on age and location pattern of the villages, natural resource base and environmental constraints, human resource base with a focus on the distribution, density, religious and caste composition as well as migration affecting population growth. The next sub-section deals with the characteristics of the rural settlements followed by housing and basic amenities, utilisation of land, economic activities of villages, trade connections, village arts and crafts. Finally the existing plans and future proposals of the region has been studied followed by a study of the Quality of Human Settlements in the district.

**Chapter 6** is titled as *A MICRO-LEVEL ANALYSIS OF POPULATION AND HUMAN SETTLEMENTS.* This chapter contains an analysis of the household characteristics in 36 villages with their representation from all the geo-ecological regions. The information included pertains to demographic characteristics of the families like age-sex pattern, marital status, age at marriage and migration. The next section, the economic profile of the households have been studied in detail followed by the social profile of the households. In the coming section, the topics that have been included are family assets, housing and basic amenities, mortality and health, environmental hazards and consequences, and the social environment of the families. The interaction pattern, commutation, frequency and purpose of family movements have been studied in great detail followed by the Quality of Housing.

Finally **Chapter 7** *SUMMARY AND CONCLUSIONS* states the summary of the observations and research findings made in the above chapters, the general conclusions drawn and the recommendations that can be suggested for the development of man in his natural and cultural surroundings in the study area.

## 1.11 OVERVIEW OF LITERATURE

The emergent problems of the study area, consequent upon different resource base, changing environment types, urbanisation and its impact, consequences of natural disasters on human activities, influence man and his habitat.

The literature reviewed has been divided into two heads viz.

I. Broad aspects of Human Settlements necessary to build up a theoretical base; and
II. Studies aimed to cover certain thematic issues, pertaining to the study area.

### I. Settlement Studies

Early contribution to the study of settlements was put forward by C. Ritter, A Meitzen and F. Von Richthofen[9] in the 19th century who prepared the foundation stones for a major focus on settlement research work.

It was Meitzen[10] who distinguished the different German settlement types based on ethnicity, and termed the well mapped cluster settlements as 'haufendorfer'.

In the early part of the twentieth century, the concept of central place theory in identifying the hierarchy of settlements was developed based on the pioneering work of W. Christaller[11] (1933). He worked out a general deductive theory explaining the horizontal as well as the vertical features of spatial organisation.

Starting from the same basic assumptions, Losch[12] developed a model of spatial organization which has a more elaborate economic base and stipulates Christaller's as a special case; but many scholars such as Hermansen point out that the models of Losch and Christaller are viewed as supplementing each other.

The most significant theoretical framework to study the complex system ranging from Man to the Universal City has been developed by Doxiadis[13] through the science of Human Settlements, which can be represented through the Ekistic Logarithmic Scale (ELS). The ELS has two dimensions, Geographic and Population, making 15 Ekistic units in a hierarchical order from Anthropos or man to 'Ecumenopolis'. The units contain 5 elements i.e. Nature, Anthropos, Society, Shells and Networks. These elements joined together form the optimization of the quality of man's relationship with his environment.

Many scholars have attempted to analyse the spatial structure and spatial system through process-type explanation. The pioneering work in this field was initiated by Erik Bylund[14] who describes the four simple types of colonization process applicable to the spread of settlements within the frame of basic assumptions of areal uniformity and equal accessibility available in all directions. His approach has been followed by workers of different countries to test the hypothesis in diverse ecological settings.

Curry[15] has adopted location theory to formulate the settlement theory with a maximum efficiency postulate based on optimizing behaviour and competition; whereas Olsson[16] tried to predict the functional and geometrical properties of the spatial phenomena.

Again the growing impact of biological sciences, has impressed some scholars to test the dispersal theory of ecology in the context of settlement colonization. Hudson[17] has developed his location theory of rural settlements presuming that human colonization can be treated as an analogue to the spread of plants and animals.

Some typological and terminological framework for the concepts of rural settlements according to form, function, genesis and development has been presented by Uhlig[18] and his team. This work is mainly oriented towards German technology which has been further elaborated by Eidt[19]. He has discussed the conceptual framework of the various settlement elements; as for example, position, form, structure, distribution etc.

One of the pioneering works regarding settlement pattern of India was done by K.H. Buschman[20], who studied the settlement pattern and housetypes in different regions of India specially in Assam, Rajasthan, Maharashtra, Mysore (Karnataka), Orissa and Andhra Pradesh. He studied meticulously the Toda Villages of the Nilgiris, the Khasi Villages of the Khasi Hills and other tribal villages in other parts of the country that mark a close relationship between natural environment and settlement type.

Specific regional studies on settlement types and pattern has been done by Indian scholars from time to time. For instance C.D. Deshpande[21] has studied the settlement types of Bombay and Karnataka, E. Ahmad[22] has studied the rural settlements of Uttar Pradesh and A.N. Bhattacharya's[23] work describes the rural settlements of the Upper Ganga Valley.

R.L. Singh's[24] contribution specially regarding rural settlements also provides an important theoretical basis for researchers. He has attempted to discuss in a scientific manner the meaning, objectives and scope of this branch[25], their evolution specially in terms of the Middle Ganga Valley[26] and the dwelling pattern in the umland of Benaras[27].

K.N. Singh's[28] work on the Medieval Town and Village settlements in Eastern Uttar Pradesh, provides an insight into the evolution of basic territorial and settlement pattern within five time periods, through simulative structural model. Further, he has pointed out how the infilling processes have given rise to three basic types of settlement units; i.e. 'pargana', 'tappa' and 'gaon'. In another paper the author tries to explain how far the morphology of the Indian villages[29] are affected by religio-spiritual and secular forces. He has also discussed about the economic distance, social space, ritual and population distances working for a long time in the rural society.

A.B. Mukherjee[30] has stated that the Siwalik Hills reveal a multiplicity of linear belts of rural settlements which are sited on 'choe' terraces and are comprised of uni-caste, uni-clan or multiclan social groups. Linear pattern has developed through the process of repetitive fission of and diffusion from the re-entrant parent settlement with which the series is linked, historically, genetically, functionally, socially and culturally; the process having been synthesised to formulate Multiple Collinear Diffusion Model.

S.P. Dasgupta and S.M. Misra[31] has discussed the different methodologies used for mapping the rural settlements in India; covering aspects such as spacing; concentration and pattern of settlements and the work done by National Atlas And Thematic Mapping Organisation in this regard.

The influence of physiography, drainage, transport and communication lines on rural settlements has been studied by D.K. Singh, B. Routray and S. Jena[32]. The study is supported by the spatial location of mean centre of settlements for the individual micro region of the state through statistical analysis.

V.K. Asthana[33] has tried to visualize the settlements around Almora through histogenesis, pattern formation and morphogenesis of settlements; which refer simultaneously to the developmental process of settlements with time, space and synthesis in an intigrated spatial unit.

The spatial characteristics of rural settlements in the Middle Ganga Plain has been studied by K.N. Singh, Rana P.B. Singh and Dinesh K. Singh[34]. The spatial arrangement has been shown on both the scales i.e. regional-showing the distributional pattern and local i.e. the structural organisation. On the basis of the latter theme a classification of rural settlements has been also attempted.

Based on the Nearest Neighbour Technique, an analysis of rural settlements of Mewar, Rajasthan has been done by C.R. Pathak and R.K. Dhabai[35]. The study also highlights whether or not the structure, pattern and tendency of separation of the rural settlements are predominantly governed by physical environment and social structure of the people.

R.Y. Singh's[36] study on the hierarchy of rural settlements of Depalpur Tahsil of Indore district, Madhya Pradesh brings out clearly that hierarchy is a product of centrality. Certain functional indicators have been selected by the author to analyse the hierarchy levels of settlements and these have been also related to the population size.

The analysis of some of the basic issues involved with the distance, direction and dimension of the spatial organisation of five different rural settlements of North India has been studied by B.B. Singh[37].

Jagdish Singh[38], gives us an all comprehensive view of the settlement characteristics of the Upper Damodar Valley Region in the light of which economic development has been analysed. The background information has been on physiographic, demographic and industrial characteristics of the region. This has been supported by a detailed study of rural and urban settlements with special reference to their spacing and morphological structures. Some case studies of individual towns like Hazaribagh, Giridih and Sindri have also been undertaken. The author has also presented quite a commendable study of the hierarchy of service centres of the region using Christaller's Central Place Theory and has concluded by portraying the problems and planning perspectives separately.

A meticulous study of the settlement pattern around Delhi has been done by Sudesh Nangia[39]. The author takes into account the unprecedented expansion of the Metropolitan City since independence, and its impact on the regional structure. A radius of 25 miles has been selected to analyse the characteristics and attributes of settlement pattern with an attempt to delimit the Delhi Region of metropolitan influence. As the metropolis expands according to the author, it uplifts the base of its region, bringing it into its web of urbanisation. It becomes necessary then to identify the spatial limit or regional boundary upto which the settlements fall within the direct impact of the metropolis, to identify the characteristics of settlements within and beyond the boundary and measure their intensity of interaction within the metropolitan city. Such a work is of necessity to envisage any plan for the integrated area development of the metropolis and its region.

Tiwari and Khan[40] have analysed the characteristics of rural service centres of Pratapgarh District. The functional inter-dependency and co-ordination within the region is organized through a number of service centres which not only act as a bridge between urban areas and the country side but are also harbingers of development and modernization. These service centres may be urban or rural in nature but they play a vital role in propagating new innovations and implementing development policies and programmes for rural upliftment. The author highlights the distribution of service centres, their hierarchical order and problems of delineation of their service zones.

The dynamics of an urban fringe has been studied by Mahanta[41] involving the changing demographic, economic, social and morphological characteristics of the fringe areas of Shillong. Here there has been a shift to permanent agriculture, phenomenal population growth rate, declining sex ratio, greater influx of immigrants and heterogeneity in speech forms.

Rank-size relationship of central places have been studied by B.L. Singh[42] in the Mithila Plains, Bihar. He has also tried to identify the pattern of central places in a temporal dimension and primacy of the primate town, based on secondary data. Average discrepancy between the actual and expected size of individual centres irrespective of their size shows that central space spectrum of the Mithila Plains deviates considerably from the presumed one on the basis of rank-size rule.

Dr P. Nag[43], in his book '*Population, Settlement and Development in Zambia*' has discussed interesting findings of Zambian Settlements. Spatial analysis and growth of population, rural development, urban settlements and urbanization, housing and squatter settlements have been studied by him in detail supported by suitable quantitative settlement analysis.

## II. Thematic Case Studies

The topics can be categorised into five groups—

1. Physical Parameters, Natural Environment, Landuse and Disasters,
2. Natural Resource Studies,
3. Population and Settlement Studies,
4. Economic Activities and Infrastructure,
5. Regional Development and Planning.

### *1. Physical Parameters, Natural Environment, Landuse and Disaster*

R. Sengupta, C.S. Murty and P.M.A. Bhattathiri[44], make certain salient observations regarding the estuarine region of River Ganga, which, they feel, has poor water quality and consequently weak recipient capacity. This report presents physical, chemical and biological observations in the last 160 Km stretch of River Ganga for a period of 3 years. A.K. Ghosh[45], draws comparison between two different types of coastal districts of Medinipur and South 24-Parganas extending over a coastal area of 0.82 m ha. The distinctly different ecological and physiographic features of the different coastal districts, however, are subject to same severe cyclonic storms. The effect of recent developmental activities by way of reclamation, intensive fishing, setting up of industries in coastal zone on one hand, and environment programme on conserving Sundarbans as a Biosphere Reserve, on the other, are discussed by the author in this paper.

K.K. Dasgupta[46] observes that the coastal belt of West Bengal is disaster prone due to the severity of cyclonic storms. The paper includes the problems created by cyclones to the coastal population, mitigation of the disaster by a more organised and scientific warning system, protection of water supply sources, construction of specifically designed coastal huts, and strengthening of the enormous stretches of coastal embankments at low cost. The author also clearly spells out that not much has yet been done to mitigate the disaster in the coastal belt with science and technology inputs and that without delay, efforts are required to be directed in that direction. K.K. Bandhyopadhay[47] also speaks of the susceptibility of coastal areas to disaster; out of which the cyclonic storms have the most destructive potential. He suggests the implementation of disaster warding methods; specially detection, tracking and prediction of cyclone movements, improved warning system and other relevant aids. A.N. Biswas[48] provides physical and numerical simulation models for an insight into the phenomena of cyclonic storms and suggests, positive and preventive measures to combat natural disasters.

S. Chattopadhyay[49], has identified the littoral fringe of West Bengal as an economically backward area. In his paper, he therefore, examined the opportunities to overcome the economic backwardness which he thinks, in this region, is an euphemism for the restrictive ecosystem that subtends between social practice and natural environment. The author also examines more fully the attributes of the ecosystem of the region, and to see in what ways the confining environments is influencing the agricultural practices in this tract.

A.K. Paul[50] has explained the physiography and dune environment of the Sundarban region. According to him the coastal area of the Sundarbans comprise monotonously flat plains of extensive fluvio-marine deposits of the Ganga. The only exceptions in this regard are the complex dune ridges and flats on the isolated islands of the South Western Sundarbans. Dune environment, evolution of the dunes, main landscape characters, and the present landuse system of the dune landscape are highlighted in this paper. The author also states that the dunes have a special importance in the low-lying coast of Sundarbans, which are frequently affected by tidal waves, cyclonic storms and high sea waves. Dunes are not sufficiently developed in the rest of the coastal region due to the prevalence of offshore wind and its low energy. In author's opinion the dune systems of the Sundarbans are unwisely used by man. They need proper prevention and management for their environmental protection in the lowlying areas of the region.

The author with M.K. Bandopadhyay[51] has also dealt with the coastal sand dunes of Sagar Island, the causes of dune formation and the dune classification (Sundarbans). The underlying morphology of this island is given in detail by the same author in the "Morphology of Sagar Island—a part of the Ganga Delta"[52].

A.K. Paul, M.K. Bandyopadhyay and A Chowdhury[53] have studied the various morpho-ecological conditions of the shallow estuarine and coastal mudflats of the Sundarban region. The findings of the article reveal that the topographical variations in the mudflats depend upon the discharge of silt and clay, hydrological stress and the process of erosion in the mudflats which varies from place to place. Morphological and ecological variations of the Sundarban mudflats are also controlled by the seasonal discharge of fresh water and fluctuations of sea level. The floristic structure and community are affected by the nature of the substratum, tidal influx, wave action and natural composition of the mud flat which controls the food chain in the Sundarban estuarine eco-system.

B. Ghosh and B.R. Ghosh[54] deal with a brief Geographical study of the Sundarbans of West Bengal and caution to the premature construction of river side embankment that has hindered the natural process of land development by spill—water filling. The article also points towards the implementation of a solid plan and programme in this part for the maintenance of the forested part, to have economic resources on one hand and deflecting the direct and severe blow of the cyclonic storms on the other.

## 2. Natural Resource Studies

S. Roy and C. Mondal[55] have portrayed a good account of the flora and fauna of the Sundarban forested area since the, play an important role in controlling the environment and are considered to be one of the most important natural resources for industry as well. The article highlights that the Sundarban forests have a tremendous influence upon the economy of the South Twenty Four Parganas District.

C. Ghosh[56] has studied the forest resources of Sundarbans and has stated how satellite data with the synoptic view and repetitive coverage may provide the best approach to monitor changes in forest cover and how it can be used to visualize an inventory of forest resources.

Kalyan Chakraborty[57] has dealt with various intricate environmental imperatives for the coastal ecosystem of Sundarban. The development of the area lies in the maintenance of an ecological balance in the fragile ecosystem. The low plant-animal diversity for Sundarban is clearly a warning signal for ensuring strict protection of this biotope for the future impending disasters. According to the author, Sundarban mangrove exhibit higher calorie concentrations and significantly high biomass productivity with low generic and specific diversity, generally both for flora and fauna. Because of locational advantages of mangroves of Indian Sundarban, biotic interference is the least here in comparison to other forest types of West Bengal. The author points that the balance of poor floral and faunal diversity in Sundarban mangroves is partially recompensated by lesser biotic influence. So he stresses on the idea of a proper balanced forest management in the Sundarbans, to build up a potentially rich natural ecosystem.

Sharmila Das[58] has studied of the forest potentiality of the Sundarban area and the products obtained from those forests. With scientific management, the author points out that this largest mangrove forest of the country has got the potentiality of a better economic development.

The same author[59] has also studied the ecological problems faced by the Active Deltaic zone of South Twenty Four Parganas like drainage congestion, water logging, salinity etc. These are the outcome of the degradation of watershed of the entire estuarine area.

The paper thus highlights the salient features of human interference and their impact on the ecology of this area.

### *3. Population and Settlement Studies*

Population studies of specific regions of West Bengal have been done by various scholars from time to time. Urban population has been studied by S. Bose[60], who has made an attempt to analyse the components of urban growth in the different districts of West Bengal from 1901 to 1986. The same author has analysed the age structure of urban population in the different districts of West Bengal during 1971 and 1981 based on the age-structure index by Caulson[61]. Single age structures vary from one district to another, an attempt has also been made to relate such spatial variations with the levels of urbanisation in the districts.

G. Rudra and K. Rudra[62] have attempted to analyse the mapping technique of human resources of North Twenty Four Parganas, West Bengal. According to the authors the mapping of the population density often furnishes a misleading picture. While calculating the density, total population and total area are taken into account, which also includes swampy and barren lands. They suggest the exclusion of uneconomic areas as well as intensive field survey methods to portray population statistics.

According to Anuradha Banerjee[63], the relationship between the natural and human resources and the development process is intricate and demands special attention from all social scientists. The author in a very simple manner has also attempted to build up an inventory of human resources of the coastal districts of India including the West Bengal coast of Medinipur and Twenty Four Parganas[64], so that priority measures can be selected for different zones in relation to other resources for human welfare.

K.N. Mukherjee[65] traces meticulously a thorough historical analysis of the development of settlements in the Sundarban area. In addition to a complete historical account, the author has for the first time prepared full 'pargana' and 'lot' maps as well as a detailed contour map (3 metre interval), for a better understanding of the micro- relief conditions associated with land formation and finally prepared a phased settlement map associated with different periods.

R. Bhattacharya[66] has stated that there are numerous settlement types in West Bengal, and any paradigm for settlements here must be a special one which will not be suitable for the neighbouring plains. He has the view that the deltaic settlements form a class by themselves.

An insight into a typical interior Sundarban village has been placed by G. N. Saha[67]. Here the study of the village was mainly undertaken to find out some aspects of socio-economic characteristics of the different caste groups and to throw some light on the changes that have taken place due to migration, contact and new environment.

P.K. Adhikari[68] has traced out the history of growth and methodology of mapping of settlement patterns, size of villages, dispersion of villages, settlement types, morphology etc. of Twenty Four Parganas District.

D. Basu[69] has dealt with the pattern of settlements of Sundarban region, their population density, density of occupied households and the ratio of persons per occupied household and have explained the causes of the variations in densities within the region.

G.N. Saha and D. Saha[70] have studied the settlements of the reclaimed parts of the Sundarbans and have dealt categorically with the people and their occupation, the economic aspects of the villages, the settlement pattern and house type.

Studies of certain police stations of Twenty Four Parganas have been conducted by certain scholars like the study by D.B. Jana and D.G. Seal[71] and by D.K. Das[72] who have probed into the settlement systems of the micro regions of these areas. Another such micro level study has been conducted by H.K. Sarkar[73]. The above mentioned paper reveals that the existing rural systems are the combined effects of physiocultural and socio economic processes in which caste based social distinctions have played a significant role. K. Mitra and G.N. Hazra[74] have presented a study of the villages of Sonarpur P.S. in South Twenty Four Parganas and have traced how far the social and economic culture of Sonarpur P.S. has been changed through migration.

Since the influence of Calcutta cannot be bypassed in any settlement studies pertaining to Twenty Four Parganas District, a selected number of articles can be mentioned in this regard. One of the most pioneering articles is by N.R. Kar[75] in which the author has studied the urban hierarchy around Calcutta in detail. The same author[76] places a special insight into the nature of rapid urban growth of Deltaic West Bengal. The nature of fringe areas around Calcutta and their identification has been studied by M. Ganguly[77].

P.B. Roy[78] has attempted to analyse the distribution pattern of urban settlements in West Bengal with the help of nearest - neighbour technique. The findings of the paper reveal that for West Bengal as a whole the distribution of urban settlements is nearly random. It is almost random in the districts of Murshidabad, Nadia, Medinipur and Bankura. There is a definite tendency towards randomness in the districts of Haora, Hugli, Barddhaman, Birbhum, Koch Behar and Purulia. In the districts of 24-Parganas, the distribution of urban settlements has all along been nearly half random, half clustered and the random element in the distribution is on the decline in the district of Darjeeling. Random element is almost absent in the districts of Maldaha, West Dinajpur and Jalpaiguri.

### *4. Economic Activities and Infrastructural Aspects*

A lot of work has been done regarding the economic activities, industrial and economic growth of the Hugli side region, including the infrastructural development of the area. Surprisingly South 24-Parganas is industrially and economically much less developed than the North 24-Parganas.

A. Sengupta[79] has studied the agriculture based economy of West Bengal since most of the region is a monocropped Kharif rice area based solely on the monsoons. He also analyses the steps of development and suggests—

(i) replacement of indigenous 'aman' rice varieties by specific High Yeilding Varieties (HYV) with certain degree of salt tolerance and preferably of a short duration;

(ii) Introducing suitable second crops with low water demand and varying degree of salt tolerance, viz, sunflower, groundnut, sugarbeet etc.;

(iii) Popularisation of the use of organic manures;

(iv) development of storage and irrigation facilities; and

(v) improvement of drainage facilities.

M.K. Sadhu, L. Saha, M. Palchaudhury, G. Chattopadhyay and K.K. Patanaik[80] explores the immense possibilities of growing vegetables followed by 'aman' paddy in coastal saline area in Sundarbans. In the present study, salt-tolerant varieties of tomatoes, chillies, okra, brinjal, have been identified, which show great promise as second crops in the Rabi season after Kharif paddy. The fertilizer requirements of the above crops under saline conditions have also been standardised. N.K. Saha and S. Kr. Halder[81] portray the technology required for agriculture in coastal West Bengal, state that the objective of agricultural development is to generate more income and to create adequate employment opportunities for the entire rural communities, with special emphasis on small and marginal farmers and agricultural labourers.

A.N. Bose[82] has studied in detail the brackish - water and marine fisheries of coastal West Bengal and has suggested their development. Similarly the authors B.N. Saigal, and Babu Lal[83] have explored the hydrographical, physical and biological characteristics of the ecosystem of coastal West Bengal and the influence of physio-chemical and biological factors affecting the estuarine and coastal productivity. K. Naskar and A. Ghosh[84] have studied the potentiality of the Mangroves and their contribution in the development of fisheries in the Sundarbans.

Sarmila Das[85] has studied systematically the fishing environment, type of fishing practised, infrastructural facilities present, problem of the fishing industry and future prospects of Twenty Four Parganas, West Bengal.

N. Chatterjee[86] has attempted an in-depth study of the impact of irrigation on the use of land, cropping pattern and crop yields of Southern West Bengal. The role of irrigation has been both qualitatively and quantitatively analysed based chiefly upon the detailed survey of twenty sample villages.

Chatterjee and Bagchi[87] have studied the transport system of the Sundarban Region. They have studied the transport conditions on sub-regional basis to diagonise the acute problems. Sub-regional demarcation is solely based on the available transport system, whether bus routes or waterways. The paper highlights that the overall network development appears to be unbalanced. The authors also recognised some intermediate nodes between Calcutta and interior Sundarbans and have computed their respective linkages.

N.R. Kar[88] has meticulously traced out the economic character of the Calcutta surroundings using modern techniques and has tried to show this city as a metropolitan centre of world importance.

### *5. Regional Development and Planning*

Developmental Plans for a backward region as South 24 Parganas is the need of the hour today. G.N. Saha[89] has pointed out to the fact that much has to be done regarding the actual measures to be employed in order to achieve desirable social and economic changes for such a problematic region. The paper also points out to the fact that planning for the development of the backward areas has got to be considered not only in terms of absolute potential that can be harnessed, but also to the historical processes. These processes have given rise to problems and challenges internal to the region and have stood in the way of any further development that might come to the region through normal private initiative.

Ghosh and Mitra[90] have stated that have various factors can build up social and economic stability in the Sundarban area. They have presented such factors as improvement of irrigation and drainage system, communications, creation of Social Forestry Scheme, establishment of small scale and cottage industries, soil, forest and wildlife protection and conservation.

## REFERENCES

1. Doxiadis, C.A.(1968), *An Introduction to the Science of Human Settlements*, Oxford University Press, New York, pp. 29-37.
2. Doxiadis, C.A. (1976), *Action for Human Settlement*, Athens, Athens Publishing Centre, pp. 19-20.
3. Leman, Alexander B. (1987), "Human Settlements: The second Definition", *Ekistics*, Vol. 325, pp. 243-248.
4. Penalosa, Enrique (1976), "Habitat", The United Nations Conference on Human Settlements published by Regional Congress of Local Authorities for Development of Human Settlements in Asia and the Pacific, 9-16 June 1982, Yokohama, Japan, p.1
5. Singh, R.L. (1961), "Meaning, Objectives and Scope of Settlement Geography," *National Geographical Journal of India*, Vol. 7, pp. 12-20.
6. Wadia, D.N. (1983), *Geology of India* , Tata McGraw - Hill Publishing Company Ltd., New Delhi, pp. 370-371.
7. Chattopadhyay, S. (1980), "Hydrology and Landuse In the Littoral Tract of Deltaic West Bengal", *Geographical Review of India*, Vol. 42, pp. 177-179.

8. Hansen, Miles M. (edited) (1978), Human Settlement System: International Perspectives on Structures, Change and Public Policy, Ballinger Publishing Company, p.1.
9. Eidt, Robert C. (1976), "Some Observations on The Role of Geography and History in the Development of a Methodology for the Analysis of Settlements", from *Geographic Dimensions of Rural Settlements*, Edited by R.L. Singh, K.N. Singh and Rana P.B. Singh, proceedings of I.G.U. Varanasi Symposium, December 1-7, 1975, published by National Geographical Society of India, Varanasi, pp. 11-12.
10. *ibid*, p. 12
11. Baskin, C.W. (1976), Central Places in Southern Germany, Eaglewood Cliffs N.J., Prentice Hall (Translation of W. Christaller, 1933) pp. 1-12.
12. Carter, Harold (1969), *Urban Geography*, Oxford University Press, pp. 24-27.
13. Doxiadis, C.A. (1968), *Ekistics : An Introduction to the Science of Human Settlements*, Oxford University Press, New York, pp. 29-37.
14. Bylund, Erik (1960), "Theoretical Considerations Regarding the Distribution of Settlement In Inner North Sweden", *Geographical Annals*, pp. 42-44, reprinted in "Readings in Rural Settlement Geography" edited by R.L. Singh, K.N. Singh and Rana P.B. Singh (1975), Varanasi, publication No. 14, pp. 43-49.
15. Singh, R.L., K.N. Singh, and Rana P.B. Singh, (Edited) (1975) Readings in Rural Settlement Geography, *op.cit.*, pp. 43-156.
16. *ibid.*
17. *ibid.*
18. Uhlig, H. *et al* (1972), "Rural Settlements", Basic Materials for the Terminology of the Agricultural Landscape, Vol. II, Giessen-Lenz. Verlong pp. 52.
19. Eidt, R.C. W.I. Woods, (1974), Abandoned Settlement Analysis, Theory and Practice, Shoreword - Wis-field Test Association pp. 2-18.
20. Buschman, K.H. (1954), "Settlements and Habitations in India", *Geographical Review of India*, XVI(3), pp. 19-33.
21. Deshpande, C.D. (1942), "Settlement Types of Bombay and Karnataka", *Indian Geographical Journal* 17(2) pp. 27-29.
22. Ahmed, E.(1952), "Rural Settlement Types in U.P." *Annals of Association of American Geographers*, XLII(3), pp.223-46.
23. Bhattacharya, A.N. (1956), Effect of Tribal and Caste Factor on Rural Settlement in U.P.", *Indian Geographical Journal*, 31 (3,4).
24. Singh, R.L. (Editor) (1972) Rural Settlements in Monsoon Asia, Proceedings of I.G.U. Symposia at Varanasi and Tokyo, National Geographical Society of India, Varanasi, pp. ix-xii.
25. Singh, R.L. (1961), "Meaning, Objectives and Scope of Settlement Geography", *National Geographical Journal of India*, Vol. 7, pp. 12-20.
26. Singh, R.L. (1955), "Evolution of Settlements in the Middle Ganga Valley, *National Geographical Journal of India*, Vol. 1(2), pp. 69-114.
27. Singh, R.L. (1957), "Typical Rural Dwellings In The Umland of Banaras", *National Geographical Journal of India*, Vol. 3(2), pp. 51-64.
28. Singh, K.N.(1972), "The Territorial Basis of Medieval Town and Village Settlement in Eastern Uttar Pradesh", *Annals of Association of American Geographers*, Vol. 58(2), pp. 203-29.

29. Singh, K.N.(1972), "An Approach to the Study of the Morphology of Indian Villages", in *Rural Settlements in Monsoon Asia*, op.cit, pp. 203-14.
30. Mukherji, A.B. (1975), "Rural Settlement in the Chandigarh Siwalik Hills : An Application of Multiple Collinear Fission Model", in *Geographic Dimensions of Rural Settlements* edited by R.L. Singh, National Geographical Society of India, pp. 54-66.
31. Dasgupta, S.P. and S.M. Mishra (1975),"An Analytical Approach to the Methodology of Mapping Rural Settlements in India", in *Geographic Dimensions of Rural Settlements, op.cit*, pp. 115-123.
32. Singh, D.K., B. Routray and S. Jena, "Spatial Analysis of Rural Settlement Pattern In Orissa", in *Geographic Dimensions of Rural Settlements*, op. cit, pp. 124-130.
33. Asthana, V.K. (1975), "Study of Rural Settlements Around Almora and Environs", in *Geographic Dimensions of Rural Settlements, op cit*, pp. 131-139.
34. Singh, K.N. , Rana P.B. Singh and D.K. Singh,(1975), "Spatial Characteristics of Rural Settlements And their Types in a part of Middle Ganga Valley", in *Geographic Dimensions of Rural Settlements, op cit*, pp. 140-148.
35. Pathak, C.R. and R.K. Dhabai, (1975), "Rural Settlement structure of Mewar", in *Geographic Dimensions of Rural Settlements, op. cit*, pp. 168-173.
36. Singh, R.Y., (1975), "Hierarchy of Rural Settlements and Identification of Locational Functional Gaps in Upper Charmanwati Basin", in *Geographic Dimensions of Rural Settlements*, op. cit., pp. 177-183.
37. Singh, B.B., (1975) "Spatial Organisation of Settlement in some North Indian Villages", in *Geographic Dimensions of Rural Settlements, op. cit.*, pp. 214-223.
38. Singh, Jagdish, (1985), *Upper Damodar Valley: A Study in Settlement Geography*, Inter-India Publications, New Delhi, pp. 1-238.
39. Nangia, Sudesh (1976), *Delhi Metropolitan Region : A Study in Settlement Geography*, K.B. Publications, New Delhi, pp. 1-173.
40. Tiwari, R.C., and N.V. Khan (1984), "Spatial Organisation of Rural Service Centres in Protapgarh District", *National Geographer*, Vol. XIX (2) December, pp.87-104.
41. Mahanta, H.B. (1986), "Dynamics of Urban Fringe: A case Study of Mawsbuit Village Near Shillong Urban Agglomeration, *Hill Geographer*, Vol. V(1,2), pp. 35-43.
42. Singh, B.L., (1985), "Rank Size Relationship in the Central Place System of Mithila Plain, North Bihar", *The National Geographical Journal of India*, Vol. 31, Pt.2, pp. 129-46.
43. Nag, P. (1990) "*Population, Settlement and Development In Zambia*", Concept Publishing Company, New Delhi-110059.
44. Sengupta, R., C.S. Murty and P.M.A. Bhattathiri,(1989), "Environmental Characteristics of the Ganga Estuary", *Coast Zone Management of West Bengal*, edited by A.N. Bose *et al.*, Sea Explorers Institute, Calcutta, pp. E19-E48.
45. Ghosh, A.K. (1989), "Ecological Profile of West Bengal", in *Coast Zone Management of West Bengal, op. cit.*, pp. E1-E9.
46. Dasgupta, K.K. (1989), "Disaster Mitigation in Coastal Area of West Bengal", *Coast Zone Management of West Bengal, op.cit*, pp. D12-D17.
47. Bandyopadhyay, K.K. (1989), "Cyclone Disaster Management of West Bengal", *Coast Zone Management of West Bengal, op. cit*, pp. D18-D38.
48. Biswas, A.N. (1989), "Disaster Management for Coastal Areas", *Coast Zone Management of West Bengal, op. cit.*, pp. D4-D11.

49. Chattopadhyay, S. (1980), "Hydrology and Landuse in the Littoral Tract of Deltaic West Bengal", *Geographical Review of India*, Vol. 42, pp. 177-179.
50. Paul, Ashis, K. (1988), "Coastal Dune Systems of Sundarbans", *Geographical Review of India*, Vol. 50(1), March, pp. 14-23.
51. Paul, Ashis K, and H.K. Bandyopadhyay (1986), "Coastal Sand Dunes of Sagar Island, West Bengal", *Geographical Review of India*, Vol. 48(2), pp. 41-48.
52. Paul, Ashis K. (1987), "Morphology of Sagar Island - A Part of Ganga Delta", *Journal of the Geological Society of India*, Bangalore, Vol. 29, No. 4, pp. 412-23.
53. Paul, Ashis K, M.K. Bandyopadhyay, and A. Chowdhury, (1987),"Morpho-Ecological Variations in the Sundarban Mudflats", *Geographical Review of India*, Vol. 49(1), pp. 1- 14.
54. Ghosh, B. and B.R. Ghosh (1989), "Geography of Sundarbans: A Unique Part of the Biggest Delta of the World", *Applied Geography*, edited by A.K. Kundu and R.K. Banerjee, National Atlas and Thematic Mapping Organisation, Monograph No.9, Government of India, pp. 297-98.
55. Roy, S. and C. Mondal (1989), "Flora and Fauna As Natural Resources of the Mangrove Forest Regions of Sundarbans", *Applied Geography, op. cit*, pp. 98-102.
56. Ghosh, C.(1989), "Application of Satellite Imagery in Monitoring and Mapping the Forest Resources of the Sundarbans", *Applied Geography, op.cit.*, pp. 352-3.
57. Chakraborti, Kalyan,(1989), "Development Perspective of Coastal Ecosystem of Sundarban forest", *Coast Zone Management of West Bengal, op. cit.*, pp. C4-C11.
58. Das, Sharmila (1992), "Mangrove forests of the Ganga Delta - A Geo-Economic Appraisal", *Indian Journal of Landscape System and Ecological Studies*, Vol.15(1), pp. 51- 58.
59. Das, Sharmila,(1990), "Human Interference on the Ecology of Sundarban, West Bengal", *Indian Journal of Landscape System and Ecological Studies*, Vol. 13(2), pp. 27- 34.
60. Bose, Sriparna, (1988), "Growth of Urban Centres and Urban Population of West Bengal", *Indian Journal of Landscape System And Ecological Studies*, Vol.11(2), pp. 45- 53.
61. Bose, Sriparna, (1989), "The Age Structure of Urban Population in West Bengal", *Applied Geography, op. cit*, pp. 197-199.
62. Rudra, Gani and Kalyan Rudra, (1988), "Mapping of Human Resource in the North 24-Parganas District", *Resource Mapping at District Level* edited by A.K. Kundu *et at.*, National Atlas and Thematic Mapping Organisation, Government of India, pp. 102-104.
63. Banerjee, Anuradha (1989), Natural and Human Resources of the Coastal Districts of India : A Geographical Analysis, unpublished M.Phil Dissertation submitted to the Jawaharlal Nehru University, pp.1.
64. Banerjee, Anuradha (1989), "The Coastal Districts of India : An Attempt Towards Building up of a Human Resource Inventory", *Applied Geography op. cit.*, pp. 265- 268.
65. Mukherjee, K.N. (1983), "History of Settlement in the Sundarban of West Bengal", *Indian Journal of Landscape System and Ecological Studies*, Vol.II(1, 2), pp. 1-19.
66. Bhattacharya, R.(1981), "Settlement Pattern in Deltaic West Bengal", *Geographical Review of India*, Vol. 37(1), pp.305-9.
67. Saha, G.N. (1979), "Putimari: A Case Study of A Rural Settlement in the Abad Area of the Sundarbans", *Geographical Review of India*, Vol.41(2), pp. 166-77.

68. Adhikari, P.K. (1987), "The History of Growth and Methodology for Mapping of Settlement Pattern of 24-Parganas District, West Bengal", *Mapping of Settlement Systems*, edited by G.K. Dutt, National Atlas and Thematic Mapping Organisation, Monograph No. 6, pp. 87-90.
69. Basu, D. (1987), "The Settlement Pattern in Sundarban Region", *Mapping of Settlement Systems, op. cit*, pp. 230-32.
70. Saha, G.N. and D. Saha (1987), "Rural Settlement in the Abad Areas of the Sundarbans", *Mapping of Settlement Systems, op. cit.*, pp. 264-66.
71. Jana, D.B. and D.G. Seal (1987), "A Study of the Rural Settlement Types in the Sagar Police Station : District 24-Parganas (South) and some considerations for Mapping", *Mapping of Settlement Systems, op.cit.*, pp. 202-4.
72. Das, D.K. (1987), "Cartographic Analysis of Rural Settlement System of Mathurapur Police Station of the Sundarban Region", *Mapping of Settlement Systems, op cit*, pp. 59-62.
73. Sarkar, H.K. (1987), "Settlement System of Harua Police Station in North Western fringe of the Sundarban Region", *Mapping of Settlement Systems, op. cit.*, pp. 59-62.
74. Mitra, K. and G.N. Hazra, (1987), "Migration in the Calcutta Metropolitan Fringe Zone in Sonarpur Police Station - A Study of Certain Selected Villages", *Mapping of Settlement Systems, op. cit.*, pp. 195-97.
75. Kar, N.R. (1960), "Urban Hierarchy and Central function around the city of Calcutta and its significance", Proceedings of the International Geographical Union Symposium on Urban Geography, Lund, Sweden, pp. 57-60.
76. Kar, N.R. (1962), "Pattern of Urban Growth in lower West Bengal", *Geographical Review of India*, Vol. 24(3-4), pp. 42-59.
77. Ganguly, Maya (1967), "The Nature of Fringe Areas of Calcutta", *Geographical Review of India*, Vol. 27(1), pp. 53- 59.
78. Roy, PhaniBhusan, (1985), "Random Element in the distribution of Urban Settlement in West Bengal 1901-71", *Indian Journal of Regional Science*, Vol. 17 (2), pp. 69-71.
79. Sengupta, Anil, (1989), "Agriculture in the Coastal Area of West Bengal", *Coast Zone Management of West Bengal* edited by A.A. Bose, *et al, op. cit*, pp. B36-B39.
80. Sadhu, M.K., et al (1989), "Possibilities of growing vegetables in saline soils", *Coast Zone Management of West Bengal, op. cit*, pp. B27-B35.
81. Saha, Nirmal Kanti and S.K. Haldar, (1989), "Technology Adoption in Agriculture in Coastal West Bengal", *Coast Zone Management of West Bengal, op. cit*, pp. B16 - B26.
82. Bose, A.N. (1989), "Fisheries Development in Coastal West Bengal : Socio-Economic Implications", *Coast Zone Management of West Bengal, op. cit.*, pp. A1-A14.
83. Saigal, B.N. and Babulal, (1989), "Physical and Biological Factors Affecting Fisheries in Estuarine and Coastal Eco-systems of West Bengal", *Coast Zone Management of West Bengal, op.cit*, pp. A25-A34.
84. Naskar, K.R. and A. Ghosh, (1989), "Mangrove Forests of Sundarban : Its impact on Estuarine Fisheries", *Coast Zone Management of West Bengal, op. cit.*, pp. A47-A-59.

85. Das, Sharmila, (1991), "Development of Fisheries in South 24 Parganas District : Problems and Prospects", *Geographical Review of India*, Vol. 52 (2), pp. 69-79.
86. Chatterjee, Nandini, (1986), "Impact of Irrigation on Agriculture in Southern West Bengal", *Geographical Review of India*, Vol. 48(1), pp. 73-81.
87. Chatterjee, S. and K.G. Bagchi, (1978), "An Analytical Study of the Transport System of the Sundarban Region", *Geographical Review of India*, Vol. 41(1), pp. 77-81.
88. Kar, N.R. (1963), "Economic Character of the Metropolitan Sphere of Influence of Calcutta", *Geographical Review of India*, Vol. 25(2), pp. 103-38. 89. Saha, Gopi Nath (1989), "Planning the Sundarban Region: Issues and Challenges", National Seminar on District Resource Mapping edited by Kundu *et al, op. cit.*, pp. 61-63.
89. Saha, Gopinath (1989), "Plenning the Sundarban Region: Issues and Challnges" National seminor on District Resource Mapping edited by Kundu *et at, op.cit.*, pp 61-63.
90. Ghosh, Mira and R. Mitra(1989), "Regional Planning in Sundarbans", *Applied Geography* edited by Kundu and Banerjee, *op. cit*, pp. 166-8.

# 2

# NATURAL ENVIRONMENT

## 2.1 INTRODUCTION

The coastal margin of Sundarbans is formed by the combined effect of fluvial and marine action. The evolution of the region can be attributed to a host of geomorphological, climatic and biotic factors; often interrupted by natural disasters. The present chapter aims to highlight the factors of the natural environment underlying the formation of the region as a special littoral case. Such background information has been used as a basework for carving the Geo-Ecological subregions required for population and settlement study.

## 2.2 GEOLOGY, TECTONICITY AND EVOLUTIONARY HISTORY

The deltaic district of South 24-Parganas is a composite landmass, the origin of which is due to a series of geologic and geomorphic events like upheaval and subsidence coupled with gradual deposition of alluvial silts brought from distant Himalayas by the Ganga-Brahmaputra river complex.

Hooker (1854) and Theobald (1881) stated that the whole of 'Lower Bengal' was originally an estuary. Historical evidences elucidate the fact that the tidal swamp once extended upto the Rajmahal Hills.[1] In the later part of the Tertiary Period (35 million years ago), this was filled up by the Himalayan drainage from the North. J. Fergusson (1863)[2] was of the opinion that during the early Pleistocene, shallow marine water condition prevailed in this part of the Bengal Basin, it was only in the late Pleistocene that sea receded completely from this area. Older sediments began to be covered with thick river borne alluvium. Very precisely Oldham[3] (1893) states, the whole area including the Sundarbans, lying between the river

Hugli in the West and Meghna (Bangladesh) in the East, is only the delta caused by the deposition of the debris carried down by the river Ganga, Brahmaputra and their tributaries. This is further substantiated by the fact that there is no trace of any marine deposits even much below the ground; but some estuarine fossils were traced at a depth of 290 meters (950 ft.) while digging a tubewell at Garden Reach under Calcutta Municipality. Oldham also suggested that this part of the Gangetic plains were formed by the sinking of the crust due to the weight of the alluvium brought down by the rivers from the Himalayas. The whole of the lower Gangetic delta as such remained somewhat trough land till today.[4]

The geologic history of the district, therefore, lies in subsidence in this part of the country followed by deposition in comparative recent times. Similar results were also obtained from the bore operation at Fort William (Calcutta) upto a depth of 140 metres. There was no trace of marine deposits proving thereby that the whole bore comprises of alluvial brackish water deposits. This view was supported by Colonel Gastrell (1868) and by Hunter (1875).

The depositional history of the region has been emphasized by the excavations of the Metro Railway Project in Calcutta, and the Second Hugli Bridge Project. Clouson[5] (1940) stated that these alluvial strata (comprising alterations of clay, sand and silt) were formed due to simultaneous depressions and elevations, proved by the occurrence of alternating peat beds (a dark brown humus formed by the partially decomposed mass of Marsh vegetation) and Kankar beds. The distinct deposition of a layer of 0.50m to 1.20m thick peat was recorded 5m below the surface, being about the mean sea level. In the excavations of the Metro Railway Project, a second layer of peat has been recorded for the first time 12m below the surface, being 7m below the mean sea level. The sequence of sediments with two distinct layers of peat and an intermediate layer of soft grey clay with decayed stumps of Sundari trees (typical of present Sundarban vegetation) has been found at several stations (Jatin Das Park, Bhowanipur and Esplanade) of the Metro Railway. As early as in June 1889 "*The Calcutta Review*" has also recorded : Stumps of Sundari trees embedded near Sealdah (Calcutta) and at Canning (South 24-Parganas) 30 feet below the ground.[6]

The palaeogeography of the district is thus associated with brackish water plants like Heritiera, Sonneratia, Avicennia, Caerisps, along with leaves, stems, radicle, mioflora and mollusc shells of Neritina, Telescopuim, etc. Radio carbon dating on some of these materials suggests that they belong to a period around 7000 years of age.

Fresh water plant deposits of pteridophytic, angiosperm and mioflora along with remnants of leaves and stems of both, some Monocotyledons and Dicotyledons have also been recovered from the older strata. The molluscan genera like Pila, Indo Planorobis Segmentina, Lamellidens etc. have also been studied and carbon dating experiments show that they were hardly about 4000 years old. All these studies reveal an ecological succession of phases like tidal mangrove, followed by sudden cessation of tidal influx, marine, and salt tolerant fresh water vegetation in conformity with the Eastward tilting of South Bengal some 300 years ago.

There is a great natural depression called "Swatch of No Ground"[7] in the Bay of Bengal, south of the Raimangal Estuary and this figures in navigation charts. The surrounding waters which are around 20 metres, change almost suddenly to 500m in depth. Fergusson's theory is that the sediments are carried away from the spot and deposition is prevented by the strong currents produced by a meeting of tides from the East and West coasts of the Bay of Bengal. Another theory attributes the depression to a local sinking. Thus the unstable condition of the area opine Oldham, Beveridge and Fergusson result in periodic subsidence, earthquakes, etc. is related to the "Swatch of no ground", the origin of which is still shrouded in mystery. Subsidence and earthquakes together with other natural hazards have been common to the region.

## 2.3 GEOMORPHIC CHARACTERISTICS

South 24-Parganas District lies within the limits of the Gangetic delta, the main channel from the Himalayas being splitted into several small channels to take the present shape of innumerable creeks and channels; to form a low flat country, little of which is raised above flood level, and a few metres rise in sea level can drown the entire landmass including Calcutta. However, 2 broad natural divisions in the district are noticeable:

(a) The more or less Stable Delta towards the North forming higher ground hardly affected by tidal action; and

(b) The most dynamic, Active Delta in the southern sea- board popularly called the low lying Sundarbans.

At present only the Eastern part of the River Matla now exists as the true core area of this dwindling mangrove forests, also known as the tidal forests. The northern inland tract of the Stable Delta is a land of sluggish rivers comprising of large amounts of clay occasionally enclosing peat beds and forming monotonous plains with a very low gradient towards the sea.

The Sundarbans, on the other hand, are a network of tidal channels, rivers, creeks and islands[8]. Gupta (1957) studied the physiography of the area in relation to tidal action. He stated that the area being subject to tidal action, a back rush of silt from the Bay occurs. The silts carried down to the sea are pushed back to the Moribund channels and get deposited there due to tidal action. The bed of the channel thus gets steadily raised ultimately blocking the flow of water and a small island is thus gradually evolved. This is the basic geographical history about the origin of innumerable islands of the region. Ray Choudhury *et al* (1963) have discussed much about the reactions of sea water in the continental shelf after analysing silts from the rivers and creeks. They have also stated that the deposits of Ganga alluvium going to the sea are turned back by tides and redeposited in the estuarine region and this alluvium is enriched with various salts. The silt and clay loads carried down into the sea beyond the delta undergo partial transformation due to exchange reaction with Sodium Chloride (NaC1) of sea water. During tides, this constituent, on suspension, rushes back through the numerous tidal creeks in the coastal region and gets partially deposited due to gravitational force which is greater than the force of suction exerted by ebb water, in the flat plain situated inland. They also opined that the Active Delta of the Sundarbans is still under formation. Presence of many small islands bear ample testimony to this condition of new land formation. Recent detection of well publicised new Moore Island (Purbasha) emphasises the fact[9].

The coastal area of the Sundarbans comprising of broad undulating indented coast line of South 24-Parganas consist of a varied morphoecological features such as mudflats, shifting sand banks, complex dune ridges and flats and mangrove swamps. Two of the most conspicuous geomorphological features of the area can be treated in greater detail.

### *(A) The Sundarban Mudflats*

Mudflats are found at the estuaries and on the deltaic islands of the Sundarbans where the sheltered spots marked by low velocity of river and tidal currents occur. (Map 2.1) Suspended sediments of finer quality get time to settle down in the sheltered areas where the disturbance of tidal currents and waves are minimized, and thus the mudflats are developed on the islands and estuarine banks. The thick mud substratum is richer in organic content and is ideal for penetration by plant roots. The flats are exposed in the low tides and are submerged in the high tides, and thus the unstable mud flat changes morphologically even in one tidal cycle[10]. The littoral parts of the mudflats have characteristic flat slopes, a resultant factor of higher velocity of tidal currents, and is thus devoid of vegetation, unlike the interior parts—that are the magnificent home of the luxuriant Mangroves. Besides, the extended mudflats of estuarine environment are important feeding grounds for marsh and estuarine birds. The mudflats are roughened by the algae mat in the monsoon and post-monsoon periods. The activities of benthic fauna on the flats develop micro-topographical variations on different islands of the Sundarbans. The composition of the mudflat is of fine silt and clay which stick together in the sea water and are generally deposited on the sandy bottom. The thick mud substratum is extremely loose and open in structure and it contains large amount of water with air gaps. The morphological features of the Sundarban mudflats have a developed profile. The profile of a shallow estuarine mudflat shows a prominent mid-tidal break of slope, almost a slopeless flat in the low velocity area, densely vegetated high mudflats or the mangrove swamps and the high velocity creek bed which is composed of solid grains of larger size. The tidal and riverine depositions are accelerated by the pneumatophores and the dense branching roots in the mangrove swamps. The morphology of the swamps is characterised by the occurrence of salt pans, ditches and banks with a thick substratum of decomposed organic

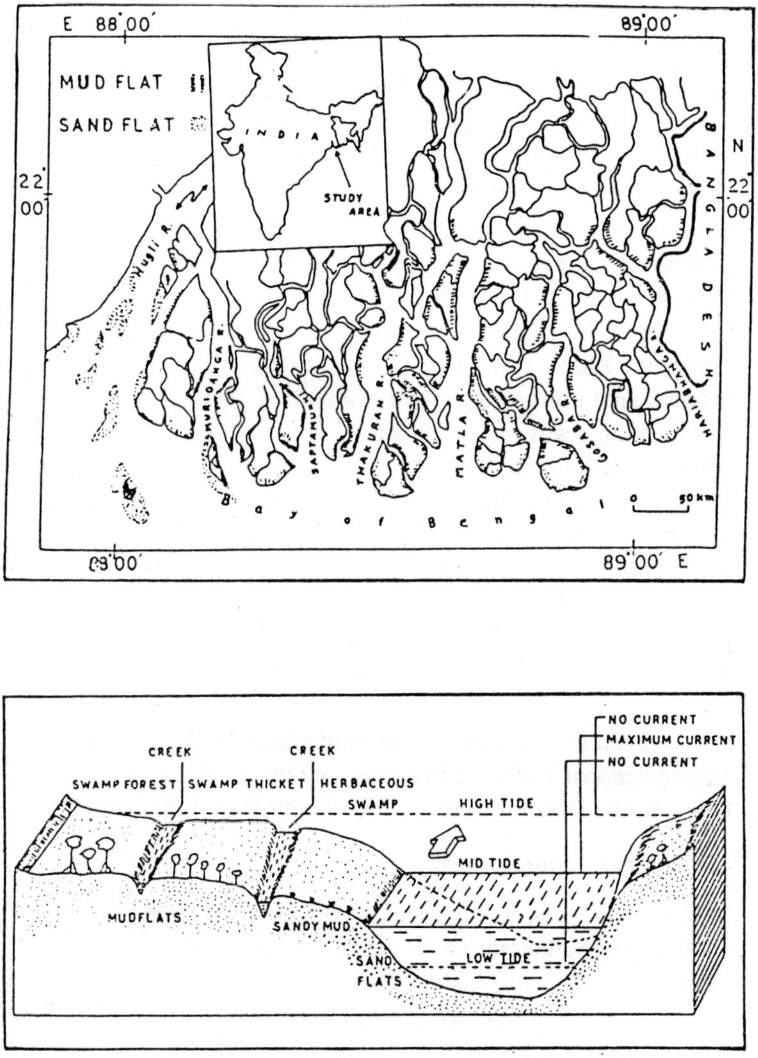


*Source* : Paul and Bandyopadhyay

**MAP 2.1** : Location of Mud-flats and Sand-flats in the Sundarbans

matter. Most of the swamp floor is totally submerged by the spring tides; and as the ebb tide starts from the highest level, the general slope of the floor become affected by lateral erosion due to ebb currents and thus the formation of new creek is initiated. The head of the creek cuts back gradually by the quick flows of spilling tides along the creek, and thus it is lengthened.

The micromorphology of the coastal mudflats is characterised by the location of peculiar mud-mounds and holes. The mounds and holes are created by the activities of a typical mud-dweller (Scylla Serrata) of the Sundarban marshes. The growing mounds and holes obstruct the flow- tide and lead to the formation of tiny swirls and eddies or sheltered patches in between these structures which favour extensive sedimentation on the floor. Some of the mudflats in this coastal area possess a pronounced break of slope at the position of the breaking waves which is marked as the beach step. The mud ridge and the microholes are the other morphological features of the coastal mudflats. The microholes of the dense mudflat are the resultant features of the activities of crustaceans in the coastal flat.

Thus the Sundarban mudflats control the food chain in the estuarine ecosystem, but excessive reclamation, however poses the greatest single threat to the shallow estuarine mudflats of the Western and Northern Sundarbans as it destroys forever the natural habitat and ecosystem.

The only exception to the monotonous flat plains of fluvio-marine deposits of the Sundarbans are the complex dune ridges and flats on the isolated islands of the South Western Sundarbans.

### *(B) Coastal Dune Systems*

Coastal dune systems are located on somewhat higher areas in the S. Western Sundarbans as for example in Sagar Island, Jambudwip, Chuksar, Fraserganj-Bakkhali Islands, Lothian and Tat Islands. Dunes are the product of sea deposition on the coast in which wave and wind processes play dominant role in the formation of dunes. The dune landscape in the Sundarbans comprises a system of low ridges parallel to the coast, separated by large dry and wet sandflats.

Dune formation in the Sundarbans is controlled by the following four major factors:

1. Insufficient source of sand on the beaches,
2. Absence of long dry season with strong wind speed (20 to 50 km per hour) on the shores,
3. High sub-surface moisture and
4. Rapid growth of vegetation on the sandy shores.

On the island of Chuksar, Jambu and Lothian, the dunes are still growing and are younger in age. The embryonic dunes, dune humps and dotted dunes (small ridges) are the special features of the dune morphology of these islands. Most of the dunes are deformed due to South West and North East winds. The dunes on these islands are mostly vegetated by heaths and grasses, height varying in between a few centimetres to 5 metres.

The dunes of Sagar Island, (Map 2.2), Fraserganj, Bakkhali and Tat Island, are mature and largely developed. In altitude these range to over 5 metres. Eight stages of dune development have been observed (Paul and Bandyopadhyay 1987)[11] on the Sagar Island, where the dune morphology and its development are controlled by the ecology of some halophytic plants. At Bakkhali, the dunes are more or less stabilized because they are largely managed through planting casurina trees. Dune areas of Tat Island are heavily settled and cultivated.

The seaward faces of the coastal dunes of these islands are now being engulfed by the encroaching sea waves with the activities of cyclones on the low lying coast. The isolated dotted dune, eroded primary dune, mobile dunes and wide bare sandflats are the important features of Sagar Island and Fraserganj coasts. The Fraserganj coast is almost destroyed by the longshore current attack from the West. Now the drier dunes are advancing inland causing damage to agricultural fields. Again, at present, the rate of coastal erosion is high on the coast of Fraserganj, Bakkhali and Sagar. Thus, the wide beaches of these coasts are gradually being narrowed and the seaward dunes are being directly attacked by the high sea waves.

A variety of dune landscape types with their associated geomorphology and vegetational types can be discernable in South Western Sundarbans that provide functions such as protection of hinterland, water storage, biotic resources and recreation.

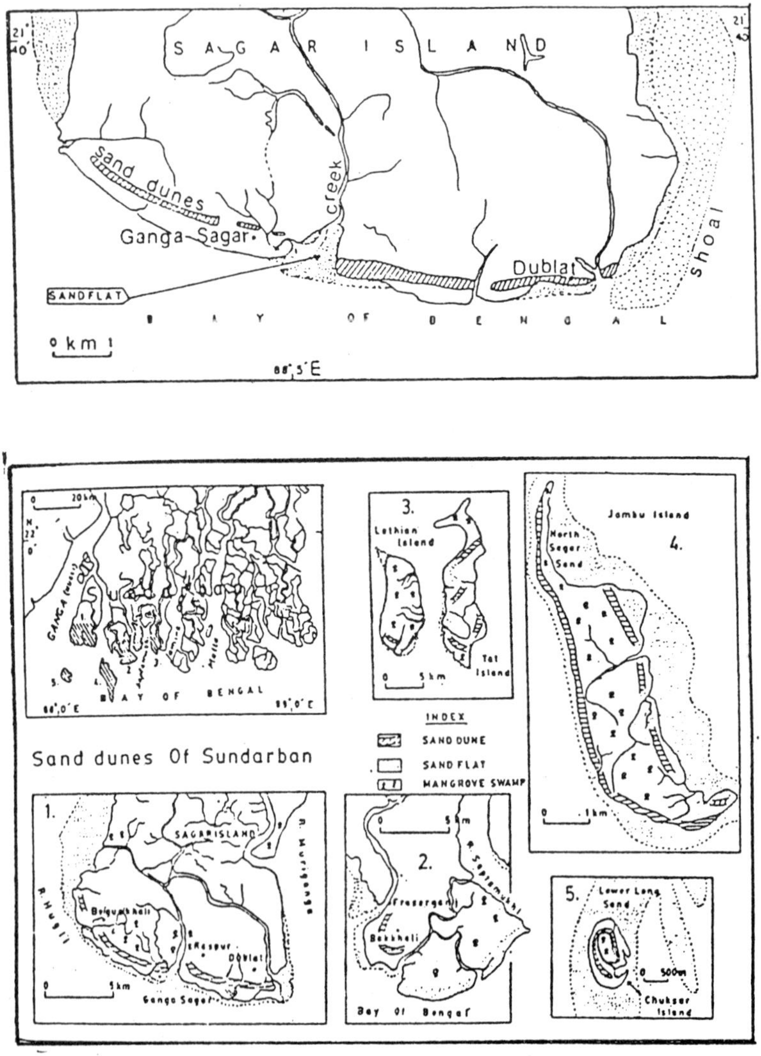


*Source* : Topographical Sheets

**MAP 2.2** : Location of Sand Dunes and Sand-flats in Sagar-Island

**TABLE 2.1 : Geo-Ecological Characteristics of Sand Dunes in the Sundarbans**

| *Type of dunes* | *Altitude above M.S.L.(in M)* | *Geomorphology* | *Stability* | *Vegetation* |
|---|---|---|---|---|
| Embryo dunes | 1 - 2 | Dotted dunes | Stable | Dune heaths |
| Fore dunes | 3 - 5 | Parallel dunes | Stable | Dune scrubs |
| Dune stacks | 1 - 1.5 | Wet hollows | Stable | Dune grass |
| Dune humps | 2 - 3 | Rounded dune top | Stable | Dune herbs |
| Dune flat | 4 - 6 | High dune flats | Stable | Wood lands |
| Primary dune complex | 2 - 3.5 | Semi-barkhans | Unstable (mobile) | Bare dunes |
| Dry sand-flat | 2.5- 4 | Dry shore flats | Unstable (mobile) | Bare dunes |

*Source* : Paul & Bandyopadhyay, 1987.

The littoral tract of South Twenty-four Parganas is therefore, the product of interaction of innumerable geomorphic and geo-ecological processes, highlighted by tidal action rather than the lone effect of waves on the seaboard. The complexity of this region, thus according to many scholars, owes its origin due to uprising of the basement complex (Pleistocene times) and consequent recession of the sea from the lower part of the Bengal basin. Thus the Geologic and various other physiographic conditions of different regional components of this delta require a complex set of analysis of tectonicity rather than depending solely on the age old hypothesis of riverine alluvial deposition.

## 2.4 FLUVIAL CHARACTERISTICS

The Geography of South Twenty Four Parganas is intimately linked with that of ever changing river courses and so the drainage pattern constitutes the underlying factor in shaping the settlement pattern of the district.

The rivers of the district (Map 2.3) were formerly distributaries of the Ganga, (i.e. they were channels by which Ganga waters were distributed and ultimately discharged into the sea); but the main current of that river got deflected eastward[12] and hence these ceased to be effective drainage channels; though a large volume of water is conveyed through the Hugli. Hence most of the rivers of the area are essentially tidal.

The Eco-geography of this deltaic coast is totally dependent on this tidal effect. There are two flow tides (in flow) and two ebb tides (out flow) daily. The intertidal zone (or the tidal limitation daily and between seasons) in the estuarine rivers ranges between 3—5 metres. However, there is a wide gap in the tidal fluctuation between the Western Bay estuaries than in the East (3m—5m Vs 1.52 m—2.13 m respectively); and this can be attributed due to a lack of fresh water drainage through Indian rivers. Moreover, the strength of the tidal current varies with the slope of the sea-bed and season. The maximum recorded velocity of tide in the Hugli estuary had been of the order of 200 cm/sec.

The main rivers of the area, most of which are estuaries are (i) the Hugli, (ii) Piyali - Bidyadhari, (iii) Muri Ganga, (iv) Saptamukhi, (v) Thakuran, (vi) Matla, (vii) Gosaba and (viii) Harinbhanga.

(i) Hugli—The Hugli (for origin see Appendix II.3) forms the western boundary of the district, by which the waters of the Ganges enter the Bay of Bengal. Entering the district from the North-East, it flows almost due South, receiving the Damodar opposite the Falta Point and Rupnarayan opposite the Hugli Point. These great tributaries deflect the stream to the East for about 13 km. and have set up in it, the dreaded moving shoals known as James and Mary Sands. Navigation in the Hugli has become difficult on account of rapid currents, shoals and shifting sandbanks. However, with some dredging operations, the river has been maintained navigable to large liners and is the gateway for the foreign trade of Eastern India.

After Diamond Harbour, the river resumes a southerly direction, until it debouches into the Bay of Bengal, its breadth at the point of junction being about 26 km., its mouth being locally known as the Burha Mantreswar. The tide of the Hugli is occasionally so strong that it gives rise

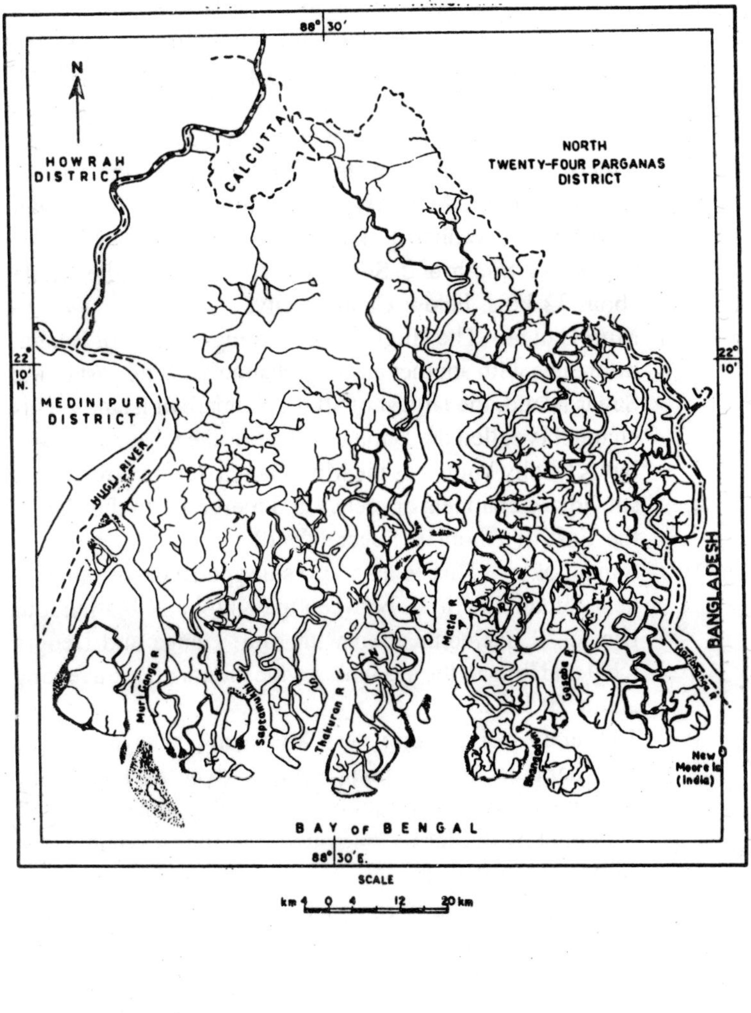


MAP 2.3 : Drainage Map of South 24-Parganas

to a phenomenon known as a bore[13]. This is the name given to the headwave which is formed when an unusually high tide is checked by the narrowing of the river channel.

(ii) The Bidyadhari and the Piyali—The Bidyadhari flows a very circuitous course and in the Northern portion of the district has nearly been silted up (in Bhangar Block) and comprises of an outfall channel for the storm- water and sewerage of Calcutta. However, south eastwards, the river widens, being joined by the Karatoya and Atharabanka and falls into the Matla river in Canning Block. The Piyali leaves the Bidyadhari 14 kms. below Bamanghata (Tiljala) and flows South and South-West till it joins the Matla about 32 kms. below Canning city.

(iii) Muri Ganga—The Hugli before joining the Bay of Bengal bifurcates with another easterly channel passing east of the Sagar Island, the largest of all the Sundarban Islands. This channel is called the Baratala River or the Channel Creek; but is locally known as the Muri Ganga. It is fed by several subsidiary channels or creeks and merges with the Bay to the East of Dhoblat (Sagar Island).

(iv) Saptamukhi—This is also an estuarine river, originating near Sultanpur, flows between the Kulpi and Mathurapur Blocks. It has connection with Muri Ganga and Deogra Khal and falls to the sea with a wide mouth after traversing about 80 kms.

(v) Thakuran—Originating near Jaynagar (Jaynagar Block) the Thakuran, another tidal estuarine river takes the name of Jamira. It has a number of connections with the Saptamukhi and forms the boundary between Mathurapur and Jaynagar Blocks.

(vi) Matla—The Matla is considered one of the most important river of South Twenty-Four Parganas due to its largest and deepest navigable channel used throughout by the ocean going vessels upto Port Canning, near which it is joined by the Bidyadhari. This river also ends up in an estuary in a wide opening to the Bay of Bengal.

(vii) Gosaba—This river is formed by the confluence of the Raimangal and Matla river and forms a broad estuary to the sea.

(viii) Harinbhanga—The Harinbhanga river forms the International Boundary of the district and is connected with the Bangladesh river Jamuna through River Kalindi in the East.

These estuarine rivers are all formed by the junction of smaller rivers, all having a general southerly course towards the sea. They are separated from one another by numerous islands, few of which are inhabited. From West to East these islands are, the largest of all, the Sagar Island (between the Hugli and the Channel Creek), the Mecklenberg Island or Fraserganj (West of Saptamukhi), Lothian Island (in the mouth of the Saptamukhi), the Bulcherry Island (between the Jamira and the Matla), the Halliday Island (in the Matla), the Dalhousie Island (between the Matla and Gosaba) and finally the Bangaduni Island (at the mouth of Gosaba).

Between the large estuaries and rivers, there are innumerable streams and water courses called "Khals", forming a perfect network of channels, drawing water from every block of land. Each block is like a saucer with high ground along the bank of the Khals surrounding it with one or more depressions and is drained off by little creeks and Khals into the larger khals and ultimately into the rivers. Many of the "Khals" connect two larger ones and as a result tide flows into them through both ends. Such Khals are called 'do-aniya khals'[14] They offer communication between the larger khals, but get silted up gradually at the point where the two tides meet because the water is stagnant there.

## 2.5 CLIMATIC CHARACTERISTICS

South Twenty-Four Parganas District is characterised by a typical tropical Monsoon Climate (as typical for the rest of India) but with excess of humidity and a little less of northern winter due to its maritime influence.

**TABLE 2.2 : Temperature and Rainfall of South 24-Parganas**

| *Particulars* | *Normal* | *1983* | *1984* |
|---|---|---|---|
| Annual Rainfall in millimetre. | 1579 | 1920 | 1997 |
| Temperature in 0°C (Dum Dum) | Maximum | 39 | 39 |
| | Minimum | 9 | 9 |

*Source* : 1. Agri, Meteorologist, Directorate of Agri: West Bengal.
2. Directorate of Regional Meteorological Centre, Calcutta.

The climatological picture is more flatenned out towards the southern seaboard, and here extreme climatic conditions do not prevail even though the region is close to the Tropic of Cancer. This is because of its locational advantage of its proximity of the sea and the constant flushing of landscape by innumerable tidal creeks and rivers. Here the maximum average temperature of 29°C is felt during June and a minimum of 20°C is recorded in December-January. The average rainfall is around 1800 mm.

The so called summer in this area prevails from middle of March to middle of June (pre-monsoon). Monsoon starts from the middle of June and prolongs upto September, sometimes extending into the middle of October. The south- west wind brings monsoon in this area.

From mid-October to November (Post-Monsoon) the cyclonic storm occasionally touches the area accompanied with high waves and tides (near the sea), which sometimes cause great disasters. The winter months are December, January and February; winds from North and North East blow from mid-October to the middle of March. The rivers become calm and quiet during this period and is the best part of the year.

In late March to May (pre-monsoon period), violent and frequent thunderstorms occur in this district, generally known as the 'Norwesters' (as they approach the land from North-Westerly direction). Hailstorms also occur accompanying the thunderstorms. Locally known as 'Kalbaishakhi', these thundersqualls are short lived, rapid shifting winds with rain and thunder accompanied by a sudden fall of temperature. The wind speed in these storms varies from 64 to 80 km. per hour and sometimes may even reach a velocity of 160 km./hour.

Therefore, the early rains of this district is mainly due to the norwesters. They are line squalls bringing thunder and lightening and intense precipitation often in the form of hail, the line regenerating several times, the down draught from the first line promoting enough turbulence, specially downward to provoke a second and so on. They are commonly associated with divergence related to the westerly Jet Streams, or to westerly disturbances in the Upper Troposphere, sometimes intensified by 'inphase superposition' of a wave in the Upper Troposphere Easterlies and develop, given an association of favourfable conditions: (1) low level convergence, (2) Upper air divergence, (3) sufficient inflow of moist air at low level; and (4) unstable lapse rates - often provided through cold air advection aloft[15].

In the early hot weather, too, as well as in the late monsoon period, cyclonic storms (Map 2.4) or tropical cyclones occur in the Bay that affect the district sometimes severely causing tidal bores and storm surges. Heavy rains associated with a storm have been known to cause floods of no mean dimesions[16]. (Appendix II.1)

**TABLE 2.3 : Frequency of Cyclonic Storms in the Bay of Bengal 1831-1960**

| *Month* | *J.* | *F.* | *M.* | *A.* | *M.* | *J.* | *J.* | *A.* | *S.* | *O.* | *N.* | *D.* | *Total* |
|---|---|---|---|---|---|---|---|---|---|---|---|---|---|
| Less-Severe | 4 | 1 | 4 | 18 | 28 | 34 | 38 | 25 | 27 | 53 | 56 | 26 | 314 |
| Severe | 1 | 1 | 2 | 7 | 18 | 4 | 7 | 1 | 8 | 19 | 23 | 9 | 100 |

*Source* : Directorate of Regional.Meteorological Centre, Calcutta.

## 2.6 SOIL CHARACTERISTICS

The natural soil associations (Map 2.5) found in this deltaic district has been formed both as a result of physical phenomena, climate, watersheds (abiotic components) as well as by the action of organic constituents (biotic components).

In general the soils of the district are derivatives of fine Gangetic deltaic alluvium borne out of terrestrial materials of the Himalayas

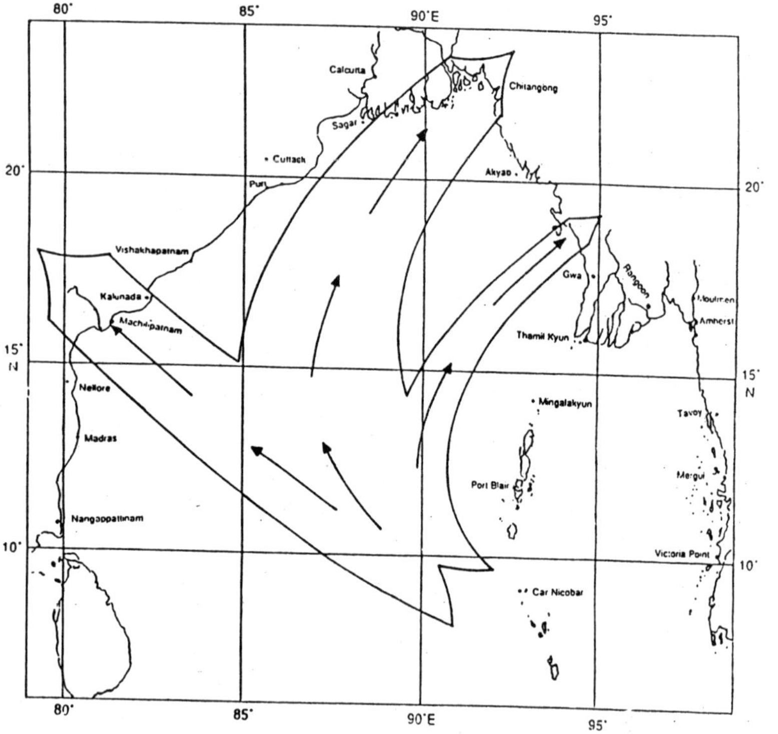


*Source* : Coast Zone Management

**MAP 2.4** : Bay of Bengal Cyclones

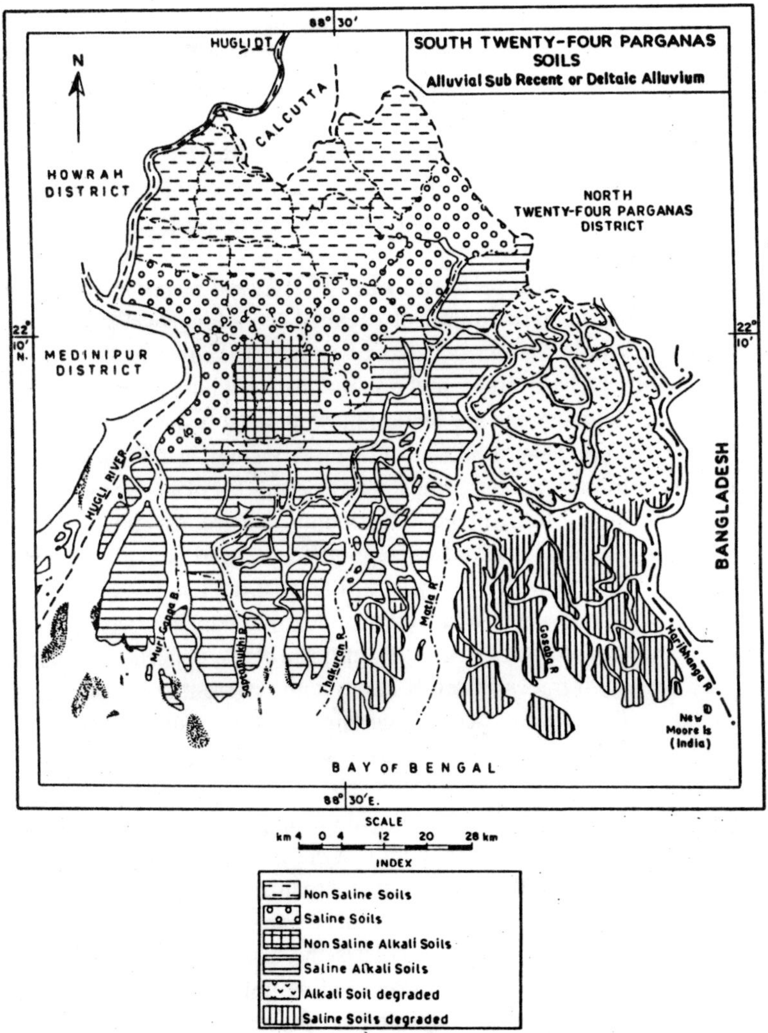


**MAP 2.5 :** Soil : South 24-Parganas

viz. (1) The Ganga alluvium and (2) Salinized Ganga alluvium[17]. The soil of this area can be well differentiated into 4 major divisions according to the factors affecting their genesis - (i) Along the Hugli and in the Northern part of the district heavy textured *silty clay loams*, with about 45 per cent clay and the rest silt with very little percentage of sand, organic content being less than one per cent. Infiltration rate is low being about 0.20 cm per day and in the monsoon this improves to about 3 cm/day.

In the Active Delta, three other soil types are noticeable (2) *Sandy clays and loams* and sand dunes are noticeable in the western estuarine parts with higher percentages of sand, organic matter and infiltration rates (3) Some *organic and peaty deposits* have been noticeable in central parts and finally (4) *Swampy and marshy soils* occur in the Eastern littoral also called the *Mangrove Soil.*

The whole district consists of *newer alluvium* but the soils of the Stable Deltaic areas are not inundated whereas in the active estuarine deltaic areas are being renewed. This results in a variation of *soil texture*. The silts (and clays) deposited in this fashion are mostly pale-brown, sometimes grey to greyish - black, with deposits of mica, very often mixed with loamy calcareous clays, and are devoid of carbonate (Kankar) segregations. Sand is available along the sea face, (specially in a part of the west depleted of the original vegetation); a result of tidal action and strong winds. The soil profile of the region portrays a grey to greyish black upperlayer whereas grey clay with traces of sands along with different kinds of silts are found in the subsoil. After a certain depth medium to fine sands having grey to bluish grey colour are noticeable. Occasionally at certain depths peat is also noticeable. The Sundarban forest proper comprises of the mangrove soil that is comparatively young and low in oxygen content. Besides humus it contains good quality of shells of forminifera, mollusca and other organisms from marine source. Calcium salts from the molluscan shells are released, related by the activity of sulphur bacteria. This is the cause of *higher alkalinity* (pH) of the silt. Mere deposition of alluvium does not always make a productive soil, complex biological process is necessary to make the soil suitable to be utilised by plants and other associates. Many organisms such as bacteria, blue-green algae, diatoms and green algae play very important role in this process. Nitrifying bacteria and sulphate reducing bacteria also have significant role (The local soil terminologies of the district is given in Appendix II.4).

The soil chemistry of the region have been studied by various scholars. Roy Choudhury *et al*[18] (1963) states that nitrogen of the soil ranges from 0.05 to 0.9 per cent, phosphate varies from 0.1 to 0.15 per cent, (0.06 to 0.1 per cent varies inside the forest), pH varies from 7.0 to 8.9. per cent, Potash varies from 0.3 to 1.0 per cent, calcium oxide ranges from 0.6 to 3.0 per cent and carbon varies from 0.50 to 1.0 per cent. Blasco (1977) states that about 40 to 60 per cent of the soil of this region are silts; organic matter varies between 1 to 1.5 per cent, pH is about 8 (alkaline) and exchangeable bases high. ($Ca^{++}$, $Mg^{++}$, $K^{+}$, $Na^{+}$). In areas of heavy rain and rapid drainage the nitrogen content of the soil decreases and the organic component increases.

The *salinity* of the surface soil and the adjoining water bodies change to a great extent throughout the year and is governed mainly by the quantity of fresh water flow. Monsoonal rainfall is also another affecting factor. On the basis of salinity in the soil, the soil types of the district can be categorised as (1) *Saline Soil* is formed where there is inundation or flushing of brackish water and is found in the flood plains of the river and creeks. Saline soils have three phases (a) *Inundated Phase*, (b) Phase rich in Calcite (CaCo3), and (c) *Phase rich in dolomite* (CaCo3, MgCo3) (2) *Saline Alkali Soils* is formed when the sodium salts flood a fresh low land enriched with alkali and sodium ions. Sometimes rain water completely removes the salt and makes the soil of the region (3) *Non-Saline Alkali*. Hence Saline Alkali Soils may have tidal or non- tidal phases. Saline alkali soils also have 3 phases (a) Rain water washed phase, (b) Sea water washed phase and, (c) Active Delta forming phase (4) *Degraded Saline Alkali soils* or *Saline Turf soil* is formed in the presence of decomposed organic matter. Organic acids and high salt content form saline unsaturated soils. These soils too have 3 phases (a) Inundated forest phase, (b) Cultivated area (above sea level) phase, and (c) cultivated area (below sea level) phase. (The physico-chemical characteristics of coastal soils of the district is given in the Appendix II.5).

Bhattacharjee[19] (1972) has studied the soil samples of the district. Saline soils have been noticeable in the blocks of Falta, Jaynagar,

Mathurapur, whereas Saline Alkali Soils are found in the Sagar Island, Kakdwip and in Namkhana - Fraserganj. Limited amounts of Saline - Alkali soils is also noticeable in parts of Kulpi, Mathurapur and in Canning. Non-Saline Alkali soils have been traced in patches in Mathurapur and degraded alkali soils in the vicinity of Port Canning.

## 2.7 FLORA AND FAUNA

The flora or natural vegetation of the district today is confined only to the forested tracts of the Active Delta, popularly known as the *Mangrove Tidal Forests* of the Sundarban Delta; with noted halo-phytic conditions. (Appendix II.6). Salinity, sandy soil, nutrients, weather hazards, cyclones, floods and above all human interference have all obstructed plant survival in this area. Therefore, only those species that have adapted themselves with high salinity, fine clayey soils and tidal currents have thrived best. The *Mangrove community* is characterised by (a) the stilt roots which both support the plants and their means of respiration. The Garjan (Rhizophora apiculata), Genwa (Excoecaria agollocha) and Jelegaren (ceriaps decandra) are examples of such plants. (b) Another noticeable feature is the pres-ence of *pneumatophores* (breathing roots) of plants such as the Kalabaen (Avicennia Marina), Keora (Sonneratia Apetala), Sundari and Passur (Xylocarpus mekongensis), (c) Plants such as the Khalsi (Aegeceras Carniculatum), Tora (Aegialitis rotundifolia) and Kala baen have salt - excretory glands, (d) The cell sap developes high osmotic pressure which helps the plants to draw water from the concentrated soil solution, (e) All these plants have *Viviparous germination* (no time gap between the formation of seed and the development of the embryo).

A wide group of the grasses, shrubs and sedges native to the initial vegetation after land evolution in these parts are also associ-ated with the mangroves. The "*Dhani*" *grass* (Porterasia Coarctata) and the *Baruna grass* (Sesuvium portula castrum) grow on fresh deposits of silt alongside the forests on freshly formed islands in the middle of rivers. Herbaceous growth is strangely absent. Plants of Genwa and Jelegaran species account of about 70 per cent of the plant species.

The Mangrove forests are adapted to a special kind of '*ecological niche*' studied widely by various scientists[20]. Prain (1903) arranged the Sundarban forests mainly into 3 categories (1) Southern coastal area with dominant mangroves (2) Central zone dominated by the Sundari, and (3) North Eastern part dominated by grasses. Curtes (1933) classified the forest cover into (1) Fresh water forest, (2) Moderately salt water forests, and (3) Salt Water Forests. Champion (1936) divided the forests into 4 types, (1) Low Mangrove forests, (2) Tree mangroves, (3) Salt water, and (4) Fresh water forests. Champion and Seth (1968) modified this division into 5 types as (1) Mangrove scrub, (2) Mangrove forests, (3) Salt water mixed forest, (4) Brakish water forest, and (5) Palm swamps. Rao and Sastry (1972, 74) proposed a modification of the former classification; dividing the Mangroves firstly into 2 broad groups as (1) Euestuarine, and (2) Proestuarine. The proestuarine group has again been divided into (i) Tidal mangrove, (ii) Euhyline, and (iii) Prohyline zones according to the topography and other edaphic factors. Chakravarty (1979) has divided the forest into (1) High tide, (2) Above the general tide level, (3) Frequently inundated by salt water, and (4) Below tide level. Naskar and Guha Bakshi (1982) have grouped the plant species into 4 major forms (1) Sea face or Beach forest, (2) Formative island flora, (3) Flora of the reclaimed and lowlying cultivated zone, and (4) Swamp forests.

In general therefore the normal pattern of vegetation in an estuarine delta, distribution of mangrove communities on tidal flats depends on the tidal intensity, the type of sediments and salinity. Three distinct zones of vegetation therefore can be recognised as (a) *A true estuarine zone,* comprising the estuarine banks along the mouths of the rivers is mainly, dominated by the 'Kala Bean', 'Tora' and 'Krippa'. These species tolerate high salinity and submergence either by developing salt excreting glands or by increasing water storage tissues in their leaves, and develop soft and porous pneumatophores (b) *A middle estuarine zone,* dominated by Garjan, Jelegaran and the taller Keora. Here salinity is lower than the true estuarine mouth, but the tidal current passing through the narrow creeks and channels is higher. Mangroves adjust to these habitats by producing stilt roots; and pneumatophores are soft and porous. (c) *An inner estuarine or riverine zone* comprising elevated areas with less aerated soil and more fresh water flow, is dominated by the Sundari, Genwa, Kankra

(Bueguiera Sexangula) and the Golepata (Nypa fruiticans). These species usually prefer more fresh water and develop hard pneumatophores to adjust to less aerated soil. This original zonation is sometimes lost due to erosional undercutting causing exposure of inner estuarine types along the mouth.

The flora of those forests has been facing *tremendous exploitation*. Over the years the "Sundari" trees (from which according to some scholars the Sundarban derive its name), noted for its valuable timber has been over-exploited. Secondly the greater part of the inner estuarine zone has become more saline due to lack of fresh water (though some of Ganga fresh water is received by the Hugli from the Farakka Barrage) and the Sundari, which prefer less saline soil, do not proliferate these days.

Of the forest products, golepata is used as roofing material for rural houses; Sundari and Passur as also Dhundul, Garjan, Tora and Mathgaran is used for house posts. Garan, Tora, Garjan, Kankra and Hental (Phoneix paludosa) are used as rafters. Branches of Garan are used for wattle. Sundari wood is good for making boats. The most favoured fuels are Garan, Khalsi, Baen and Singara. In addition some mangrove trees of the region give shelter to migratory rock bees from the Himalayas to built many beehives. On an average 500 quintals of honey and 30 quintals of wax are been collected from these forests.

The fauna of these forests play generally *amphibious role*. The food-chain (Map 2.6), of the Sundarbans brings into focus the factor that the famous Royal Bengal Tiger is at the apex of the hierarchy of terrestrial as well as aquatic animals. Here the tiger's prey includes pig, deer, monkey, water monitor, bird, crab and fish.

The Sundarbans is one of the tiger reserves having the largest tiger population of India and where Project Tiger (Appendix II.7) was launched in 1973 to save the tiger from extinction. The Sundarbans Tiger Reserve covering 2585 sq.km. over the whole of South Twenty four Parganas had 135 tigers at that time, has 264 (1984 Census) at present, the annual rate of growth being 8.7 per cent [21]. There are also two more Sanctuaries at Halliday and Lothan Islands. There are no major co-predators to share the source of food with the tiger even adapted to swimming and drinking honey from the beehives.

The jungle cat (Felis chaus) and the civet cat (Viverra zibatha) and the fishing cat (Felis Viverina) are found in plenty. The chital

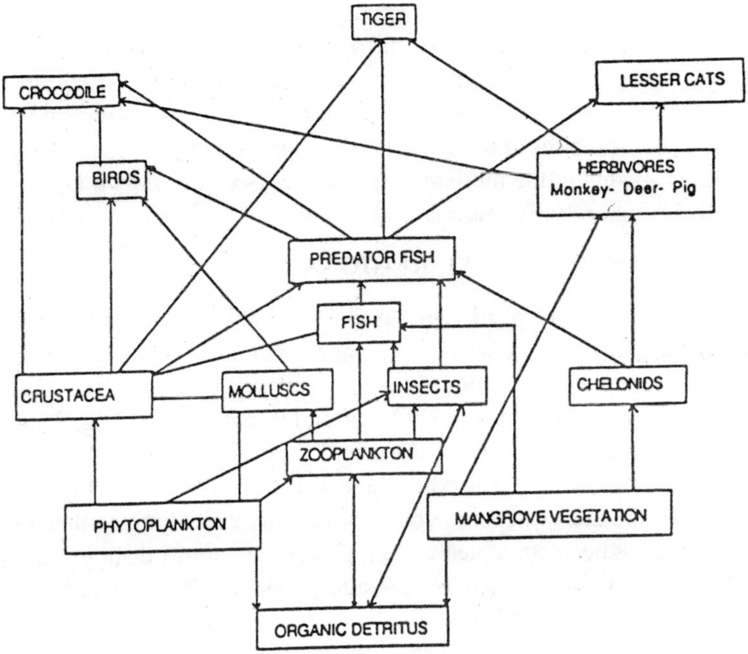


*Source :* Coast Zone Management, West Bengal

**Fig. 2.6 :** Food Chain in the Mangrove Eco-system

or the axis deer (Cervus axis) has been estimated to be 30,000 in the forest. Besides the rhesus monkey, barking deer, wild pig, otter, water monitor are also prominent.

The fluvial habitats of the region are utilized by the estuarine crocodile (now also being reared here in the crocodile project) sharks, dolphins and crabs. Of the snakes, the king cobra, common cobra, banded krait, russel's viper and some sea snakes are venomous while the python is the most prominent non-venomous snake of the forest.

The Sajnekhali Bird Sanctuary is alive with birds specially during the monsoon. The open bill stork, little egret, large egret, grey heron, purple heron, night heron and cormorant are the local birds whereas the pelican is migratory. Besides these forests are also the abode of local birds as the stork, lapwing, dove, parakeet, cuckoo, etc. Fishes abound in the nutrient enriched creeks and so prawn farming and fishing are very important activities.

## 2.8 GEO-ECOLOGICAL REGIONS

The regional concept though based on mental judgement has long been regarded as "inherently geographic work"[22]. Much debate has been undertaken right from Hettner, Whittlesey to more recent scholars like Woolridge and East, C.C. Carter, I.G. Joerg, K. Young, Stamp and Baker, Mathieson, Roger Minshull[23] and Indian authors like K.S. Ahmad, Pithawala, Asok Mitra, and R.L. Singh[24], on this topic. In view of the above national complexities the present regionalization scheme has been attempted to incorporate the various distinguishing and meaningful regional factors and assess their role in different subregions in this area.

Based on the physical and ecological parameters of the natural environment, an attempt has been made here to classify South Twenty-Four Parganas (a part of the Ganges-Hugli Delta), into different regions. (Table 2.4)

I. **The Stable Delta of the North**; comprising of slight higher elevations and the land of sluggish rivers and depressions[25] in contrast to—

II. **The Active Delta of the Southern part**; comprising a composite of tidal channels, rivers, creeks, islands. (Map 2.7) Each of these two broad divisions can be further subdivided based on micro variations as (I) The Stable Delta of the

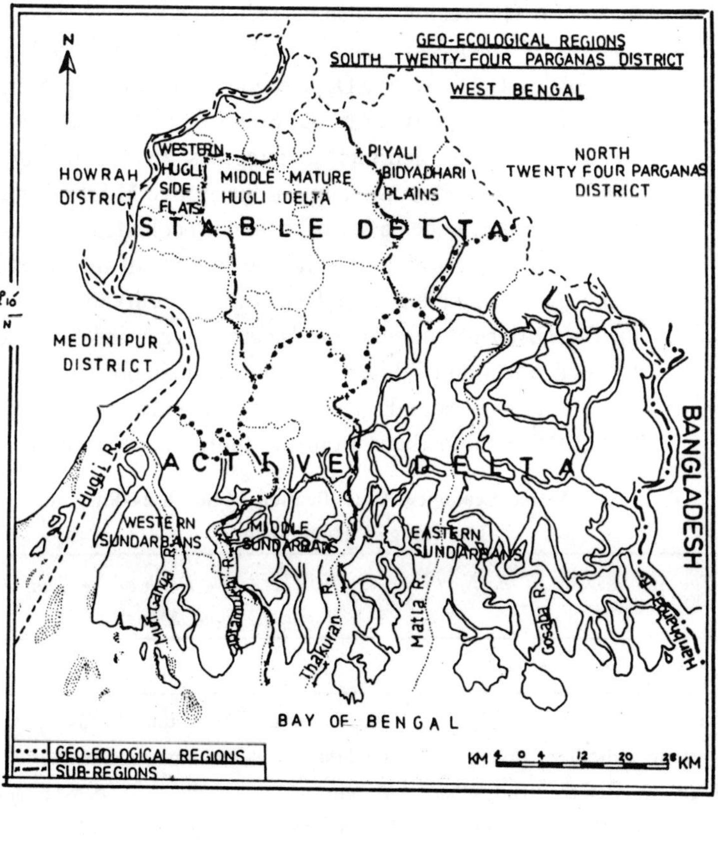


**MAP 2.7 :** Geo-Ecological Regions South 24-Parganas District, West Bengal

North can be divided into *(i) The Western Hugli Side Flats*; comprising a narrow strip of flat alluvial land along the stretch of the Hugli in the west, *(ii) The Mature Delta of the Hugli* in the Middle bordering the Hugli Side Flats, sloping southwards, and *(iii) The Piyali - Bidyadhari Plains* in the East also forming a plain area with land sloping to the south. This region is also characterised by swamps and marshes of which Salt Water Lake (Dhapa) is one of the best examples. (II) The Active Delta of the South (or the present day 'Sundarbans'), lying to the South of the Stable Delta can again be classified into 3 subregions. *(iv)The Western Sundarban Margin,* comprising of the Active Mouth of the Hugli; exposed under a set of different ecological factors. *(v) The Middle Sundarbans* and the Fringes of the Active Delta (Bordering the Mature Delta of the North) and finally the *(vi) Eastern or Interior Sundarbans* comprising of dense forested tracts and saline soils lying in juxtaposition with the international boundary (Bangladesh); and separating the Bangladeshi Sundarbans from the Indian counterpart.

**TABLE 2.4 : A Geo-Ecological Classification of South 24-Parganas : The Ganga - Hugli Delta**

| *I. The Stable Delta of the North* | | | *II. The Active Delta of the South or the Sundarbans* | | |
|---|---|---|---|---|---|
| *(i)* | *(ii)* | *(iii)* | *(iv)* | *(v)* | *(vi)* |
| The Western Hugli Side Flats. | The Middle Mature Delta of the Hugli. | The Piyali-Bidyadhari Plains of the East. | The Western Sundarbans Margin, comprising of the the Active Mouth of the Hugli. | The Middle Sundarbans and the Fringes of Active Delta. | Eastern or interior Sundarbans of Dense Tidal Forested Tracts. |

*Note* : Classification is based on physical and ecological factors.

For simplicity and data computation, the regional divisions consist of separate blocks, (1991 Census), given as follows :

(i) The Western Hugli Side Flats consist of the blocks of (1) Thakurpukur-Metiaburuz, (2) Maheshtala, (3) Budge Budge, (4) Falta, (5) Diamond Harbour and (6) Kulpi;

(ii) The Middle Mature Delta of the Hugli consist of 6 blocks of (7) Sonarpur, (8) Bishnupur, (9) Baruipur, (10) Mograhat, (11) Mandir Bazar and (12) Jaynagar;

(iii) The Piyali Bidhyadhari Plains of the Eastern part of the district falls in the (13) Bhangar and (14) Canning blocks;

(iv) The Western Sundarban Margin consists of 3 blocks of (15) Sagar Island, (16) Kakdwip and (17) Namkhana;

(v) The Middle Sundarbans consist of again (18) Mathurapur and (19) Patharpratima; and

(vi) The Eastern Sundarbans also comprises of 3 blocks of (20) Kultali, (21) Basanti and (22) Gosaba.

The characteristics and attributes of area, population and settlements of the District has been portrayed in Table 2.5 which depicts a marked contract between the Stable and the Active Delta. The Middle Mature Hugli Delta is the largest subregion in areal extent exemplified by contributing 20.91% of the total area, and also contributes the highest proportion of human numbers i.e. 33.92% in 1991. Within the Active Delta, the Western Sundarbans depicts the largest areal size i.e. 19.06% but the lowest population size of 8.21% only.

Population density figures reveal the highest 1991 density of 1914/sq.km in the Western Hugli Side Flats and the lowest i.e. 393/sq.km again in the Western Sundarbans. The highest growth rate of population is seen in the Piyali- Bidyadhari Plains having a 1981-1991 growth rate of 36.58%. The Eastern Sundarbans reveal the lowest rate of 19.70%. Sex -Ratio figures in general are in the favour of males but lower figures are noticeable in the Stable Delta.

The total number of settlements of the district has exibited a rise from 2124 in 1981 to 2151 in 1991. The highest number or 803 settlements occur in the Middle Mature Hugli Delta, followed by 618 settlements of the Western Hugli Side Flats. The lowest number of settlements, all villages, 122 in number are seen in the Western Sundarbans.

In general the highest number of villages, 789 in number, occur in the Middle Mature Delta, whereas the lowest i.e. 122 occur in Western Sundarbans. The Active Delta in general has no town or city. Within the Stable Delta the highest number of towns i.e. 27 in number occur in the Western Hugli Side Flats. Again average area per settlement is greater in general in the Active Delta, being largest in the Western Sundarbans, being 9.98 sq.km. in 1991 and smallest in the Stable Delta, being 1.31 sq.km. in the Western Hugli Side Flats. The average population per settlement also portrays a similar picture.

The Scheduled Castes and Tribes are more concentrated in the Active Delta, the Eastern Sundarbans depict the highest i.e. 52.03% of Scheduled castes in 1991, and 6.46% of the Scheduled tribes in 1991. The lowest proportion of scheduled castes and tribes in 1991 are noticeable in the Western Hugli Side Flats and the Middle Mature Hugli Delta respectively. Literacy figures of 1991 reveal the highest in the Western Hugli Side Flats, being 50.62% and the lowest in the Piyali-Bidyadhari Plains i.e. 32.98%. Again work participation show higher rates in the Active Delta in comparison to the Stable Delta; the highest rate of 1991 being seen in the Western Sundarbans i.e. 33.05%. In terms of area, population growth rates, settlements and literacy, the Middle Mature Delta of the Hugli and the Western Hugli Side Flats constitute two important sub-regions of the Stable Delta that stand ahead of others.

## 2.9 CONCLUSION

From the above study it can therefore be concluded that the Geo-Ecological characteristics of South 24-Parganas are responsible for regional contrasts in the district. The coastal area is a typical littoral type with deltaic estuarine and tidal complicacies. Recently, the entire area of the Sundarbans, south of the Dampier - Hodges line has been declared as a "Biosphere Reserve"–– the fifth one in the country. From the margin of the coast towards the interior of the district, changing natural environments and ecosystems are observed. The littoral margin has high salinity, periodic innundations, storms, forests and wild animals. Even within this region, micro contrasts arise from the west to the East. All these factors contribute to marked variation in the characteristics of human settlements in the region.

**TABLE 2.5 : Characteristics and Attributes of Settlements in the Geo-Ecological Regions 1981-1991**

| *Geo-ecological Region* | *Name of the Block* | *Area in (sq.km.)* | *Proportion of area* | *Number of Villages (inhabited)* | | *Number of towns* | | *Total no of Settlements* | | *Average area per Settlement (sq.km)* | |
|---|---|---|---|---|---|---|---|---|---|---|---|
| | | | | 1981 | 1991 | 1981 | 1991 | 1981 | 1991 | 1981 | 1991 |
| 1 | 2 | 3 | 4 | 5 | 6 | 7 | 8 | 9 | 10 | 11 | 12 |
| **STABLE DELTA** | | | | | | | | | | | |
| (I) THE WESTERN HUGLI-SIDE FLATS | 1. Thakurpukur - Metiaburuz | 32.0 | 0.50 | 19 | 31 | 3 | 5 | 22 | 36 | 1.45 | 0.89 |
| | 2. Maheshtala | 53.1 | 0.83 | 28 | 12 | 9 | 12 | 37 | 24 | 1.44 | 2.21 |
| | 3. Budge Budge | 142.5 | 2.23 | 83 | 80 | 5 | 9 | 88 | 89 | 1.62 | 1.60 |
| | 4. Falta | 135.7 | 2.12 | 133 | 133 | 0 | 0 | 133 | 133 | 1.02 | 1.02 |
| | 5. Diamond Harbour | 196.3 | 3.07 | 165 | 163 | 1 | 1 | 166 | 164 | 1.18 | 1.20 |
| | 6. Kulpi | 250.7 | 3.92 | 170 | 172 | 0 | 0 | 170 | 172 | 1.47 | 1.46 |
| | **TOTAL** | **810.3** | **12.69** | **598** | **591** | **18** | **27** | **616** | **618** | **1.32** | **1.31** |
| (II) THE MIDDLE MATURE DELTA OF THE HUGLI | 7. Sonarpur | 170.7 | 2.67 | 92 | 93 | 4 | 8 | 96 | 101 | 1.78 | 1.69 |
| | 8. Bishnupur | 213.4 | 3.34 | 154 | 155 | 1 | 3 | 155 | 158 | 1.38 | 1.35 |
| | 9. Baruipur | 214.5 | 3.36 | 132 | 137 | 1 | 2 | 133 | 139 | 1.61 | 1.54 |
| | 10. Mcgrahat | 255.1 | 3.99 | 170 | 176 | 0 | 0 | 170 | 176 | 1.50 | 1.45 |
| | 11. Mandir Bazar | 117.3 | 1.84 | 110 | 113 | 0 | 0 | 110 | 113 | 1.07 | 1.04 |
| | 12. Jay Nagar | 364.4 | 5.70 | 113 | 115 | 1 | 1 | 114 | 116 | 3.20 | 3.14 |
| | **TOTAL** | **1335.4** | **20.91** | **771** | **789** | **7** | **14** | **778** | **803** | **1.72** | **1.66** |

**TABLE 2.5 : (Contd.)**

| *Geo-ecological Region* | *Name of the Block* | *Area in (sq.km.)* | *Propor-tion of area* | *Number of Villages (inhabited)* | | *Number of towns* | | *Total no of Settlements* | | *Average area per Settlement (sq.km)* | |
|---|---|---|---|---|---|---|---|---|---|---|---|
| | | | | 1981 | 1991 | 1981 | 1991 | 1981 | 1991 | 1981 | 1991 |
| 1 | 2 | 3 | 4 | 5 | 6 | 7 | 8 | 9 | 10 | 11 | 12 |
| (III) The PIYALI- | 13 Bhangar | 299.3 | 4.69 | 143 | 145 | 0 | 0 | 143 | 145 | 2.09 | 2.06 |
| BIDYADHARI | 14. Canning | 886.7 | 7.62 | 199 | 121 | 1 | 1 | 120 | 122 | 4.06 | 3.99 |
| PLAINS(EAST) | **Total** | **786.0** | **12.30** | **262** | **266** | **1** | **1** | **263** | **267** | **2.99** | **2.94** |
| **ACTIVE DELTA** | | | | | | | | | | | |
| (IV) THE WESTERN | 15. Sagar Island | 580.9 | 9.09 | 44 | 46 | 0 | 0 | 44 | 46 | 13.20 | 12.63 |
| SUNDARBAN | 16. Kakdwip | 476.8 | 7.46 | 48 | 48 | 0 | 0 | 48 | 48 | 9.92 | 9.93 |
| MARGIN | 17. Namkhana | 159.8 | 2.50 | 28 | 28 | 0 | 0 | 28 | 28 | 5.7 | 5.71 |
| | **TOTAL** | **1217.5** | **19.06** | **120** | **122** | **0** | **0** | **120** | **122** | **10.15** | **9.98** |
| (V) THE MIDDLE | 18 Mathurapur | 611.8 | 9.58 | 121 | 125 | 0 | 0 | 121 | 125 | 5.06 | 4.89 |
| SUNDARBANS | 19 Pathar Pratima | 484.6 | 7.59 | 86 | 90 | 0 | 0 | 86 | 90 | 5.63 | 5.38 |
| | **TOTAL** | **1096.4** | **17.16** | **207** | **215** | **0** | **0** | **207** | **215** | **5.30** | **5.10** |
| (VI) THE EASTERN | 20 Kultali | 361.1 | 5.65 | 51 | 51 | 0 | 0 | 51 | 51 | 7.08 | 7.08 |
| INTERIOR | 21 Basanti | 409.7 | 6.41 | 65 | 67 | 0 | 0 | 65 | 67 | 6.30 | 6.11 |
| SUNDARBANS | 22 Gosaba | 371.4 | 5.81 | 50 | 50 | 0 | 0 | 50 | 50 | 7.43 | 7.43 |
| | **TOTAL** | **1142.2** | **17.88** | **166** | **168** | **0** | **0** | **166** | **168** | **6.88** | **6.80** |
| | **DISTRICT TOTAL** | **6387.8** | **100** | **2124** | **2151** | **26** | **42** | **2150** | **2193** | **2.97** | **2.91** |

**TABLE 2.5** : (*Contd.*)

| *Geo-ecological Region* | *Name of the Block* | *Total Population* 1981 | 1991 | *Proportion of pop. to Total* 1981 | 1991 | *Density Population* 1981 | 1991 | *Growth Rates* 1981-91 |
|---|---|---|---|---|---|---|---|---|
| | | 13 | 14 | 15 | 16 | 17 | 18 | 19 |
| **STABLE DELTA** | | | | | | | | |
| (I) THE WESTERN HUGLI-SIDE FLATS | 1. Thakurpukur - Metiaburuz | 110,606 | 176,456 | 2.51 | 3.03 | 3456 | 5514 | 59.54 |
| | 2. Maheshtala | 194,094 | 331,142 | 4.41 | 5.68 | 3655 | 6236 | 70.61 |
| | 3. Budge Budge | 295,350 | 342,924 | 6.71 | 5.88 | 2073 | 2406 | 16.11 |
| | 4. Falta | 161,181 | 199,596 | 3.66 | 3.42 | 1188 | 1471 | 23.83 |
| | 5. Diamond Harbour | 229,167 | 288,601 | 5.21 | 4.95 | 1167 | 1470 | 25.93 |
| | 6. Kulpi | 167,640 | 211,851 | 3.81 | 3.63 | 669 | 845 | 26.37 |
| | **TOTAL** | **1,158,038** | **1,550,570** | **26.32** | **26.60** | **1429** | **1914** | **33.90** |
| (II) THE MIDDLE MATURE DELTA OF THE HUGLI | 7. Sonarpur | 241,434 | 346,520 | 5.49 | 5.94 | 1414 | 2030 | 43.53 |
| | 8. Bishnupur | 287,811 | 357,253 | 6.54 | 6.13 | 1349 | 1674 | 24.13 |
| | 9. Baruipur | 230,238 | 312,071 | 5.23 | 5.35 | 1073 | 1455 | 35.54 |
| | 10. Mograhat | 318,136 | 419,464 | 7.23 | 7.19 | 1247 | 1644 | 31.85 |
| | 11. Mandir Bazar | 126,947 | 159,585 | 2.89 | 2.74 | 1082 | 1360 | 25.71 |
| | 12. Jay Nagar | 254,478 | 382,823 | 5.78 | 6.57 | 698 | 1051 | 50.43 |
| | **TOTAL** | **1,459,043** | **1,977,716** | **33.16** | **33.92** | **1093** | **1481** | **35.55** |
| (III) THE PIALI-BIDYADHARI PLAINS(EAST) | 13. Bhangar | 248,071 | 330,613 | 5.64 | 5.67 | 829 | 1105 | 33.27 |
| | 14. Canning | 248,754 | 347,930 | 5.65 | 5.97 | 511 | 715 | 39.87 |
| | **TOTAL** | **496,825** | **678,543** | **11.29** | **11.64** | **632** | **863** | **36.58** |

**TABLE 2.5 : (*Contd.*)**

| *Geo-ecological Region* | *Name of the Block* | *Total Population* | | *Proportion of pop. to Total* | | *Density Population* | | *Growth Rates* |
|---|---|---|---|---|---|---|---|---|
| | | 1981 | 1991 | 1981 | 1991 | 1981 | 1991 | 1981-91 |
| | | 13 | 14 | 15 | 16 | 17 | 18 | 19 |
| **ACTIVE DELTA** | | | | | | | | |
| (IV) THE WESTERN | 15. Sagar Island | 115,228 | 154,190 | 2.62 | 2.64 | 198 | 265 | 33.82 |
| SUNDARBAN | 16. Kakdwip | 166,777 | 227,692 | 3.79 | 3.91 | 350 | 473 | 36.52 |
| MARGIN | 17. Namkhana | 74,156 | 96,750 | 1.69 | 1.66 | 464 | 605 | 30.47 |
| | **TOTAL** | **356,161** | **478,632** | **8.09** | **8.21** | **293** | **·393** | **34.39** |
| (V) THE MIDDLE | 18. Mathurapur | 244,609 | 314,870 | 5.56 | 5.40 | 400 | 515 | 28.72 |
| SUNDARBANS | 19. Pathar Pratima | 197,686 | 245,821 | 4.49 | 4.22 | 408 | 507 | 24.35 |
| | **TOTAL** | **442,295** | **560,691** | **10.05** | **9.62** | **403** | **511** | **26.77** |
| (VI) THE EASTERN | 20. Kultali | 147,147 | 156,450 | 3.34 | 2.68 | 407 | 433 | 6.32 |
| INTERIOR | 21. Basanti | 172,353 | 226,974 | 3.92 | 3.89 | 421 | 554 | 31.69 |
| SUNDARBANS | 22. Gosaba | 168,335 | 200,514 | 3.82 | 3.44 | 453 | 540 | 19.12 |
| | **TOTAL** | **487,835** | **583,938** | **11.09** | **10.01** | **427** | **511** | **19.70** |
| | **DISTRICT TOTAL** | **4,400,197** | **5,830,090** | **100** | **100** | **689** | **913** | **32.50** |

**TABLE 2.5** : (*Contd.*)

| *Geo-ecological Region* | *Name of the Block* | *Sex Ratio (no. of Females per 1000 males)* | | *Average Population per Settlement* | | *Proportion of Scheduled castes to total pop.* | | *Proportion of Schduled tribes to total pop.* | |
|---|---|---|---|---|---|---|---|---|---|
| | | 1981 | 1991 | 1981 | 1991 | 1981 | 1991 | 1981 | 1991 |
| | | 20 | 21 | 22 | 23 | 24 | 25 | 26 | 27 |
| **STABLE DELTA** | | | | | | | | | |
| (I) THE WESTERN HUGLI-SIDE FLATS | 1. Thakurpukur - Metiaburuz | 928 | 857 | 5028 | 4902 | 30.11 | 28.62 | 0.63 | 0.24 |
| | 2. Maheshtala | 882 | 882 | 5246 | 13798 | 22.94 | 19.78 | 0.23 | 0.33 |
| | 3. Budge Budge | 844 | 874 | 3356 | 3853 | 22.27 | 18.91 | 0.39 | 0.35 |
| | 4. Falta | 931 | 939 | 1212 | 1501 | 25.20 | 22.96 | — | ... |
| | 5. Diamond Harbour | 935 | 937 | 1381 | 1760 | 23.18 | 20.67 | — | 0.01 |
| | 6. Kulpi | 952 | 1066 | 986 | 1232 | 39.09 | 32.56 | — | ... |
| | **TOTAL** | **903** | **918** | **1880** | **2509** | **26.15** | **22.91** | **0.20** | **1.18** |
| (II) THE MIDDLE MATURE DELTA OF THE HUGLI | 7. Sonarpur | 899 | 923 | 2514 | 3431 | 38.77 | 38.32 | 0.96 | 0.94 |
| | 8. Bishnupur | 928 | 952 | 1857 | 2261 | 35.93 | 35.89 | 0.03 | 0.01 |
| | 9. Baruipur | 935 | 924 | 1731 | 2245 | 44.99 | 44.75 | 0.33 | 0.34 |
| | 10. Mograhat | 937 | 931 | 1871 | 2383 | 30.52 | 32.46 | 0.01 | ... |
| | 11. Mandir Bazar | 949 | 932 | 1154 | 1412 | 47.72 | 47.65 | — | ... |
| | 12. Jay Nagar | 939 | 936 | 2232 | 3300 | 43.12 | 41.12 | 0.04 | 0.23 |
| | **TOTAL** | **930** | **933** | **1875** | **2463** | **38.93** | **38.81** | **0.23** | **0.27** |
| (III) THE PIYALI-BIDYADHARI PLAINS(EAST) | 13. Bhangar | 946 | 949 | 1735 | 2280 | 27.22 | 25.00 | 1.76 | 1.24 |
| | 14. Canning | 963 | 954 | 2073 | 2852 | 43.42 | 42.53 | 3.98 | 3.93 |
| | **TOTAL** | **954** | **952** | **1889** | **2541** | **35.33** | **33.99** | **2.87** | **2.62** |

TABLE 2.5 : *(Contd.)*

| *Geo-ecological Region* | *Name of the Block* | *Sex Ratio (no. of Females per 1000 males)* | | *Average Population per Settlement* | | *Proportion of Scheduled castes to total pop.* | | *Proportion of Schduled tribes to total pop.* | |
|---|---|---|---|---|---|---|---|---|---|
| | | 1981 | 1991 | 1981 | 1991 | 1981 | 1991 | 1981 | 1991 |
| | | 20 | 21 | 22 | 23 | 24 | 25 | 26 | 27 |
| **ACTIVE DELTA** | | | | | | | | | |
| (IV) THE WESTERN | 15. Sagar Island | 950 | 946 | 2119 | 3352 | 26.67 | 28.44 | 0.36 | 0.35 |
| SUNDARBAN | 16. Kakdwip | 948 | 1017 | 3475 | 4744 | 29.10 | 33.74 | 0.68 | 0.49 |
| MARGIN | 17. Namkhana | 947 | 947 | 2648 | 3455 | 25.22 | 26.28 | 0.47 | 0.55 |
| | **TOTAL** | **948** | **979** | **2968** | **3923** | **27.51** | **30.32** | **0.53** | **0.46** |
| (V) THE MIDDLE | 18. Mathurapur | 932 | 927 | 2022 | 2519 | 20.00 | 35.25 | 1.06 | 0.99 |
| SUNDARBANS | 19. Pathar Pratima | 944 | 952 | 2299 | 2731 | 23.95 | 25.92 | 0.78 | 0.75 |
| | **TOTAL** | **937** | **938** | **2137** | **2608** | **29.91** | **31.16** | **0.93** | **0.89** |
| (VI) THE EASTERN | 20. Kultali | 937 | 943 | 2885 | 3068 | 48.53 | 50.27 | 2.69 | 2.81 |
| INTERIOR | 21. Basanti | 947 | 950 | 2652 | 3388 | 41.48 | 41.75 | 6.26 | 6.00 |
| SUNDARBANS | 22. Gosaba | 934 | 941 | 3368 | 4010 | 64.13 | 65.04 | 9.71 | 9.82 |
| | **TOTAL** | **939** | **945** | **2939** | **3476** | **51.42** | **52.03** | **6.37** | **6.46** |
| | **DISTRICT TOTAL** | **929** | **937** | **2047** | **2658** | **34.71** | **33.93** | **1.30** | **1.21** |

TABLE 2.5 : *(Contd.)*

| *Geo-ecological Region* | *Name of the Block* | *Proportion of Literates to total Population* | | *Work Participation rate (to total Population)* | |
|---|---|---|---|---|---|
| | | *1981* | *1991* | *1981* | *1991* |
| | | *28* | *29* | *30* | *31* |
| **STABLE DELTA** | | | | | |
| (I) THE WESTERN HUGLI-SIDE FLATS | 1. Thakurpukur - Metiaburuz | 70.54 | 55.39 | 34.08 | 41.24 |
| | 2. Maheshtala | 52.17 | 57.78 | 25.24 | 27.71 |
| | 3. Budge Budge | 43.18 | 51.67 | 26.95 | 26.93 |
| | 4. Falta | 42.84 | 49.07 | 24.50 | 31.46 |
| | 5. Diamond Harbour | 42.54 | 47.72 | 26.29 | 27.34 |
| | 6. Kulpi | 36.78 | 39.15 | 25.45 | 27.07 |
| | **TOTAL** | **46.20** | **50.62** | **26.66** | **29.40** |
| (II) THE MIDDLE MATURE DELTA OF THE HUGLI | 7. Sonarpur | 48.52 | 61.66 | 26.07 | 27.31 |
| | 8. Bishnupur | 39.18 | 47.23 | 26.20 | 27.66 |
| | 9. Baruipur | 40.52 | 50.19 | 26.20 | 26.60 |
| | 10. Mograhat | 32.55 | 40.44 | 25.08 | 26.59 |
| | 11. Mandir Bazar | 34.16 | 41.11 | 24.79 | 24.87 |
| | 12. Jay Nagar | 32.77 | 37.94 | 25.68 | 25.72 |
| | **TOTAL** | **37.94** | **46.46** | **25.79** | **26.60** |
| (III) THE PIYALI-BIDYADHARI PLAINS(EAST) | 13. Bhangar | 29.06 | 34.01 | 27.75 | 27.02 |
| | 14. Canning | 26.44 | 32.01 | 27.02 | 27.32 |
| | **TOTAL** | **27.75** | **32.98** | **27.38** | **27.17** |

**TABLE 2.5 :** *(Contd.)*

| *Geo-ecological Region* | *Name of the Block* | *Proportion of Literates to total Population* | | *Work Participation rate (to total Population)* | |
|---|---|---|---|---|---|
| | | *1981* | *1991* | *1981* | *1991* |
| | | *28* | *29* | *30* | *31* |
| **ACTIVE DELTA** | | | | | |
| (IV) THE WESTERN | 15. Sagar Island | 40.58 | 35.59 | 26.90 | 27.41 |
| SUNDARBAN | 16. Kakdwip | 35.94 | 43.26 | 27.38 | 31.26 |
| MARGIN | 17. Namkhana | 41.34 | 50.96 | 27.41 | 45.76 |
| | **TOTAL** | **38.56** | **41.38** | **27.23** | **33.05** |
| (V) THE MIDDLE | 18. Mathurapur | 34.15 | 41.63 | 26.73 | 30.87 |
| SUNDARBANS | 19. Pathar Pratima | 37.89 | 43.54 | 27.39 | 32.65 |
| | **TOTAL** | **35.82** | **42.46** | **27.04** | **31.65** |
| (VI) THE EASTERN | 20. Kultali | 19.02 | 32.19 | 27.39 | 26.30 |
| INTERIOR | 21. Basanti | 25.27 | 31.52 | 27.14 | 29.87 |
| SUNDARBANS | 22. Gosaba | 35.78 | 44.07 | 28.81 | 35.93 |
| | **TOTAL** | **27.01** | **36.01** | **27.79** | **30.99** |
| | **DISTRICT TOTAL** | **37.59** | **44.15** | **26.66** | **28.87** |

**REFERENCES**


1. Wadia, D.N. (1973), *Geology of India*, Tata Mc Graw Hill Publishing Company, New Delhi, pp. 370-371.
2. Fergusson, J. (1983), "Delta of The Ganges" *Quarterly Journal of the Geological Society* XIX, pp. 28-32.
3. Oldham, R.D. (1917),"Structure of The Gangetic Plains", *Memoirs of the Geological Society of India*, Vol.XIII, Pt.1, pp. 16-18.
4. Mitra Asok (1951), Census of India: District Handbook 24-Parganas, West Bengal Government Press, Alipore, pp. VIII - IX.
5. De, Rabindranath (1990), *The Sundarbans*, Oxford University Press, Calcutta, pp. 8-9.
6. *ibid.*, pp. 8-9.
7. Mandal, A.K., R.K. Ghosh (1989), Sundarban - *A Socio Bio-Ecological Study*, Bookland Pvt. Ltd., Calcutta, pp. 8-9.
8. Mitra, Ashok (1951), Census of India, *op.cit.* pp. IV and V.
9. Mandal A.K., R.K. Ghosh (1989), *op.cit.*, pp. 7-8.
10. Paul, A.K., M.K. Bandyopadhyay and A. Chowdhury (1987), "Morpho-ecological variations in the Sundarban Mudflats", *Geographical Review of India* Vol 49, No 1, pp. 1-15.
11. Paul, A.K. and M.K. Bandyopadhyay (1986), "Coastal sand dunes of Sagar Island, *West Bengal Geographical Review of India*, Vol 48, No 2, pp. 41-48.
12. Mitra, Asok (1953), An Account of Land Management In West Bengal 1870-1890, Census of India 1951, West Bengal Government Press, Alipore, pp. 128-129.
13. Mitra Asok (1951), Census of India District Handbook 24-Parganas, *op.cit.* pp. VI-VII.
14. *Ibid*, pp. VII - VIII.
15. Spate, O.H.K. and A.T.A. Learmouth (1957), *India and Pakistan - A General and Regional Geography*, Methuen and Co. Ltd., U.K., pp. 52-53.
16. Das, P.K. (1968), *The Monsoon*, National Book Trust, India, pp. 113-114.
17. Lahiri, T.B. (Member - Secretary) (1979), Project Report On Sundarban Development, Government of India, pp. 12-13.
18. *Ibid.*, pp. 19-22.
19. Mandal, A.K., R.K. Ghosh (1989) *Sundarban - A Socio Bio-Ecological Study, op.cit*, pp. 33-36.
20. *Ibid.*, pp. 38-41.
21. De, Rabindranath (1990), *The Sundarbans, op.cit*, p.2.
22. Broek, Jan, O.M. (1965), *Geography: Its Scope And Spirit*, Columbus C.E. Merril Books, p. 58.
23. Minshull, Roger (1967), *Regional Geography, Theory and Practice*, Hutchinson University Library, London, pp.26-28.
24. Singh, R.L. (1971), *India : A Regional Geography*, National Geographical Society of India, pp. 26-28.
25. Roy, B.K., Vijay S. Verma (1988), *Regional Divisions of India : A Cartographic Analysis*, Vol. XXII West Bengal, Census of India, pp.170-172.

# POPULATION PROFILE

## 3.1 INTRODUCTION

In India, as elsewhere (a) the distribution of population in space, (b) the composition of population and (c) the growth and density of population[1] is conditioned by the interplay of historical and geographical factors. Ancient cultures and imperial regimes have influenced population dynamics in our country over a long past and their impact is visible on the pattern of today. The present geographical distribution is a product of history and there is no doubt that the current history too is causing the pattern of distribution to change[2]. Hence, the population profile of the region has been viewed here to bring out the regional variations in (a) *Spatial distribution, density* (b) *Composition* of population and (c) The *growth* of population between 1981-1991.

The state of West Bengal constituting the Lower Ganga Plains is one of the most populous states of India covering an area of 88,752 sq. km and a total population of 54,580,647 persons in 1981 i.e. with only 2.70% of India's total area, West Bengal supported 7.97% of the total country's population and ranked fourth after Uttar Pradesh, Bihar and Maharashtra. In 1991 this figure rose to 68,077,965 covering 8.12% of India's total population.

The net decadal increase of 13 million people in West Bengal should be viewed in the light of the fact that with a limited portion of India's land resources, West Bengal supports a considerable amount of human numbers thereby creating a considerable pressure on land and natural resources.

Littoral South 24-Parganas is one of the populous districts of West Bengal. Of the 17 districts of the state, with 15.86% of the total area, Medinipur ranked first in 1991, comprising 12.88% of the total West Bengal population. With 4.61% of total area, North 24-Parganas ranked second supporting 10.71% of the population. The third rank goes to Barddhaman district that supports 7.9% of total area and 8.79% of the total population. This is closely followed by the district under concern. South 24-Parganas ranked *fourth* in 1991, with 11.22% of the total state area supporting 8.40% of the total population. South-24 Parganas comprised of a total population of 4,400,197 in 1981 that rose to 5,830,090 in 1991. The net addition of 1.4 million people in the district in 1991 is the resultant of the interplay of various factors. The aim of the present chapter is therefore to assess the processes that are continuously at work in delimiting and determining the population characteristics of the 6 geo-ecological regions from 1981 to 1991.

## 3.2 SPATIAL DISTRIBUTION AND DENSITY OF POPULATION 1981-1991

South Twenty-Four Parganas shows a remarkable contrast in the spatial distribution of population. The different Geo-ecological regions exhibit different human numbers attributed to the contrasting physical characteristics and ever changing historical factors. From the total figures, it is clearly discernable that with 45.90% of the total area of the district, the Stable Delta in the North supported 70.77% of the district's total population in 1981; but this figure has risen to 72.16% in 1991. By contrast, the Active Delta of the district with 54.10% of the total district's area supported 29.23% of the total population of the district and 27.84% in 1991.

Table 3.1 depicts the different proportions of area and population of the 6 sub-regions in 1981 and 1991. The highest proportion of the total district's *area* is represented by the *Middle Mature Hugli Delta*, i.e. 20.91% and the lowest by the Piyali Bidyadhari Plains i.e. 12.30%, both in the Stable Delta. The Active Delta regions share 19.06%, 17.88% and 17.16% of the districts area in the Western, Eastern and Middle Sundarbans respectively. The blockwise breakup reveal that higher proportions of area are exhibited by the Active Delta, being as high as 9.58% in Mathurapur.

Population wise too 1981 figures exhibit that the Middle Mature Delta of the Hugli covers the largest share of population i.e. 33.16% followed by the Western Hugli Side Flats 26.32%, the Piyali

**TABLE 3.1 : Spatial Distribution of Popualtion 1981-91**
**(Proportion of Area And Population to District Total)**

| | | | *1981* *Population* | | | *1991* *Population* | | |
|---|---|---|---|---|---|---|---|---|
| *Regions/Blocks* | | *Area* | *Person* | *Male* | *Female* | *Person* | *Male* | *Female* |
| | *1* | *2* | *3* | *4* | *5* | *6* | *7* | *8* |
| **STABLE DELTA** | | | | | | | | |
| *I.* | *THE WESTERN HUGLI SIDE FLATS* | | | | | | | |
| 1. | Metiaburuz | 0.50 | 2.51 | 2.52 | 2.51 | 3.03 | 3.16 | 2.89 |
| 2. | Mahestala | 0.83 | 4.41 | 4.52 | 4.29 | 5.68 | 5.85 | 5.50 |
| 3. | Budge Budge | 2.23 | 6.71 | 7.02 | 6.38 | 5.88 | 6.08 | 5.67 |
| 4. | Falta | 2.12 | 3.66 | 3.66 | 3.67 | 3.42 | 3.42 | 3.43 |
| 5. | Diamond Harbour | 3.07 | 5.21 | 5.19 | 5.23 | 4.95 | 4.95 | 4.95 |
| 6. | Kulpi | 3.92 | 3.81 | 3.76 | 3.86 | 3.63 | 3.41 | 3.88 |
| | **TOTAL** | **12.69** | **26.32** | **26.67** | **25.94** | **26.60** | **26.85** | **26.32** |
| *II.* | *THE MIDDLE MATURE DELTA OF THE HUGLI* | | | | | | | |
| 7. | Sonarpur | 2.67 | 5.49 | 5.57 | 5.40 | 5.94 | 5.99 | 5.90 |
| 8. | Bishnupur | 3.34 | 6.54 | 6.54 | 6.54 | 6.13 | 6.08 | 6.18 |
| 9. | Baruipur | 3.36 | 5.23 | 5.23 | 5.25 | 5.35 | 5.39 | 5.31 |
| 10. | Mograhat | 3.99 | 7.23 | 7.20 | 7.26 | 7.19 | 7.21 | 7.17 |
| 11. | Mandir - Bazar | 1.84 | 2.89 | 2.86 | 2.92 | 2.74 | 2.74 | 2.73 |
| 12. | Jaynagar | 5.70 | 5.78 | 5.75 | 5.82 | 6.57 | 6.57 | 6.56 |
| | **TOTAL** | **20.91** | **33.16** | **33.14** | **33.18** | **33.92** | **33.98** | **33.86** |
| *III.* | *THE PIYALI BIDYADHARI PLAINS IN THE EAST* | | | | | | | |
| 13. | Bhangar | 4.69 | 5.64 | 5.59 | 5.69 | 5.67 | 5.64 | 5.71 |
| 14. | Canning | 7.62 | 5.65 | 5.55 | 5.76 | 5.97 | 5.91 | 6.03 |
| | **TOTAL** | **12.30** | **11.29** | **11.14** | **11.45** | **11.64** | **11.55** | **11,73** |
| **ACTIVE DELTA** | | | | | | | | |
| *IV.* | *THE WESTERN SUNDARBANS* | | | | | | | |
| 15. | Sagar Island | 9.09 | 2.62 | 2.59 | 2.65 | 2.64 | 2.63 | 2.66 |
| 16. | Kakdwip | 7.46 | 3.79 | 3.75 | 3.83 | 3.91 | 3.75 | 4.07 |
| 17. | Namkhana | 2.50 | 1.69 | 1.67 | 1.70 | 1.66 | 1.65 | 1.67 |
| | **TOTAL** | **19.06** | **8.09** | **8.01** | **8.18** | **8.21** | **8.03** | **8.40** |
| *V.* | *THE MIDDLE SUNDARBANS* | | | | | | | |
| 18. | Mathurapur | 9.58 | 5.46 | 5.55 | 5.57 | 5.40 | 5.43 | 5.37 |
| 19. | Pathar Pratima | 7.59 | 4.49 | 4.46 | 4.53 | 4.22 | 4.18 | 4.25 |
| | **TOTAL** | **17.16** | **10.05** | **10.10** | **9.62** | **9.61** | **9.62** | **9.62** |
| *VI.* | *EASTERN SUNDARBANS* | | | | | | | |
| 20. | Kultali | 5.65 | 3.34 | 3.33 | 3.36 | 2.68 | 2.67 | 2.69 |
| 21. | Basanti | 6.41 | 3.92 | 3.88 | 3.96 | 3.89 | 3.87 | 3.92 |
| 22. | Gosaba | 5.81 | 3.82 | 3.82 | 3.84 | 3.44 | 3.43 | 3.45 |
| | **TOTAL** | **17.88** | **11.09** | **11.03** | **11.15** | **10.01** | **9.97** | **10.06** |
| **DISTRICT TOTAL** | | **100** | **100** | **100** | **100** | **100** | **100** | **100** |

Bidyadhari Plains 11.29%. The Active Delta exhibit the highest 1981 percentage in the Eastern Sundarbans 11.09%, followed by the Middle Sundarban 10.05% and lastly the Western Sundarban 8.09%. These figures in 1991 exhibit an increase in the Stable Delta region in the order of 33.92% in the Middle Mature Delta of the Hugli followed by 26.60% in the Western Hugli Side Flats and 11.64% in the Piyali Bidyadhari Plains. But the Active Delta apart from the Western Sundarbans, shows declining proportions in both Middle and Eastern Sundarbans (the figures being 9.62% and 10.01% respectively).

Therefore, from the above analysis, it is evident that the Blocks with higher areal proportions i.e. the Active Deltaic areas exhibit lower proportions of population in 1981 which had again further declined in 1991. Environmental constraints like dense forested tracts, menace of wild life (in the Eastern Sundarbans), cyclonic storms, tidal bores, rigorous salinity both in water and soil, are the factors that have limited the growth of population in these areas.

By contrast, the Stable Delta region to the north having a smaller areal proportion has higher proportions of population that has increased from 1981 to 1991. The proximity of this region to the city of Calcutta. with various urban facilities also seem to have promoted its population growth.

The 1981 block level population reveal that Mograhat in the Middle Mature Delta represents the highest proportion, 7.23%, closely followed by Budge Budge, 6.71%, whereas the lowest proportion is represented by Namkhana Block of the Western Sundarbans, 1.69%. The male and female proportions also exhibit similar trends. In 1991, Mograhat block still retains the first position but with a slight decline to 7.19% followed here by Bishnupur 6.13%, whereas Namkhana still stands at the lowest 1.66% , with a further lowering of the proportion in 1991.

The proportion of total population, therefore, exhibit a general increase over 1981 in almost all the subregions, except in the Middle and the Eastern Sundarbans. At the block level only 9 blocks out of 22 blocks have shown an increase. These are Thakurpukur - Metiaburuz and Maheshtala of the Western Hugli Side Flats, Sonarpur, Baruipur and Jaynagar of the Middle Mature Hugli Delta, Bhangar and Canning comprising the Piyali-Bidyadhari Plains in the East, and Sagar and Kakdwip blocks of the Western Sundarbans.

The total population of 1991 exhibit therefore four size groups for choroplething purpose. (Map 3.1) A very high proportion (6.1 to 7.5%) is found in 3 blocks of Bishnupur, Mograhat and Jaynagar of the Stable Delta. A high proportion (4.6 to 6.0% ) is noticeable in Maheshtala, Budge Budge, Diamond Harbour, Sonarpur, Baruipur, Bhangar, Canning and Mathurapur blocks. A medium proportion (3.1-4.5%) is discernable in Falta, Kulpi, Kakdwip, Pathar Pratima, Basanti and Gosaba and finally, a low proportion (1.6 to 3.0%) is seen in Thakurpukur-Metiaburuz, Sagar Island, Mandir Bazar, Namkhana and Kultali.

### 3.2.1. Rural Urban Distribution of 1981-1991

Table 3.2 represents the distribution of population in rural areas. Here, the Middle Mature Hugli Delta has the highest areal proportion with 20.61% of the total district's area, followed by the Western Sundarbans, 19.49%; the Eastern Sundarbans, 18.28%; and the Middle Sundarbans 17.55%. The Piyali-Bidyadhari Plains with 12.37% and the Western Hugli Side Flats have the smallest proportion of rural area. Here, the 1981 proportions reveal again the highest figure in the Middle Mature Delta i.e. 34.19%, followed by 20.39% in the Western Hugli Side Flats. The lowest is noticeable in the Western Sundarbans i.e. 9.22%. 1991 figures reveal a similar picture, the respective proportions being 35.18, 19.36 and 9.59%. Decline in rural proportions being noticeable in the Western Hugli Side Flats and in the Middle Sundarbans. The male and female counterparts also exhibit a similar ranks. Blocks level information of 1991 portrays Mograhat at the highest level 8.41%, followed in this case by Jaynagar 7.27%, Bishnupur 6.88%, Bhangar 6.63% and Mathurapur 6.31%. The lowest proportions are exhibited by Thakurpukur 1.22% and Maheshtala, 1.38%, lying in close juxtaposition with the Greater Calcutta Region.

The 1981 and 1991 comparative rural pictures portray an increase in the rural population proportions in only 10 blocks out of the 22 blocks. viz. Thakurpukur - Metiaburuz, Baruipur, Mograhat, Jaynagar, Bhangar, Canning, Sagar, Kakdwip, Namkhana and in Basanti. Declining rural proportions are noticeable in Maheshtala, Budge Budge, Falta, Diamond Harbour, Kulpi, Sonarpur, Bishnupur, Mandir Bazar, Mathurapur, Pathar Pratima, Kultali and Gosaba.

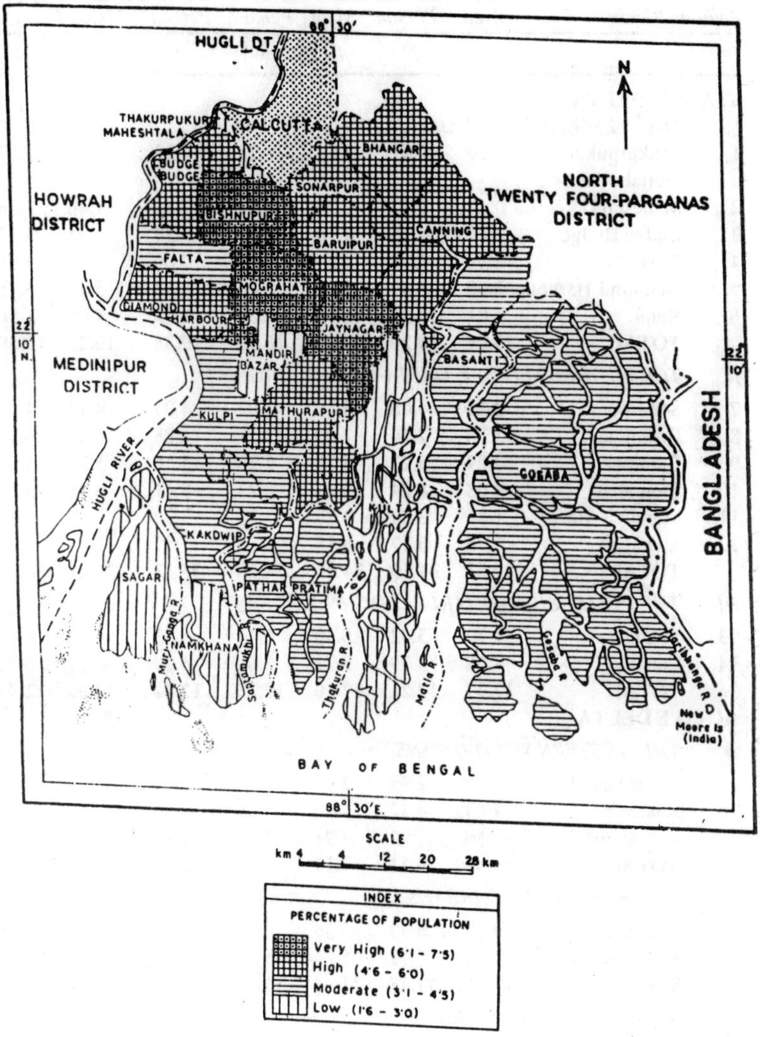


**MAP 3.1 :** South 24-Parganas : Spatial Distribution of Population 1991.

**TABLE 3.2 : Spatial Distribution of Rural Population 1981-91 (Proportion of Rural Area And Population)**

| | | | *1981 Population* | | | *1991 Population* | | |
|---|---|---|---|---|---|---|---|---|
| *Regions/Blocks* | | *Area* | *Person* | *Male* | *Female* | *Person* | *Male* | *Female* |
| *1* | | *2* | *3* | *4* | *5* | *6* | *7* | *8* |
| **STABLE DELTA** | | | | | | | | |
| *I.* | *THE WESTERN HUGLI SIDE FLATS* | | | | | | | |
| 1. | Thakurpukur-Metiaburuz | 0.29 | 0.81 | 0.84 | 0.78 | 1.22 | 1.26 | 1.17 |
| 2. | Mahestala | 0.44 | 1.42 | 1.43 | 1.40 | 1.38 | 1.40 | 1.36 |
| 3. | Budge Budge | 1.77 | 4.15 | 4.18 | 4.11 | 3.34 | 3.34 | 3.33 |
| 4. | Falta | 2.17 | 4.17 | 4.19 | 4.16 | 4.00 | 4.02 | 3.98 |
| 5. | Diamond Harbour | 3.00 | 5.41 | 5.41 | 5.40 | 5.18 | 5.20 | 5.15 |
| 6. | Kulpi | 4.01 | 4.34 | 4.31 | 4.38 | 4.25 | 4.00 | 4.50 |
| | **TOTAL** | **11.69** | **20.29** | **20.36** | **20.22** | **19.36** | **19.23** | **19.49** |
| *II.* | *THE MIDDLE MATURE DELTA OF THE HUGLI* | | | | | | | |
| 7. | Sonarpur | 2.25 | 4.08 | 4.18 | 3.97 | 4.07 | 4.12 | 4.01 |
| 8. | Bishnupur | 3.36 | 7.14 | 7.17 | 7.11 | 6.88 | 6.85 | 6.91 |
| 9. | Baruipur | 3.29 | 5.28 | 5.29 | 5.28 | 5.36 | 5.42 | 5.29 |
| 10. | Mograhat | 4.08 | 8.24 | 8.24 | 8.23 | 8.41 | 8.48 | 8.33 |
| 11. | Mandir - Bazar | 1.88 | 3.29 | 3.27 | 3.31 | 3.20 | 3.22 | 3.17 |
| 12. | Jaynagar | 5.75 | 6.17 | 6.15 | 6.18 | 7.27 | 7.31 | 7.22 |
| | **TOTAL** | **20.61** | **34.19** | **34.29** | **34.08** | **35.18** | **35.41** | **34.94** |
| *III.* | *THE PIYALI BIDYADHARI PLAINS IN THE EAST* | | | | | | | |
| 13. | Bhangar | 4.79 | 5.42 | 6.40 | 6.40 | 6.63 | 6.62 | 6.63 |
| 14. | Canning | 7.58 | 5.79 | 5.71 | 5.68 | 6.29 | 6.27 | 6.32 |
| | **TOTAL** | **12.37** | **12.21** | **12.10** | **12.33** | **12.22** | **12.90** | **12.95** |
| **ACTIVE DELTA** | | | | | | | | |
| *IV.* | *THE WESTERN SUNDARBANS* | | | | | | | |
| 15. | Sagar Island | 9.30 | 2.98 | 2.97 | 3.00 | 3.09 | 3.09 | 3.09 |
| 16. | Kakdwip | 7.63 | 4.32 | 4.30 | 4.34 | 4.56 | 4.41 | 4.73 |
| 17. | Namkhana | 2.56 | 1.92 | 1.91 | 1.93 | 1.94 | 1.94 | 1.94 |
| | **TOTAL** | **19.49** | **9.22** | **9.17** | **9.28** | **9.59** | **9.44** | **9.76** |
| *V.* | *THE MIDDLE SUNDARBANS* | | | | | | | |
| 18. | Mathurapur | 9.79 | 6.33 | 6.35 | 6.31 | 6.31 | 6.38 | 6.24 |
| 19. | Pathar Pratima | 7.76 | 5.12 | 5.10 | 5.14 | 4.93 | 4.92 | 4.94 |
| | **TOTAL** | **17.55** | **11.45** | **11.45** | **11.45** | **11.24** | **11.30** | **11.18** |
| *VI.* | *EASTERN SUNDARBANS* | | | | | | | |
| 20. | Kultali | 5.78 | 3.81 | 3.81 | 3.81 | 3.14 | 3.14 | 3.13 |
| 21. | Basanti | 6.56 | 4.46 | 4.44 | 4.49 | 4.55 | 4.55 | 4.55 |
| 22. | Gosaba | 5.95 | 4.36 | 4.37 | 4.35 | 4.02 | 4.03 | 4.00 |
| | **TOTAL** | **18.28** | **12.63** | **12.62** | **12.64** | **11.71** | **11.72** | **11.69** |
| **DISTRICT TOTAL** | | **100** | **100** | **100** | **100** | **100** | **100** | **100** |

The 1991 rural population distribution displays four groups. (Map 3.2)

(i) A very high group (8-10%) is represented by Mograhat,
(ii) A high group (4-8%) is seen in a large number of blocks Diamond Harbour, Kulpi, Sonarpur, Bishnupur, Baruipur, Jayanagar, Bhangar, Canning, Kakdwip, Mathurapur, Pathar Pratima, Basanti and Gosaba,.
(iii) A medium group (2 - 4%) is seen in Budge Budge, Falta, Mandir Bazar, Sagar Island, and Kutali and finally,
(iv) A low group of (1 - 2%) seen in Thakurpukur,.Maheshtala and Namkhana.

Urban areas (Table 3.3) located only in the Stable Delta, where the Hugli Side Flats with 57.04% of the total district's area has the highest proportion, followed by 33.76% of the Middle Mature Delta and only 9.20% of the Piyali-Bidyadhari Plains that ranks last. Both 1981 and 1991 figures reveal that the Western Hugli Sides Flats have the highest urban population, 69.54% in 1981 and 69.51% in 1991; followed by the Middle Mature Hugli Delta, i.e. 25.78% in 81 and 26.46% in 1991. The Piyali-Bidyadhari Plains rank last with 4.68% in 1981 and 4.03% in 1991. Total urban proportions have declined slightly in all three subregions. At the block level, only 9 blocks have urban areas. The highest proportion of urban area is noticeable in Budge Budge, 22.95%, and the lowest in Bishnupur, 2.34%. The 1981 urban population proportions reveal the highest in Maheshtala, 25.89% followed by Budge Budge 25.12% and the lowest in Bishnupur, 2.27%. In general urban regions in contiguity with the Calcutta Region show higher figures. The male and female urban 1981 proportions exhibit similar trends, though female proportions are slightly higher in the blocks of Thakurpukur - Metiaburuz, Diamond Harbour, Sonarpur, Baruipur, Jaynagar and Canning. In 1991, the highest proportion is also noticeable in Maheshtala, 31.19%, and the lowest in Bishnupur, 1.67%.

Thus the 1981-1991 comparative study reveals that though in actual figures the population has increased over the decade the general proportions have declined in the rural areas for the district as a whole from 87.76% in 1981 to 85.57% in 1991. But urban areas on the other hand has shown an increase from 12.24% in 1981 to 14.43% in 1991.

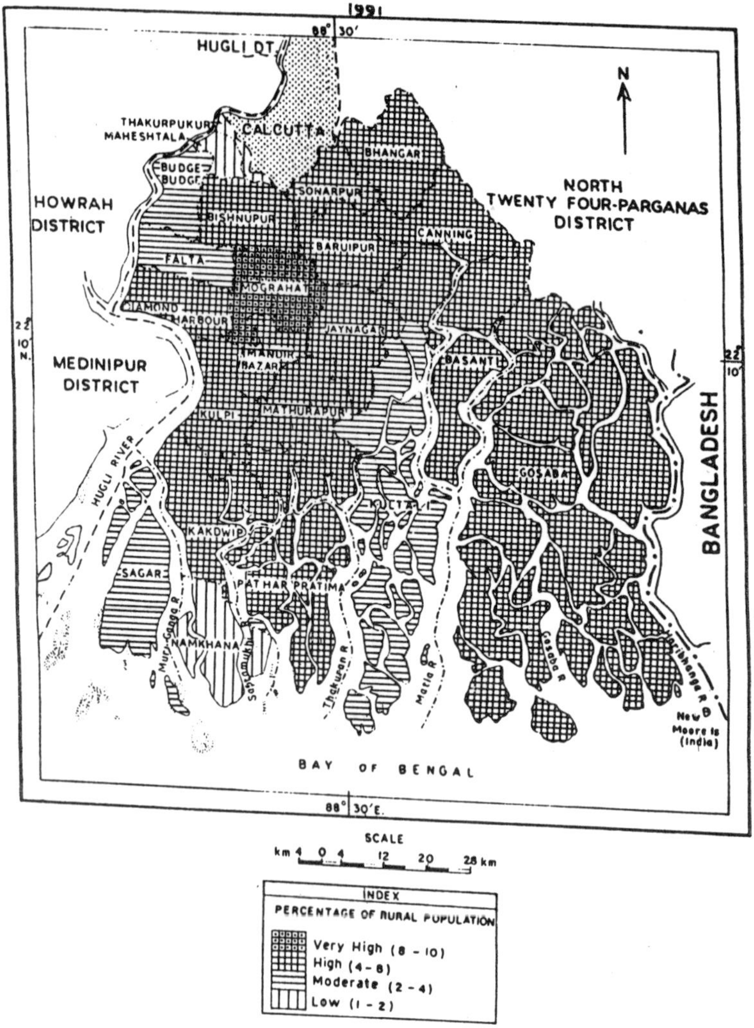


MAP 3.2 : South 24-Parganas : Spatial Distribution of Rural Population

**TABLE 3.3 : Spatial Distribution of Urban Population 1981-91 (Proportion of Urban Population and Area)**

| Regions/Blocks | | Prop. of Urban Area to Total Area | 1981 | | | 1991 | | |
|---|---|---|---|---|---|---|---|---|
| | | | Person | Male | Female | Person | Male | Female |
| *1* | | *2* | *3* | *4* | *5* | *6* | *7* | *8* |
| **STABLE DELTA** | | | | | | | | |
| *I.* | *THE WESTERN HUGLI SIDE FLATS* | | | | | | | |
| 1. | Thakurpukur-Metiaburuz | 9.91 | 14.76 | 14.14 | 15.48 | 13.75 | 13.94 | 13.54 |
| 2. | Mahestala | 18.12 | 25.89 | 31.98 | 25.89 | 31.19 | 31.21 | 31.16 |
| 3. | Budge Budge | 22.25 | 25.12 | 26.68 | 23.32 | 20.91 | 21.66 | 20.19 |
| 4. | Falta | — | — | — | — | — | — | — |
| 5. | Diamond Harbour | 6.37 | 3.77 | 3.66 | 3.90 | 3.60 | 3.49 | 3.72 |
| 6. | Kulpi | — | — | — | — | — | — | — |
| | **TOTAL** | **57.04** | **69.54** | **70.37** | **68.58** | **69.51** | **70.30** | **68.60** |
| *II.* | *THE MIDDLE MATURE DELTA OF THE HUGLI* | | | | | | | |
| 7. | Sonarpur | 21.30 | 15.60 | 15.21 | 16.05 | 17.06 | 16.59 | 17.61 |
| 8. | Bishnupur | 2.34 | 2.27 | 2.23 | 2.31 | 1.67 | 1.67 | 1.66 |
| 9. | Baruipur | 6.44 | 4.87 | 4.72 | 5.05 | 5.33 | 5.23 | 5.45 |
| 10. | Mograhat | — | — | — | — | — | — | — |
| 11. | Mandir - Bazar | — | — | — | — | — | — | — |
| 12. | Jaynagar | 3.68 | 3.04 | 3.04 | 2.38 | 3.10 | 2.40 | 2.48 |
| | **TOTAL** | **33.76** | **25.78** | **25.14** | **26.51** | **26.46** | **25.82** | **27.20** |
| *III.* | *THE PIYALI BIDYADHARI PLAINS IN THE EAST* | | | | | | | |
| 13. | Bhangar | — | — | — | — | — | — | — |
| 14. | Canning | 2.90 | 4.68 | 4.48 | 4.91 | 4.03 | 3.88 | 4.20 |
| | **TOTAL** | **9.20** | **4.68** | **4.49** | **4.91** | **4.03** | **3.88** | **4.20** |
| **DISTRICT TOTAL** | | **100** | **100** | **100** | **100** | **100** | **100** | **100** |

(Active Delta is Entirely Rural)

### 3.2.2. Density of Population

Population density is a method of analysing the distribution of population, overpopulation, underpopulation and optimum population can be assessed by comparing population densities through statistical methods. It is impossible to discuss the distribution of population without indicating that there are more people in some places, leading to relatively higher densities and fewer in others leading to lower densities[3]. Table 3.4 depicts the 1981-1991 densities. The 1981 density picture reveals that the Stable Delta has conspicuously higher densities compared to the district's average,

689 and 913 persons per sq. km. in 1981 and 1991 respectively.

Located far away from the environmental constraints, the Stable Deltaic regions have experienced a more developed agricultural change, urbanization, industrialization, good communication facilities; as well as historically these areas have been settled much prior to a date when forest reclamation started in the southern parts in the Active Delta for the creation of 'abad' lands for agricultural purposes. Hence human numbers have gathered in the Stable Delta for ages thereby contributing to the present picture of today. Lastly, the impact of the Calcutta Conurbation on these areas is worth mentioning. A typical commuter's zone has been extended into these areas thereby *inflating the density* of this region.

**Density Distribution 1981-1991**

The *highest population density* both in 1981 and 1991 is seen in the *Western Hugli Side Flats*, the respective figures being 1429 and 1914 persons per sq. km. This is followed by the Middle Mature Hugli Delta, figures being 1093 and 1481/sq.km. respectively. The lower densities characterise the Active Delta with the lowest in Western Sundarbans, the figures being 293 and 393/sq.km. respectively.

The block level, 1981 figures reveal a very high contrast; *Maheshtala* having the *highest density* of 3655 sq.km. to the *lowest density* of 198/sq.km in the Sagar Island. The 1991 total density figures reveal a similar trend and also that densities have increased in all the blocks with the order more or less remaining the same. Maheshtala leads the density figures with a 1991 density as high as 6236/sq.km., followed by Thakurpukur - Metiaburuz 5514/sq.km, and Budge Budge 2406/sq.km. In the Active Delta though the 1991 total densities have shown a general increase, they are in general *below* the *district's total density* of 913/sq.km. In this sub-region Sagar Island again depicts the lowest of 265/sq.km. Within the Active Delta region of the Sundarban the highest 1991 densities are located in Namkhana 605/sq.km, Basanti 554/sq.km. and Gosaba 540/sq.km. Environmental constraints and recent settlement of the region are responsible for the lower densities exhibited by these regions.

The 1991 (Map 3.3) total density figures represent four groups of - (i) very high density (6000/sq.km.) in the Maheshtala Block, (ii) a high density (3001 - 6000/sq.km,) is noticeable in Thakurpukur-

**TABLE 3.4 : Density of Population 1981-91**

| Region/Blocks | 1981 | | | 1991 | | |
|---|---|---|---|---|---|---|
| | *Total* | *Rural* | *Urban* | *Total* | *Rural* | *Urban* |
| *1* | *2* | *3* | *4* | *5* | *6* | *7* |
| **STABLE DELTA** | | | | | | |
| *I. THE WESTERN HUGLI SIDE FLATS* | | | | | | |
| 1. Thakurpukur-Metiaburuz | 3456 | 1701 | 5676 | 5514 | 3321 | 8263 |
| 2. Mahestala | 3655 | 1989 | 5445 | 6236 | 2500 | 10250 |
| 3. Budge Budge | 2073 | 1449 | 4225 | 2406 | 1506 | 5515 |
| 4. Falta | 1188 | 1188 | — | 1471 | 1471 | — |
| 5. Diamond Harbour | 1167 | 1115 | 2255 | 1470 | 1379 | 3363 |
| 6. Kulpi | 669 | 669 | — | 845 | 845 | — |
| **TOTAL** | **1429** | **1073** | **4645** | **1914** | **1323** | **7256** |
| *II. THE MIDDLE MATURE DELTA OF THE HUGLI* | | | | | | |
| 7. Sonarpur | 1414 | 1120 | 2790 | 2030 | 1443 | 4770 |
| 8. Bishnupur | 1349 | 1312 | 3702 | 1674 | 1634 | 4251 |
| 9. Baruipur | 1073 | 993 | 2882 | 1455 | 1301 | 4927 |
| 10. Mograhat | 1247 | 1247 | — | 1644 | 1644 | — |
| 11. Mandir-Bazar | 1082 | 1082 | — | 1360 | 1360 | — |
| 12. Jaynagar | 698 | 663 | 3143 | 1051 | 1009 | 3888 |
| **TOTAL** | **1093** | **1025** | **2910** | **1481** | **1363** | 4668 |
| *III. THE PIYALI BIDYADHARI PLAINS IN THE EAST* | | | | | | |
| 13. Bhangar | 829 | 829 | — | 1105 | 1105 | — |
| 14. Canning | 511 | 472 | 1939 | 715 | 663 | 2608 |
| **TOTAL** | **632** | **610** | **1939** | **863** | **834** | **2608** |
| **ACTIVE DELTA** | | | | | | |
| *IV. THE WESTERN SUNDARBANS* | | | | | | |
| 15. Sagar Island | 198 | 198 | — | 265 | 265 | — |
| 16. Kakdwip | 350 | 350 | — | 473 | 473 | — |
| 17. Namkhana | 464 | 464 | — | 605 | 605 | — |
| **TOTAL** | **223** | **293** | **—** | **393** | **393** | **—** |
| *V. THE MIDDLE SUNDARBANS* | | | | | | |
| 18. Mathurapur | 400 | 400 | — | 515 | 515 | — |
| 19. Pathar Pratima | 408 | 408 | — | 507 | 507 | — |
| TOTAL | 403 | 403 | — | 511 | 511 | — |
| *VI. EASTERN SUNDARBANS* | | | | | | |
| 20. Kultali | 407 | 407 | — | 433 | 433 | — |
| 21. Basanti | 421 | 421 | — | 554 | 554 | — |
| 22. Gosaba | 453 | 453 | — | 540 | 540 | — |
| **TOTAL** | **427** | **427** | **—** | **511** | **511** | **—** |
| **DISTRICT TOTAL** | **689** | **618** | **3810** | **913** | **799** | **5955** |

Metiaburuz, (iii) a Medium density (1000 - 3000/sq.km.) is found in a large number of blocks, viz. Budge Budge, Falta, Diamond Harbour, Sonarpur, Bishnupur, Baruipur, Mograhat, Mandir Bazar, Jaynagar and Bhangar, finally (iv) a very low density of (less than 1000 per sq.km) in Kulpi, Canning, Sagar Island, Kakdwip, Namkhana, Mathurapur, Pathar Pratima, Kultali, Basanti and Gosaba.

## Rural-Urban Differential

### *Rural Density Distribution 1981-1991*

The rural density of the district was 618/sq.km in 1981 and 799 in 1991. The Stable Delta regions show densities more than this figure. The Western Hugli Side Flats ranks first again with the respective figures of 1981 and 1991 being 1073 and 1323/sq.km.

13 blocks of the Stable Delta have rural densities greater than the district's total in 1991, with the highest in Thakurpukur - Metiaburuz i.e. 3321/sq.km followed by Maheshtala 2500/sq.km, Mograhat 1644/sq.km and Bishnupur 1634/sq.km, the order in the Active Delta remaining the same as the total density figures. The 1991 Rural density figures portray four density groups. A very high density (greater than 3000/sq.km) is seen in Thakurpukur - Metiaburuz. A high density of (2000-3000/sq.km) is seen in Maheshtala. A Medium density (1000-2000/sq.km.) is noticeable in Budge Budge, Falta, Diamond Harbour, Sonarpur, Bishnupur, Baruipur, Mograhat, Mandir Bazar, Jaynagar and Bhangar. Finally, a low density of (1000 /sq.km) is discernable in Kulpi, Canning, Sagar Island, Kakdwip, Namkhana, Mathurapur, Pathar Pratima, Kultali, Basanti and Gosaba.

### *Urban Density Distribution 1981 - 1991*

The Urban densities are much higher than their rural counterparts. Here also the Western Hugli Side Flats reveal the highest both in 81 and 91, the respective figures being 4645 and 7256/sq.km. The Middle Mature Delta is the next important region also having high urban densities followed by the Piyali-Bidyadhari Plains. Of the 9 blocks having urbanized tracts, 3 have densities more than the districts total of 3810/sq. km. in 1981, these being Thakurpukur - Metiaburuz 5676/sq.km, Maheshtala 5445/sq.km and Budge Budge

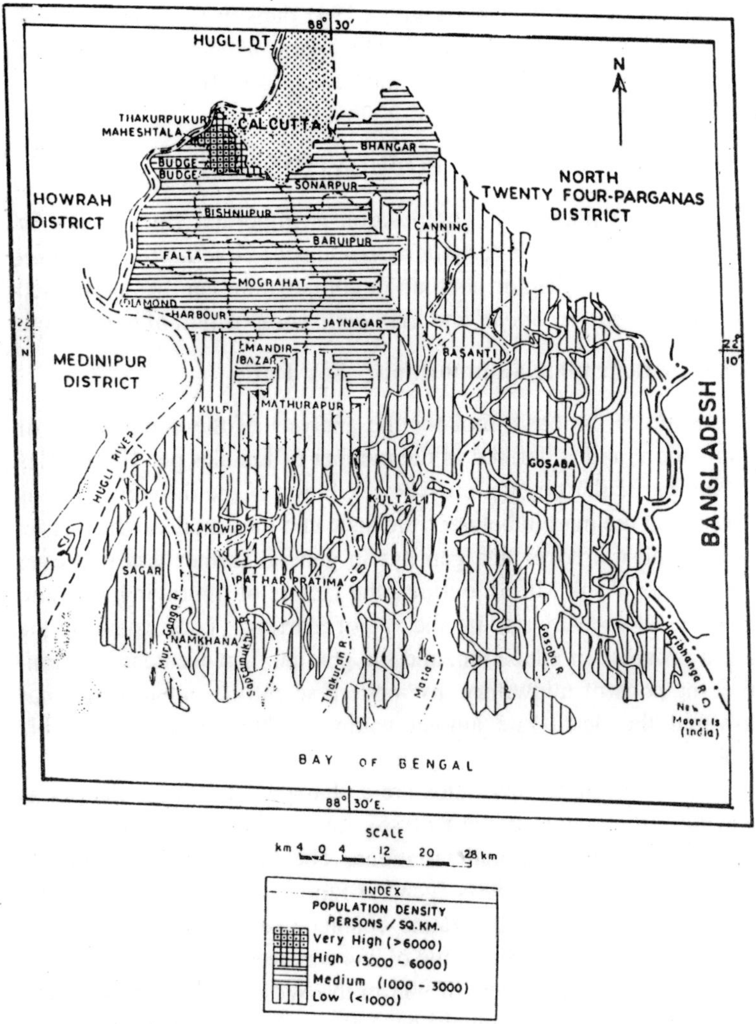


**MAP 3.3** : South 24-Parganas : Density of Population 1991.

4225/sq.km. Canning portrays the lowest urban density of 1939/ sq.km. The district's total urban density in 1991 increased to 5955/ sq.km. Here also 3 blocks out of 9 exhibit higher densities, the first being in this case Maheshtala with a 1991 density as high as 10,250/ sq.km, followed by Thakurpukur - Metiaburuz 8263/sq.km and Budge Budge 5515/sq.km. Here also the lowest density is portrayed by Canning block with a figure of 2608/sq.km.

## 3.3 COMPOSITION OF POPULATION 1981-91

The study of population composition is important since it can be viewed as an *active factor that determines or conditions population growth*[4]. In this chapter population composition can be subdivided into *Demographic, Social* and *Economic* composition of population.

### 3.3.1 Demographic Composition - Sex Ratio

Sex Ratio is the basic tool for the analysis of the composition of population; and is defined as the number of females per 1000 males of any particular population. The sex ratios of the different regions reveal that the margin between the male and the female in the district is less and moreover this gap has in general further lessened over the decade. Asok Mitra[5] outlines the factors of improving sex ratio of India as a steady rise in the age of marriage consequent on the rapid progress of education, and the gradual displacement of primitive methods of midwifery by modern scientific methods, that has lowered the death rate among young mothers to an appreciable extent.

Though higher sex ratios are a characteristic of the district as a whole, the spatial pattern of sex ratio of the district represents considerable inter-regional variations. The 1981 total figures (Table 3.5) represent the district's general ratio at 929 females per 1000 males. In general, higher ratios characterise the Active Delta. In 1981, however, the highest ratio of 954 was seen in the Piyali Bidyadhari Plains and the lowest of 903 in the Western Hugli Side Flats. 17 blocks out of the 22 blocks have ratios above the district average in 1981. The highest ratio of 952 is noticeable in Kulpi block in 1981, in the urbanised and industrialized blocks of Budge Budge i.e. 844. The 1991 figures in general represent a somewhat increase in

**TABLE 3.5 : Sex Ratio 1981 - 1991**

| Regions/Blocks | | 1981 | | | 1991 | | | Change in Sex Ratio | | |
|---|---|---|---|---|---|---|---|---|---|---|
| | | Total | Rural | Urban | Total | Rural | Urban | Total | Rural | Urban |
| | 1 | 2 | 3 | 4 | 5 | 6 | 7 | 8 | 9 | 10 |
| **STABLE DELTA** | | | | | | | | | | |
| *I.* | *THE WESTERN HUGLI SIDE FLATS* | | | | | | | | | |
| 1. | Thakurpukur-Metiaburuz | 928 | 870 | 951 | 857 | 877 | 848 | -71 | 7 | -103 |
| 2. | Mahestala | 882 | 918 | 869 | 882 | 923 | 871 | 0 | 5 | 2 |
| 3. | Budge Budge | 844 | 921 | 759 | 874 | 943 | 814 | 30 | 22 | 55 |
| 4. | Falta | 931 | 931 | — | 939 | 939 | — | 8 | 8 | — |
| 5. | Diamond Harbour | 935 | 935 | 927 | 937 | 938 | 928 | 2 | 3 | 1 |
| 6. | Kulpi | 952 | 952 | — | 1066 | 1066 | — | 114 | 114 | — |
| | **TOTAL** | **903** | **931** | **847** | **918** | **961** | **852** | **15** | **30** | **5** |
| *II.* | *THE MIDDLE MATURE DELTA OF THE HUGLI* | | | | | | | | | |
| 7. | Sonarpur | 899 | 890 | 916 | 923 | 921 | 926 | 24 | 31 | 10 |
| 8. | Bishnupur | 928 | 930 | 901 | 952 | 956 | 865 | 24 | 26 | -36 |
| 9. | Baruipur | 935 | 935 | 929 | 924 | 926 | 910 | -11 | - 9 | -19 |
| 10. | Mograhat | 937 | 937 | — | 931 | 931 | — | -6 | - 6 | — |
| 11. | Mandir-Bazar | 949 | 949 | — | 932 | 932 | — | -17 | -17 | — |
| 12. | Jaynagar | 939 | 942 | 904 | 936 | 936 | 926 | -3 | - 6 | 22 |
| | **TOTAL** | **930** | **931** | **916** | **933** | **935** | **919** | **3** | **4** | **3** |
| *III.* | *THE PIYALI BIDYADHARI PLAINS IN THE EAST* | | | | | | | | | |
| 13. | Bhangar | 946 | 946 | — | 949 | 949 | — | 3 | 3 | — |
| 14. | Canning | 963 | 965 | 951 | 954 | 955 | 945 | -9 | -10 | -5 |
| | **TOTAL** | **954** | **955** | **951** | **952** | **952** | **945** | **-2** | **-3** | **-6** |

TABLE 3.5 : (*Contd.*)

| *Regions/Blocks* | | *1981* | | | *1991* | | | *Change in Sex Ratio* | | |
|---|---|---|---|---|---|---|---|---|---|---|
| | | *Total* | *Rural* | *Urban* | *Total* | *Rural* | *Urban* | *Total* | *Rural* | *Urban* |
| | *1* | *2* | *3* | *4* | *5* | *6* | *7* | *8* | *9* | *10* |
| **ACTIVE DELTA** | | | | | | | | | | |
| *IV.* | *THE WESTERN SUNDARBANS* | | | | | | | | | |
| 15. | Sagar Island | 950 | 950 | — | 946 | 946 | — | -4 | -4 | — |
| 16. | Kakdwip | 948 | 948 | — | 1017 | 1047 | — | 69 | 69 | — |
| 17. | Namkhana | 947 | 947 | — | 947 | 947 | — | 0 | 0 | — |
| | **TOTAL** | **948** | **948** | — | **979** | **979** | — | **31** | **31** | — |
| *V.* | *THE MIDDLE SUNDARBANS* | | | | | | | | | |
| 18. | Mathurapur | 932 | 932 | — | 927 | 927 | — | -5 | -5 | — |
| 19. | Pathar Pratima | 944 | 944 | — | 952 | 952 | — | 8 | 8 | — |
| | **TOTAL** | **937** | **937** | — | **938** | **938** | — | **1** | **1** | — |
| *VI.* | *EASTERN SUNDARBANS* | | | | | | | | | |
| 20. | Kultali | 937 | 937 | — | 943 | 943 | — | 6 | 6 | — |
| 21. | Basanti | 947 | 947 | — | 950 | 950 | — | 3 | 3 | — |
| 22. | Gosaba | 934 | 934 | — | 941 | 941 | — | 7 | 7 | — |
| | **TOTAL** | **939** | **939** | — | **945** | **945** | — | **6** | **6** | — |
| | **DISTRICT TOTAL** | **929** | **937** | **869** | **937** | **949** | **873** | **8** | **12** | **4** |

the ratios, the trend remaining almost similar. The highest ratio among the subregions, however is seen in the Western Sundarbans, i.e. 979, followed by 952 of the Piyali-Bidyadhari Plains. The lowest ratio of 918 occurs in the Western Hugli Side Flats. In general, the district's total represent a ratio of 937 females per 1000 males. 12 blocks in 1991 exhibit a ratio above this figure. Kulpi and Kakdwip represent very high ratios in the order of 1066 and 1017 respectively indicating in most probability male selective outmigration to the Greater Calcutta Region for economic pursuits. The blocks in the Active Delta in general represent higher ratios compared to the Stable Delta in the north, further supporting the above mentioned fact.

### *Rural Urban Difference in Sex Ratio 1981 - 1991*

Both the 1981 and 1991 figures again represent contrasting ratios between the rural and the urban areas, the rural ratios being usually higher than the urban counterparts. For instance the Western Hugli Side Flat represent a gap of 84 females in 1981 between the rural and urban areas, that has increased to 109 in 1991. For the Middle Mature Delta these respective figures are 15 in 1981 and 16 in 1991. Only a minor difference is noticeable in the Piyali Bidyadhari Plains between the rural and urban areas. At the block level in 1981 higher urban ratios have been observed in Thakurpukur-Metiaburuz and in Sonarpur. Budge Budge in 1981 portrays a gap as high as 162 females between rural and urban areas, which has falled to 129 in 1991. Maheshtala again depicts a difference of 49 females in 1981 that had risen to 52 in 1991. According to Asok Mitra, in urban areas there is a predominance of non-agricultural occupations in the organised sector, engaging more males than females. Moreover, the urban population consists of a number of students and job seekers most of whom are males. This reduces the number of urban females and lowers the sex ratio.

The 1981-1991 change in sex ratio reveal that apart from the Piyali-Bidyadhari Plains, all subregions, have registered rising ratios. At the block level 13 blocks have registered rising sex ratios, 2 blocks have shown stable ratios and 7 blocks have shown declining sex ratios both in rural and urban areas. The district on the whole exhibits rising ratios both in rural and urban areas. Improving sex ratios reflect a better situation in favour of females with the improvement of the minimum facilities of education, health, nutrition and female status. Sex ratio of the 22 blocks of South 24-Parganas can be grouped into five classes. (Map 3.4) A very high ratio of more than 1050 is noticeable is Kulpi. A high ratio of 1000-1050 is found in Kakdwip. The medium ratio of 950-1000 can be located in Bishnupur, Canning and Pathar Pratima. The low group of 900-950 covers the maximum blocks (14) viz. Falta, Diamond Harbour, Sonarpur, Baruipur, Mograhat, Mandir Bazar, Jaynagar, Bhangar, Sagar Island, Namkhana, Mathurapur, Kultali, Basanti, and Gosaba. Finally, a very low ratio of less than 900 is found in Thakurpukur - Metiaburuz, Maheshtala and Budge Budge.

### 3.3.2 Social Composition of Population

Data on social characteristics of population are significant and meaningful for a wide variety of purposes because they are the indices of *cultural background* and legal or social status differences within the population at the local, regional, national or international level[6]. In this section therefore two indicators chosen according to data availability viz Literacy and Scheduled Caste and Tribe.

#### *Spatial Perspective on Literacy*

In the modern context, a wide diffusion of literacy and education is indispensable to the process of development, both in economic and social terms[7]. Though education by itself does not generate socio-economic progress, the lack of it can certainly be an impediment in the developmental process. A certain minimum level of literacy is therefore, a basic requirement for the people to get out of ignorance and backwardness. The distributional spread of literacy in all the 6 geo-ecological regions covering the 22 blocks have been highlighted in this section; as well as the progress of literacy over the decadal span of 1981-1991 has been taken into account.

The total literacy figures for the district as a whole, Table 3.6, represents 37.59%, that has increased to 44.15% in 1991. In 1981, the Western Hugli Side Flats with 46.20% of the district's population

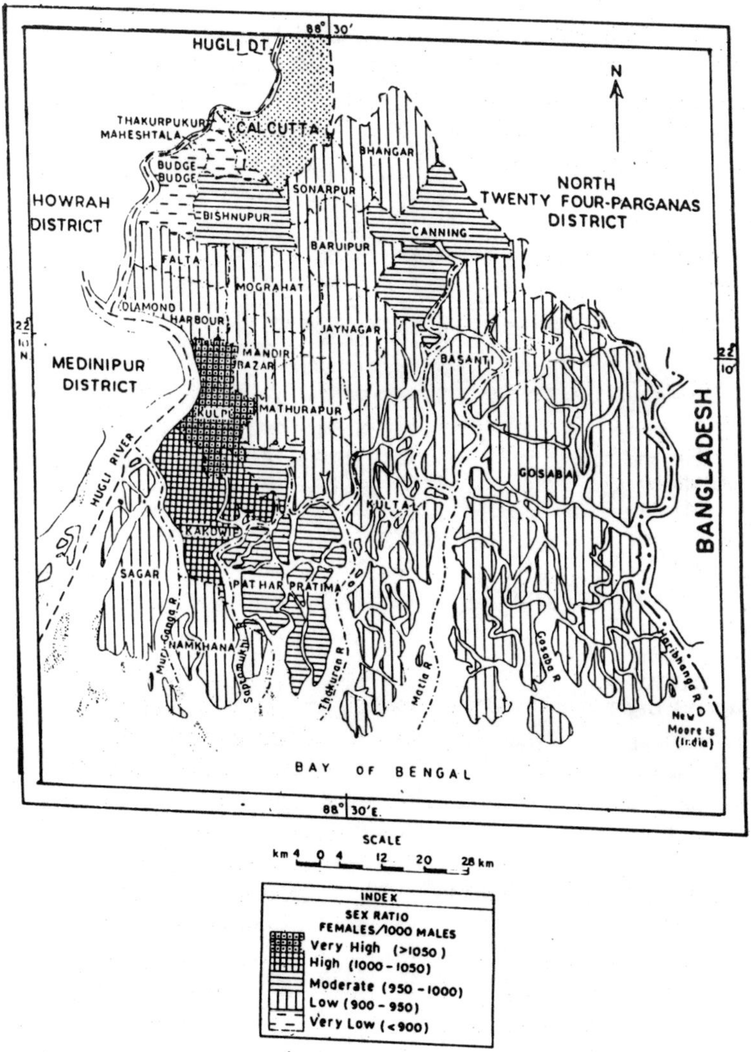


**MAP 3.4 :** South 24-Parganas : Sex Ratio 1991.

**TABLE 3.6 : LITERACY 1981-1991**
**Proportion of total Literate to total Population**

| Regions/Blocks | | 1981 | | | 1991 | | |
|---|---|---|---|---|---|---|---|
| | | Person | Male | Female | Person | Male | Female |
| 1 | | 2 | 3 | 4 | 5 | 6 | 7 |
| **STABLE DELTA** | | | | | | | |
| *I.* | *THE WESTERN HUGLI SIDE FLATS* | | | | | | |
| 1. | Thakurpukur-Metiaburuz | 70.54 | 85.43 | 54.48 | 55.39 | 59.46 | 50.65 |
| 2. | Mahestala | 52.17 | 61.02 | 42.14 | 57.78 | 64.89 | 49.73 |
| 3. | Budge Budge | 43.18 | 54.43 | 29.85 | 51.67 | 59.53 | 42.69 |
| 4. | Falta | 42.84 | 56.50 | 28.15 | 49.07 | 60.41 | 36.98 |
| 5. | Diamond Harbour | 42.54 | 55.04 | 29.16 | 47.72 | 57.39 | 37.41 |
| 6. | Kulpi | 36.78 | 49.57 | 23.34 | 39.15 | 52.98 | 26.17 |
| | **TOTAL** | **46.20** | **58.19** | **32.92** | **50.62** | **59.57** | **40.86** |
| *II.* | *THE MIDDLE MATURE DELTA OF THE HUGLI* | | | | | | |
| 7. | Sonarpur | 48.52 | 55.21 | 41.08 | 61.46 | 70.19 | 52.00 |
| 8. | Bishnupur | 39.18 | 51.94 | 25.42 | 47.23 | 58.42 | 35.47 |
| 9. | Baruipur | 40.52 | 52.20 | 28.03 | 50.19 | 62.12 | 37.27 |
| 10. | Mograhat | 32.55 | 46.20 | 17.99 | 40.44 | 51.36 | 28.72 |
| 11. | Mandir - Bazar | 34.16 | 49.03 | 18.50 | 41.11 | 54.26 | 26.98 |
| 12. | Jaynagar | 32.77 | 46.65 | 17.99 | 37.94 | 50.90 | 24.10 |
| | **TOTAL** | **37.94** | **50.11** | **24.84** | **46.46** | **57.79** | **34.32** |
| *III.* | *THE PIYALI BIDYADHARI PLAINS IN THE EAST* | | | | | | |
| 13. | Bhangar | 29.06 | 37.63 | 20.00 | 34.01 | 43.85 | 23.63 |
| 14. | Canning | 26.44 | 39.10 | 13.30 | 32.01 | 44.22 | 19.21 |
| | **TOTAL** | **27.75** | **38.36** | **16.62** | **32.98** | **44.04** | **21.36** |
| **ACTIVE DELTA** | | | | | | | |
| *IV.* | *THE WESTERN SUNDARBANS* | | | | | | |
| 15. | Sagar Island | 40.58 | 55.25 | 25.12 | 32.59 | 37.25 | 27.66 |
| 16. | Kakdwip | 35.94 | 49.38 | 21.76 | 43.26 | 57.37 | 29.39 |
| 17. | Namkhana | 41.34 | 55.96 | 25.91 | 50.96 | 63.84 | 37.36 |
| | **TOTAL** | **38.56** | **52.65** | **23.71** | **41.38** | **52.11** | **30.43** |
| *V.* | *THE MIDDLE SUNDARBANS* | | | | | | |
| 18. | Mathurapur | 34.15 | 48.34 | 18.91 | 41.63 | 55.00 | 27.19 |
| 19. | Pathar Pratima | 37.89 | 52.44 | 22.47 | 43.54 | 56.19 | 30.25 |
| | **TOTAL** | **35.82** | **50.17** | **20.51** | **42.46** | **55.52** | **28.54** |
| *VI.* | *EASTERN SUNDARBANS* | | | | | | |
| 20. | Kultali | 19.02 | 22.12 | 9.50 | 32.19 | 46.45 | 17.06 |
| 21. | Basanti | 25.27 | 37.00 | 12.88 | 31.52 | 43.48 | 18.92 |
| 22. | Gosaba | 35.78 | 48.66 | 22.00 | 44.07 | 55.97 | 31.43 |
| | **TOTAL** | **27.01** | **38.30** | **15.00** | **36.01** | **48.57** | **22.71** |
| | **DISTRICT TOTAL** | **37.59** | **49.86** | **24.37** | **44.15** | **55.09** | **32.47** |

TABLE 3.6 (*Contd.*)

**Proportion of Rural Literate to Total Rural Population**

| Regions/Blocks | 1981 | | | 1991 | | |
|---|---|---|---|---|---|---|
| | Person | Male | Female | Person | Male | Female |
| *1* | *2* | *3* | *4* | *5* | *6* | *7* |
| **STABLE DELTA** | | | | | | |
| *I. THE WESTERN HUGLI SIDE FLATS* | | | | | | |
| 1. Thakurpukur Metiaburuz | 53.43 | 62.08 | 43.48 | 28.90 | 29.47 | 28.23 |
| 2. Mahestala | 44.52 | 55.13 | 32.97 | 57.12 | 66.30 | 47.71 |
| 3. Budge Budge | 35.50 | 50.37 | 23.53 | 47.00 | 55.50 | 37.99 |
| 4. Falta | 42.84 | 56.50 | 28.15 | 49.07 | 60.41 | 36.98 |
| 5. Diamond Harbour | 40.09 | 53.88 | 27.21 | 45.86 | 55.73 | 35.35 |
| 6. Kulpi | 36.78 | 49.57 | 23.34 | 39.15 | 52.98 | 26.17 |
| **TOTAL** | **40.50** | **53.19** | **26.84** | **44.98** | **55.14** | **34.41** |
| *II. THE MIDDLE MATURE DELTA OF THE HUGLI* | | | | | | |
| 7. Sonarpur | 40.13 | 46.77 | 32.66 | 52.03 | 62.78 | 40.35 |
| 8. Bishnupur | 38.33 | 51.19 | 24.50 | 46.30 | 58.01 | 34.04 |
| 9. Baruipur | 36.69 | 48.91 | 23.62 | 46.40 | 49.24 | 32.55 |
| 10. Mograhat | 32.55 | 46.20 | 17.99 | 40.40 | 51.36 | 28.72 |
| 11. Mandir - Bazar | 34.16 | 49.03 | 18.50 | 41.11 | 54.26 | 26.98 |
| 12. Jaynagar | 30.66 | 44.89 | 15.55 | 36.42 | 25.66 | 22.24 |
| **TOTAL** | **35.12** | **47.76** | **21.54** | **43.06** | **55.10** | **30.19** |
| *III. THE PIYALI BIDYADHARI PLAINS IN THE EAST* | | | | | | |
| 13. Bhangar | 29.06 | 37.63 | 20.00 | 34.01 | 43.85 | 23.63 |
| 14. Canning | 24.12 | 37.03 | 10.74 | 29.73 | 42.29 | 16.53 |
| **TOTAL** | **26.72** | **37.34** | **15.58** | **31.92** | **43.09** | **20.19** |
| **ACTIVE DELTA** | | | | | | |
| *IV. THE WESTERN SUNDARBANS* | | | | | | |
| 15. Sagar Island | 40.58 | 55.25 | 25.12 | 32.59 | 37.25 | 27.66 |
| 16. Kakdwip | 35.94 | 49.38 | 21.76 | 43.26 | 57.37 | 29.39 |
| 17. Namkhana | 41.34 | 55.96 | 25.91 | 50.96 | 63:84 | 37.36 |
| **TOTAL** | **38.56** | **52.65** | **23.71** | **41.38** | **52.11** | **30.43** |
| *V. THE MIDDLE SUNDARBANS* | | | | | | |
| 18. Mathurapur | 34.15 | 48.34 | 18.91 | 41.63 | 55.00 | 27.19 |
| 19. Pathar Pratima | 37.98 | 52.44 | 22.47 | 43.54 | 56.19 | 30.25 |
| **TOTAL** | **35.82** | **50.17** | **20.51** | **42.46** | **55.52** | **28.54** |
| *VI. EASTERN SUNDARBANS* | | | | | | |
| 20. Kultali | 19.02 | 22.12 | 9.50 | 32.19 | 46.45 | 17.06 |
| 21. Basanti | 25.27 | 37.00 | 12.88 | 31.52 | 43.48 | 18.92 |
| 22. Gosaba | 35.78 | 48.66 | 22.00 | 44.07 | 55.97 | 31.43 |
| **TOTAL** | **27.01** | **38.30** | **15.00** | **36.01** | **48.57** | **22.71** |
| **DISTRICT TOTAL** | **34.56** | **47.14** | **21.13** | **40.94** | **52.56** | **28.68** |

**TABLE 3.6 : (*Contd.*)**

**Proportion of Urban Literate to Total Urban Population**

| Regions/Blocks | 1981 | | | 1991 | | |
|---|---|---|---|---|---|---|
| | Person | Male | Female | Person | Male | Female |
| 1 | 2 | 3 | 4 | 5 | 6 | 7 |
| **STABLE DELTA** | | | | | | |
| *I. THE WESTERN HUGLI SIDE FLATS* | | | | | | |
| 1. Thakurpukur-Metiaburuz | 77.24 | 94.98 | 58.59 | 69.31 | 74.97 | 43.79 |
| 2. Mahestala | 55.17 | 63.27 | 45.84 | 57.96 | 64.53 | 50.42 |
| 3. Budge Budge | 49.92 | 58.84 | 38.16 | 56.09 | 63.08 | 47.50 |
| 4. Falta | 49.92 | 58.84 | 38.16 | 56.09 | 63.08 | 47.50 |
| 5. Diamond Harbour | 58.47 | 66.96 | 49.31 | 63.60 | 71.47 | 55.11 |
| 6. Kulpi | | | | | | |
| TOTAL | **58.14** | **68.16** | **46.30** | **59.93** | **66.81** | **52.22** |
| *II. THE MIDDLE MATURE DELTA OF THE HUGLI* | | | | | | |
| 7. Sonarpur | 64.25 | 71.24 | 56.63 | 74.78 | 80.68 | 68.42 |
| 8. Bishnupur | 58.18 | 68.71 | 46.51 | 70.01 | 67.96 | 72.38 |
| 9. Baruipur | 70.35 | 77.67 | 62.48 | 72.71 | 79.11 | 65.68 |
| 10. Mograhat | | | | | | |
| 11. Mandir - Bazar | | | | | | |
| 12. Jaynagar | 63.51 | 71.84 | 54.30 | 65.35 | 72.55 | 57.56 |
| TOTAL | **64.79** | **72.29** | **56.59** | **73.21** | **78.80** | **67.12** |
| *III. THE PIYALI BIDYADHARI PLAINS IN THE EAST* | | | | | | |
| 13. Bhangar | | | | | | |
| 14. Canning | 47.00 | 57.33 | 36.13 | 53.11 | 61.98 | 43.72 |
| TOTAL | **47.00** | **57.33** | **36.13** | **53.11** | **61.98** | **43.72** |
| DISTRICT TOTAL | **59.33** | **68.71** | **48.53** | **63.17** | **69.50** | **55.92** |

as literates ranked first, followed in order by 38.56% of the Western Sundarbans, 37.94% of Middle Mature Hugli Delta, 35.82% of the Eastern Sundarbans, 27.75% of the Piyali-Bidyadhari Plains and finally 27.01% of the Eastern Sundarbans. At the block level Thakurpukur - Metiaburuz in 1981 represents the highest literacy 70.54%, followed by Maheshtala 52.17%; the lowest proportions however being noticeable in Kultali 19.02% and Basanti 25.27%.

The 1991 data reveal a somewhat change in rank, though the proportions have shown a general increase over the decade. Here also the Western Hugli Side Flats with 50.62% literate stands first, followed in order by 46.46% of the Middle Mature Hugli Delta, 42.46% of the Middle Sundarbans, 41.38% of the Western

Sundarbans, 36.01% of the Eastern Sundarban and finally 32.98% of the Piyali Bidyadhari Plains. Thakurpukur - Metiaburuz and Sagar Island have registered a decline in the proportions at the block level. Here, Sonarpur takes the lead with 61.46%, followed by Maheshtala 57.78%; the lowest literacy proportions being noticeable in Basanti 31.52% and Canning 32.01%. Thus both 1981 and 1991 data reveal that literacy rates are in general higher in the Stable Delta in marked contract to the Active Delta. Even within the Stable Delta, the two subregions viz. the Western Hugli Side Flats and the Middle Mature Delta stand out predominantly over the relatively lower literacy region of the Piyali - Bidyadhari Plains. These are also the areas having larger urban tracts and close proximity to the Calcutta conurbation. Most of the blocks in the Stable Delta exhibit figures higher to the district's total of 44.15% in 1991. 9 blocks of the Stable Delta viz. Thakurpukur - Metiaburuz, Maheshtala, Budge Budge, Falta, Diamond Harbour, Sonarpur, Bishnupur and Baruipur and only one block of the Active Delta viz. Namkhana stand above this figure.

Five size groups can be delineated with the 1991 total literacy data. (Map 3.5) A very high literacy rate (of 57 to 62%) is noticeable in the blocks of Sonarpur and Maheshtala. The high literacy (51 to 56%) covers the blocks of Thakurpukur - Metiaburuz, Budge Budge, and Namkhana. The medium literacy rate (45 to 50%) covers Falta, Diamond Harbour, Baruipur and Bishnupur. The low literacy rate (39 to 44%) prevails in the blocks of Kulpi, Mograhat, Mandir Bazar, Kakdwip, Mathurapur, Pathar Pratima and Gosaba, whereas the very low rate (32 to 38%) prevails in Kultali, Basanti, Canning, Sagar Island, Bhangar and Jaynagar.

### *Male - Female Differential in Literacy Rates 1981-1991*

In the modern context, it is by the position of women in society that we judge the progress of a community towards socio economic advancement. But the female literacy proportions display much lower figures than their male counterparts revealing *constraints* in the way of *female education.*

In 1981, while 49.86% of the total males were literates the position of females was 24.37% only for the district as a whole; in

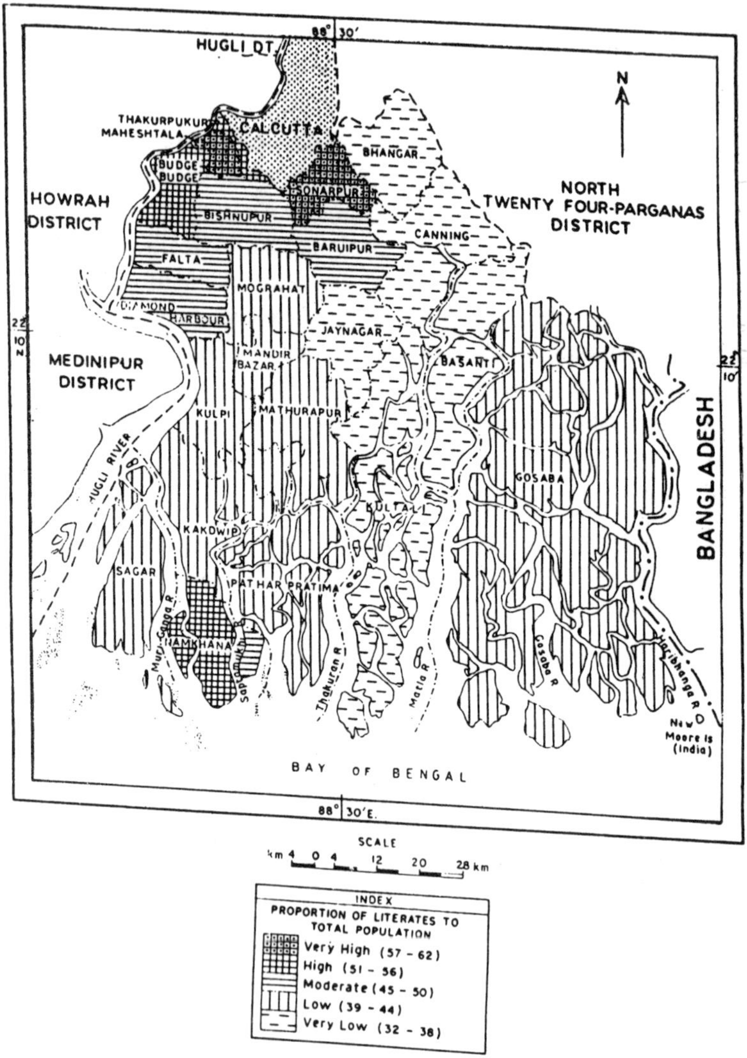


**MAP 3.5** : South 24-Parganas : Literacy 1991

1991 these figures had risen to 55.09% and 32.47% respectively. 1981 figures reveal that the highest difference of 29.66% is discernable in the Middle Sundarbans, followed by 28.94% of the Western Sundarbans, the lowest difference of 21.74% in the Piyali - Bidyadhari Plains. At the block level in 1981, Thakurpukur - Metiaburuz and Mandir Bazar, display a difference of 31%. Sagar Island, Namkhana and Pathar Pratima exhibit a difference of 30%, the lowest however being noticeable in Kultali i.e. 13%.

In 1991 the male, female proportions have increased considerably and the male - female difference in literacy has decreased except in the Piyali Bidyadhari and Eastern Sundarbans (the difference here have slightly increased) indicating that the impediments against female literacy have been gradually disappearing. At the sub-regional level, the highest difference here is noticed again in the Middle Sundarbans, 26.98% in this case, followed by 25.86% of the Eastern Sundarbans. The lowest difference of 18.71% is seen in the Western Hugli Side Flats. At the block level, in 1991, however male - female difference is highest in Kultali, 29% and the lowest of 9% in Thakurpukur, just the reverse of the 1981 trend.

In general the Active Delta exhibits not only lower rates than the first two subregions but also greater differentials highlighting impediments in the way of female education, and also against their employment outside the home. But inspite of comparative lower proportion, the female literacy has gone up considerably during the 1981- 1991 decade exhibiting a positive development.

The 1991 male literacy rates ( Map 3.6) display a high literacy rate (66 - 72%) in Thakurpukur - Metiaburuz, Maheshtala, Budge Budge, Falta, Baruipur and Namkhana; A medium rate (52-58%) in Diamond Harbour, Kulpi, Bishnupur, Mandir Bazar, Kakdwip, Mathurapur, Pathar Pratima and Gosaba; a low rate (46-51%) in Mograhat, Jaynagar, and Kultali; and finally, a very low rate (37-44%) in Bhangar, Canning, Sagar Island and Basanti. The 1991 female literacy rates (Map 3.7) portray a very high rate (46-52%) noticeable in Thakurpukur - Metiaburuz, Maheshtala and Sonarpur. A high rate (39-45%) in Budge Budge; a medium rate (32-38%) in Falta, Diamond Harbour, Bishnupur, Baruipur and Namkhana. Low rate (25-31%) is discernable in Kulpi, Mograhat, Mandir Bazar, Sagar Island, Kakdwip, Mathurapur, Pathar Pratima and Gosaba. A

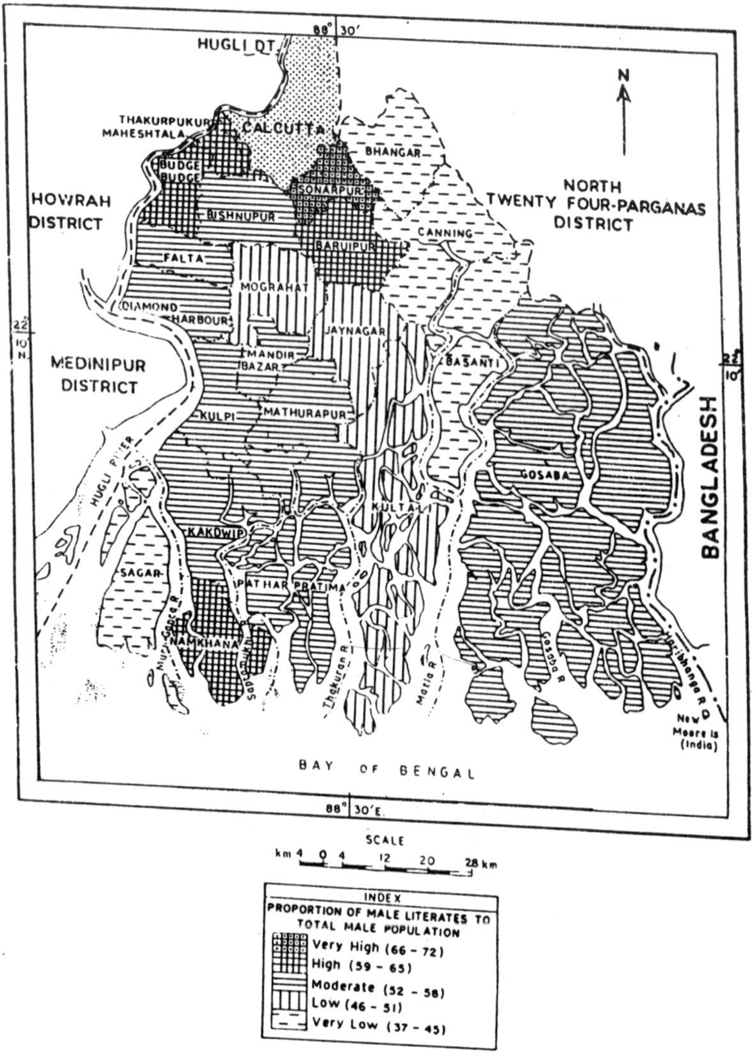


**MAP 3.6 :** South 24-Parganas : Male Literacy 1991

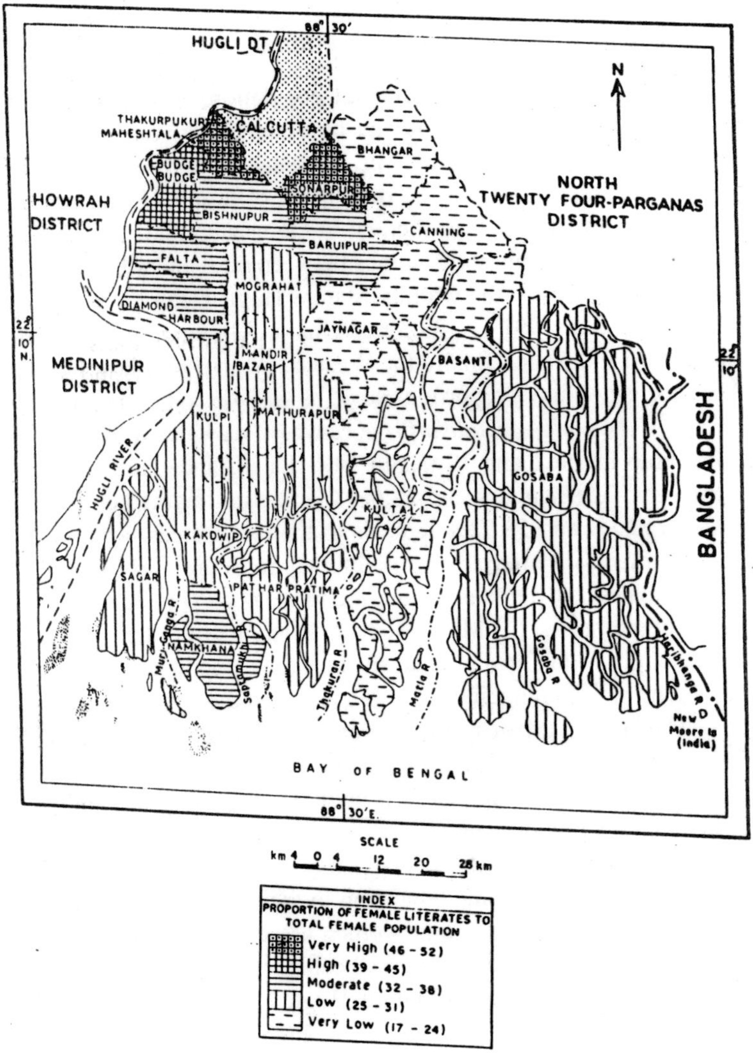


**MAP 3.7 :** South 24-Parganas : Female Literacy 1991

very low rate (17-24%) is finally seen in Jaynagar, Bhangar, Canning, Kultali and Basanti.

### *Rural Urban Difference in Literacy Rates*

As in several other characteristics of population, so in literacy and education, the villages and towns of South 24-Parganas stand in marked contrast to each other. In 1981 the proportion of 34.36% literacy was reported from the rural areas of South 24-Parganas in marked contrast to 59.33% literacy in the urban areas. At the sub-regional level the highest difference between rural and urban literacy rates is portrayed by the Middle Mature Hugli Delta both in 1981 i.e. 30.15% and 1991 i.e. 29.59%. This is followed by the Piyali-Bidyadhari Plains and finally the Western Hugli Side Flats. In 1991 these corresponding proportions stood as 40.94% (rural) and 63.17% (urban). The *male - female difference* was *more marked* in the *rural areas* both in 1981 and 1991. In 1991 for instance the rural areas displayed 52.56% males and 28.68% females in marked contrast to 69.50% males and 55.92% females in the urban areas. From Table 3.7 it is therefore inferred that (i) literacy rates are fairly high both among males and females in the urban areas as compared to their rural counterparts, (ii) Male - female differential in literacy among rural people is far greater than in the urban population, (iii) areal variations in urban literacy are much less than those in rural literacy.

The higher urban rates may be resultant of various facts. (i) Urban areas are the centres of administration of higher hierachical order (ii) where non-agricultural activities requiring the ability to read and write predominate (iii) which are the centres of newer ideas, and (iv) where people are socially more aware and economically more capable of providing education to their children, high rates of literacy both among men and women are expected.

Both in 1981 and in 1991, the highest rural literacy rate is discernable in the Middle Mature Hugli Delta, the figures being 34.74% and 37.01% respectively. The highest urban rates are seen in the Western Hugli Side Flats, the figures here being 68.14 and 65.94 respectively. At the block level in 1981, Thakurpukur - Metiaburuz represents the highest rural literacy of 53.43% and Kultali, the lowest of 19.02%; whereas the 1991 data represents Canning with the highest rural literacy of 58.13% and Basanti having the

**TABLE - 3.7 : Chance in Literacy 1981 - 1991**
**(Proportion of change in Literate Popultion Among Total Popultion)**

| Regions/Blocks | Total | | | Rural | | | Urban | | |
|---|---|---|---|---|---|---|---|---|---|
| | Person | Male | Female | Person | Male | Female | Person | Male | Female |
| 1 | 2 | 3 | 4 | 5 | 6 | 7 | 8 | 9 | 10 |
| **STABLE DELTA** | | | | | | | | | |
| *I. THE WESTERN HUGLI SIDE FLATS* | | | | | | | | | |
| 1. Thakurpukur-Metiaburuz | -15.15 | -25.83 | -3.78 | -24.53 | -32.61 | -15.25 | -7.93 | -20.01 | -14.80 |
| 2. Mahestala | 5.61 | 3.87 | 7.59 | 12.60 | 11.70 | 14.20 | 2.79 | 1.26 | 4.58 |
| 3. Budge Budge | 8.49 | 5.10 | 12.84 | 11.50 | 5.13 | 12.46 | 6.17 | 4.24 | 0.34 |
| 4. Falta | 6.23 | 3.91 | 8.83 | 6.23 | 3.91 | 8.83 | | | |
| 5. Diamond Harbour | 5.18 | 2.35 | 7.80 | 5.77 | 1.85 | 8.14 | 5.13 | 4.51 | 5.80 |
| 6. Kulpi | 2.37 | 3.41 | 2.83 | 2.37 | 3.41 | 2.83 | | | |
| **TOTAL** | **4.42** | **1.38** | **7.94** | **4.48** | **1.95** | **7.57** | **1.79** | **-1.35** | **5.92** |
| *II. THE MIDDLE MATURE DELTA OF THE HUGLI* | | | | | | | | | |
| 7. Sonarpur | 12.94 | 14.98 | 10.92 | 11.90 | 16.01 | 7.69 | 10.53 | 9.44 | 11.79 |
| 8. Bishnupur | 8.05 | 6.48 | 10.05 | 7.97 | 6.82 | 9.54 | 11.83 | -0.75 | 25.87 |
| 9. Baruipur | 9.67 | 9.92 | 9.24 | 9.71 | 10.33 | 8.93 | 2.36 | 1.44 | 3.20 |
| 10. Mograhat | 7.89 | 5.16 | 10.73 | 7.89 | 5.16 | 10.73 | | | |
| 11. Mandir - Bazar | 6.95 | 5.23 | 8.48 | 6.95 | 5.23 | 8.48 | | | |
| 12. Jaynagar | 5.17 | 4.25 | 6.11 | 5.76 | -19.23 | 6.69 | 1.84 | 0.71 | 3.26 |
| **TOTAL** | **8.52** | **7.68** | **9.48** | **7.94** | **7.34** | **8.65** | **8.42** | **6.51** | **10.53** |
| *III. THE PIYALI BIDYADHARI PLAINS IN THE EAST* | | | | | | | | | |
| 13. Bhangar | 4.95 | 6.22 | 5.63 | 4.95 | 6.22 | 3.63 | | | |
| 14. Canning | 5.57 | 5.12 | 5.91 | 5.61 | 5.27 | 5.84 | 6.11 | 4.65 | 7.59 |
| **TOTAL** | **5.23** | **5.68** | **4.74** | **5.20** | **5.75** | **4.61** | **6.11** | **4.65** | **7.59** |

**TABLE - 3.7:** *(Contd.)*

**(Proportion of change in Literate Popultion Among Total Popultion)**

| Regions/Blocks | Total | | | Rural | | | Urban | | |
|---|---|---|---|---|---|---|---|---|---|
| | *Person* | *Male* | *Female* | *Person* | *Male* | *Female* | *Person* | *Male* | *Female* |
| *1* | *2* | *3* | *4* | *5* | *6* | *7* | *8* | *9* | *10* |
| **ACTIVE DELTA** | | | | | | | | | |
| *IV. THE WESTERN SUNDARBANS* | | | | | | | | | |
| 15. Sagar Island | -7.99 | -18.00 | 2.54 | -7.99 | -18.00 | 2.54 | — | — | — |
| 16. Kakdwip | 7.32 | 7.99 | 7.63 | 7.32 | 7.99 | 7.63 | — | — | — |
| 17. Namkhana | 9.62 | 7.88 | 11.45 | 9.62 | 7.88 | 11.45 | — | — | — |
| TOTAL | 2.82 | - 0.54 | 6.72 | 2.82 | - 0.54 | 6.72 | — | — | — |
| *V. THE MIDDLE SUNDARBANS* | | | | | | | | | |
| 18. Mathurapur | 7.48 | 6.66 | 8.28 | 7.48 | 6.66 | 8.28 | — | — | — |
| 19. Pathar Pratima | 5.65 | 3.75 | 7.78 | 5.65 | 3.75 | 7.78 | — | — | — |
| TOTAL | 6.64 | 5.35 | 8.03 | 6.64 | 5.35 | 8.03 | — | — | — |
| *VI. EASTERN SUNDARBANS* | | | | | | | | | |
| 20. Kultali | 13.17 | 24.33 | 7.56 | 13.17 | 24.33 | 7.56 | — | — | — |
| 21. Basanti | 6.25 | 6.48 | 6.04 | 6.25 | 6.48 | 6.04 | — | — | — |
| 22. Gosaba | 8.29 | 7.31 | 9.43 | 8.29 | 7.31 | 9.43 | — | — | — |
| TOTAL | 9.00 | 10.27 | 7.71 | 9.00 | 10.27 | 7.71 | — | — | — |
| **DISTRICT TOTAL** | **6.56** | **5.23** | **8.10** | **6.38** | **5.42** | **7.55** | **3.84** | **0.79** | **7.39** |

lowest rural literacy rate of 31.52%. The rural literacy figures here also are higher in the Stable Delta region than in the Active Delta. The urban literacy rates are much higher. The 1981 highest occurs in Thakurpukur - Metiaburuz 77.24% and the lowest in Canning being 47.00%. In 1991 the highest urban literacy is portrayed by Sonarpur 74.18% and the lowest by Canning 53.11%.

The rural literacy rates can be classified into Five groups. A very high rate (55 to 60% literacy) is noticeable in Maheshtala and Canning; Canning in the Piyali - Bidyadhari Plains representing highest rural literacy due to its strategic importance. A high rate (49.54%) occurs in Falta, Sonarpur and Namkhana. A large number of blocks represent a medium rate (43-48%) in Budge Budge, Diamond Harbour, Bishnupur, Baruipur, Kakdwip, Pathar Pratima, and Gosaba. Lower rates (37-42%) are noticeable in Kulpi, Mograhat, Mandir Bazar and Mathurapur; and finally the lowest rate (30 - 36%) are found in Thakurpukur - Metiaburuz, Jaynagar, Bhangar, Sagar Island, Kultali and Basanti.

The urban literacy rates 1991 also can be represented by five groups. Sonarpur falls in the very high group (of 75 - 80%) literacy, the high group (69 - 74%) is represented by Thakurpukur - Metiaburuz, Bishnupur and Baruipur. The medium rate (63 - 68%) occurs in Diamond Harbour and Jaynagar, the low rate (57 - 62%) in Maheshtala and finally the very low rate (50 - 56%) in Budge Budge and Canning.

### *Literacy Rates Among Literate Population*

Another way of measuring literacy distribution and rates is to judge the literacy rates among the total literate population both for total, male, female and for rural and urban areas. Such rates (Appendix III.1) revealing the following facts (i) *literacy rates have increased in nearly all the regions* (except the first) and nearly all blocks over the decade 1981 and 1991 (ii) *The rural literacy rates are considerably lower than the urban counterpart* and finally (iii) *the literacy rates among the total literates are in general lower in the Active Delta* than in the Stable Delta of the Hugli.

Among the regions, the highest 1981 total literacy is seen in the Middle Mature Delta i.e. 33.47% and the lowest of 7.97% in the Eastern Sundarbans. In 1991 the first rank is still retained by the same region with 35.70% literates, the lowest of 7.69% in this case being depicted by the Western Sundarbans. At the block level the highest 1981 total literacy is seen in Budge Budge, 7.71%, and the lowest in Kultali 1.69%, the corresponding rank for 1991 being represented by Sonarpur, the 1991 highest 8.27%; and Namkhana 1.92% the lowest.

### *Growth in Literacy 1981 - 1991*

Considering the proportion of literates among the total population, changes in literacy has been estimated in Table 3.7. Nearly all the *subregions* depict *positive changes in literacy rates*, the highest rate being depicted by the Eastern Sundarbans; 9.00% and Middle Mature Delta depicts the highest urban rate of 8.42% .

At the block level all blocks have registered considerable increase apart from 2 blocks of Thakurpukur - Metiaburuz and Sagar Island. Kultali exhibits the highest increase of + 13.17% followed by Sonarpur + 12.94%. The total male literacy also depicts similar ranks. It is also discernable that the increase in total female literacy rates is higher than the male rate, here Budge Budge ranks the highest of + 12.84% followed by Sonarpur + 10.92%.

The rural growth in literacy over the decade 1981 - 1991 is seen in 20 blocks and in 8 blocks in urban areas out of a total of 9.

## 3.3.3 Social Composition: Regional Contrast in the Distribution of Scheduled Caste and Tribe

### *Spatial Pattern of Scheduled Caste 1981 - 1991*

Scheduled Caste form an important component of the district's population with 33.90% of the total 1981 population belonging to this category and the proportion rising slightly to 33.93% in 1991 (Table -3.8)

In 1981, the *Eastern Sundarbans* displayed the highest Scheduled Caste population of 51.42% and the Western Hugli Side Flats the lowest of 26.15%. This rank remained the same in 1991; only with the respective change in proportions as 52.03% and 22.91%. 10 blocks have proportions higher than the districts total in 1981, Gosaba representing the highest of 64.13% and Mathurapur the lowest with 20.00%. The male and female counterparts exhibit similar trends in

**TABLE 3.8 : Scheduled Caste to Total Population 1981-1991 (Proportion of Scheduled Caste Population to Total Population)**

| *Regions/Blocks* | | *1981* | | | *1991* | | |
|---|---|---|---|---|---|---|---|
| | | *Person* | *Male* | *Female* | *Person* | *Male* | *Female* |
| *1* | | *2* | *3* | *4* | *5* | *6* | *7* |
| **STABLE DELTA** | | | | | | | |
| *I.* | *THE WESTERN HUGLI SIDE FLATS* | | | | | | |
| 1. | Thakurpur-Metiaburuz | 30.11 | 30.62 | 29.55 | 28.62 | 27.90 | 29.46 |
| 2. | Mahestala | 22.94 | 22.78 | 23.12 | 19.78 | 19.37 | 20.25 |
| 3. | Budge Budge | 22.27 | 20.88 | 23.92 | 18.91 | 18.40 | 19.50 |
| 4. | Falta | 25.20 | 25.18 | 25.22 | 22.96 | 25.66 | 20.07 |
| 5. | Diamond Harbour | 23.18 | 23.26 | 23.09 | 20.67 | 22.20 | 17.57 |
| 6. | Kulpi | 39.09 | 43.58 | 34.37 | 32.56 | 32.54 | 32.58 |
| | **TOTAL** | **26.15** | **26.38** | **25.90** | **22.91** | **23.40** | **22.39** |
| *II.* | *THE MIDDLE MATURE DELTA OF THE HUGLI* | | | | | | |
| 7. | Sonarpur | 38.77 | 38.62 | 38.94 | 38.32 | 38.39 | 38.25 |
| 8. | Bishnupur | 35.93 | 35.90 | 35.96 | 35.89 | 36.38 | 35.37 |
| 9. | Baruipur | 44.99 | 45.51 | 44.42 | 44.75 | 44.41 | 43.31 |
| 10. | Mograhat | 30.52 | 33.15 | 27.72 | 32.46 | 32.73 | 31.16 |
| 11. | Mandir - Bazar | 47.72 | 47.97 | 47.47 | 47.65 | 47.99 | 47.29 |
| 12. | Jaynagar | 43.12 | 43.65 | 42.58 | 41.12 | 41.39 | 40.83 |
| | **TOTAL** | **38.93** | **39.66** | **38.15** | **38.81** | **39.14** | **38.46** |
| *III.* | *THE PIYALI BIDYADHARI PLAINS IN THE EAST* | | | | | | |
| 13. | Bhangar | 27.22 | 27.00 | 27.45 | 25.00 | 24.98 | 25.03 |
| 14. | Canning | 43.42 | 44.08 | 42.73 | 42.53 | 42.98 | 42.05 |
| | **TOTAL** | **35.33** | **35.52** | **35.13** | **33.99** | **34.20** | **33.75** |
| **ACTIVE DELTA** | | | | | | | |
| *IV.* | *THE WESTERN SUNDARBANS* | | | | | | |
| 15. | Sagar Island | 26.67 | 26.54 | 26.81 | 28.44 | 27.92 | 28.98 |
| 16. | Kakdwip | 29.10 | 29.32 | 28.88 | 33.74 | 34.96 | 32.53 |
| 17. | Namkhana | 25.22 | 25.22 | 25.22 | 26.28 | 27.17 | 25.34 |
| | **TOTAL** | **27.51** | **27.57** | **27.45** | **30.52** | **31.05** | **29.98** |
| *V.* | *THE MIDDLE SUNDARBANS* | | | | | | |
| 18. | Mathurapur | 37.92 | 34.74 | 34.70 | 35.25 | 35.21 | 35.30 |
| 19. | Pathar Pratima | 23.95 | 23.87 | 24.04 | 25.92 | 24.59 | 24.81 |
| | **TOTAL** | **29.91** | **29.90** | **29.92** | **31.16** | **30.59** | **30.67** |
| *VI.* | *EASTERN SUNDARBANS* | | | | | | |
| 20. | Kultali | 48.53 | 48.35 | 48.72 | 50.27 | 50.52 | 50.00 |
| 21. | Basanti | 41.48 | 41.80 | 41.15 | 41.75 | 42.33 | 41.13 |
| 22. | Gosaba | 64.13 | 64.46 | 63.78 | 65.04 | 65.26 | 64.80 |
| | **TOTAL** | **51.42** | **51.62** | **51.21** | **52.03** | **51.42** | **52.67** |
| | **DISTRICT TOTAL** | **34.71** | **35.03** | **36.08** | **33.93** | **34.19** | **33.54** |

TABLE 3.8 : (*Contd.*)
**(Proportion of Rural Scheduled Caste Population to Total Rural Population)**

| Regions/Blocks | | 1981 Person | 1981 Male | 1981 Female | 1991 Person | 1991 Male | 1991 Female |
|---|---|---|---|---|---|---|---|
| *1* | | *2* | *3* | *4* | *5* | *6* | *7* |
| **STABLE DELTA** | | | | | | | |
| *I.* | *THE WESTERN HUGLI SIDE FLATS* | | | | | | |
| 1. | Thakurpukur-Metiaburuz | 44.50 | 43.35 | 46.87 | 48.00 | 46.85 | 49.32 |
| 2. | Mahestala | 49.83 | 49.46 | 50.22 | 49.62 | 49.33 | 49.93 |
| 3. | Budge Budge | 30.08 | 25.70 | 34.85 | 26.12 | 25.83 | 26.43 |
| 4. | Falta | 25.20 | 25.18 | 25.22 | 22.96 | 25.66 | 20.07 |
| 5. | Diamond Harbour | 24.49 | 24.59 | 24.38 | 21.56 | 24.82 | 18.08 |
| 6. | Kulpi | 39.09 | 43.58 | 34.37 | 32.56 | 32.54 | 32.58 |
| | **TOTAL** | **31.49** | **31.48** | **31.50** | **28.71** | **30.01** | **27.36** |
| *II.* | *THE MIDDLE MATURE DELTA OF THE HUGLI* | | | | | | |
| 7. | Sonarpur | 51.64 | 51.22 | 52.12 | 51.75 | 51.71 | 51.79 |
| 8. | Bishnupur | 37.26 | 37.26 | 37.25 | 36.63 | 37.12 | 36.13 |
| 9. | Baruipur | 47.60 | 47.32 | 47.91 | 46.58 | 47.24 | 45.87 |
| 10. | Mograhat | 30.52 | 33.15 | 27.22 | 32.45 | 32.73 | 32.16 |
| 11. | Mandir - Bazar | 47.72 | 47.97 | 47.47 | 47.65 | 47.99 | 47.29 |
| 12. | Jaynagar | 44.89 | 45.09 | 44.67 | 42.54 | 42.79 | 42.26 |
| | TOTAL | 41.33 | 41.95 | 40.67 | 41.12 | 41.48 | 40.74 |
| *III.* | *THE PIYALI BIDYADHARI PLAINS IN THE EAST* | | | | | | |
| 13. | Bhangar | 27.22 | 27.00 | 27.45 | 25.00 | 24.98 | 25.03 |
| 14. | Canning | 42.71 | 43.48 | 41.93 | 41.58 | 42.04 | 41.10 |
| | **TOTAL** | **34.56** | **34.77** | **34.35** | **33.08** | **33.28** | **32.88** |
| **ACTIVE DELTA** | | | | | | | |
| *IV.* | *THE WESTERN SUNDARBANS* | | | | | | |
| 15. | Sagar Island | 26.67 | 26.54 | 26.81 | 28.44 | 27.92 | 28.98 |
| 16. | Kakdwip | 29.10 | 29.32 | 28.88 | 33.74 | 34.96 | 32.53 |
| 17. | Namkhana | 25.22 | 25.22 | 25.22 | 26.28 | 27.17 | 25.34 |
| | **TOTAL** | **27.51** | **27.54** | **27.45** | **30.52** | **31.05** | **29.98** |
| *V.* | *THE MIDDLE SUNDARBANS* | | | | | | |
| 18. | Mathurapur | 37.72 | 34.74 | 34.70 | 35.25 | 35.21 | 35.30 |
| 19. | Pathar Pratima | 23.95 | 23.87 | 24.04 | 25.92 | 24.59 | 24.81 |
| | **TOTAL** | **29.91** | **29.90** | **29.92** | **31.16** | **30.59** | **30.67** |
| *VI.* | *EASTERN SUNDARBANS* | | | | | | |
| 20. | Kultali | 48.53 | 48.35 | 48.72 | 50.27 | 50.52 | 50.00 |
| 21. | Basanti | 41.48 | 41.80 | 41.15 | 41.75 | 42.33 | 41.13 |
| 22. | Gosaba | 64.13 | 64.46 | 63.78 | 65.04 | 65.26 | 64.80 |
| | **TOTAL** | **51.42** | **51.62** | **51.21** | **52.03** | **51.42** | **52.67** |
| | **DISTRICT TOTAL** | **37.20** | **37.47** | **38.94** | **36.82** | **37.28** | **36.21** |

**TABLE 3.8 :** (Contd.)
**(Proportion of Urban Scheduled Caste Population to Total Urban Population)**

| *Regions/Blocks* | | *1981* | | | *1991* | | |
|---|---|---|---|---|---|---|---|
| | | *Person* | *Male* | *Female* | *Person* | *Male* | *Female* |
| | *1* | *2* | *3* | *4* | *5* | *6* | *7* |
| **STABLE DELTA** | | | | | | | |
| *I.* | *THE WESTERN HUGLI SIDE FLATS* | | | | | | |
| 1. | Thakurpukur-Metiaburuz | 24.28 | 25.42 | 23.07 | 18.46 | 18.09 | 18.84 |
| 2. | Mahestala | 12.39 | 12.58 | 15.26 | 11.96 | 11.73 | 12.22 |
| 3. | Budge Budge | 13.02 | 15.67 | 9.54 | 12.11 | 12.12 | 12.42 |
| 4. | Falta | — | — | — | — | — | — |
| 5. | Diamond Harbour | 9.63 | 9.59 | 9.68 | 12.90 | 12.66 | 13.16 |
| 6. | Kulpi | — | — | — | — | — | — |
| | **TOTAL** | **14.99** | **16.17** | **13.60** | **13.34** | **13.08** | **13.64** |
| *II.* | *THE MIDDLE MATURE DELTA OF THE HUGLI* | | | | | | |
| 7. | Sonarpur | 14.64 | 14.67 | 14.61 | 19.34 | 19.49 | 19.17 |
| 8. | Bishnupur | 6.04 | 5.71 | 6.40 | 17.65 | 19.12 | 15.95 |
| 9. | Baruipur | 24.61 | 31.54 | 17.17 | 27.81 | 27.70 | 27.93 |
| 10. | Mograhat | — | — | — | — | — | — |
| 11. | Mandir - Bazar | — | — | — | — | — | — |
| 12. | Jaynagar | 17.43 | 23.07 | 11.20 | 15.72 | 16.35 | 15.05 |
| | **TOTAL** | **16.10** | **18.04** | **13.98** | **20.61** | **20.84** | **20.36** |
| *III.* | *THE PIYALI BIDYADHARI PLAINS IN THE EAST* | | | | | | |
| 13. | Bhangar | — | — | — | — | — | — |
| 14. | Canning | 49.68 | 49.46 | 49.92 | 51.28 | 51.64 | 50.90 |
| | **TOTAL** | **49.68** | **49.46** | **49.92** | **51.28** | **51.64** | **50.90** |
| | **DISTRICT TOTAL** | **16.90** | **18.14** | **15.48** | **16.79** | **16.58** | **17.03** |

this regard with marginal difference between the two. In 1991 also 10 blocks exhibit proportions above the district's total. Here also Gosaba stands at the highest of 65.04% and Budge Budge the lowest at 18.91%. 9 blocks have registered an increase in scheduled caste population, 8 are found in the Active Delta. 13 blocks all in the Stable Deltaic area have registered a decline in the decadal growth of scheduled castes; thereby exhibiting growing proportion in the Active Delta.

The spatial pattern of scheduled caste population can be best depicted by regrouping the blocks into five size groups. (Map 3.8) A very high proportion (59 to 68%) occurs in Gosaba. A high proportion (49 to 58%) is found in Kultali. In the medium category

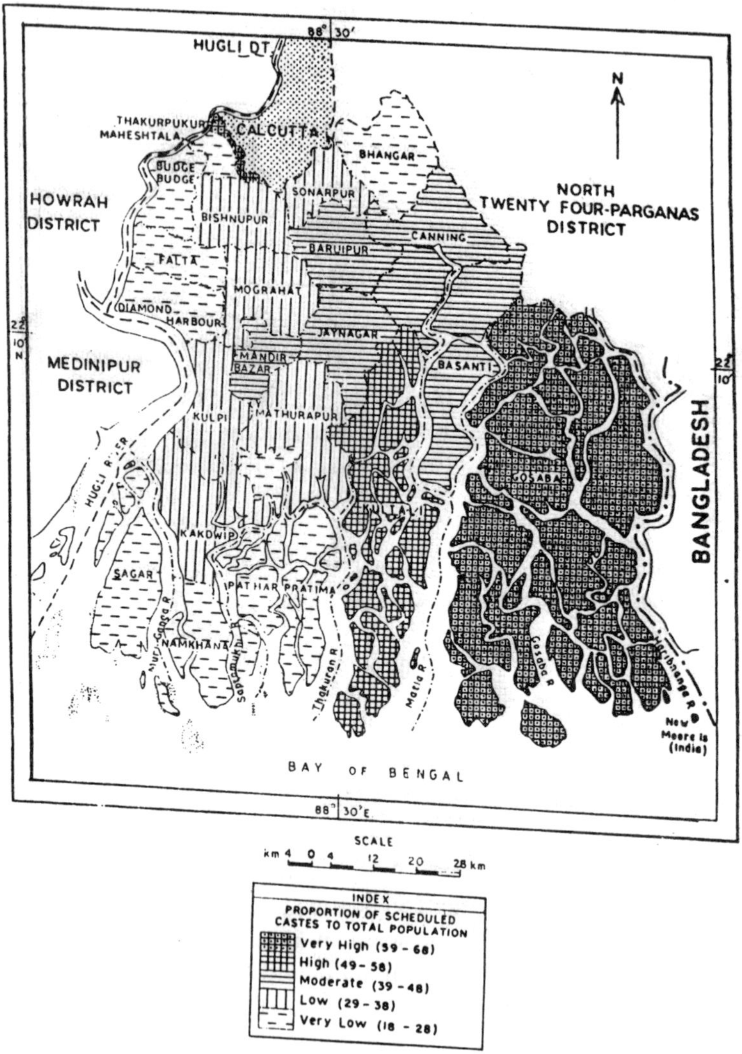


**MAP 3.8 :** South 24-Parganas : Scheduled Caste Population 1991

(39 to 48%) fall the blocks of Baruipur, Mandir Bazar, Jaynagar, Canning and Basanti. In the low proportion group (29-38%) fall the blocks of Thakurpukur, Metiaburuz, Kulpi, Sonarpur, Bishnupur, Mograhat, Kakdwip and Mathurapur. Finally in the very low proportion (18 to 28%) fall the blocks of Maheshtala Budge Budge, Falta, Diamond Harbour, Bhangar, Sagar Island, Namkhana and Pathar Pratima.

## Male Female Difference in Scheduled Caste 1981 - 1991

The male female portions exhibit slight differences both in 1981 and 1991 in both rural and urban areas. However, in the rural areas this difference is a little bit more accentuated than in the urban counterparts. In 1991 higher male proportions are noticeable in all regions except Eastern Sundarbans. The urban, male female components are much lower compared to the rural areas exhibiting the fact that scheduled caste population are concentrated more in the rural areas. Moreover there exists hardly any difference in the male - female counterparts in the urban areas.

## Rural Urban Difference in Scheduled Caste 1981-1991

The rural proportions of scheduled caste population exhibit not only higher figures but this proportion has been declining over the decade in the Stable Delta. Declining proportions in 1991 is the result of an increase in the total population at a greater rate than an increase in the scheduled caste population.

In the rural areas too, Gosaba has the highest scheduled caste proportion both in 1981 and 1991 the figures being 64.13% and 65.04% respectively. In 1981, 12 blocks stand above the district's total of 36.27% and this has changed to 11 blocks in 1991 that lies above the 1991 total of 36.82% in rural areas.

The rural size groups in 1991 can be classed as (i) A very high proportion (61-70%) in Gosaba, (ii) A high proportion (51-60%) in Sonarpur, (iii) A medium proportion (41-50%) covering the 8 blocks of Thakurpukur - Metiaburuz, Maheshtala, Baruipur, Mandir Bazar, Jaynagar, Canning, Kultali and Basanti, (iv) A low proportion (31-40%) is seen in 5 blocks of Kulpi, Bishnupur, Mograhat, Kakdwip and Mathurapur and finally (v) A very low proportion (20-30%) is discernable in the 7 blocks of Budge Budge, Falta, Diamond Harbour, Bhangar, Sagar Island, Namkhana and Pathar Pratima.

The urban areas on the other hand depict very low rates both in 1981 and 1991, the district's figure being 16.90% for 1981 and 16.79% for 1991. Highest proportion is located in the Piyali Bidyadhari Plains with 51.28% (urban Canning 51.28% in 1991) and lowest in the Western Hugli Side Flats 13.34% (Maheshtala a lowest of 11.96%).

## Distribution of Scheduled Caste among total Scheduled Caste Population

The components of scheduled castes among the total scheduled castes (Appendix III.2) in the different subregions and blocks in rural and urban areas and among the males and females both in 1981 and 1991, indicates a concentration in the Middle Mature Hugli Delta in both the decades, and also in the Western Hugli Side Flats and Eastern Sundarbans. Blockwise, Canning and Gosaba have the highest concentration of over 5 per cent.

## Spatial Distribution of Scheduled Tribe

The scheduled tribes also belong to the backward section of the society thereby exert a frictional drag in the overall development process, the study of which becomes necessary to judge the composition of the total population of an area.

From Table 3.9, it is evident that the *scheduled tribes are very few in number* in the district of South 24-Parganas. Even within the district *striking contrasts* occur among the blocks of the *Stable* and the *Active Delta*. Their proportions are negligeable in the Western Hugli Side Flats and in the Middle Mature Delta of the Hugli. Highest proportions occur in the Eastern Interior Sundarbans 6.37% in 1981 and 6.46% in 1991, followed by the Piyali Bidyadhari Plains, 2.87% in 1981 and 2.62% in 1991.

In 1981 the district's total proportion was only 1.30% and this further declined to 1.21% in 1991. In 1981 only 5 blocks had proportions above this level, *highest* in *Gosaba* i.e. 9.71% and lowest in Bhangar 1.76%. In Falta, Diamond Harbour and Kulpi, Mograhat and Mandir Bazar there was no scheduled tribes. In 1991, too there was 5 blocks above the districts total, viz. highest in Gosaba 9.82%, and also lowest in Bhangar 1.24%. Most of the blocks register a fall

**TABLE 3.9 : Proporation of Scheduled Tribe to Total Population (Proportion of Scheduled Tribe Population to Total Urban population)**

| *Regions/Blocks* | *1981* | | | *1991* | | |
|---|---|---|---|---|---|---|
| | *Person* | *Male* | *Female* | *Person* | *Male* | *Female* |
| *1* | *2* | *3* | *4* | *5* | *6* | *7* |
| **STABLE DELTA** | | | | | | |
| *I. THE WESTERN HUGLI SIDE FLATS* | | | | | | |
| 1. Thakurpukur-Metiaburuz | 0.43 | 0.65 | 0.61 | 0.24 | 0.24 | 0.25 |
| 2. Mahestala | 0.23 | 0.22 | 0.24 | 0.33 | 0.35 | 0.32 |
| 3. Budge Budge | 0.39 | 0.33 | 0.45 | 0.35 | 0.30 | 0.40 |
| 4. Falta | 0.00 | 0.00 | 0.00 | 0.00 | 0.00 | 0.00 |
| 5. Diamond Harbour | 0.00 | 0.00 | 0.00 | 0.00 | 0.01 | 0.01 |
| 6. Kulpi | 0.00 | 0.00 | 0.00 | 0.00 | 0.00 | 0.00 |
| **TOTAL** | **0.20** | **0.19** | **0.21** | **0.18** | **0.17** | **0.18** |
| *II. THE MIDDLE MATURE DELTA OF THE HUGLI* | | | | | | |
| 7. Sonarpur | 0.96 | 1.00 | 0.93 | 0.94 | 0.99 | 0.89 |
| 8. Bishnupur | 0.03 | 0.04 | 0.02 | 0.01 | 0.01 | 0.01 |
| 9. Baruipur | 0.33 | 0.32 | 0.33 | 0.34 | 0.34 | 0.34 |
| 10. Mograhat | 0.01 | 0.00 | 0.01 | 0.00 | 0.00 | 0.00 |
| 11. Mandir - Bazar | 0.00 | 0.00 | 0.00 | 0.00 | 0.00 | 0.00 |
| 12. Jaynagar | 0.04 | 0.04 | 0.03 | 0.23 | 0.23 | 0.24 |
| **TOTAL** | **0.23** | **0.23** | **0.22** | **0.27** | **0.28** | **0.26** |
| *III. THE PIYALI BIDYADHARI PLAINS IN THE EAST* | | | | | | |
| 13. Bhangar | 1.76 | 1.74 | 1.79 | 1.24 | 1.20 | 1.20 |
| 14. Canning | 3.98 | 3.90 | 4.07 | 3.93 | 3.83 | 4.04 |
| **TOTAL** | **2.87** | **2.82** | **2.94** | **2.62** | **2.55** | **2.69** |
| **ACTIVE DELTA** | | | | | | |
| *IV. THE WESTERN SUNDARBANS* | | | | | | |
| 15. Sagar Island | 0.36 | 0.36 | 0.38 | 0.35 | 0.34 | 0.37 |
| 16. Kakdwip | 0.68 | 1.53 | 0.69 | 0.49 | 0.51 | 0.48 |
| 17. Namkhana | 0.47 | 0.50 | 0.43 | 0.55 | 0.55 | 0.55 |
| **TOTAL** | **0.53** | **0.54** | **0.53** | **0.46** | **0.46** | **0.46** |
| *V. THE MIDDLE SUNDARBANS* | | | | | | |
| 18. Mathurapur | 1.06 | 1.04 | 1.07 | 0.99 | 0.99 | 1.01 |
| 19. Pathar Pratima | 0.78 | 0.74 | 0.82 | 0.75 | 0.74 | 0.76 |
| **TOTAL** | **0.93** | **0.91** | **0.96** | **0.89** | **0.88** | **0.90** |
| *VI. EASTERN SUNDARBANS* | | | | | | |
| 20. Kultali | 2.69 | 2.59 | 2.79 | 2.81 | 2.80 | 2.83 |
| 21. Basanti | 6.26 | 6.16 | 6.36 | 6.00 | 5.95 | 6.06 |
| 22. Gosaba | 9.71 | 9.50 | 9.94 | 9.82 | 9.58 | 10.01 |
| **TOTAL** | **6.37** | **6.24** | **6.52** | **6.46** | **6.35** | **6.57** |
| **DISTRICT TOTAL** | **1.30** | **1.26** | **1.33** | **1.21** | **1.19** | **1.24** |

**TABLE 3.9** (*Contd.*)
**(Proportion of Rural Scheduled Tribe Population to Total Rural Population)**

| Regions/Blocks | | 1981 | | | 1991 | | |
|---|---|---|---|---|---|---|---|
| | | Person | Male | Female | Person | Male | Female |
| 1 | | 2 | 3 | 4 | 5 | 6 | 7 |
| **STABLE DELTA** | | | | | | | |
| *I.* | *THE WESTERN HUGLI SIDE FLATS* | | | | | | |
| 1. | Thakurpukur-Metiaburuz | 0.82 | 0.84 | 0.80 | 0.21 | 0.20 | 0.22 |
| 2. | Mahestala | 0.05 | 0.09 | 0.02 | 0.07 | 0.08 | 0.05 |
| 3. | Budge Budge | 0.67 | 0.59 | 0.76 | 0.13 | 0.12 | 0.14 |
| 4. | Falta | 0.00 | 0.00 | 0.00 | 0.00 | 0.00 | 0.00 |
| 5. | Diamond Harbour | 0.00 | 0.00 | 0.00 | 0.00 | 0.00 | 0.00 |
| 6. | Kulpi | 0.00 | 0.00 | 0.00 | 0.00 | 0.00 | 0.00 |
| | **TOTAL** | **0.17** | **0.16** | **0.19** | **0.04** | **0.04** | **0.04** |
| *II.* | *THE MIDDLE MATURE DELTA OF THE HUGLI* | | | | | | |
| 7. | Sonarpur | 1.27 | 1.27 | 1.27 | 1.49 | 1.56 | 1.41 |
| 8. | Bishnupur | 0.03 | 0.04 | 0.02 | 0.01 | 0.01 | 0.01 |
| 9. | Baruipur | 0.33 | 0.33 | 0.32 | 0.32 | 0.33 | 0.31 |
| 10. | Mograhat | 0.01 | 0.00 | 0.01 | 0.00 | 0.00 | 0.00 |
| 11. | Mandir - Bazar | 0.00 | 0.00 | 0.00 | 0.00 | 0.00 | 0.00 |
| 12. | Jaynagar | 0.04 | 0.04 | 0.04 | 0.24 | 0.24 | 0.24 |
| | TOTAL | 0.22 | 0.22 | 0.21 | 0.27 | 0.28 | 0.26 |
| *III.* | *THE PIYALI BIDYADHARI PLAINS IN THE EAST* | | | | | | |
| 13. | Bhangar | 1.79 | 1.74 | 1.79 | 1.24 | 1.20 | 1.20 |
| 14. | Canning | 4.37 | 4.29 | 4.46 | 4.31 | 4.21 | 4.42 |
| | **TOTAL** | **3.00** | **2.94** | **3.06** | **2.74** | **2.66** | **2.81** |
| **ACTIVE DELTA** | | | | | | | |
| *IV.* | *THE WESTERN SUNDARBANS* | | | | | | |
| 15. | Sagar Island | 0.36 | 0.36 | 0.38 | 0.35 | 0.34 | 0.37 |
| 16. | Kakdwip | 0.68 | 1.53 | 0.69 | 0.49 | 0.51 | 0.48 |
| 17. | Namkhana | 0.47 | 0.50 | 0.43 | 0.55 | 0.55 | 0.55 |
| | **TOTAL** | **0.53** | **0.54** | **0.53** | **0.46** | **0.46** | **0.46** |
| *V.* | *THE MIDDLE SUNDARBANS* | | | | | | |
| 18. | Mathurapur | 1.06 | 1.04 | 1.07 | 0.99 | 0.99 | 1.01 |
| 19. | Pathar Pratima | 0.78 | 0.74 | 0.82 | 0.75 | 0.74 | 0.76 |
| | **TOTAL** | **0.93** | **0.91** | **0.96** | **0.89** | **0.88** | **0.90** |
| *VI.* | *EASTERN SUNDARBANS* | | | | | | |
| 20. | Kultali | 2.69 | 2.59 | 2.79 | 2.81 | 2.80 | 2.83 |
| 21. | Basanti | 6.26 | 6.16 | 6.36 | 6.00 | 5.95 | 6.06 |
| 22. | Gosaba | 9.71 | 9.50 | 9.94 | 9.82 | 9.58 | 10.01 |
| | **TOTAL** | **6.37** | **6.24** | **6.52** | **6.46** | **6.35** | **6.57** |
| **DISTRICT TOTAL** | | **1.44** | **1.41** | **1.47** | **1.36** | **1.34** | **1.38** |

**TABLE 3.9** (*Contd.*)
**(Proportion of Urban Scheduled Tribe Population to Total Urban Population)**

| *Regions/Blocks* | | *1981* | | | *1991* | |
|---|---|---|---|---|---|---|
| | *Person* | *Male* | *Female* | *Person* | *Male* | *Female* |
| *1* | *2* | *3* | *4* | *5* | *6* | *7* |
| **STABLE DELTA** | | | | | | |
| *I. THE WESTERN HUGLI SIDE FLATS* | | | | | | |
| 1. Thakurpukur-Metiaburuz | 0.53 | 0.57 | 0.53 | 0.26 | 0.26 | 0.26 |
| 2. Mahestala | 0.30 | 0.27 | 0.33 | 0.40 | 0.42 | 0.39 |
| 3. Budge Budge | 0.05 | 0.05 | 0.05 | 0.56 | 0.46 | 0.67 |
| 4. Falta | 0.00 | 0.00 | 0.00 | 0.00 | 0.00 | 0.00 |
| 5. Diamond Harbour | 0.00 | 0.00 | 0.00 | 0.07 | 0.06 | 0.08 |
| 6. Kulpi | 0.00 | 0.00 | 0.00 | 0.00 | 0.00 | 0.00 |
| TOTAL | **0.25** | **0.23** | **0.26** | **0.40** | **0.38** | **0.43** |
| *II. THE MIDDLE MATURE DELTA OF THE HUGLI* | | | | | | |
| 7. Sonarpur | 0.40 | 0.49 | 0.31 | 0.16 | 0.18 | 0.15 |
| 8. Bishnupur | 0.03 | 0.03 | 0.03 | 0.00 | 0.00 | 0.00 |
| 9. Baruipur | 0.30 | 0.28 | 0.40 | 0.45 | 0.42 | 0.49 |
| 10. Mograhat | 0.00 | 0.00 | 0.00 | 0.00 | 0.00 | 0.00 |
| 11. Mandir - Bazar | 0.00 | 0.00 | 0.00 | 0.00 | 0.00 | 0.00 |
| 12. Jaynagar | 0.00 | 0.00 | 0.00 | 0.07 | 0.08 | 0.07 |
| TOTAL | **0.31** | **0.35** | **0.27** | **0.20** | **0.21** | **0.20** |
| *III. THE PIYALI BIDYADHARI PLAINS IN THE EAST* | | | | | | |
| 13. Bhangar | — | — | — | — | — | — |
| 14. Canning | 0.52 | 0.47 | 0.58 | 0.39 | 0.33 | 0.45 |
| TOTAL | **0.52** | **0.47** | **0.58** | **0.39** | **0.33** | **0.45** |
| DISTRICT TOTAL | **0.27** | **0.27** | **0.08** | **0.35** | **0.33** | **0.37** |

in the proportion over the decade. Another fact is that the female scheduled tribes are more or less equal to their male counterparts, in some cases being slightly more. Again their proportion is more in rural areas than in the urban areas.

The 22 blocks of the district can be grouped into four classes. A very High Group (greater than 6.0%) is discernable in Gosaba. A high group (4.01-6.0%) in Basanti, A medium group (2.01-4.0%) in Canning and Kultali. The low group (2.01-4.0%) covers most of the blocks in Thakurpukur - Metiaburuz, Maheshtala, Budge Budge, Diamond Harbour, Sonarpur, Bishnupur, Baruipur, Jaynagar, Bhangar, Sagar Island, Kakdwip, Namkhana, Mathurapur and Pathar Pratima; and finally the very low group (less than 0.01%) in Falta, Kulpi, Mograhat and Mandir Bazar.

The proportion of Scheduled Tribes among the total Scheduled Tribes population also reveals a similar picture (Appendix III.3). In 1981 the highest proportion occurs in Eastern Sundarbans 54.57% (in Gosaba block 28.69%) and this remains true for 1991 but with a decline in proportion. Here also the male female differential is marginal.

### 3.3.4 Economic Characteristics of Population

The total population comprises of two sections mainly (a) economically active and (b) economically inactive. To the first group belong the *workers* who are producers of economic goods or services, hence they are said to be gainfully employed. They are the breadwinners or livelihood earners. Other terms such as "work force", "gainfully employed" or "labour force" are used to refer to the "economically active" portion of the population.[8]

#### *Spatial Distribution of Workers 1981 - 1991*

In 1981, the total work participation rate was 26.66% for the district as a whole that rose to 28.87% in 1991. Surprisingly the *Active Delta* regions have *a higher rate;* the highest 27.79% noticeable in 1981 in Eastern Sundarbans and the highest in 1991 in the Western Sundarbans i.e. a rate of 33.05%. The lowest rates in both the decades being seen in the Western Hugli Side Flats. Blockwise information states in 1981 only 12 blocks had a proportion above the district's total. The highest proportion is seen in Thakurpukur - Metiaburuz (34.08%) and the lowest in Falta (24.50%) in 1981. In 1991 only 8 blocks stood above the district's total figure. Here Namkhana retained the highest rank (45.76%) but the lowest was seen in Mandir Bazar (24.87%).

Five size groups can be discerned in 1991 (Map 3.9). In the very high group (44-49%), falls Namkhana. In the high group (39-44%) is found Thakurpukur - Metiaburuz. Gosaba falls within the medium group (34 - 39%), 5 blocks come under the low group (29-34%) viz. Falta, Kakdwip, Mathurapur, Pathar Pratima and Basanti. Finally a majority i.e. 14 blocks come under the very low group (24-29%). These are Maheshtala, Budge Budge, Diamond Harbour, Kulpi, Sonarpur, Bishnupur, Baruipur, Mograhat, Mandir Bazar, Jaynagar, Bhangar, Canning, Sagar Island and Kultali.

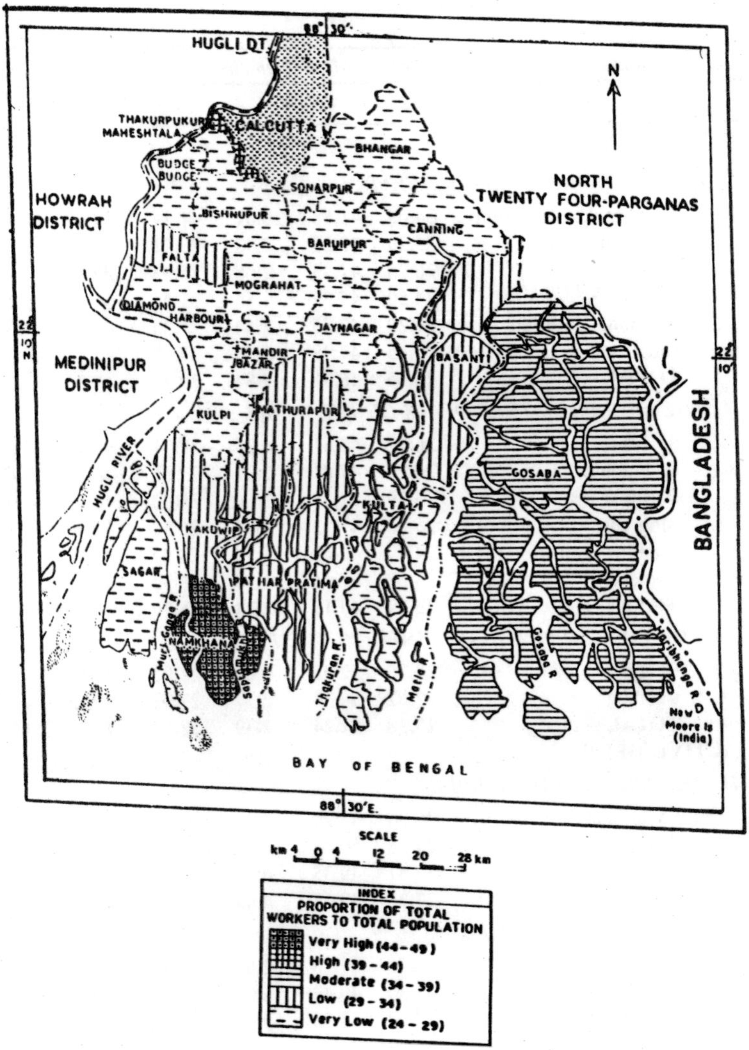


MAP 3.9 : South 24-Parganas : Work Participation 1991.

**TABLE 3.10 : Work Participation Rate 1981 - 1991**
**Proporation of Workers to Total Population**

| Regions/Blocks | 1981 | | | 1991 | | |
|---|---|---|---|---|---|---|
| | Person | Male | Female | Person | Male | Female |
| 1 | 2 | 3 | 4 | 5 | 6 | 7 |
| **STABLE DELTA** | | | | | | |
| *I. THE WESTERN HUGLI SIDE FLATS* | | | | | | |
| 1. Thakurpukur-Metiaburuz | 34.08 | 41.58 | 26.01 | 41.24 | 57.93 | 21.77 |
| 2. Mahestala | 25.24 | 45.28 | 2.53 | 27.71 | 47.67 | 5.08 |
| 3. Budge Budge | 26.95 | 47.43 | 2.68 | 26.93 | 47.11 | 3.84 |
| 4. Falta | 24.50 | 45.57 | 1.86 | 31.46 | 53.09 | 8.42 |
| 5. Diamond Harbour | 26.29 | 47.55 | 3.54 | 27.34 | 48.35 | 4.92 |
| 6. Kulpi | 25.45 | 47.98 | 1.78 | 27.07 | 45.23 | 10.04 |
| **TOTAL** | **26.66** | **46.36** | **4.84** | **29.40** | **49.25** | **7.78** |
| *II. THE MIDDLE MATURE DELTA OF THE HUGLI* | | | | | | |
| 7. Sonarpur | 26.07 | 45.61 | 4.35 | 27.31 | 47.31 | 5.65 |
| 8. Bishnupur | 26.20 | 47.81 | 2.92 | 27.66 | 46.71 | 7.35 |
| 9. Baruipur | 26.20 | 47.27 | 3.66 | 26.60 | 46.61 | 4.93 |
| 10. Mograhat | 25.08 | 47.22 | 1.44 | 26.59 | 31.90 | 5.11 |
| 11. Mandir - Bazar | 24.79 | 46.48 | 1.94 | 24.87 | 45.86 | 2.34 |
| 12. Jaynagar | 25.68 | 47.94 | 1.98 | 25.72 | 46.68 | 3.34 |
| **TOTAL** | **25.79** | **47.13** | **2.84** | **26.70** | **46.70** | **5.07** |
| *III. THE PIYALI BIDYADHARI PLAINS IN THE EAST* | | | | | | |
| 13. Bhangar | 27.75 | 52.08 | 2.01 | 27.02 | 49.52 | 3.30 |
| 14. Canning | 27.02 | 50.39 | 2.77 | 27.32 | 49.25 | 4.34 |
| **TOTAL** | **27.38** | **51.24** | **2.39** | **27.17** | **49.39** | **3.84** |
| **ACTIVE DELTA** | | | | | | |
| *IV. THE WESTERN SUNDARBANS* | | | | | | |
| 15. Sagar Island | 26.90 | 48.74 | 3.90 | 27.41 | 48.23 | 5.41 |
| 16. Kakdwip | 27.38 | 50.42 | 3.07 | 31.46 | 48.70 | 14.51 |
| 17. Namkhana | 27.41 | 49.35 | 4.24 | 45.76 | 55.45 | 35.54 |
| **TOTAL** | **27.23** | **49.65** | **4.03** | **33.05** | **49.94** | **15.80** |
| *V. THE MIDDLE SUNDARBANS* | | | | | | |
| 18. Mathurapur | 26.76 | 49.26 | 2.61 | 30.87 | 49.19 | 11.10 |
| 19. Pathar Pratima | 27.39 | 49.42 | 4.07 | 32.65 | 51.28 | 13.10 |
| **TOTAL** | **27.04** | **49.33** | **3.27** | **31.65** | **50.10** | **11.98** |
| *VI. EASTERN SUNDARBANS* | | | | | | |
| 20. Kultali | 27.39 | 50.75 | 2.46 | 26.30 | 47.55 | 2.76 |
| 21. Basanti | 27.14 | 50.83 | 2.10 | 29.87 | 50.36 | 8.30 |
| 22. Gosaba | 28.81 | 51.85 | 4.14 | 35.93 | 53.28 | 17.50 |
| **TOTAL** | **27.79** | **51.16** | **2.91** | **30.99** | **50.60** | **10.24** |
| **DISTRICT TOTAL** | **26.66** | **48.25** | **3.42** | **28.87** | **48.67** | **7.73** |

**TABLE 3.10 : (*Contd*)**

**Proporation of Rural Workers to Rural Population**

| *Regions/Blocks* | *1981* | | | *1991* | | |
|---|---|---|---|---|---|---|
| | *Person* | *Male* | *Female* | *Person* | *Male* | *Female* |
| *1* | *2* | *3* | *4* | *5* | *6* | *7* |
| **STABLE DELTA** | | | | | | |
| *I. THE WESTERN HUGLI SIDE FLATS* | | | | | | |
| 1. Thakurpukur | 56.32 | 59.63 | 52.52 | 67.63 | 77.57 | 56.29 |
| 2. Mahestala | 25.15 | 46.16 | 2.27 | 27.85 | 49.48 | 4.42 |
| 3. Budge Budge | 25.06 | 45.02 | 3.39 | 25.42 | 45.00 | 4.66 |
| 4. Falta | 24.50 | 45.57 | 1.86 | 31.46 | 53.09 | 8.42 |
| 5. Diamond Harbour | 26.27 | 47.70 | 3.35 | 27.20 | 48.30 | 4.69 |
| 6. Kulpi | 25.45 | 47.98 | 1.78 | 27.07 | 45.23 | 10.04 |
| **TOTAL** | | | | | | |
| *II. THE MIDDLE MATURE DELTA OF THE HUGLI* | | | | | | |
| 7. Sonarpur | 26.80 | 46.70 | 4.46 | 27.45 | 47.41 | 5.77 |
| 8. Bishnupur | 26.61 | 47.97 | 2.89 | 27.56 | 46.62 | 7.31 |
| 9. Baruipur | 26.43 | 47.80 | 3.59 | 26.75 | 46.90 | 5.00 |
| 10. Mograhat | 25.08 | 47.22 | 1.44 | 26.59 | 31.90 | 5.11 |
| 11. Mandir - Bazar | 24.79 | 46.48 | 1.94 | 24.87 | 45.86 | 2.34 |
| 12. Jaynagar | 25.73 | 48.20 | 1.88 | 25.69 | 46.73 | 3.23 |
| **TOTAL** | **25.90** | **47.51** | **2.71** | **26.56** | **46.70** | **5.03** |
| *III. THE PIYALI BIDYADHARI PLAINS IN THE EAST* | | | | | | |
| 13. Bhangar | 27.75 | 52.08 | 2.01 | 27.02 | 49.52 | 3.30 |
| 14. Canning | 27.07 | 50.83 | 2.45 | 27.33 | 49.41 | 4.21 |
| TOTAL | 27.42 | 51.70 | 2.22 | 27.17 | 49.47 | 3.74 |
| **ACTIVE DELTA** | | | | | | |
| *IV. THE WESTERN SUNDARBANS* | | | | | | |
| 15. Sagar Island | 26.90 | 48.74 | 3.90 | 27.41 | 48.23 | 5.41 |
| 16. Kakdwip | 27.38 | 50.42 | 3.07 | 31.46 | 48.70 | 14.51 |
| 17. Namkhana | 27.41 | 49.35 | 4.24 | 45.76 | 55.45 | 35.54 |
| **TOTAL** | **27.23** | **49.65** | **4.03** | **33.05** | **49.94** | **15.80** |
| *V. THE MIDDLE SUNDARBANS* | | | | | | |
| 18. Mathurapur | 26.76 | 49.26 | 2.61 | 30.87 | 49.19 | 11.10 |
| 19. Pathar Pratima | 27.39 | 49.42 | 4.07 | 32.65 | 51.28 | 13.10 |
| **TOTAL** | **27.04** | **49.33** | **3.27** | **31.65** | **50.10** | **11.98** |
| *VI. EASTERN SUNDARBANS* | | | | | | |
| 20. Kultali | 27.39 | 50.75 | 2.46 | 26.30 | 47.55 | 2.76 |
| 21. Basanti | 27.14 | 50.83 | 2.10 | 29.87 | 50.36 | 8.30 |
| 22. Gosaba | 28.81 | 51.85 | 4.14 | 35.93 | 53.28 | 17.50 |
| **TOTAL** | **27.79** | **51.16** | **2.91** | **30.99** | **50.60** | **10.24** |
| **DISTRICT TOTAL** | **26.72** | **48.78** | **3.18** | **29.08** | **48.86** | **8.22** |

TABLE 3.10 *(Contd.)*

**Proporation of Urban Workers to Urban Population**

| Regions/Blocks | 1981 Person | 1981 Male | 1981 Female | 1991 Person | 1991 Male | 1991 Female |
|---|---|---|---|---|---|---|
| *1* | *2* | *3* | *4* | *5* | *6* | *7* |
| **STABLE DELTA** | | | | | | |
| *I. THE WESTERN HUGLI SIDE FLATS* | | | | | | |
| 1. Thakurpukur-Metiaburuz | 25.37 | 35.20 | 16.08 | 27.37 | 47.78 | 3.30 |
| 2. Mahestala | 25.28 | 44.94 | 2.64 | 27.68 | 47.20 | 5.26 |
| 3. Budge Budge | 29.20 | 50.05 | 1.73 | 28.35 | 48.97 | 3.01 |
| 4. Falta | — | — | — | — | — | — |
| 5. Diamond Harbour | 26.53 | 46.04 | 5.47 | 28.58 | 48.76 | 6.82 |
| 6. Kulpi | — | — | — | — | — | — |
| TOTAL | **26.78** | **44.78** | **5.53** | **27.86** | **47.94** | **4.30** |
| *II. THE MIDDLE MATURE DELTA OF THE HUGLI* | | | | | | |
| 7. Sonarpur | 24.70 | 43.55 | 4.14 | 27.12 | 47.17 | 5.47 |
| 8. Bishnupur | 25.08 | 44.41 | 3.63 | 30.12 | 48.81 | 8.51 |
| 9. Baruipur | 24.38 | 43.17 | 4.16 | 25.69 | 44.91 | 4.53 |
| 10. Mograhat | — | — | — | — | — | — |
| 11. Mandir - Bazar | — | — | — | — | — | — |
| 12. Jaynagar | 24.87 | 44.14 | 3.54 | 26.26 | 45.64 | 5.32 |
| TOTAL | **24.69** | **43.62** | **4.03** | **26.94** | **46.68** | **5.46** |
| *III. THE PIYALI BIDYADHARI PLAINS IN THE EAST* | | | | | | |
| 13. Bhangar | — | — | — | — | — | — |
| 14. Canning | 26.59 | 46.51 | 5.64 | 27.30 | 47.83 | 5.56 |
| TOTAL | **26.59** | **46.5** | **5.64** | **27.30** | **47.83** | **5.56** |
| DISTRICT TOTAL | **26.23** | **44.57** | **5.14** | **27.60** | **47.61** | **4.66** |

The 1981 and 1991 difference in *work participation* rates exhibit a +2.21% change in the district over 1981 with *a general increase in most of the region.* 9 blocks exhibit positive changes above this figure. The highest change is noticeable in Namkhana +18.35%.

### *Male Female Difference 1981 - 1991*

Male Female portions of the workforce represent striking contrasts (Table 3.10). The male rate is much higher than the female counterpart in all the regions.

In 1981 the male participation rate was 48.25%, that rose to 48.67% in 1991 for the whole district. In stark contrast the female rate was 3.37% in 1981 and rose to only 7.71% in 1991. The age old concepts of females dedicating themselves to domestic chores, child bearing, lower literacy levels, and they being specially shut off from the organised sectors of the industry; are the factors responsible for their low work participation rates. Moreover the census data regarding females are not always adequate specially where they are working as domestic help, these being unrecorded.

### *Rural Urban Difference 1981 - 1991*

Table 3.10 exhibits the work participation rates for rural and urban areas. 1981 data reveal hardly any difference between the two in South 24-Parganas. For instance the total rates were 26.72% in rural areas and 26.23% in urban areas. The male rates were 48.78% in rural areas and 44.57% in urban areas and finally the female rates were 3.13% in rural areas and 5.14% in urban areas. But in 1991 the rural rates have surpassed the urban rates in all total, male and female categories. The total 1991 rates was 29.08% in rural areas and 27.60% in urban areas; and for male and female portions these were 48.86, 47.61; 8.20 and 4.66% respectively.

From the above discussion it is evident that two points emerge clearly (i) *Male rates are conspicuously higher* than the female counterparts and (ii) The *rural participation rates are higher* than the urban portions pointing clearly to agrarian base of the region. Entirely rural blocks have in general higher work participation rates as Gosaba, Namkhana, Pathar Pratima, Mathurapur etc. within the Active Delta thereby pointing unmistakably to the factor that the agriculture and primary activities contribute a good amount to the work force.

The proportion of workers to total workers reveal the highest participation in 1991 in the Middle Mature Delta i.e. 31.26% and the lowest in Kultali i.e. 2.44% (Appendix III.4).

### 3.3.5 Worker-Non-Worker Ratio

Table 3.11 shows the dependency rates of worker to non-worker both in rural and urban areas for 1981 as well as 1991. The rate was 2.75 for the district as a whole in 1981 that had fallen to 2.46 in 1991. The *highest ratio* of 2.88 in 1981 is exhibited by *the Western Hugli Side Flats* whereas *the Piyali-Bidyadhari Plains* overtook this rank in 1991 with a ratio of 2.78. The highest ratio at the block level

**TABLE 3.11 : Worker Non Worker Ratio 1981 - 1991**
**Total Ratio**

| *Regions/Blocks* | *1981* Person | *1981* Male | *1981* Female | *1991* Person | *1991* Male | *1991* Female |
|---|---|---|---|---|---|---|
| *1* | *2* | *3* | *4* | *5* | *6* | *7* |
| **STABLE DELTA** | | | | | | |
| *I. THE WESTERN HUGLI SIDE FLATS* | | | | | | |
| 1. Thakurpukur Metiaburuz | 1.93 | 1.40 | 2.84 | 1.42 | 0.73 | 3.59 |
| 2. Mahestala | 2.96 | 1.21 | 38.52 | 2.61 | 1.09 | 18.68 |
| 3. Budge Budge | 2.71 | 1.11 | 36.31 | 2.82 | 1.12 | 25.04 |
| 4. Falta | 3.08 | 1.19 | 52.76 | 2.18 | 0.88 | 10.88 |
| 5. Diamond Harbour | 2.80 | 1.10 | 27.81 | 2.66 | 1.07 | 19.32 |
| 6. Kulpi | 2.93 | 1.08 | 55.18 | 2.69 | 1.21 | 8.96 |
| **TOTAL** | **2.75** | **1.16** | **19.67** | **2.40** | **1.01** | **11.85** |
| *II. THE MIDDLE MATURE DELTA OF THE HUGLI* | | | | | | |
| 7. Sonarpur | 2.84 | 1.19 | 21.99 | 2.66 | 1.11 | 16.70 |
| 8. Bishnupur | 2.82 | 1.09 | 33.25 | 2.61 | 1.14 | 12.61 |
| 9. Baruipur | 2.82 | 1.12 | 26.32 | 2.76 | 1.15 | 19.28 |
| 10. Mograhat | 2.99 | 1.12 | 68.44 | 2.76 | 2.13 | 18.57 |
| 11. Mandir - Bazar | 3.03 | 1.15 | 50.55 | 3.02 | 1.18 | 41.74 |
| 12. Jaynagar | 2.89 | 1.09 | 49.51 | 2.89 | 1.14 | 28.94 |
| **TOTAL** | **2.88** | **1.12** | **34.30** | **2.76** | **1.14** | **18.70** |
| *III. THE PIYALI BIDYADHARI PLAINS IN THE EAST* | | | | | | |
| 13. Bhangar | 2.60 | 0.92 | 48.75 | 2.70 | 1.02 | 29.30 |
| 14. Canning | 2.70 | 0.98 | 35.10 | 3.56 | 1.03 | 22.04 |
| **TOTAL** | **2.65** | **0.95** | **40.80** | **2.78** | **1.05** | **26.24** |
| **ACTIVE DELTA** | | | | | | |
| *IV. THE WESTERN SUNDARBANS* | | | | | | |
| 15. Sagar Island | 2.72 | 1.05 | 24.64 | 2.65 | 1.07 | 17.48 |
| 16. Kakdwip | 2.65 | 0.98 | 31.57 | 2.18 | 1.05 | 5.89 |
| 17. Namkhana | 2.65 | 1.03 | 22.58 | 1.19 | 0.80 | 1.81 |
| **TOTAL** | **2.68** | **1.01** | **27.10** | **2.03** | **1.00** | **5.33** |
| *V. THE MIDDLE SUNDARBANS* | | | | | | |
| 18. Mathurapur | 2.74 | 1.03 | 37.31 | 2.24 | 1.03 | 8.01 |
| 19. Pathar Pratima | 2.65 | 1.02 | 23.57 | 2.06 | 0.95 | 6.63 |
| **TOTAL** | **2.70** | **1.03** | **29.63** | **2.16** | **1.00** | **7.34** |
| *VI. EASTERN SUNDARBANS* | | | | | | |
| 20. Kultali | 2.65 | 0.97 | 39.65 | 2.80 | 1.10 | 35.23 |
| 21. Basanti | 2.68 | 0.97 | 46.62 | 2.35 | 0.99 | 11.05 |
| 22. Gosaba | 2.47 | 0.[illegible] | 23.15 | 1.78 | 0.88 | 4.71 |
| **TOTAL** | **2.60** | **0.95** | **33.32** | **2.23** | **0.98** | **8.77** |
| **DISTRICT TOTAL** | **2.75** | **1.07** | **28.67** | **2.46** | **1.05** | **11.97** |

**TABLE 3.11** (*Contd.*)

**Rural Ratio**

| *Regions/Blocks* | *1981* | | | *1991* | | |
|---|---|---|---|---|---|---|
| | *Person* | *Male* | *Female* | *Person* | *Male* | *Female* |
| *1* | *2* | *3* | *4* | *5* | *6* | *7* |
| **STABLE DELTA** | | | | | | |
| *I. THE WESTERN HUGLI SIDE FLATS* | | | | | | |
| 1. Thakurpukur-Metiaburuz | 0.77 | 0.68 | 0.90 | 0.48 | 0.29 | 0.78 |
| 2. Mahestala | 2.98 | 1.17 | 43.05 | 2.59 | 1.02 | 21.62 |
| 3. Budge Budge | 2.99 | 1.22 | 28.50 | 2.93 | 1.22 | 20.39 |
| 4. Falta | 3.08 | 1.19 | 52.76 | 2.18 | 0.88 | 10.88 |
| 5. Diamond Harbour | 2.81 | 1.10 | 28.85 | 2.68 | 1.07 | 20.32 |
| 6. Kulpi | 2.93 | 1.08 | 55.18 | 2.69 | 1.21 | 8.96 |
| **TOTAL** | **2.76** | **1.12** | **21.11** | **2.30** | **1.00** | **9.25** |
| *II. THE MIDDLE MATURE DELTA OF THE HUGLI* | | | | | | |
| 7. Sonarpur | 2.70 | 1.14 | 21.42 | 2.64 | 1.11 | 16.33 |
| 8. Bishnupur | 2.76 | 1.08 | 33.60 | 2.63 | 1.15 | 12.68 |
| 9. Baruipur | 2.78 | 1.09 | 26.86 | 2.74 | 1.13 | 19.00 |
| 10. Mograhat | 2.99 | 1.12 | 68.44 | 2.76 | 2.13 | 18.57 |
| 11. Mandir - Bazar | 3.03 | 1.15 | 50.55 | 3.02 | 1.18 | 41.74 |
| 12. Jaynagar | 2.89 | 1.07 | 52.19 | 2.89 | 1.14 | 29.96 |
| **TOTAL** | **2.86** | **1.01** | **35.92** | **2.76** | **1.14** | **18.89** |
| *III. THE PIYALI BIDYADHARI PLAINS IN THE EAST* | | | | | | |
| 13. Bhangar | 2.60 | 0.92 | 48.75 | 2.70 | 1.02 | 29.30 |
| 14. Canning | 2.69 | 0.97 | 39.82 | 2.66 | 1.02 | 22.75 |
| **TOTAL** | **2.65** | **0.94** | **44.06** | **2.79** | **1.05** | **26.96** |
| **ACTIVE DELTA** | | | | | | |
| *IV. THE WESTERN SUNDARBANS* | | | | | | |
| 15. Sagar Island | 2.72 | 1.05 | 24.64 | 2.65 | 1.07 | 17.48 |
| 16. Kakdwip | 2.65 | 0.98 | 31.57 | 2.18 | 1.05 | 5.89 |
| 17. Namkhana | 2.65 | 1.03 | 22.58 | 1.19 | 0.80 | 1.81 |
| **TOTAL** | **2.68** | **1.01** | **27.10** | **2.03** | **1.00** | **5.33** |
| *V. THE MIDDLE SUNDARBANS* | | | | | | |
| 18. Mathurapur | 2.74 | 1.03 | 37.31 | 2.24 | 1.03 | 8.01 |
| 19. Pathar Pratima | 2.65 | 1.02 | 23.57 | 2.06 | 0.95 | 6.63 |
| **TOTAL** | **2.70** | **1.03** | **29.63** | **2.16** | **1.00** | **7.34** |
| *VI. EASTERN SUNDARBANS* | | | | | | |
| 20. Kultali | 2.65 | 0.97 | 39.65 | 2.80 | 1.10 | 35.23 |
| 21. Basanti | 2.68 | 0.97 | 46.62 | 2.35 | 0.99 | 11.05 |
| 22. Gosaba | 2.47 | 0.93 | 23.15 | 1.78 | 0.88 | 4.71 |
| **TOTAL** | **2.60** | **0.95** | **33.32** | **2.23** | **0.98** | **8.77** |
| **DISTRICT TOTAL** | **2.74** | **1.05** | **30.95** | **2.44** | **1.05** | **11.20** |

TABLE 3.11 : (*Contd.*)

**Urban Ratio**

| Regions/Blocks | 1981 | | | 1991 | | |
|---|---|---|---|---|---|---|
| | Person | Male | Female | Person | Male | Female |
| 1 | 2 | 3 | 4 | 5 | 6 | 7 |
| **STABLE DELTA** | | | | | | |
| *I. THE WESTERN HUGLI SIDE FLATS* | | | | | | |
| 1. Thakurpukur-Metiaburuz | 2.94 | 1.84 | 5.22 | 2.65 | 1.09 | 29.30 |
| 2. Mahestala | 2.96 | 1.22 | 36.88 | 2.61 | 1.12 | 18.01 |
| 3. Budge Budge | 2.42 | 1.00 | 56.80 | 2.53 | 1.04 | 32.22 |
| 4. Falta | — | — | — | — | — | — |
| 5. Diamond Harbour | 2.77 | 1.17 | 17.28 | 2.50 | 1.05 | 13.66 |
| 6. Kulpi | — | — | — | — | — | — |
| **TOTAL** | **2.73** | **1.23** | **17.09** | **2.59** | **1.09** | **22.28** |
| *II. THE MIDDLE MATURE DELTA OF THE HUGLI* | | | | | | |
| 7. Sonarpur | 3.05 | 1.30 | 23.15 | 2.69 | 1.12 | 17.25 |
| 8. Bishnupur | 2.99 | 1.25 | 26.55 | 2.32 | 1.05 | 10.75 |
| 9. Baruipur | 3.10 | 1.32 | 23.04 | 2.89 | 1.23 | 21.55 |
| 10. Mograhat | — | — | — | — | — | — |
| 11. Mandir - Bazar | — | — | — | — | — | — |
| 12. Jaynagar | 3.02 | 1.27 | 28.81 | 2.81 | 1.19 | 17.80 |
| **TOTAL** | **3.05** | **1.29** | **23.82** | **2.71** | **1.14** | **17.33** |
| *III. THE PIYALI BIDYADHARI PLAINS IN THE EAST* | | | | | | |
| 13. Bhangar | — | — | — | — | — | — |
| 14. Canning | 2.76 | 1.15 | 16.73 | 2.66 | 1.09 | 16.99 |
| **TOTAL** | **2.76** | **1.15** | **16.73** | **2.66** | **1.09** | **16.99** |
| **DISTRICT TOTAL** | **2.81** | **1.24** | **18.46** | **2.62** | **1.10** | **20.46** |

i.e. 3.08, was seen in Falta in 1981 and 3.56 in Canning in 1991. By contrast, the lowest ratio was seen in Thakurpukur - Metiaburuz in 1981; the figure being 1.93, and in 1991 the lowest ratio was seen in Namkhana i.e. a figure of 1.19.

Five size groups can be discerned in 1991. (i) A very High Ratio ( greater than 3.01) is discernable in Mandir Bazar and Canning. (ii) A High Ratio (2.51 - 3.00) is seen in most of the blocks in Maheshtala, Budge Budge, Diamond Harbour, Kulpi, Sonarpur, Bishnupur, Baruipur, Mograhat, Jaynagar, Bhangar, Sagar-Island and Kultali. (iii) A Moderate Ratio (2.01 - 2.50) is found in Falta, Kakdwip, Mathurapur, Pathar Pratima and Basanti. (iv) A very low Ratio of (less than 1.50) is seen in Thakurpukur - Metiaburuz and Namkhana.

### Male Female Difference

The male - female portions of the worker-nonworker ratio represent marked contrasts. The male ratios are much lower than their female counterparts. In 1981, the male ratio for the state as a whole was 1.97 and that for females was 28.67. In 1991 these respective figures were 1.05 and 11.97. Therefore though female ratio is higher it has actually declined over the decade, exhibiting a healthy sign that the dependency burden of non-working community over the bread earners has lessened. In 1991 the Stable Delta regions specially in the Piyali Bidyadhari Plains have registered accentuated gaps between the male and the female.

### Rural Urban Difference

The rural - urban worker - nonworker ratio does not differ much in the Stable Deltaic area as in the case of males and females. The urban ratios are slightly on the higher side showing the dependency of non-workers here is greater. For instance the total district's 1981 rural ratio stood at 2.74 but the urban one was 2.81. In 1991 these corresponding figures changed to 2.44 and 2.62, thereby indicating a general overall fall in the rates both in rural and urban areas over 1981. In this case also striking differences between the male and the female counterparts is discernable.

## 3.4 GROWTH OF POPULATION 1981 - 1991

The changing pattern of the distribution of population and its composition as discussed above can be reflected by the differentials in the decennial rate of growth over time which can be announced partly through differentials in the rate of natural increase (birth rate/death rate) and partly through the varying pattern of in and out migration.

### 3.4.1 Spatial Pattern of Population Change

The decennial growth rate of the total population for the district as a whole was 32.50%, 31.96% in case of males and 33.08% in the case of females (Table 3.12) over the span of 1981 - 1991. The *highest total growth* rate is seen in the *Piyali Bidyadhari Plains*, 36.58%. The Middle Mature Hugli Delta 35.55% and in the Western Sundarbans 34.39%.

**TABLE 3.12 : Population Grwoth Rate 1981 - 1991**

| Regions/Blocks | Total | | | Rural | | | Urban | | |
|---|---|---|---|---|---|---|---|---|---|
| | Person | Male | Female | Person | Male | Female | Person | Male | Female |
| *1* | *2* | *3* | *4* | *5* | *6* | *7* | *8* | *9* | *10* |
| **STABLE DELTA** | | | | | | | | | |
| *I. THE WESTERN HUGLI SIDE FLATS* | | | | | | | | | |
| 1. Thakurpukur- Metiaburuz | 59.54 | 65.56 | 53.04 | 95.17 | 94.53 | 95.90 | 45.58 | 53.72 | 37.01 |
| 2. Maheshtala | 70.61 | 70.66 | 70.55 | 25.69 | 25.35 | 26.06 | 88.23 | 87.98 | 88.52 |
| 3. Budge Budge | 16.11 | 14.21 | 18.35 | 3.94 | 2.77 | 5.21 | 30.52 | 26.62 | 35.65 |
| 4. Falta | 23.83 | 23.32 | 24.38 | 23.83 | 23.32 | 24.38 | — | — | — |
| 5. Diamond Harbour | 25.93 | 25.79 | 26.09 | 23.68 | 23.52 | 23.85 | 49.10 | 49.00 | 49.21 |
| 6. Kulpi | 26.37 | 19.37 | 33.73 | 26.37 | 19.37 | 33.73 | — | — | — |
| **TOTAL** | **33.90** | **32.85** | **35.05** | **23.23** | **21.38** | **24.23** | **56.21** | **55.81** | **56.68** |
| *II. THE MIDDLE MATURE DELTA OF THE HUGLI* | | | | | | | | | |
| 7. Sonarpur | 43.53 | 41.75 | 45.50 | 28.90 | 26.85 | 31.20 | 70.94 | 70.06 | 71.89 |
| 8. Bishnupur | 24.13 | 22.60 | 25.77 | 24.54 | 22.85 | 26.36 | 14.81 | 17.04 | 12.34 |
| 9. Baruipur | 35.54 | 36.29 | 34.74 | 30.99 | 31.60 | 30.34 | 70.95 | 72.72 | 69.05 |
| 10. Mograhat | 31.85 | 32.23 | 31.45 | 31.85 | 32.23 | 31.45 | — | — | — |
| 11. Mandir - Bazar | 25.71 | 26.82 | 24.54 | 25.71 | 26.82 | 24.54 | — | — | — |
| 12. Jaynagar | 50.43 | 50.72 | 50.14 | 52.27 | 52.71 | 51.81 | 71.25 | 71.05 | 71.15 |
| **TOTAL** | **35.55** | **35.31** | **35.80** | **32.93** | **32.68** | **33.21** | **60.44** | **60.19** | **60.70** |
| *III. THE PIYALI BIDYADHARI PLAINS IN THE EAST* | | | | | | | | | |
| 13. Bhangar | 33.23 | 33.07 | 33.49 | 33.27 | 33.07 | 33.49 | — | — | — |
| 14. Canning | 39.87 | 40.52 | 39.19 | 40.47 | 41.16 | 39.76 | 34.52 | 34.94 | 34.09 |
| **TOTAL** | **36.58** | **36.78** | **36.36** | **36.69** | **36.88** | **36.48** | **34.52** | **34.94** | **34.09** |

TABLE 3.12 : (*Contd.*)

| Regions/Blocks | Total | | | Rural | | | Urban | | |
|---|---|---|---|---|---|---|---|---|---|
| | *Person* | *Male* | *Female* | *Person* | *Male* | *Female* | *Person* | *Male* | *Female* |
| *1* | *2* | *3* | *4* | *5* | *6* | *7* | *8* | *9* | *10* |
| **ACTIVE DELTA** | | | | | | | | | |
| *IV. THE WESTERN SUNDARBANS* | | | | | | | | | |
| 15. Sagar Island | 33.82 | 34.07 | 33.55 | 33.82 | 34.07 | 33.55 | — | — | — |
| 16. Kakdwip | 36.52 | 31.84 | 41.46 | 36.52 | 31.84 | 41.46 | — | — | — |
| 17. Namkhana | 30.47 | 30.52 | 30.42 | 30.47 | 30.52 | 30.42 | — | — | — |
| **TOTAL** | **34.39** | **32.29** | **36.60** | **34.39** | **32.29** | **36.60** | — | — | — |
| *V. THE MIDDLE SUNDARBANS* | | | | | | | | | |
| 18. Mathurapur | 28.72 | 29.08 | 28.35 | 28.72 | 29.08 | 28.35 | — | — | — |
| 19. Pathar Pratima | 24.35 | 23.82 | 24.91 | 24.35 | 23.82 | 24.91 | — | — | — |
| **TOTAL** | **26.77** | **26.73** | **26.81** | **26.77** | **26.73** | **26.81** | — | — | — |
| *VI. EASTERN SUNDARBANS* | | | | | | | | | |
| 20. Kultali | 6.32 | 5.99 | 6.68 | 6.32 | 5.99 | 6.68 | — | — | — |
| 21. Basanti | 31.69 | 31.49 | 31.91 | 31.69 | 31.49 | 31.91 | — | — | — |
| 22. Gosaba | 19.12 | 18.65 | 19.62 | 19.12 | 18.65 | 19.62 | — | — | — |
| **TOTAL** | **19.70** | **19.34** | **20.08** | **19.70** | **19.34** | **20.08** | — | — | — |
| **DISTRICT TOTAL** | **32.50** | **31.96** | **33.08** | **29.18** | **28.49** | **29.92** | **56.29** | **55.98** | **56.64** |

Maheshtala Block records highest growth of 70.61% and the lowest is seen in Kutlali i.e. 6.32%. The male and female proportions also exhibit same ranks. The growth rates for the 22 blocks can be classed into five broad groups. (Map 3.10)

(i) *A very High Intercensal Change* (58.33 - 71.32) is seen in Thakurpukur -Metiaburuz and in Maheshtala.

(ii) *A High Rate* (45.33 - 58.32) is seen in Jaynagar.

(iii) *A Moderate Rate* (32.33 - 45.32) is discernable in 5 blocks of Sonarpur, Baruipur, Bhangar, Canning, Sagar Island and in Kakdwip.

(iv) *A Low Rate* (19.33 - 32.32) is seen in most of the blocks like Falta, Diamond Harbour, Kulpi, Bishnupur, Mograhat, Mandir Bazar, Namkhana, Mathurapur, Pathar Pratima and Basanti and finally,

(v) *A very Low Rate* (6.32 - 19.32) in Budge Budge, Kultali and Gosaba.

The above distribution thus highlights that growth rates are in general on the higher side in the Stable Delta due to infrastructural and developmental facilities; nearness to the Calcutta Conurbation, as well as the recent urban development of this area.

### 3.4.2 Rural and Urban Growth Rate and URGD

The Rural and Urban Growth represents striking intercensal changes. The district in general represents a rate of 29.18% in the rural areas but the corresponding figure in urban areas is 56.29%. In case of males the rural areas exhibit 28.49% and the corresponding figure for urban areas is 55.98%. Again in case of females the corresponding figures are 29.92 and 56.64% for rural and urban areas respectively.

The *Urban - Rural Growth Differential* show *positive changes* in the Western Hugli Side Flats and in the Middle Mature Delta. Five blocks out of the 9, having urbanised areas also have positive changes. Therefore, in other words it can be said that *urbanisation is active*[10] in Maheshtala with a URGD of 62.54, Budge Budge 26.58, Diamond Harbour 39.96, all in the Stable Delta of South Twenty-Four Parganas.

### 3.4.3 Spatial Distribution of Changes in Population Density

Another way of explaining the dynamism of population growth is through *changing densities*. The intercensal density change of the district represents clearly three facts (Table 3.13).

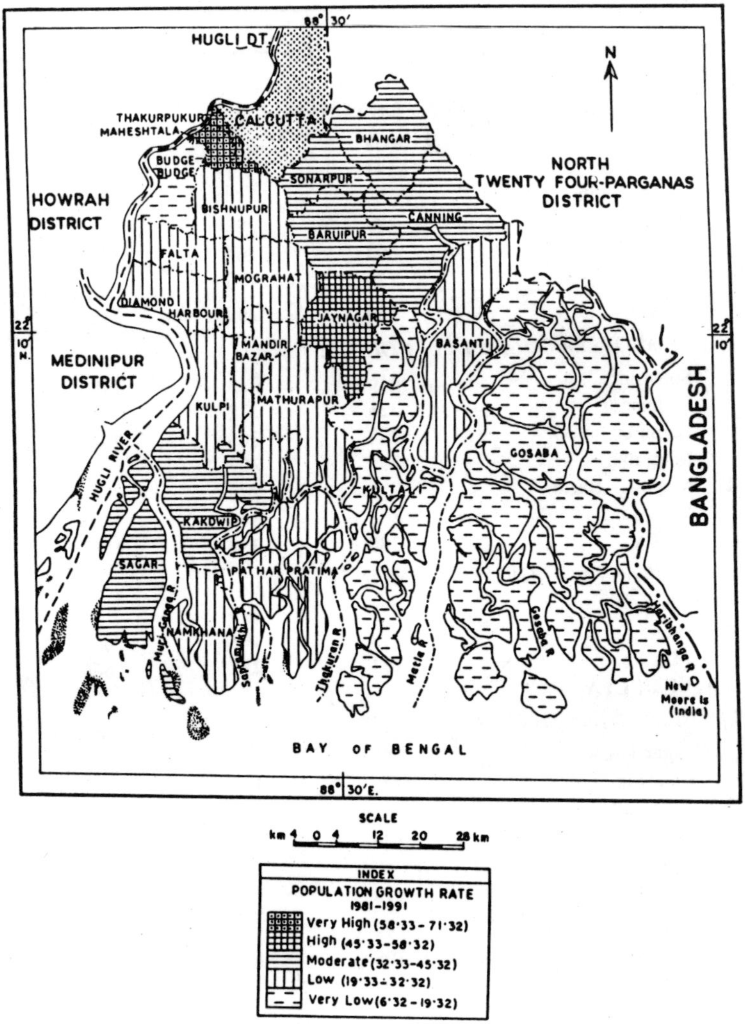


**MAP 3.10 :** South 24-Parganas : Growth of Population 1981-91

**TABLE 3.13 : Chance in Density 1981 - 1991**

| Regions/Blocks | Density of Population | | |
|---|---|---|---|
| | Total | Rural | Urban |
| 1 | 2 | 3 | 4 |
| **STABLE DELTA** | | | |
| *I. THE WESTERN HUGLI SIDE FLATS* | | | |
| 1. Thakurpukur-Metiaburuz | 2058 | 1620 | 2587 |
| 2. Mahestala | 2581 | 511 | 4805 |
| 3. Budge Budge | 333 | 57 | 1290 |
| 4. Falta | 283 | 283 | — |
| 5. Diamond Harbour | 303 | 264 | 1108 |
| 6. Kulpi | 176 | 176 | — |
| **TOTAL** | **485** | **250** | **2611** |
| *II. THE MIDDLE MATURE DELTA OF THE HUGLI* | | | |
| 7. Sonarpur | 616 | 323 | 1980 |
| 8. Bishnupur | 325 | 322 | 549 |
| 9. Baruipur | 382 | 308 | 2045 |
| 10. Mograhat | 397 | 397 | — |
| 11. Mandir - Bazar | 278 | 278 | — |
| 12. Jaynagar | 853 | 346 | 745 |
| **TOTAL** | **388** | **338** | **1758** |
| *III. THE PIYALI BIDYADHARI PLAINS IN THE EAST* | | | |
| 13. Bhangar | 276 | 276 | — |
| 14. Canning | 204 | 191 | 669 |
| **TOTAL** | **231** | **224** | **669** |
| **ACTIVE DELTA** | | | |
| *IV. THE WESTERN SUNDARBANS* | | | |
| 15. Sagar Island | 67 | 67 | — |
| 16. Kakdwip | 128 | 128 | — |
| 17. Namkhana | 141 | 141 | — |
| **TOTAL** | **100** | **100** | — |
| *V. THE MIDDLE SUNDARBANS* | | | |
| 18. Mathurapur | 115 | 115 | — |
| 19. Pathar Pratima | 99 | 99 | — |
| **TOTAL** | **108** | **108** | — |
| *VI. EASTERN SUNDARBANS* | | | |
| 20. Kultali | 26 | 26 | — |
| 21. Basanti | 133 | 133 | |
| 22. Gosaba | 87 | 87 | — |
| **TOTAL** | **84** | **84** | — |
| **DISTRICT TOTAL** | **224** | **181** | **2145** |

(i) All blocks represent *positive changes* exhibiting a *tremendous growth of population* and consequently *a great pressure on land.*

(ii) Change in density as usual is *greater* in the *Stable Delta* to the North than in the Active Delta of the Sundarbans and finally,

(iii) The *urban density changes* are far more *greater* than the rural counterparts, thus exhibiting the greater pressure on land in the urban areas than in the rural areas.

The density change represents +224 for the district as a whole. At the regional level, the Western Hugli Side Flats represents the highest density change of +485 persons/sq.km, followed by 388/sq.km of the Middle Mature Hugli Delta, 231/sq.km. of the Piyali Bidyadhari Plains, 108/sq.km of the Middle Sundarbans, 100/sq.km of the Western Sundarbans and finally 84/sq.km of the Eastern Sundarbans. The Stable Delta thereby exhibit strikingly high density changes. Blockwise Maheshtala 2058/sq.km. has highest change, the lowest is seen in Kultali 26/sq.km. The district represents a change in density of 181/sq.km. in rural and 2145/sq.km in urban areas. The highest change in rural density occurs in the Middle Mature Hugli Delta i.e. +338/sq. km and the highest urban density change of +2611/sq.km. is discernable in the Western Hugli Side Flats.

## 3.5 CONCLUSION

After analysing the population distribution, composition and growth of population of South 24-Parganas 1981-1991, it is evident that certain facts emerge clearly,

(i) A striking contrast regarding population distribution and density between the Stable and Active Delta;

(ii Strikingly high population densities in the urban areas accompanied by a high change in density;

(iii) A balanced sex ratio in most of the region accompanied by an increase in sex ratio in most of the region indicative of a healthy situation;

(iv) A higher male literacy but the female literacy has been improving over the decade, thereby exhibiting development in favour of females; as well as higher urban literacies;

(v) The district's scheduled caste population being much higher than the tribal population, has portrayed small growth over the decade;

(vi) The work participation rates are clearly in favour of males and very depressing in case of females, but in overall terms they are not on the very high side; though growth in work participation has taken place over the decade;

(vii) The dependency burden of non-workers of the district is greater in the urban areas and in the females; thereby relegating the females to the background wherever employment is concerned; and

(viii) High Growth Rates of Population are a characteristic of this Delta, growth rates being higher in the Stable Delta in general. Here the change in density is also more marked thereby creating a tremendous pressure on land.

## REFERENCES

1. Premi M.K. and R.P. Tyagi (1985), in *"Distribution and growth of population"* in *Contribution to Indian Geography* VI: Population Geography (Ed K.V. Sundaram and Sudesh Nangia) Heritage Publishers p. 7
2. *Ibid.*
3. Mandal R.B. Joseph Uyanga, Hanuman Prasad. (1989), *Introductory Methods in Population Analysis,* Concept Publishing Co. p. 172.
4. Bogue Donald J, (1969), *Principles of Demography*, in John Wiley and Sons Inc p. 147.
5. Mitra, Ashok (1985) *"Implications of the Sex Ratio in India's Population" op.cit* 1.
6. Gosal, Gurdev Singh (1985) *"Spatial Perspective on Literacy in India" op.cit.*1.
7. *ibid.*
8. Bogue, D.J. (1969), *op.cit.* p. 214-215.
9. Urban Growth in India Pt. 1&2 Census of India, 1981.
10. Clarke, John I. (1976) *Population Geography.* Pergamon International Library p.76.

# 4

# SETTLEMENT PATTERN

## 4.1 INTRODUCTION

Considering the ecological and human factors, it now becomes imperative to place an insight into the study of settlements, their origin, evolution and growth, their spatial organisation and distributional pattern, external forms, their degree of cohesion or concentration, clustering as well as their changes over time. This involves the understanding of the entire processes, phenomena and factors of the entire physical, biospheric and ecological system on one hand and human behavioural systems on the other.[1]

With such objectives in mind, the present chapter attempts to study the settlements of the region in the view of —

(i) their origin and evolution through history,
(ii) their site and location factors,
(iii) their definite patterns in the geo-ecological regions,
(iv) A probe into selected quantitative techniques used for this pattern analysis,
(v) their concentration and density analysis in order to measure changes over time, and finally
(vi) the estimation of the rank size rule to study urban primacy.

Though we maintain separate categories as hamlets, villages, towns, cities, metropolis etc., in reality there actually exists a 'settlement continuum'[2] more so marked in case of the urban settlements where one type merges imperceptibly into the other.

## 4.2 EVOLUTION OF SETTLEMENTS

The evolution of settlements through historical period is an important aspect specially because of the nature of transformation of the region during the last few decades. Initially most of the region was under virigin forests. Forest clearance started during the British rule and settlements were established, land grants being common. Later, after independence with the abolition of the Zamindary system the cultivators became the proprietors and villages took a permanent shape. But sad enough, human agencies started interfering with the land in its premature delta building stage (Chapter - 2). Today the settlements of the region is widely different from those under different ecological set up expected of a tropical deltaic coastal situation.

### 4.2.1 Rural Settlements

#### *Ancient and Medieval Periods*

Though the cultural landscape of South Twenty-Four Parganas began changing sharply in recent times, anthropological evidences conclusively prove that the early settlers were of Negroid stock (Hutton -1931) followed by Pro-Australoid and Homo-Alpinus group. Proto-Nordic or Aryans occupied the area much later, after their first advent and settlement in the whole of Northern India.

However, hardly any reference to lower Bengal is available in the old literature of the Aryans. In *Mahabharata*, this region has been referred as *Vanaparva*. Panini, the historian, also referred to the eastern boundary of the Aryan occupation upto *Kalikaban* which may include the southern limits of South 24-Parganas. However, early evidences of the region has disappeared due to the great subsidence of the whole of lower Bengal during the middle of the 6th Century AD. This made many popular ports and cities disappear from this area (*Epigraphica Indica* 18 p 85).

Though references about lower Bengal can be obtained from the old records of the Greek and Chinese travellers who termed the region as *Gangaridi*, the history of settlements of this area can be traced with greater authenticity after the invasion by Alexander. Jainism and Buddhism, is also said to have spread to this area. In Hieun-Tsang's account mention has been made of his visit in 639 AD to *Samatata*[3] or lower Bengal, including the littoral tract. The Sen Dynasty ruled during 1200 AD after the Pal Dynasty (770-810

AD) in Bengal and during this time Southern Bengal fell into the hands of the Sen rulers upto the second half of the 13th century.

During the Muslim Rule in India, the whole period of 1338 to 1576 AD is known in the history as period of independent Bengal, because Turkish rulers identified themselves closely with the local inhabitants and became Bengalees by large. This period also witnessed the fall of Jainism, Buddhism and Hinduism. It is said that a large number of foreigners such as Turks, Arabs, Persians, Pakhtuns came and settled in this region. Khan Jahan Ali is singularly most famous as far as Southern Bengal is concerned, being one of the first person to rule and develop a large tract of the Sundarban forest during the fifteenth century; the forest limits then spreading far interior covering nearly the whole of 24-Parganas (including North and South).

From the early sixteenth century European travellers and traders as well as pirates began their frequent visits to Bengal through the ports of Southern Bengal. (Portuguese early 16th century, Dutch 1632, French 1673, Danish 1676 and British 1690). The Portuguese are said to have occupied Tardaha in Bhangar block on the Bidyadhari a century before the foundation of Calcutta.

By the end of the fifteenth century therefore the history of settlements in Bengal can be traced out in greater detail. From the *Ain-i-Akbari* we find that the district formed part of the Sarkar, or revenue division, of *Satgaon*, which extended from near Sagar Island to near Plassey.(Appendix IV.1) During the later part of Akbar's rule a few Zamindars in the name of Bara Bhuiyas became very powerful, Pratapaditya was one of them who was the actual ruler of South 24-Parganas at this time. Pratapaditya and his uncle Basanta Roy made many constructive works in some part of Southern Bengal. *Chandikan* is in all probability the present day Sagar Island, was the old capital of Pratapaditya. *Reclamation of forest land* for agriculture and human settlements was most successfully done during his regime.

In the later half of the sixteenth century, the emporium of sea borne trade was Satgaon on the Saraswati (near Hugli town). Four families of Bysakhs and Seths founded the village of *Gobindapur* (on the site of the present Fort William Calcutta), and another market was established at *Sutanuti*. It was here that the English under Job Charnock, sought a refuge after their abandonment of the Hugli factory in 1686 and thus out of the marshes of lower Bengal sprung up *Calcutta in August 1690* out of three small villages of *Sutanuti, Kalikata, and Govindapur*.

During the decline of the Mughal rule the Marathas locally known as Bargis (pirates) invaded lower Bengal, thus restricting prosperity and expansion of the settlements in the region.

Not only the *historical events* and political upheavals disturbed the settlements of this area but *natural calamities* and changes in river courses also played a very important role in the histogenesis of settlements of this region. In addition, the Maugh and Portuguese pirates repeatedly invaded the area during the first half of the 17th century AD which made the *Sundarban* part of the district *a desolate area* shown by Renald in the Map of Bengal, Sheet No. XX.

Alivardi Khan (1740-1756) was the last ruler of Bengal who fought many a battles to restore stability in the region. Independence of Bengal was ultimately lost when Sirajuddaulah, the then King of Bengal, was treacherously defeated in the battle of Plassey by the East India Company's army in 1757. On 20th December 1757, Mirjafar, the defamed new Nawab made an assignment to the East India Company of the Zamindary or landholder's rights over a tract of country known as the *Zamindari of Calcutta or the Twenty Four Parganas* from the number of Parganas included in it.

### *Modern Period*

The early part of the British rule, the need for various forest products increased to a great extent and the virgin forests of South 24 Parganas began to draw the attention of the then British rulers. Records are available from around 1770 that private parties were entrusted with the duties to reclaim the forest land. Prior to that, Calcutta had come into existence and certain settlements such as Budge Budge and Falta existed. *Falta* was then "a place of some importance" (during 1756), "having a town with a large bazar, and was moreover the station of all the Dutch shipping".[4]

Soon after the grant of 24-Parganas to the East India Company, Collector General Mr. Claude Russell granted leases between 1770-

1773 AD to individuals to reclaim the land for cultivation and supply of timber. Mr. Tilman Henckell, judge and Magistrate (Jessore, now in Bangladesh) submitted a detailed proposal to secure peace and control of the South 24-Parganas and Sundarban in December 20th, 1783 to Warren Hastings, Governor General who accorded the approval in 1784 and *land leases* were given (144 grants) to develop the area between Raimongal (now in Bangladesh) and Haringhata.

The survey of the Sundarban from the river Hugli to river Passar (Bangladesh Sundarban) was initiated by Lieutenant W.E. Morrison during 1811-1814 AD. The course between the Hugli and river Thakuran was surveyed by Lt. Blane during 1813-1814. In 1816 Mr. D. Scalt was appointed as the Commissioner of the area and was vested with the power of collector of land revenue. Mr. Princep (1822-23 AD) also conducted surveys and designed the area into *blocks* and numbered them, which is regarded as *the beginning of designating various parts of South 24-Parganas as lots or lats*[5] (Map 4.1), existing in Sundarbans even today. In the year 1829 Lt. Hodges began to survey the boundary of the forest region and Morrison's Map of 1814 was made mainly on the basis of this Survey. It was completed in the year 1831 and is known as *Hodges Map of Sundarban.* Rennel also published a series of Maps of the area. In 1829-1830, Mr. Dampier the then Commissioner and Lt. Hodges, Surveyor, defined and surveyed the line of forests, the limit of which came to be known as the *Dampier Hodges Line.* Since 1830, 3737 sq.km of the region to the South of the Dampier Hodges Line had been cleared for cultivation and settlement. This line denoting the then forest limit extended from Kulpi to Bashirhat (North 24-Parganas) and comprised of (a) *deforested colonised area* and (b) *the residual forested land.*

As per jarip of land in 1839, the Zamindars were given some rights over the forest land with 99 years of lease agreement. Out of a total of 178 grants, 105 belonged to Hindus, 30 to Muslims and rest to Europeans. The leases were commonly known as "latdars" or tenure holders. They could sublet their holdings to "Chakdars" who could sublet to the "raiyats" and they in turn could further sublet to "Under raiyats". The out right sales were allowed from 1865. Survey and mapping also continued during this period. Ellison pre-

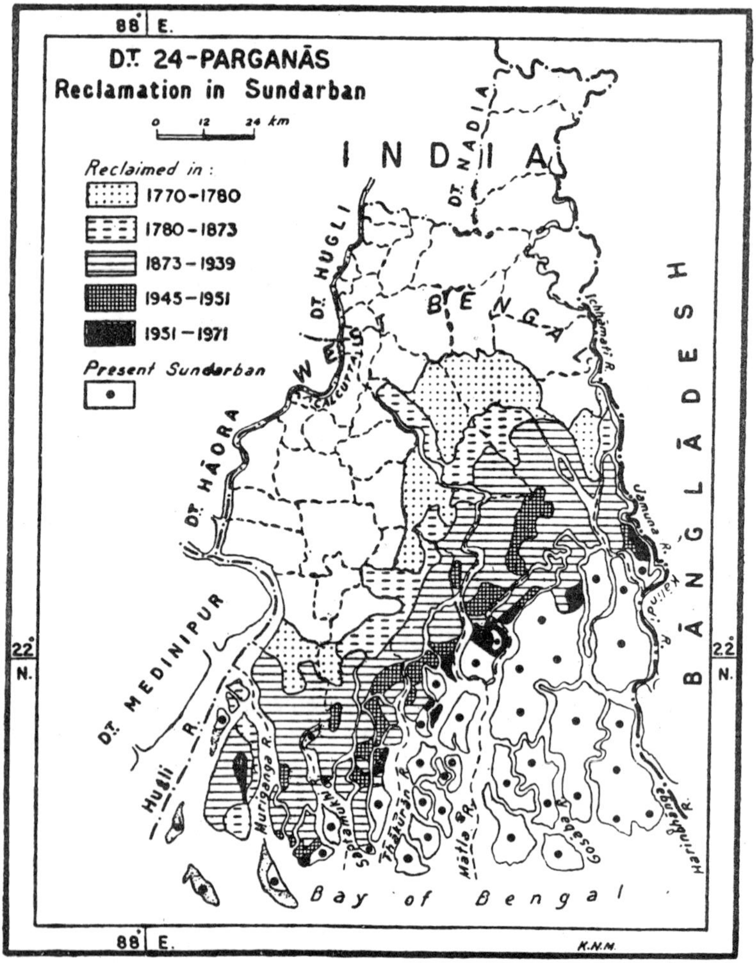


*Source* : K.N. Mukherjee (1983)

**MAP 4.1** : South 24-Parganas : Reclamation in Sundarbans

pared a map of the area under Surveyor General Col. H.I. Thuillier (1873). The last survey of the region was probably that of A.W. Stuart's during 1905-1908.

Certain names stand out in initiating some projects of land reclamation of the area. Mr. Trower, Collector of 24 Parganas reclaimed part of the *Sagar Island* during 1812 and he formed a company known as the "Sagar Island Society". In order to prevent cyclones, *safety measures were introduced* in the island by constructing a high embankment and a still functioning light house at Beguakhali, Sagar; the remanants of the embankment exist even today.

Sagar Island is almost synonymous with the age old pilgrimage and *Kapil Muni's temple* situated there. A fair is held at the occasion of "Makar Sankranti" (middle of January). The most heinous superstition of sacrificing the first child by Hindu parents, if the child was born after taking oath at Sagar Sangam continued till 1801, stopped only by reforms introduced by Mr. Marquess Wellesly.

Some persons of their own also dedicated to the cause of developing inaccessible areas and are remembered by place names such as *Canning*.

*Gosaba* owes its origin to the pioneering works of Sir Daniel Hamilton. In 1916 he took three islands of Gosaba - Satjalia, Rangabalia and Gosaba from the Government and formed the "*Gosaba Estate*". He also established Co-operative Credit Society (for providing loans to cultivators and the distribution of food grains), schools and a charitable dispensary.

Along with land reclamation certain drainage and embankment schemes also existed in the area during the British rule, like for instance the *Magrahat Drainage Scheme* of 1901-11 and the construction of a sluice in the neighbourhood of Diamond Harbour in 1909.

Mr. K.N. Mukherjee (1983)[6], who studied the reclamation and settlement of this area has stated that 1780-1873 reclamation was confined in the areas of Bhangar and Kulpi Block, which was initiated earlier. Quite a major portion of reclamation was carried out during these periods in Canning, Mathurapur, and Jaynagar. Reclamation almost stopped between 1800 to 1830. In the northern and south western sectors, extensive reclamation took place during the years 1873 to 1939. The whole of Kakdwip, residual portion of Canning and Sagar, Namkhana, Pathar Pratima, Basanti, Mathurapur, Kultali and Gosaba were also covered.

Therefore, today the region is by and large settled and initially *the majority of the early settlers were low caste migrants apart from the migrant tribals* (Oraon, Munda, Santhals) of the Sundarbans. Later, before and after partition, refugees from East Pakistan (Bangladesh) settled in Northern part of the district and in Gosaba (East). Development of the Sundarbans started from 1950 onwards after independence.

### 4.2.2 Urban Settlements

The urban development of the region can be traced only during the expansion of British political control in India, (Map 4.2). The need for various forest products and the chance emergence of Calcutta in 1690 by Job Charnock, were the two factors fostering urban development here. Despite its distance from Europe, Calcutta remained the British capital from 1773 to 1912, and this had a profound influence on the settlements of this region.

W. W. Hunter[7] (1875) reports that *in the British days also with the exception of Calcutta, the population of the area was almost wholly rural*, and the so called towns were mere collections of villages. The census report of 1872 states "It may naturally be expected that the metropolitan division, if so styled should posses a large number of important towns. Such however, is not the case. Even in the neighbourhood of Calcutta, the so called townships are mere collection of villages—*villages closely studded and densely populated*, it is true, but still with small pretensions to be designated towns. The villages are grouped together for municipal purposes, and are thus shown in the Census table as towns; but cattle graze, and rice is sown and reaped, in their very midst".

The *British period* therefore records the outcome of *very few towns* mainly portraying agrarian characteristics. Such is common in a region where agriculture is the mainstay specially in the absence of any strategic mineral and industrial base. The census of 1872 records the presence of the South Suburban Town (South of Calcutta)

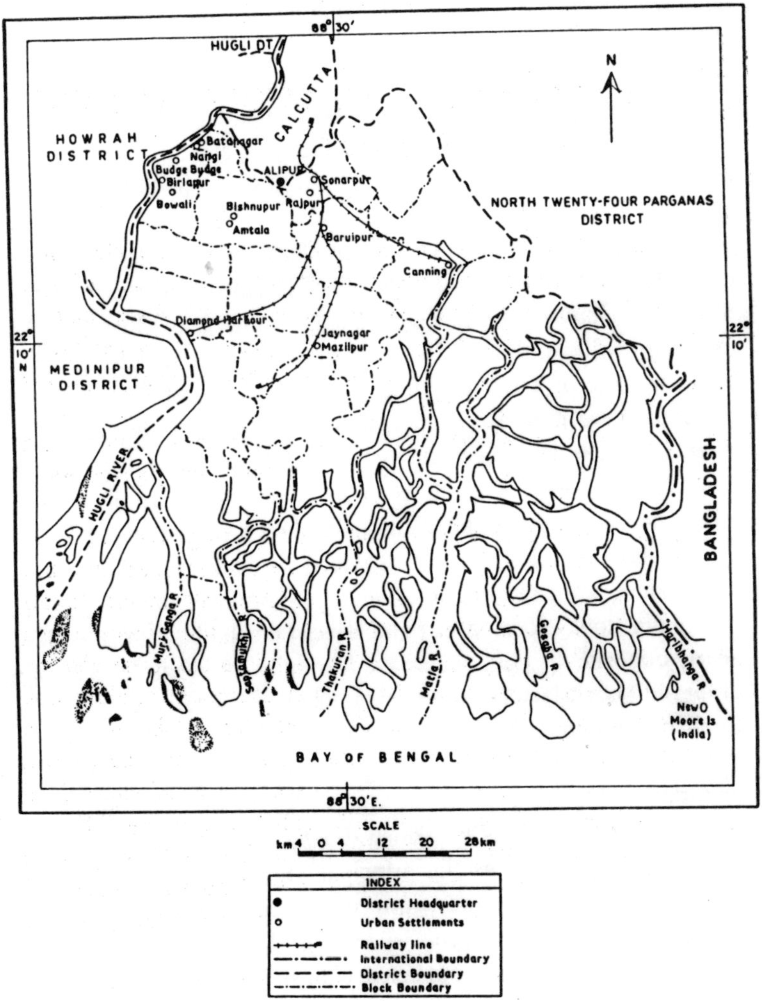


**MAP 4.2 :** South 24-Parganas, Urban Settlements

with an 1869 population of 46,494 persons; Jaynagar (Jaynagar Block), had a population of 5372 in 1872; Port and Town Canning (Canning Block) situated on the Matla River representing an unsuccessful effort to create an auxiliary harbour to Calcutta by the Britishers with a 1870 population of only 714 persons. The other towns and notable villages which later on emerged as small towns include Baruipur, (Baruipur Block) with a 1869 population of 3231 persons and a municipality, Alipur the civil headquarters of the district within the South Suburban Municipality), Garden Reach, a fashionable suburb of Calcutta, situated on the river side a few kilometres to the South of the city, Kalighat today well situated within the limits of South Calcutta was then a place of religious significance as the site of a temple in honour of the Goddess Kali, situated according to 1872 census, on the bank of the old bed of the Ganges, a few miles South of Calcutta. Budge Budge (Budge Budge Block) was another important village about 12 miles below Garden Reach, noted as being the site of a fort captured from the forces of Siraj-ud-daula by Lord Clive in 1756. Rajpur, a short distance further down the river, is said to have been many years ago the field of one of the contests which took place between the Dutch and the English. Garia today incorporated within Calcutta was then a village on the Tolly's Canal, about 8 miles South of Calcutta, containing a large market for produce from the interior.

Falta (today located in Falta Block) on the bank of the Hugli nearly opposite the point where the Damodar flows into it, is the site of an old Dutch factory, and is also noted as the place to which the English fleet retreated on the capture of Calcutta by Siraj-ud-daula, still today remains a village, though once being a place of strategic importance. Diamond Harbour, was well known as the anchorage of the Company's ships in British times emerged as a small town. Khari was developed as the principal village of the small Fiscal division of the same name within the Diamond Harbour sub-division. The Revenue Surveyor reported in 1857 that it contained a small Christian Church, connected with the Society for the propagation of the Gospel and an English school. It still remains a village.

Important settlements of the British time include Masat, famous for its fair in honour of Saint Manik Pir (1872 Census) is now incorporated within Calcutta; Bhangarhat and Mograhat famous for their hats or bazars. Mograhat had a Christian Church for native converts capable of holding 150 persons. Basra, another village in Baruipur sub-division on the Bidyadhari was an important depot of the timber trade of the Sundarbans and also a station on the Calcutta and South Eastern State Railway running to Port Canning.

Thus during this period the South Suburban town emerged as ranking first, population wise. *Many of the notable villages mentioned in this section took the characteristics of towns while others did not.* But the organisational nature of towns can be still traced today.

During the turn of the present century, i.e. in 1901, there was only 5 towns, in the district and their number remained the same during 1911 and 1921. These 5 towns include Batanagar (Maheshtala Block), Budge Budge (Budge Budge), Jaynagar - Mazilpur (Jaynagar), Rajpur (Sonarpur), and South Suburban town (now incorporated within Calcutta). Most of these towns belonged to the class III, IV and V categories (Table 4.1). In 1931 and 1941 the number of towns increased to 6 with the inclusion of Baruipur as class IV town (in the Baruipur Block).

The *post independence period* marked the rise in the number of towns (Table 4.1), specially in the decades of 51-61, 61-71, 71-81 and 81-91. This period also marked the evolution of class I and class II towns in the history of urbanisation and the change in the status in case of many towns.

Beginning with 1951, the number of towns increased to 8. New inclusions were that of Port Canning (Canning Block) and Diamond Harbour (Diamond Harbour Block) in the class V category. In 1961 their number increased to 12 and the 4 new towns included in this census were Birlapur (Budge Budge, class IV), Jadavpur (now in Calcutta, class II), Nangi (Mahestala, class III) and Panchur (Metiaburuz, class III).

Similarly, 4 more towns were added during the 61-71 decade marking the appearance of 16 towns, that includes Jagannathgarh (Maheshtala, class IV), Kanyanagar, (Bishnupur, class V), Krishnagar (Maheshtala, class V) and Uttar Raypur (Budge Budge, class IV).

**TABLE 4.1 : Class and Number of Town in South 24-Parganas 1981-1991**

| *Class* | *1981* | *1911* | *1921* | *1931* | *1941* | *1951* | *1961* | *1971* | *1981* | *1991* |
|---|---|---|---|---|---|---|---|---|---|---|
| I | | | | | | 1 | 1 | 2 | 2 | 0 |
| II | | | | | 1 | | 2 | 3 | 5 | 4 |
| III | 1 | 1 | 2 | 3 | 2 | 2 | 4 | 3 | 3 | 6 |
| IV | 3 | 3 | 2 | 2 | 3 | 3 | 5 | 6 | 11 | 11 |
| V | 1 | 1 | 1 | 1 | | 2 | | 2 | 5 | 19 |
| VI | | | | | | | | | | 2 |
| TOTAL | 5 | 5 | 5 | 6 | 6 | 8 | 12 | 16 | 26 | 42 |

I = Greater than 1,00,000
II = 50,000 - 1,00,000
III = 20,000 - 50,000
IV = 10,000 - 20,000
V = 5,000 - 10,000
VI = Less than - 5,000

1971-81 period marked *a sudden spurt in urbanisation* when the number of towns shot up from 16 in 1971 to 26 in 1981. The 10 new entrants were Bowali (Birlapur, class IV), Chak Kasipur (Budge Budge, class IV), Chandannagar (Maheshtala, class IV), Chota Kalikapur (Maheshtala, class IV), Gobindapur (Maheshtala, class IV), Laskarpur (Sonarpur, class IV), Maheshtala (Maheshtala, class V), Naipara (Maheshtala, class V), Sonarpur (Sonarpur Block, class IV), and Sripur Bagherghol (Sonarpur, class V).

The *maximum increase* in the number of towns however have been registered during the 1981-91 period, when the total number of towns rose from 26 in 1981 to 42 in 1991. Two Class I towns of 1981 i.e. Jadavpur (Jadavpur Block and South Suburban town of Behala) were merged with the Calcutta Municipal district during 1991. Irrespective of this, the new towns added during this Census were 18 in number thus giving rise to a total figure of 42. These new towns are - Gopalpur (Thakurpukur, class IV), Barhans Fartabad (Sonarpur, class - IV), Pujali (Budge Budge, class - IV), Jalkura (Maheshtala, class - V), Tetulberia (Sonarpur, class -V), Memanpur (Sonarpur, class - V), Daulatpur (Maheshtala, class - V), Nischintapur (Sonarpur, class - V), Raypur (Maheshtala, class - V), Kumarakhali (Sonarpur, class - V), Joka (Behala, class - VI), Champahati (Baruipur, class - V), Parui (Behala, class - V), and Tentulkhuli (Maheśhtala, class - VI).

## 4.3 RURAL SETTLEMENTS

Rural settlements portray an intrinsic form of man's interaction with the nature. Villages in India, where there seems to have been nothing like a planned rural settlement are a sort of natural growth in their physical and cultural setting[8], and villages of South 24-Parganas are no exception to it. Although the villages do not possess well - defined shapes and a distinct internal plan, there is a considerable arrangement both in the internal structure and external outline of the villages, which is very clearly related to the nature of their site and cultural features. *Every settlement is unique, and has a personality of its own.* A village is more closely related to its immediate surroundings than a town and it more completely typifies the kind of region in which neither manufacturing industry nor commerce are highly significant.[9] Though it is generally seen that the rural settlements of South 24-Parganas are mainly agricultural, but fishing villages, forest villages and dormitory villages, serving nearby towns are not uncommon.

### 4.3.1 Site and Location of Rural Settlement

A descriptive approach[10] has been undertaken based on topographical sheet analysis forming the basis of settlement study. The site factors of the rural settlements of South 24-Parganas are exceptionally simple because of the deltaic and fertile nature of the country with an almost ubiquitious supply of water, as stated in Chapter 2.

The histogenesis of rural settlments has clearly revealed that the forest cover (initially occupying the whole area) had to be cleared first, and naturally certain favoured spots initially had to be selected. Two such advantage that were invariably sought after, and that acted as the initial siting factors are :

(i) a fairly *raised stretch of land* well above the high tide level, so that swampy and marshy stretches of land could be avoided. Such sites are more prevalent today in the littoral parts of the district may be termed as "dry point settlement"; as also found in other regions where water is too plentiful.

(ii) Another of the initial site factor was the *presence of navigable waterways* or drainage lines including rivers such as the Hugli, Bidyadhari, Muriganga, Thakuran, Matla, Saptamukhi, Gosaba etc. The Hugli being the most important artery of this region, the Hugli Side Flats provided sites for *pioneer settlements* of this area. Even today, navigable arteries provide preferential site factors in the southern Sundarban part of the district, since river communication provides the only form of transport in these parts, as for instance in Gosaba.

(iii) Presence of *suitable flat stretches of land and fertile soil* provide another favourable site for settlements. Sandy soils, as in certain littoral fringes of Sagar Island, are generally avoided. Sometimes uneven stretches have been utilised for homesteads whereas the surrounding flat lands have been used for agricultural purposes. In Sundarban area, the whole length of the rivers, khals and creeks have been artifically embanked to protect the land from tidal bores and to fight the problem of rigorous salinity.

Together with the initial siting factors, creation of *transport arteries*, creation of *tourist resorts* and the creation of *large inland fisheries* mainly in the coastal areas have also affected the location of settlements.

(i) Settlements have sprung up in a linear fashion along the major transport arteries like Sealdah - Diamond Harbour broad-guage line which was completed in 1883 with a branch line from Sonarpur towards Canning. Afterwards another line from Baruipur was extended upto Lakshmikantapur in Mathurapur Block. The major bus routes include :

(a) Esplanade (Calcutta) via Garia - Sonarpur to Baruipur.
(b) Esplanade to Basanti, via - Ghatakpukur in Bhangar Block.
(c) Esplanade to Namkhana, via - Kakdwip.
(d) Esplanade to Diamond Harbour, via - Amtala,Bishnupur etc.

The transport lines, not only affected the location of settlements but also penetrated the urban influence into the rural area.

(ii) The emergence of tourist spots in the Sundarbans have also given rise to settlements. Fraserganj, Bakkhali, in Namkhana Block, Sajnakhali in Gosaba are examples of such settlements.

(iii) The emergence of large inland fisheries as for instance in Tiljala (South East of Calcutta) has given rise to nearby settlements (after the reclamation of marshy area in those parts) and also to fish 'mandis' like Choubagha in Bhangar Block for instance.

### 4.3.2 Type, Form and Distribution of Rural Settlements

Geography is often defined as the study of 'spatial organization expressed as patterns and processes'[11] , concerning essentially 'man-environment relationship and emerging cultural landscape'[12]. 'The conceptual framework of areal association is intimately linked with pattern analysis'[13]..It gives a base for the identification of type, form and classification of rural settlements.

In regional context the word "type" 'identifies the relationship between settlements within organized space'[14], this means that it symbolizes a set of relatively homogenous units defined by specific criteria[15], thus expressing in other words the view of the spatial organisation. The concept of 'pattern' basically meaning 'design' is borrowed from Plant Ecology, is sometimes used as synonymous with 'shape', but there is no geometrical similarities between these two, because according to Bunge "any close curve has a shape and any non-closed collections of points has a pattern"[16].

In the following sections the settlement "types" has been discussed together with the external forms of settlements as expressed through topographical sheets (Map 4.3), in the six geo-ecological regions. (Table 4.2)

#### *Settlements of the Western Hugli Side Flats*

This region being situated on higher ground and having favourable factors such as fertile soil conditions and good connectivity with Calcutta have developed *compact settlements with an agglomeration of dwellings uniformly spaced over the area.* The compact settlements are situated extermely close to each other. Such settlements

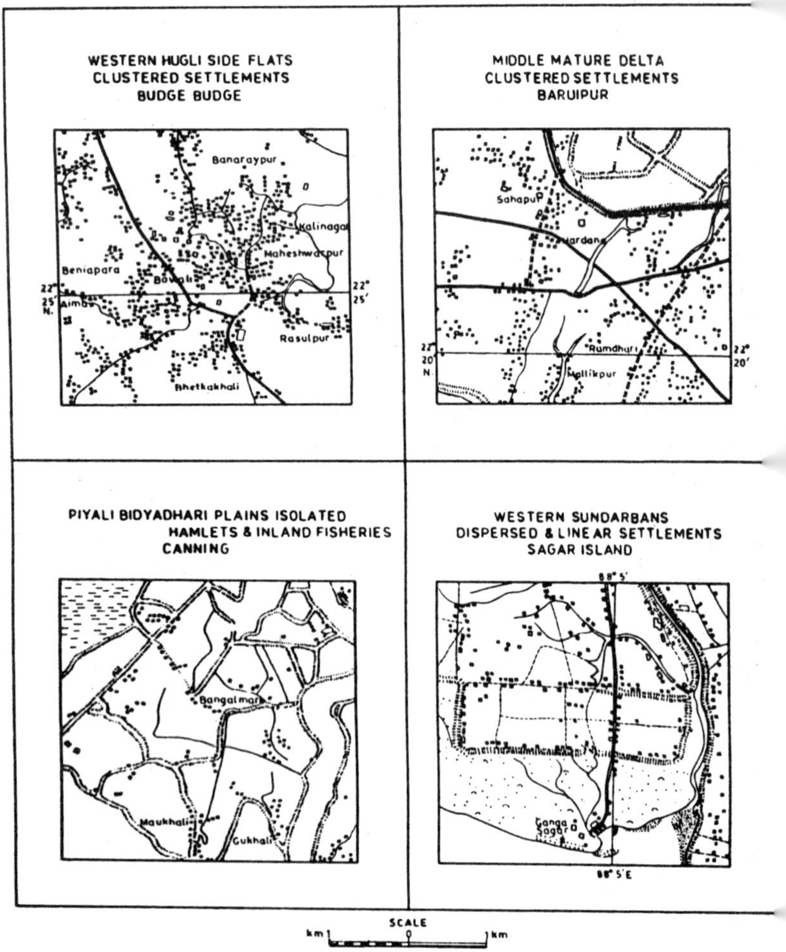


**Map 4.3 :** South 24-Parganas : Rural Settlements-I

**TABLE 4.2 : Geo Ecological Regions**
**Intersettlement Pattern**

| STABLE DELTA<br>Highly Agglomerated and Semi Nucleated | | | ACTIVE DELTA<br>Semi-Nucleated and Highly Dispersed | | |
|---|---|---|---|---|---|
| I | II | III | IV | V | VI |
| WESTERN HUGLI SIDE FLATS | MIDDLE MATURE HUGLI DELTA | PIYALI BIDYADHARI PLAINS | WESTERN SUNDARBANS | MIDDLE SUNDARBANS | EASTERN SUNDARBANS |
| Highly Agglomerated in the North | Highly Agglomerated in the North | Semi-Nucleated | Semi-Nucleated in the North and West | Semi-Nucleated in the North and | Highly dispersed |
| Semi-Nucleated in the South | Semi-Nucleated in the South | | Moderately dispersed in South and East | Moderately dispersed in the South | |

(*Source* : Topographical Sheets of R.F. 1: 50,000)

are the result of articulatory centripetal force operating in the village territory with a tendency towards *nucleation*. Such type of settlements in the region is also due to the close proximity of Calcutta and its sub-urbanized fringe areas apart from the general fertility of the land and flatness of the terrain.

In the blocks next to Metropolitan Calcutta, agglomeration is found to such an extent that they have given rise to an external form of *shapeless clusters* as noticeable in the Maheshtala and Budge Budge blocks. In the vicinity of the urban centres of Maheshtala and Budge Budge have sprung up linear agglomerated clusters. The *linear shapeless agglomeration* in these parts have sprung up mainly along major arteries of metalled roads and rail tracts connecting the area with Calcutta. Shapelessness is the keynote of the suburbanized blocks of Thakurpukur, Maheshtala and Budge Budge.

From the Southern part of the Budge Budge block towards Falta and Diamond Harbour we find compact settlements uniformly spread with an increase of interstitial spaces. Usually the settlements are located at the central point or focus surrounded by cultivated fields on all sides, giving rise to easy accessibility from residence to the workplace. In Budge Budge, Falta and Diamond Harbour blocks the agglomerated clusters have also sprung up all along the Hugli Front sometimes in a linear fashion as for example the settlements of Gadakhali (Budge Budge), Falta and Nainan (Diamond Harbour).

Though the external form of the villages here is generally amorphous and irregular due to extreme congestion in these parts, occasionally well-defined geometric shapes are also noticeable. Square villages are noticeable as for instance Barkali (Falta), Kheto (Diamond Harbour), Ramdebpur (Kulpi). Rectangular and square form is due to the operation of the rectangular division of land, i.e. the "Bigha system' which has been in practice since early time.[17] Circular or Round Villages (akin to "Rundling") in this part is exhibited by Sanpukuria (Maheshtala), Birpana, Majherhat, Jonktabla (Diamond Harbour), and Bhagabanpur (Kulpi). Apart from these types the 'Strassendorf' type of street Village are noticeable in Harishpur (Falta), Double Village like Paschim Durgapur (Falta), Cruciform Village in Kulpi etc.

### The Middle Mature Delta Region of the Hugli

In this region too *amporphous (shapeless) agglomerated clusters* are generally the rule in the Northern part having close proximity to Calcutta; the settlements, usually giving rise to certain shapes, forming compact clusters towards the south and east (near the Piyali Bidyadhari plains). All along the main metalled road connecting Calcutta with Sonarpur, Baruipur, Jaynagar with Lakshmikantapur in Mandir Bazar, as well as along the branch of the Eastern Railway connecting Calcutta with Sonarpur, Baruipur, Jaynagar - Mazilpur with Lakshmikantapur have sprung up a continuous belt of elongated shapeless clusters, exemplified by Sarmastapur, Bade Hugli, Chandpur and others. In Bishnupur also such settlements are noticeable but a lesser degree of agglomeration is noticeable along the Diamond Harbour Road.

In the North Eastern part of Sonarpur and Western part of Tiljala we find extensive stretches of marshy land (occupying the original channel of the Adi Ganga and Bidyadhari) now utilized in the form of inland fisheries. Isolated clusters are also noticeable in these parts.

Though shapelessness and irregularity is the usual form, occasionally the round external form is noticeable as for instance in Atapara, Achna, Inyatpur, Khelarampur, Katiberia of Mandir Bazar. Semi circular forms are often noticeable along small rivers or Khals in this area like Chak Haradhanpur of Mograhat. The intervillage distance increase towards the South and South East in Mograhat, and in Eastern Baruipur. Apart from the main arteries already stated, the transport lines comprise mainly of semimetalled and unmetalled roads often giving rise to footpaths and cart tracts in these parts; hence giving rise to smaller clusters than in the Northern and North Western part of the region.

### The Piali - Bidyadhari Plains of the East

This region exhibits a *considerable variation in agglomeration from North to South.* Bhangar to the north of Canning exhibits more agglomeration than Canning.

Though shapeless clusters is also the rule in Bhangar, the uniformity increases here; the agglomerations often giving rise to

**Plate 1 :** Kutcha House : Middle Mature Delta (Mandir Bazar)

**Plate 2 :** Kutcha House : Western Hugliside Flats (Diamond Harbour)

**Plate 3 :** Semi-Kutcha House : Middle Mature Delta (Mandir Bazar)

**Plate 4 :** Pucca House : Western Hugliside Flats (Diamond Harbour)

*semi-compact* type of settlements as exhibited by Pakhimara, KobilJanga, Goalbati, Gangati here. Along the Bhangar Kata Khal and along the Bidyadhari Khal have sprung up *loose knit* clusters like Anantapur, Goptala, Hatisala on the Bidyadhari Khal and Karaidanga, Krolberia, Ghojernath, Bhangar on the Bhangar Khal. Along portions of the main metalled road connecting Calcutta with Basanti via Bhatipota, Ghatakpukur, also show shapeless clusters identified in Bhatipota, Kharamba, Ghunimeghi, Phulbari- Bamunia, Chandipur and Rangsara. In the Western part of Bhangar, low lying lands occupying the former courses of the Bidyadhari are occupied by fisheries. Here also semi compact settlements are noticeable as for instance in Beder Ait and Bagan Ati. Small Khals or river courses in this region like Bobaler Khal, Karaibagan Khal have given rise to semi circular, semi compact villages following circuitous river courses. Otherwise shapelessness is the usual rule even in semi compact villages and hence definite geometrical forms are not noticeable. Some of the settlements developed along the main road artery however represent the Strassendorf type of street village.

Semi nucleation and isolated dispersed settlement types reach their fullest form in Canning. Settlements though uniformly spaced are placed far apart from each other. The Bidyadhari after traversing Bhangar ulitimately joins the Matla in Canning. External forms representing Loose - Knit villages are seen along the Matla, North of Port Canning. Portions of the low lying Matla Flood Plain has been extensively embanked and this region represents the *isolated homesteads* mainly engaged in fishing pursuits exemplified by the settlements of Jalghata, Baghmari, Baintala and Kochhari. Otherwise the semicompactness of the area does not give rise to any well defined external form.

In stark contrast to the Stable Delta, the settlement pattern of the Active Delta or the Sundarbans exhibit different types, form and pattern, settlements being highly dispersed all over the area.

### *The Western Sundarban Margin comprising of the Active Mouth of the Hugli*

Here (Map 4.4) Sagar Island represents highly dispersed semicompact and hamleted settlements giving rise to different external forms. The

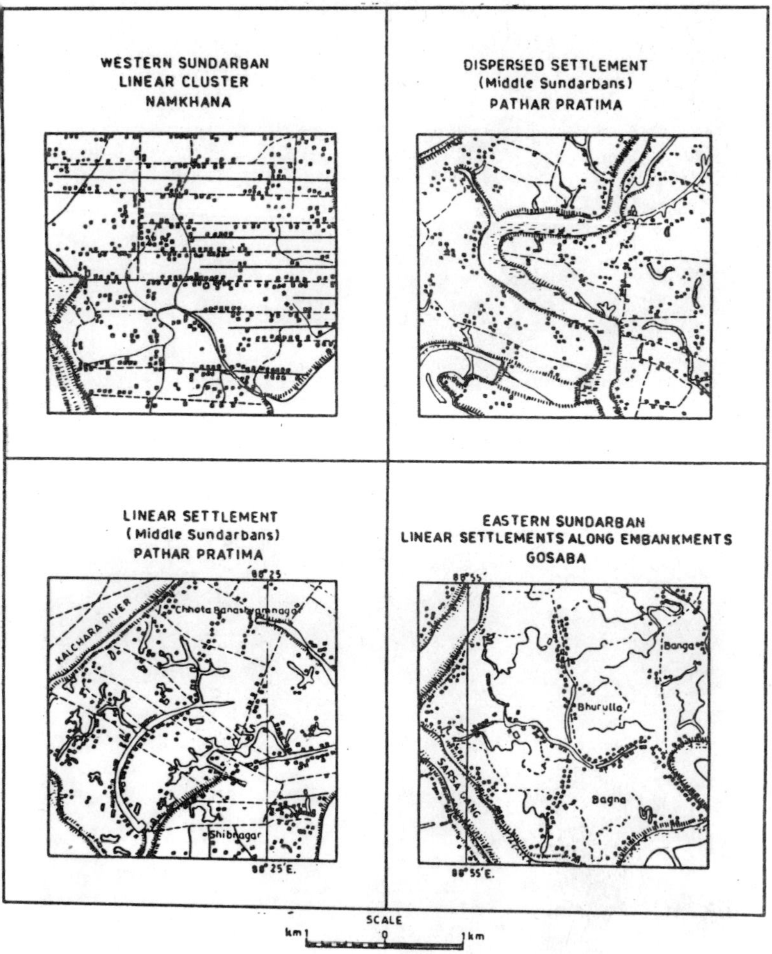


**Map 4.4 :** South Twenty-Four ?arganas : Rural Settlements-II

**Plate 5 :** Bathing Water : Middle Mature Delta (Mandir Bazar)

**Plate 6 :** Semi Kutcha House : Piyali-Bidyadhari Plains (Narayanpur-Bhangar)

*linear type* is most predominant along numerous lengthy, embankments of the area, along local "Khals" and along all metalled and unmetalled roads. Along the Phuldubi Gang, Jamuna Khal, Chemaguri Gang, Maragoalia Khal, Shankar Khal, Gangasagar Khal, Beguakhali Khal, Marichkhali Khal and Satbanki Khal in Sagar have sprung up linear settlements. All these Khals are either directly linked to the Hugli River, (in the West), or Baratala River (in the East) and get filled up at high tide. Such fluvial and marine deposits results in good spawning and breeding ground for fish. The main metalled road traversing the whole length of the island from Kachuberia in the North to Gangasagar in the South have also given rise to linear settlements. Banstala - Mahendraganj, Khasramkar, Khansaheb Abad are such typical linear settlments.

Apart from linearity, settlements of Sagar Island exhibit a variety of shapes and forms. Semicircular types along river meanders are exemplified by Kailapara, along Kailapara Khal and Chak Phuldubi along the Phuldubi Khal, Cruciform village is exhibited by Naraharipur; Checkerboard form by Dhaspara (due to the existence of crisscrossed footpaths) and hollow-square type by Magrahat, Harinbari, Mandirtala etc.

The hollow square in these parts are a outcome of the existence of a tank or pond in the central part around which settlments have sprung up. Starshaped settlement is exhibited by Purushottampur.

In the Northern part of Kakdwip, the settlements are nucleated or agglomerated and *semi-nucleated* in nature, giving way to *dispersed and isolated clusters* to the East and Southern part of the block and in Namkhana lying to the South of Kakdwip area. Examples of agglomerated clusters to the North West of Kakdwip block are exemplified by Nischintapur, Ramtanunagar, Tetultala, Madhabnagar and Raghunathpur. Along the numerous "Khals" of this area the banks of which are embanked, have sprung up linear clusters as for example Rajnagar along the Jhinger Khal and Betalpara along the Gurlial Khal. The settlement of Kakdwip also exhibit linear cluster along the main metalled road connecting Kakdwip with Calcutta via Kulpi block.

*Dispersed* settlements are the rule of the Eastern, Southern Kakdwip and Namkhana. Here the linear pattern is noticeable along the embanked Khals and the main metalled road connecting Kakdwip

**Plate 7** : Kutcha House : Western Sundarbans Gangasagar

**Plate 8** : Bird's Eye view of Sagar Island from Beguakhali Light-house.

with Narayanpur. Apart from these, the settlements here do not portray any well defined external forms and shapes. Dispersion reaches its highest extent in Western Namkhana block (which comprises of various islands) as for example in Mahsani Island, Palibunia Island with a tendency towards linearity along footpaths. Here uniformity is the general rule. Uneven dispersion is noticeable in Eastern Namkhana and the settlements also exhibit semi-circular forms along river bends as for example along the Bagkhali River, Edward's Creek and Sundaria Doanna. Hamleted settlments are also seen here.

### *The Middle Sundarbans And the Fringes of the Active Delta*

North Mathurapur lying in the fringe of the Stable Delta exhibits agglomerated settlment types uniformly distributed. Along the main metalled roads the villages are linear, agglomerated and compact such as, Satghara, Debipur, Belgachhi, Shibgaj, Krishnachandrapur, Kashinagar, Mathurapur being the examples. External forms, such as square villages are exemplified by Radhakantapur, Raghabpur, rectangular villagles by Purandharpur, Rajpur Haldarpara, circular or round villages by Tilian, Bahirchak, Urarpol, Uluberia, Kille, Nayapara etc.

Agglomeration gives way to *highly dispersed and hamleted villages* as we approach the littoral margin in Southern Mathurapur and Patharpratima. Here linear settlements are also noticeable along numerous tidal embanked Khals, the settlements giving rise to circular external forms along river meanders. Hamlets are usually small nucleation or tiny foci, incapable of exerting any attraction. Such type of settlements have sprung up due to ecological restraints in these parts.

In Mathurapur linear settlements are exemplified along the Chhatua Khal, Simultala Khal, Pirkhali Khal, and in PatharPratima they are identified along Curzon Creek, Kuemuri Khal, Kakmara Khal etc. In Patharpratima dispersion reaches its maximum extent due to the existence of numerous Khals, Creeks, 'Doaniya Khals' responsible for the existence of numerous islands forming the block. Dakshin Gopalnagar, Kabidebnagar, Indraprastha, Heremba Gopalpur, are examples of some dispersed and hamleted settlements in Patharpratima.

### *The Eastern Interior Sundarbans (of Dense Tidal Forests)*

Eastern Sundarbans consist of dense tidal reserved forests in the Southern and South Eastern parts, therefore only the Northern part of these blocks are inhabited. The inhabited portions consist of a sum total of numerous islands separated from each other by innumerable khals, rivers and creeks. Kultali is separated from Basanti by the Matla river and Basanti from Gosaba by the Bidya River.

The Northern part of Kultali exhibit semi-nucleated and dispersed settlements taking usually a *linear pattern* along the Khals. Herobhanga on the Jamuna Khal, Talaberia No. 2 along the Nimania Khal, Durgapur along the Ural Khal are such examples in Kultali and Bharatgarh along the Shiyalpheli Khal, Hiranmaipur along the Bidya Khal, Garanbos, along the Haldhoa Khal are such examples in Basanti. Dispersion increases towards the South and East of the area and in Basanti Block, though linearity is still the rule. Curvilinear settlement forms are noticeable along river bends and abandoned water courses, like Deulbari in Kultali.

*Linearity along with dispersion* reaches its maximum in Gosaba block. Here, along the numerous embanked khals, linear settlements is the only rule giving rise to a few *scattered hamlets*. Linear clusters are also noticeable occasionally as exemplified by the settlement of Gosaba on the Bidya river and Rangabalia village. A few examples of the numerous linear villages here are Battali, Bipradaspur, Surjyaberi along the Maukhali Khal, Baramolla-Khali, Taranagar along the Durgamandal Khal, Chota-Mollakhali along the Mollakhali Khal, and Sonagan, Dulki along the Durgadauna Khal. The settlements in this area are spread over enormous area, often *one island comprising of one village only*.

Thus to conclude, the following settlments types, (Table 4.2), have been recognised in the area. The Stable Delta lying in close proximity with Calcutta usually portrays agglomerated, shapeless, compact clusters and compact settlements in marked contrast to the semi-nucleated, dispersed and hamleted settlements of the Active Delta or the Sundarbans. In the suburbanised blocks near Calcutta as for example in Mahestala, Budge Budge, Sonarpur, Northern Baruipur, agglomerated shapeless clusters of compact nature is the general rule. Proceeding a bit southwards in the blocks of Diamond

Harbour, Falta, Kulpi, Bishnupur, Bhangar, North Mathurapur, Magrahat, Mandir Bazar, and Jaynagar both the agglomerated and seminucleated settlements dominate the scenario. The semi-nucleated settlments are noticeable in Canning, West Northern Kakdwip and Northern Kultali. In Southern Kakdwip, Southern Mathurapur, and in Kultali, moderately dispersed and hamleted settlements are noticeable. Highly dispersed and hamleted settlements are found in the littoral margins of Namkhana and Gosaba. Thus we see a change in settlement types, from the littoral margin (of Bay of Bengal) to the interior.

### 4.3.3 Spacing of Rural Settlements

After the examination of the existence of a variety of distributional patterns of rural settlements, it now becomes imperative to analyse the methodology applied in the statistical interpretation of settlements and this has been used for mapping in the present chapter. The distribution pattern of the settlements and their types as has been noticed is intimately related to the geo-ecological factors along with the cultural landscape of the area, their groupings and allocation being an outcome of the time sequence. To study the same, *a quantitative approach* has been applied in this chapter, after considering various indices of spacing, dispersion of settlements, size and density. Through these indices an attempt has been made to measure the degree of concentration and dispersion of settlements.

Spacing denotes the relative locational arrangement of settlements in a given space[18], and is often used as a unit for the measurement of concentration and dispersion of settlements[19]. Two factors have been taken into account regarding the spacing of rural settlements in South-24 Parganas.

(a) the *density* i.e. the number of settlements per unit area and
(b) *the distance apart* of settlements using topographical sheet information of the whole area at scale 1 : 50,000.

The density figures have been grouped into 3 classes of less than 25 settlements/100 sq.km, 25 - 50 settlements/100 sq.km and finally more than 50 settlements per 100 Sq.Km. It has been observed that most of the blocks of the Stable Delta exhibit higher densities than the Active Delta region that occupy the lowest category.

**Plate 9** : Pucca and Semi Pucca House : Eastern Sundarbans (Gosaba)

**Plate 10** : Kutcha House : Eastern Sundarbans (Basanti)

Since just settlement density may not always reveal the best picture of the spacing of settlements (as it gives us a crude picture), a reformed theoretical basis of the transformation of settlement density into spacing was first initiated by Robinson and Barnes [20] formula as modified by Mather.

The formula reads as $Hd = 1.0746 / \sqrt{d}$

($d$ = density of settlements per units area).

The computation of the hypothetical inter-settlement distances denotes the mean spacing, ranging from 1.22 km to 4.48 km. In map, spacing is grouped into the following 4 categories: (Map 4.5)

(a) *Low Spacing* (less than 2 km) : This is noticeable in Falta, Diamond Harbour, Kulpi, and Mandir Bazar located in the Hugli Side Flats and Hulgi Delta proper. This zone covers 11.35% of the total rural area and 18.02% of the total rural population. The lowest spacing is noticeable in Thakurpukur lying next to Calcutta and it is here that the inter-village distance is the least due to pressure of population on land resulting in small villages, closely spaced. Falta, Kulpi, Diamond Harbour and Mandir Bazar have a good connectivity with Calcutta and hence inter-village space is low due to creation of a large number of closely spaced villages. The highest value of this group is noticeable in Kulpi (1.92 km). Here factors of restricted scope of expansion and good communication facilities including river transport has resulted in such spacing.

(b) *Moderate Spacing* (2-3 Km) is discerned in Mahestala, Budge Budge, Sonarpur, Bishnupur, Baruipur, Mograhat, Jaynagar, Bhangar, Kakdwip, Mathurapur, Basanti and Gosaba.

Most of the blocks in this group lie in the Stable Delta (Middle Mature Hugli Delta) and in some portions of the Sundarbans. Here due to availability of flat land and the penetration of urban influence due to better communication facilities, villages have sprung up nearly everywhere and hence village spacings are less. In some portions of the Sundarbans too as for instance in Kakdwip, Mathurapur, (Northern Sundarbans) and in Basanti and Gosaba (Eastern

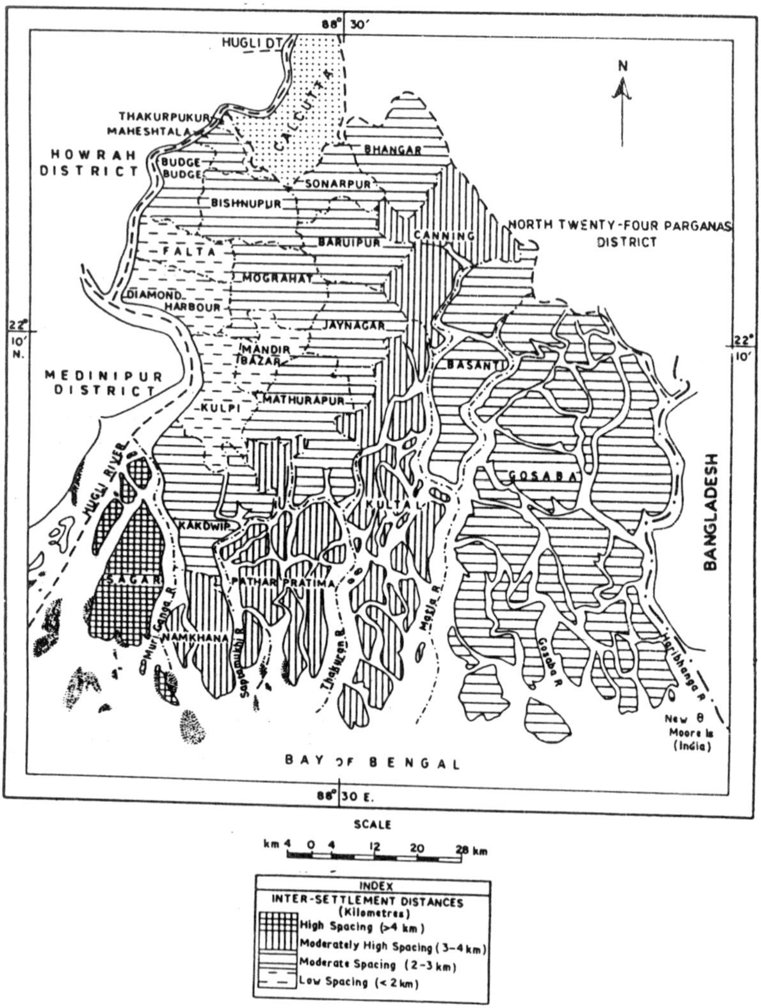


**MAP 4.5** : South 24-Parganas : Spacing of Rural Settlements

Sundarbans), due to restrictions imposed by the nature of land and the forest covered area, settlements grew up in a restricted area and hence the intervillage spacings are moderate. Such spacing cover nearly 55.67% of the rural area supporting 62.36% of the total rural population. Here the lowest spacing is seen in Budge Budge and Baruipur, (2.03 km) and the highest in Mathurapur, of the Sundarbans, (2.99 km).

(c) *Moderately High Spacing* (3 - 4 Km) covers Canning, Namkhana, Patharpratima and Kultali in the Piyali Bidyadhari Plains and in the Sundarbans. Canning is crossed by large streams and it is here that the intervillage distances have increased considerably. Namkhana, Patharpratima and Kultali of the Sundarban are also larger blocks crisscrossed by a number of distributaries and Khals. Forest cover does not exist in Namkhana or Patharpratima but only a part of Southern Kultali comes under the reserved forests. All these factors are responsible for dispersed settlements placed far apart from one another often one island comprising of one village only. Namkhana shows the highest spacing in this group of 3.84 km and Canning the least of 3.07 km. The region covers 23.68% of the total rural area, having 16.64% of the total rural population.

(d) *High Spacing* (of over 4 km) is seen in Sagar Island of Western Sundarbans. This island contains only 2.98% of the total rural population on 9.30% of the total rural area with a maximum distance of 4.48 kms. between two villages. This explains *a close inter-relationship among the density of village (d), and hypothetical spacing (Hd)*. For instance the density increases in the Stable Delta where the Hypothetical distance is less and the vice versa holds true for the Active Delta.

### 4.3.4 Dispersion of Rural Settlements

Dispersion may be defined "as the degree of deviation of a set of points from random, relative to some delimited area."[21]

Settlements are not always evenly spaced nor on the other hand, they are spaced in a strictly random pattern[22]. In the present text dispersion[23] has been measured through *'Nearest Neighbour Analysis'*[24]. The nearest neighbour statistic ($R_n$) i.e., the index of randomness[25] which shows the level of association between observed mean spacing ($^rO$) and expected spacing ($^rE$) in random situation, has been computed with the mathematical expression advanced by Clark and Evans as

$$^Rn = {}^rO/{}^rE = 2\,{}^rO\sqrt{d}$$

where $^rE = 0.5\sqrt{d}$

Based on this formula, the standard Rn value ranges have been fixed for the dispersion of settlements which are 0.0 for complete clustering, 1.0, for random and 2.15 for ideal or uniform.

$R_n$ statistics can also be compared with the *index of randomness disturbance* which is measured by the correlative ratio of actual spacing ($^rO$) and hypothetical spacing (*Hd*). The ratio between $^rO$ and *Hd* varies from 0.0 (aggregation) to 1.0 (uniform).

For the present analysis, Blocks have been considered as the standard areal unit for the measurement of Rn values, and 50% of the settlements were taken as samples from the topographical sheets for computation. Considering the *homogeneity* of the landscape, settlements are found *uniformly distributed in an ubiquitous manner* all over the land. Therefore, it is noticeable that *the dispersion trend is flatenning towards uniformity* from random and there is conspicuous absence of clustering. On the basis of the results obtained, however, 4 regions can be dilineated after classification of data, (Map 4.6) based on Table 4.3

a) *Very Low Uniformity* or nearing randomness (Rn values less than 1.30) - This covers Thakurpukur in Hugli Side Flats and Sonarpur in the Middle Mature Hugli Delta covering 2.54% of rural area, 5.22% of villages and 4.89% of rural population. The lower uniformity in these areas may be due to penetration of urban influence and the low rural proportion of area. The observed mean intervillage spacing comes to 1.04 km and the percentage ratio between mean observed spacing and hypothetical spacing ranges from 58 to 59.

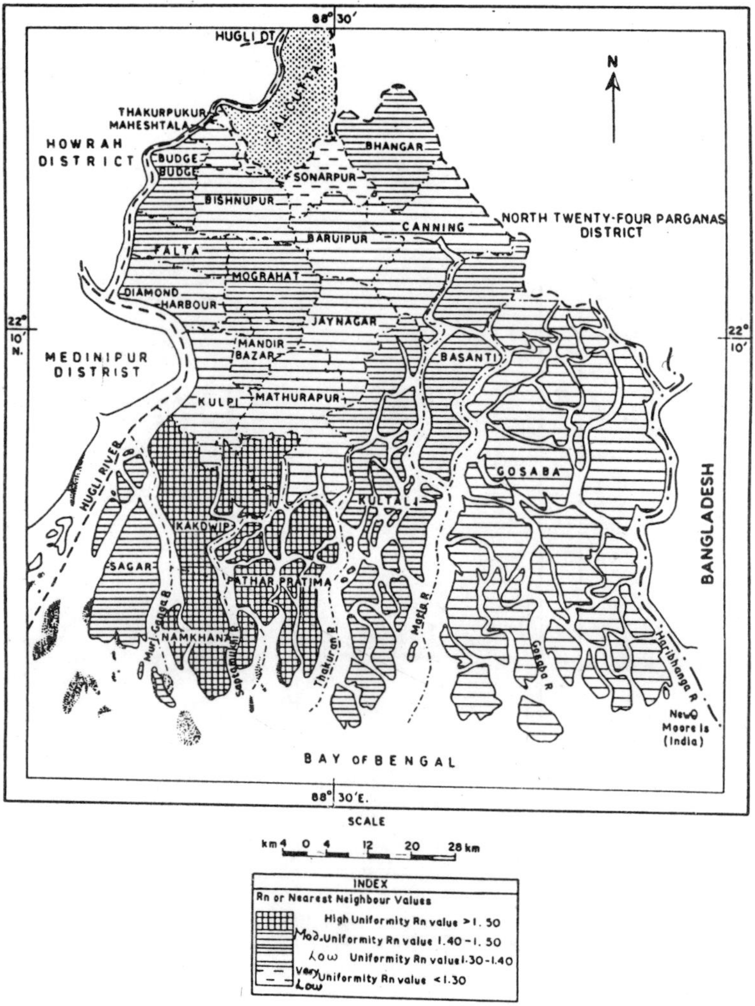


**MAP : 4.6 :** South 24-Parganas : Nature of Dispersion of Rural Settlements.

**TABLE 4.3 : Spatial Characteristics of Villages**

| *Geo-Ecological Region* | *Blocks* | *Density of Village/ Sq.km.* | *Hypo-thetical spacing (Hd,km)* | *Mean Obser-ved spacing $r_O$ Km.* | *Expec-ted spacing $r_E$ Km.* | *Nature of dispersion error* $R_n$ | *Di%* | *Stand-ard error* $\sigma_{re}$ | *Z value* |
|---|---|---|---|---|---|---|---|---|---|
| *1* | *2* | 3 | 4 | 5 | 6 | 7 | 8 | 9 | 10 |
| **STABLE DELTA** | | | | | | | | | |
| *I. THE WESTERN HUGLI SIDE FLATS* | | | | | | | | | |
| 1. | Thakurpukur Metiaburuz | 0.78 | 1.22 | 0.71 | 0.57 | 1.25 | 58 | 0.03 | 4.85 |
| 2. | Mahestala | 0.24 | 2.19 | 1.36 | 1.02 | 1.33 | 62 | 0.12 | 2.70 |
| 3. | Budge Budge | 0.28 | 2.03 | 1.40 | 0.94 | 1.49 | 69 | 0.08 | 5.75 |
| 4. | Falta | 0.33 | 1.89 | 1.28 | 0.87 | 1.47 | 68 | 0.07 | 6.59 |
| 5. | Diamond Harbour | 0.38 | 1.73 | 1.06 | 0.81 | 1.31 | 61 | 0.06 | 4.15 |
| 6. | Kulpi | 0.31 | 1.92 | 1.23 | 0.90 | 1.37 | 64 | 0.08 | 4.10 |
| *II. THE MIDDLE MATURE DELTA OF THE HUGLI* | | | | | | | | | |
| 7. | Sonarpur | 0.21 | 2.34 | 1.37 | 1.09 | 1.26 | 59 | 0.09 | 3.10 |
| 8. | Bishnupur | 0.24 | 2.19 | 1.37 | 1.02 | 1.34 | 63 | 0.08 | 4.54 |
| 9. | Baruipur | 0.28 | 2.03 | 1.25 | 0.94 | 1.33 | 62 | 0.09 | 3.39 |
| 10. | Mograhat | 0.25 | 2.15 | 1.42 | 1.00 | 1.42 | 66 | 0.08 | 5.27 |
| 11. | Mandir - Bazar | 0.34 | 1.85 | 1.22 | 0.86 | 1.42 | 66 | 0.07 | 5.12 |
| 12. | Jaynagar | 0.20 | 2.39 | 1.48 | 1.12 | 1.32 | 62 | 0.13 | 2.75 |
| *III THE PIYALI BIDYADHARI PLAINS* | | | | | | | | | |
| 13. | Bhangar | 0.19 | 2.44 | 1.64 | 1.15 | 1.43 | 67 | 0.12 | 1.87 |
| 14. | Canning | 0.12 | 3.07 | 1.90 | 1.44 | 1.32 | 62 | 0.07 | 6.14 |

TABLE 4.3 : (*Contd.*)

| *Geo-Ecological Region* | *Blocks* | *Density of Village/ Sq.km.* | *Hypo-thetical spacing (Hd,km)* | *Mean Obser-ved spacing $r_O$ km.* | *Expec-ted spacing $r_E$ km.* | *Nature of dispersion error* $R_n$ | *Di%* | *Stand-ard error* $\sigma_{re}$ | *Z value* |
|---|---|---|---|---|---|---|---|---|---|
| 1 | 2 | 3 | 4 | 5 | 6 | 7 | 8 | 9 | 10 |
| **ACTIVE DELTA** | | | | | | | | | |
| *IV. THE WESTERN SUNDARBANS* | | | | | | | | | |
| 15. | Sagar Island | 0.06 | 4.48 | 2.80 | 2.04 | 1.37 | 63 | 0.21 | 3.81 |
| 16. | Kakdwip | 0.18 | 2.56 | 1.79 | 1.18 | 1.52 | 70 | 0.11 | 5.55 |
| 17. | Namkhana | 0.08 | 3.84 | 2.66 | 1.77 | 1.50 | 69 | 0.33 | 2.71 |
| *V. THE MIDDLE SUNDARBANS* | | | | | | | | | |
| 18. | Mathurapur | 0.13 | 2.99 | 1.88 | 1.39 | 1.35 | 63 | 0.14 | 3.60 |
| 19. | Pathar Pratima | 0.09 | 3.58 | 2.57 | 1.67 | 1.54 | 72 | 0.22 | 4.06 |
| *VI. THE EASTERN SUNDARBANS* | | | | | | | | | |
| 20. | Kultali | 0.11 | 3.26 | 2.19 | 1.51 | 1.45 | 67 | 0.17 | 4.45 |
| 21. | Basanti | 0.18 | 2.56 | 1.70 | 1.18 | 1.44 | 66 | 0.23 | 1.68 |
| 22. | Gosaba | 0.15 | 2.76 | 1.76 | 1.29 | 1.36 | 64 | 0.13 | 4 15 |

b) *Low Uniformity* than randomness ($R_n$ values 1.30 to 1.40)— Quite a large number of blocks fall in this group, denoting the homogeneity of the land and almost uniform location of the villages in space. Though uniformity is the rule of the compact and semicompact settlements of the Stable Delta, it is also the rule of the dispersed settlements of the Sundarbans. Here we find the settlements to be uniformly dispersed, giving rise to higher uniform $R_n$ values as well. Maheshtala, Diamond Harbour, Kulpi, Bishnupur, Baruipur, Jaynagar, Canning of the Stable Delta as well as Sagar Island, Mathurapur, and Gosaba of the Active Delta; fall in this group covering 51.58% villages, 52.47% of the total rural area and 49.22% of the total rural population. The observed mean spacing of the villages in this case comes to 1.61 km and ratio between mean observed spacing and hypothetical distance or $D_i$ % ranges between 61 and 64.

c) *Moderate Uniformity* ($R_n$ values 1.40 to 1.50) is noticeable mostly in the Stable Delta blocks of Budge Budge, Falta, Mograhat, Mandir Bazar, Bhangar as well Kultali, Basanti of Sundarbans covering 35.53% of the villages, 27.03% of the total rural area and 34.54% of the total rural population. Ample fertile land in these parts and the ubiquitous supply of water is responsible for the high and uniform growth of villages all over the area. The actual or observed mean spacing of villages in this group is 1.55 and $D_i$ here ranges from 66 to 69.

d) *High uniformity* ($R_n$ value greater than 1.50) is noticeable in the Sundarban blocks of Kakdwip, Namkhana and Pathar Pratima. Here we find that very uniform dispersed settlements have sprung up on every parcel of land available for cultivation, hence the $R_n$ values here portray a very high uniformity compared to other areas. This group covers 7.67% of the villages sharing 17.95% of the total rural area and 11.36% of the total rural population. The mean observed spacing of the villages stand as 2.43 km and $D_i$% ranges from 69 to 72.

The above dispersion analysis clearly reveals that the settlements are tending towards uniformity than being perfectly random except in Thakurpukur-Metiaburuz and Sonarpur where the trend is lesser when compared to other Blocks. Monotony and homogeneity of this aggradational deltaic plain is responsible for such a pattern. After computing the $R_n$ values, the Standard Error and the $Z$ values have been computed for each case. The standard error or

$$\sigma^r_E = \frac{0.26136}{\sqrt{N^2/A}}$$

$N^2/A$ Where $N$ = number of settlements
and $A$ = *total area*, and

$$Z = \frac{\overline{r_o} - \overline{r_e}}{\sigma^r_E}$$

This is a normal variate statistic used to test the significance of the difference between $^r o$ and $^r e$. The settlements of all the blocks have not only shown a trend towards uniformity at various grades but the $Z$ test has also shown that the results are significant for most of the blocks,. apart from a few in Bhangar and Basanti. So the characteristic of uniformity becomes an established fact.

### 4.3.5 Concentration of Rural Settlements

After studying the spatial arrangement of settlements, it is now imperative to probe into the concentration of settlements in South 24-Parganas (Table 4.4), the areal size of villages, the population size as well as the settlement groupings in this area. It has been also observed that village size, density of rural settlements and intervillage spacing (already computed) are the closely interwoven, attributes of the rural landscape.

It is seen that most of that the Stable Delta region has low areal sizes of settlements (Map 4.7) compared to those of the Active Delta regions. The lowest areal concentration in 1991 occurs in the Western Hugli Side Flats of 1.24 sq.km per settlement. The highest occurs in the Western Sundarbans in the order of 9.98 sq.km. Most of the regions exhibit a marginal declining concentration of area. The very low category of less than 3 sq.km per village is noticeable in most of the blocks of the Active Delta among its 3 subregions. The whole of Western Hugli Side Flats, together with the blocks of Baruipur, Mandir Bazar and Bhangar covering 31.34 per cent of the total rural area and 54.74 per cent of the total rural population fall in this category. The smallest areal size in this group are however notice-

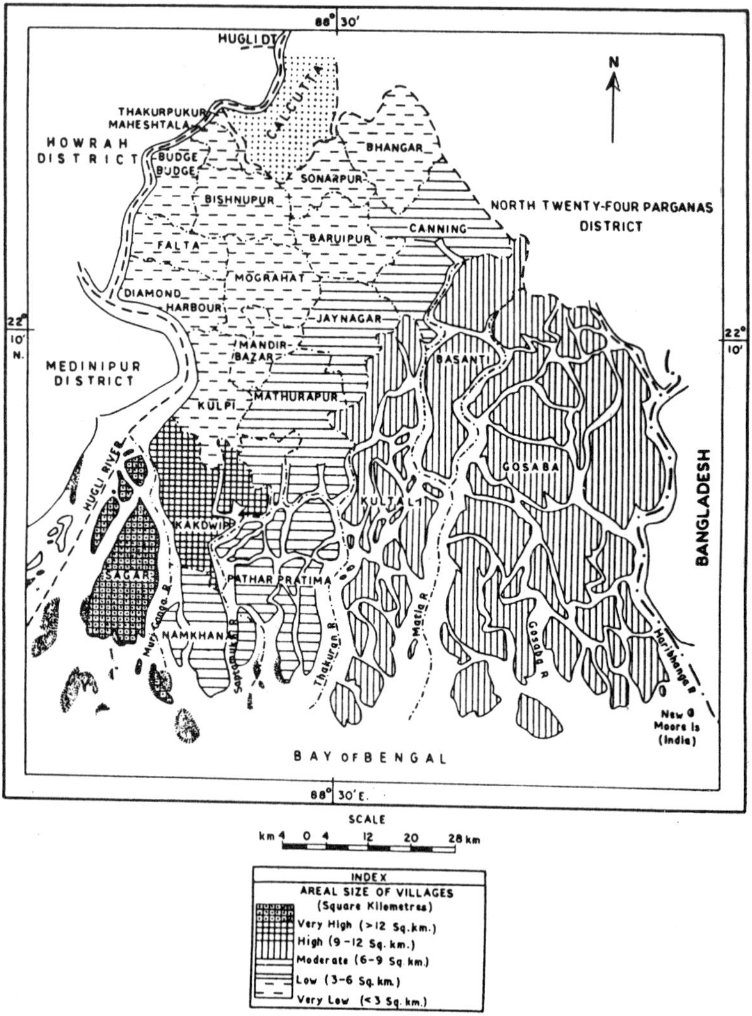


**MAP 4.7** : South 24-Parganas : Areal Size of Villages 1991

able in Thakurpukur 0.58 sq.km, 1991, lying next to Calcutta Metropolitan District, therefore indicating the intensive use of land in these parts.

The next category on the lower side 3-6 sq. km per village is seen in Jaynagar, Canning, Namkhana, Mathurapur, and Pathar Pratima, covering a total rural area of 33.44% and a population of 25.33% .

In the medium category of 6-9 Sq.km/village is noticeable three of the Active Delta blocks of Kultali, Basanti and Gosaba covering 18.28 per cent of the total rural area and 12.63 per cent of the rural population.

The high category of 9-12 sq.km/village and very high category i.e. greater than 12 sq.km/village groups include one block each also of the Active Sundarban Delta viz. Kakdwip and Sagar Island and sharing only 7.63 and 9.30 per cent of the area and 4.32 and 2.98 per cent of the rural population. Thus the villages of the Sundarban Delta cover greater area or are large areal size villages particularly in Kakdwip and Sagar Island.

Based on the rural population size (Table 4.4) the concentration of settlements have been calculated following Monkhouse's Method[27]

$$C = \frac{\text{Number of inhabitants in the parish}}{\text{Number of Settlements in the parish}}$$

C = Co-efficient of grouping.

The figures of the six sub-regions reveal the highest 1991 concentration of 1634 persons per village in the Western Hugli Side Flats, and the highest of 3923 persons in Western Sundarban. The table also reveals that the highest concentration of area as well as of population occurs in the Active Delta regions. The blockwise distributional pattern (Map 4.8) reveals a low concentration of less than 1500 persons per village in Thakurpukur, Kulpi, Mandir Bazar and Kultali covering 11.96 per cent of the total rural area and 11.80 per cent of the total rural population. A moderate concentration of 1500 - 3000 persons occurs in Budge Budge, Falta, Diamond Harbour, Sonarpur, Bishnupur, Baruipur, Mograhat, Bhangar, Canning, Basanti, Mathurapur, Pathar Pratima covering 56.42 per cent of the total rural area and 65.94 per cent of the total rural population. High concentration of 3000-4500 persons occur in Jaynagar, Sagar Island, Namkhana and Gosaba covering 23.55 per cent of total rural area

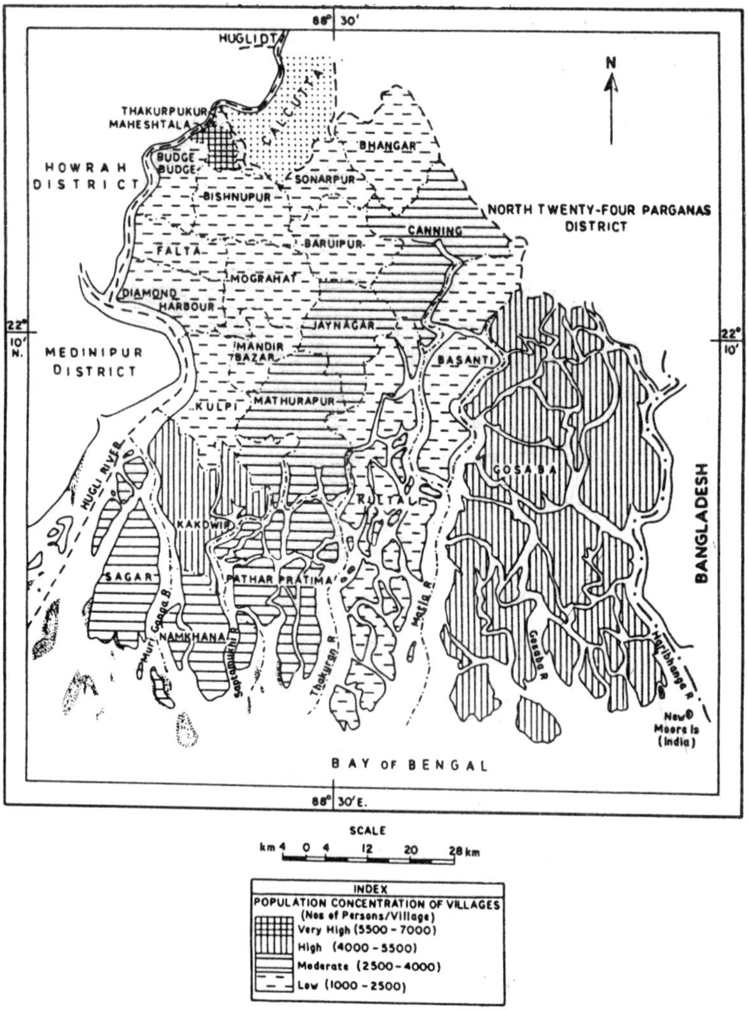


**MAP 4.8** : South 24-Parganas : Population Size of Villages 1991

**TABLE 4.4 : Area and Population Concentration of Rural Settlements 1981 - 1991**

| *Region/Blocks* | *Area / Village* 1981 | *Area / Village* 1991 | *Population / Village* 1981 | *Population / Village* 1991 |
|---|---|---|---|---|
| **STABLE DELTA** | | | | |
| *I. THE WESTERN HUGLI SIDE FLATS* | | | | |
| 1. Thakurpukur-Metiaburuz | 0.96 | 0.58 | 1639 | 1960 |
| 2. Mahestala | 0.98 | 2.29 | 1953 | 5729 |
| 3. Budge Budge | 1.33 | 1.38 | 1929 | 2081 |
| 4. Falta | 1.02 | 1.02 | 1212 | 1501 |
| 5. Diamond Harbour | 1.14 | 1.15 | 1266 | 1585 |
| 6. Kulpi | 1.47 | 1.46 | 986 | 1232 |
| **TOTAL** | **1.22** | **1.24** | **1310** | **1634** |
| *II. THE MIDDLE MATURE DELTA OF THE HUGLI* | | | | |
| 7. Sonarpur | 1.53 | 1.51 | 1711 | 2182 |
| 8. Bishnupur | 1.36 | 1.36 | 1790 | 2214 |
| 9. Baruipur | 1.56 | 1.50 | 1546 | 1951 |
| 10. Mograhat | 1.50 | 1.45 | 1871 | 2383 |
| 11. Mandir - Bazar | 1.07 | 1.04 | 1154 | 1412 |
| 12. Jaynagar | 3.18 | 3.12 | 2107 | 3153 |
| **TOTAL** | **1.67** | **1.63** | **1712** | **2224** |
| *III. THE PIYALI BIDYADHARI PLAINS IN THE EAST* | | | | |
| 13. Bhangar | 2.09 | 2.06 | 1735 | 2280 |
| 14. Canning | 3.98 | 3.91 | 1879 | 2595 |
| **TOTAL** | **2.95** | **2.91** | **1800** | **2423** |
| **ACTIVE DELTA** | | | | |
| *IV. THE WESTERN SUNDARBANS* | | | | |
| 15. Sagar Island | 13.20 | 12.63 | 2119 | 3352 |
| 16. Kakdwip | 9.92 | 9.93 | 3475 | 4744 |
| 17. Namkhana | 5.71 | 5.71 | 2648 | 3455 |
| **TOTAL** | **10.45** | **9.98** | **2968** | **3923** |
| *V. THE MIDDLE SUNDARBANS* | | | | |
| 18. Mathurapur | 5.06 | 4.89 | 2022 | 2519 |
| 19. Pathar Pratima | 5.63 | 5.38 | 2299 | 2731 |
| **TOTAL** | **5.30** | **5.10** | **2137** | **2608** |
| *VI. EASTERN SUNDARBANS* | | | | |
| 20. Kultali | 7.08 | 7.08 | 2885 | 3068 |
| 21. Basanti | 6.30 | 6.11 | 2652 | 3388 |
| 22. Gosaba | 7.43 | 7.43 | 3368 | 4010 |
| **TOTAL** | **6.88** | **6.80** | **2939** | **3476** |
| **DISTRICT TOTAL** | **2.94** | **2.91** | **1818** | **2319** |

and 16.32 per cent of total rural population. Finally a very high concentration of more than 4500 persons occur in Maheshtala and Kakdwip covering 8.07 per cent and 5.94 per cent of the total rural area and population respectively.

### 4.3.6 Size Classification of Villages

Table 4.5 represents the classification of 2151 villages of South 24 Parganas according to their 1991 population size. 29.52 per cent of the total villages of the district fall in the category of 1000-1999 population group followed by 25.57 per cent in the 2000 - 4999 group. The regionwise picture reveals greater proportion of villages of the Western Hugli Side Flats and the Middle Mature Hugli Delta, range in population size of 500-1999, whereas in the other four regions, the size ranges between 1000-4999. In other words higher population sizes of villages are noticeable to the East and South of the region.

## 4.4 URBAN SETTLEMENTS

Urban settlements by virtue of themselves being the most sizeable human occupance and possessing different attributes occupy a place of considerable significance. The town provides meaningful clues about the economic and social health of the region and also reflects the transformation of the physio-socio-cultural landscape. It is a source of change in its own right. It is also a centre of diffusion of modern civilization, thereby providing a milleau in which social ferment and innovation can take place. Its expansion therefore, helps to determine the trend towards more modern condition.

### 4.4.1 Site and Situation of Urban Settlements

All the 42 towns of the district are situated in the Stable Delta, mostly *clustered around the Calcutta District* specially in the blocks of Thakurpukur-Metiaburuz, Maheshtala, Budge Budge and Sonarpur. 27 are located in the Western Hugli Side Flats, 14 in the Middle Mature Hugli Delta and 1 only, in the Piyali Bidyadhari Plains.

***The Western Hugli Side Flats***

The towns here are located along the Hugli River, having close proximity and connectivity with Calcutta, themselves being part of

**TABLE 4.5 : Size Classification of Villages - 1991**

| *Resion/Blocks* | *Population* | | *Size* | | *Groups - 1991* | | | |
|---|---|---|---|---|---|---|---|---|
| | *Less than 200* | *200-499* | *500-999* | *1000-1999* | *2000-4999* | *5000-9999* | *More than 10,000* | *Total No. of villages* |
| **STABLE DELTA** | | | | | | | | |
| *I. THE WESTERN HUGLI SIDE FLATS* | | | | | | | | |
| 1. Thakurpukur-Metiaburuz | — | 4 | 10 | 7 | 6 | 4 | — | 31 |
| 2. Mahestala | — | — | — | 10 | 2 | — | — | 12 |
| 3. Budge Budge | 3 | 7 | 21 | 28 | 19 | 2 | — | 80 |
| 4. Falta | 6 | 19 | 41 | 48 | 18 | 1 | — | 133 |
| 5. Diamond Harbour | 3 | 23 | 54 | 58 | 24 | 1 | — | 163 |
| 6. Kulpi | 23 | 43 | 56 | 34 | 13 | 2 | 1 | 172 |
| **TOTAL** | **35** | **96** | **182** | **185** | **82** | **10** | **1** | **591** |
| % Distribution | (5.92) | (16.24) | (30.80) | (31.30) | (13.87) | (1.69) | (0.17) | (100) |
| *II. THE MIDDLE MATURE DELTA OF THE HUGLI* | | | | | | | | |
| 7. Sonarpur | 3 | 10 | 23 | 30 | 24 | 3 | — | 93 |
| 8. Bishnupur | 1 | 12 | 36 | 57 | 43 | 6 | — | 155 |
| 9. Baruipur | 4 | 18 | 42 | 45 | 23 | 4 | 1 | 137 |
| 10 Mograhat | 4 | 18 | 40 | 60 | 39 | 14 | 1 | 176 |
| 11. Mandir - Bazar | 10 | 22 | 38 | 25 | 16 | 2 | — | 113 |
| 12. Jaynagar | 4 | 11 | 25 | 36 | 30 | 6 | 3 | 115 |
| **TOTAL** | **26** | **91** | **204** | **253** | **175** | **35** | **5** | **789** |
| **% Distribution** | **(3.30)** | **(11.53)** | **(25.86)** | **(32.07)** | **(22.18)** | **(4.44)** | **(0.62)** | **(100)** |

TABLE 4.5 : (*Contd.*)

| *Resion/Blocks* | *Population Size Groups - 1991* | | | | | | | |
|---|---|---|---|---|---|---|---|---|
| | *Less than 200* | *200-499* | *500-999* | *1000-1999* | *2000-4999* | *5000-9999* | *More than 10,000* | *Total No. of villages* |
| *III. THE PIYALI BIDYADHARI PLAINS IN THE EAST* | | | | | | | | |
| 13. Bhangar | 4 | 11 | 30 | 53 | 42 | 5 | — | 145 |
| 14. Canning | 8 | 15 | 21 | 35 | 34 | 7 | 1 | 121 |
| **TOTAL** % Distribution | **12** (4.51) | **26** (9.77) | **51** (19.17) | **88** (33.08) | **76** (28.57) | **12** (4.51) | **1** (0.38) | **266** (100) |
| **ACTIVE DELTA** | | | | | | | | |
| *IV. HE WESTERN SUNDARBANS* | | | | | | | | |
| 15. Sagar Island | — | 4 | 4 | 9 | 29 | — | — | 46 |
| 16. Kakdwip | — | — | 4 | 10 | 27 | 6 | 1 | 48 |
| 17. Namkhana | 3 | — | 1 | 3 | 20 | 1 | — | 28 |
| **TOTAL** % Distribution | **3** (2.46) | **4** (3.28) | **9** (7.38) | **22** (18.0) | **76** (62.30) | **7** (5.74) | **1** (0.82) | **122** (100) |
| *V. THE MIDDLE SUNDARBANS* | | | | | | | | |
| 18. Mathurapur | 10 | 30 | 29 | 23 | 20 | 9 | 4 | 125 |
| 19. Pathar Pratima | 3 | 5 | 9 | 25 | 45 | 3 | — | 90 |
| **TOTAL** % Distribution | **13** (6.05) | **35** (16.28) | **38** (17.67) | **48** (22.33) | **65** (30.23) | **12** (5.58) | **4** (1.86) | **215** (100) |
| *VI. EASTERN SUNDARBANS* | | | | | | | | |
| 20. Kultali | 1 | 4 | 6 | 11 | 20 | 9 | — | 51 |
| 21. Basanti | — | 6 | 9 | 19 | 24 | 9 | — | 67 |
| 22. Gosaba | — | — | 1 | 9 | 32 | 7 | 1 | 50 |
| **TOTAL** % Distribution | **1** (0.59) | **10** (5.95) | **16** (9.52) | **39** (23.21) | **76** (45.24) | **25** (14.88) | **1** (0.59) | **168** (100) |
| **TOTAL OF S.24 Parganas % Dist. of Total Villages.** | **90 (4.18)** | **262 (12.18)** | **500 (23.25)** | **635 (29.52)** | **550 (25.57** | **101 (4.70)** | **13 (0.60)** | **2151 (100)** |

the Hugli Industrial Belt. Their connectivity is mainly through two branches of the local railway. One branch connects Calcutta with Budge Budge and the other connects Diamond Harbour with Calcutta. The towns here include Pachur, Gopalpur, Gobindpur, Parui and Joka of Thakurpukur - Metiaburuz. In Maheshtala they include Nangi, Batanagar, Jagannathgarh, Raypur, Chata Kalikapur, Noapara, Krishnagar, Jalkhura, Maheshtala, Memanpur, Chandannagar, and Daulatpur. Budge Budge includes the towns of Uttar Raypur, Budge Budge, Birlapur, Bowali, Dakshin Raypur, Pujali, Chak Alampur, Chak Kasipur and Nischintapur. Diamond Harbour includes only one town by the same name. Budge Budge is the most important class II town here, on the Hugli. Its locational advantage supports a base comprising of loading of petroleum and ancillary industries. Other industrial towns include Batanagar and Birlapur, both class III. Diamond Harbour, class III is the sub-divisional headquarters, the town originally developing as an ancient fishing port, at the mouth of Hugli.

### *The Middle Mature Delta of the Hugli*

The towns of this region also have close proximity with Calcutta, and good connectivity. Two branches of the local railway connects Sonarpur, Baruipur, Mograhat with Diamond Harbour; its branch line passes through Jaynagar into Kulpi via Mandir Bazar. The towns of this region include Rajpur, Sonarpur, Laskarpur, Barhans Fartabad, Sripur Bagherghol, Tentulberia, Chauhati and Kumrakhali of Sonarpur. In Bishnupur they are Bishnupur, Kanyanagar and Amtala, and in Baruipur they are Baruipur and Champahati. The important towns of the region include Baruipur, class III, situated on the bank of the now silted Adi Ganga. Market gardening around the town specializing in fruits to cater to the Calcutta market, has increased its importance as a market gardening centre. Rajpur, class II is a satellite township of Calcutta. Jaynagar-Mazilpur, class IV is the block headquarters with a strong agrarian base. Sonarpur, class IV is another satellite town of Calcutta. Bishnupur, class V constitutes the block headquarters.

### *The Piyali Bidyadhari Plains*

Lying to the East, this region is relatively far from Calcutta has only one urban centre. Port Canning, class III has grown up into a town from the British days. It has a river front location, being located on the Matla and forming the gateway and break of bulk town catering to the interior Sundarbans. It is also the end terminus of the local railway line running from Calcutta. Agricultural items and fish constitute the most important commodities handled by the town.

### 4.4.2 Spacing of Urban Settlements

As in case of rural settlements, here also the density of urban settlements i.e. the number of towns per sq.km and their hypothetical distances have been computed. Most of the towns are concentrated around the Calcutta Metropolitan District in the Western Hugli Flats and in the Middle Mature Delta region. Here the areal densities are 23 towns per 100 sq. km. in Maheshtala, 16 in Thakurpukur Metiaburuz, 6 in Budge Budge, 5 in Sonarpur and one each in Bishnupur and Baruipur. In Diamond Harbour, Jaynagar and Canning the figure is extremely low since they contain 1 town per block each.

The hypothetical distances or Hd reveal lowest urban spacing of 6.20 km in the Western Hugli Side Flats and highest of 10.75 in the Middle Mature Delta. Blockwise the gradation reveals 2.24 km. in Maheshtala, 2.69 km in Thakurpukur, 4.39 km in Budge Budge, 4.81 km in Sonarpur, 10.75 km in Bishnupur and 11.33 km in Baruipur.

### 4.4.3 Dispersion of Urban Settlements

The nearest neighbour statistic of the 42 towns of the district also represents a $R_n$ value of 0.19, indicative of *nearing complete clustering*

Mean observed spacing or $r_o$, km = 0.81190
and expected spacing $r_e$, km = 4.1776
The standard error or $\sigma r_e$ value = 0.34
and the $Z$ stands at 9.90 being significant at 1% level.

### 4.4.4 Size and Concentration of Urban Settlements

Table 4.6 reveals the concentration of area and population of the urban settlements at the region and block level. In 1991, the highest areal concentration, 13 sq.km is seen in Canning and lowest of 2.13 sq.km in Maheshtala. The highest population concentration in 1991 is seen in Canning, and the lowest in Bishnupur. Thus both area and opulation-wise Canning Town of the Piyali Bidyadhari Plains stands ighest.

**TABLE 4.6 : Concentration of Urban Settlements 1981 - 1991 (Based on area and Population)**

| *Geo-Ecological Region/Block* | *Area / 1981* | *Town 1991* | *Population / Town 1981* | *1991* |
|---|---|---|---|---|
| 2 | 3 | 4 | 5 | 6 |
| **STABLE DELTA** | | | | |
| *I. THE WESTERN HUGLI SIDE FLATS* | | | | |
| 1. Thakurpukur-Metiaburuz | 4.67 | 2.80 | 26,490 | 23,138 |
| 2. Mahestala | 2.84 | 2.13 | 15,489 | 21,866 |
| 3. Budge Budge | 6.40 | 3.56 | 27,043 | 19,609 |
| 4. Diamond Harbour | 9.00 | 9.00 | 20,299 | 30,266 |
| **TOTAL** | **4.48** | **2.99** | **20,799** | **21,660** |
| *II. THE MIDDLE MATURE DELTA OF THE HUGLI* | | | | |
| 5. Sonarpur | 7.53 | 3.76 | 20,999 | 17,947 |
| 6. Bishnupur | 3.30 | 1.10 | 12,218 | 4,676 |
| 7. Baruipur | 9.10 | 4.55 | 26,229 | 22,420 |
| 8. Jaynagar | 5.20 | 5.20 | 16,343 | 20,217 |
| **TOTAL** | **6.81** | **3.41** | **19,826** | **15,904** |
| *III. THE PIYALI BIDYADHARI PLAINS IN THE EAST* | | | | |
| 9. Canning | 13.00 | 13.00 | 25,203 | 33,904 |
| **TOTAL** | **13.00** | **13.00** | **25,203** | **33,904** |
| **DISTRICT AVERAGE** | **5.43** | **3.36** | **20,707** | **20,033** |

### 4.4.5 Size Classification of Urban Settlements

Table 4.7 depicts the population size classes of the towns. Nineteen towns fall in the size group of 5000 to 10,000 persons, class V, highest number being seen in the Western Hugli Side Flats, class IV occupies the next category followed by class III. There are only four class II towns with over 50,000 persons and three of them are located in the Western Hugli Side Flats.

South 24-Parganas besides showing a clustering of towns in a particular region, also exhibit the lack of class I towns and a fewer upper class town exists. The engulfment of higher class towns as for example that of South Suburban and Jadavpur, class I each, into the Calcutta Municipality is the main reason for this. The smaller towns remain to function under the urban shadow imposed by the CMD. Again the Active Delta with a good areal extent lacks urban development in general.

**TABLE 4.7 : Size Classification of Urban Settlements - 1991**

| *Geo-Ecological Region/Block* | | *Class II* | *Class III* | *Class IV* | *Class V* | *Class VI* |
|---|---|---|---|---|---|---|
| *1* | *2* | *3* | *4* | *5* | *6* | *7* |
| *I.* | *THE WESTERN HUGLI SIDE FLATS* | | | | | |
| 1. | Thakurpukur Metiaburuz | 1 | — | 1 | 2 | 1 |
| 2. | Mahestala | 1 | 1 | 3 | 8 | — |
| 3. | Budge Budge | 1 | 1 | 3 | 3 | — |
| 4. | Diamond Harbour | — | 1 | — | — | — |
| | **TOTAL** | **3** | **3** | **7** | **13** | **1** |
| *II.* | *THE MIDDLE MATURE DELTA* | | | | | |
| 5. | Sonarpur | 1 | — | 4 | 3 | — |
| 6. | Bishnupur | — | — | — | 2 | 1 |
| 7. | Baruipur | — | 1 | — | 1 | — |
| 8. | Jaynagar Mazilpur | — | 1 | — | — | — |
| | **TOTAL** | **1** | **2** | **4** | **6** | **1** |
| *III.* | *THE PIYALI BIDYADHARI PLAINS* | | | | | |
| 9. | Canning | — | 1 | — | — | — |
| | **TOTAL** | **0** | **1** | — | — | — |
| | **DISTRICT TOTAL** | **4** | **6** | **11** | **19** | **2** |

## 4.4.6 Rank Size Distribution of Urban Settlements

In the next section, a rank size relationship of the 42 urban centres has been worked out according to 1991 data by using the formula

$$Pr = KR - b^{28}.$$

For the 42 urban centres of South 24-Parganas in 1991, the equation of log *Pr* (*y*) and *R* (*x*) is as follows:

$$\log P_r = 5.17 - 0.87 \log R$$

where $\log K = 5.17$ and $b = 0.87$

The values of *b* here is significant at .01 per cent level of significance. The coefficient of determination of the equation was found to be 0.9846; i.e. 98.46 per cent variations in log *Pr* are being explained by log *R*. This is a very high level of explanation, which is rarely found in any bivariate case. The population of the 42 cities and towns of South 24-Parganas is given in the following table in the form of their estimated population, according to their rank size rule, actual population, difference and per cent difference.

From Table 4.8 it is evident that Budge Budge stands as the primate town of South 24-Parganas reaching nearly double the population strength of Panchur (Thakurpukur - Metiaburuz block). Both of these towns exhibit lower population than the estimated one. This fact is seen both at the upper and the lower ends specially where actual population fall short of the expected population. In 24 cases, however the actual population are greater than the estimated ones. Average discrepancy between the actual and expected size of the individual centres irrespective of their size show that central place spectrum of South-24 Parganas deviates slightly from the Rank Size Rule. Among the block headquarters, Budge Budge ranks highest, followed by Baruipur, (5th), then Port Canning (6th), Diamond Harbour (7th), Jaynagar-Mazilpur (10th), Sonarpur (13th), Maheshtala (30th) and lastly Bishnupur (41st) all in the Stable Delta.

Thus Khan and Wanmali (1972) states that, “Population distribution patterns emerge in frameworks ranging from very simple to very complex forms of spatial economic organisation. In the first case, the resultant distribution tends to have greater degree of primary and in latter the outcome approximates the Rank Size Rule and can be summed up in the form of a stochastic process. Movement from less complex to more complex economic organisation is also likely to be a movement towards Rank Size Regularity”.

## 4.5 CONCLUSION

The Sundarban Delta provides a micro level diversified picture amidst the overall monotony. The region ranges in all forms, shapes and types of settlements starting from individual dispersed hamlets, to tightly nucleated clusters, local factors of natural and cultural landscape affecting the type in each case. The nearest neighbour statistics again underlies the uniformity in the spacing, whereas the village size analysis has helped us to recognize the concentration of settlements. In this regard the Active Delta has exhibited highest areal concentration.

The case with the urban settlements had been somewhat different. Lack of higher class towns, their clustering in particular pockets and absence in others is a striking feature irrespective of its rich historical past. The overshadowing influence of the Calcutta District is a major hinderance lying in the way of their development.

**TABLE 4.8 : Rank Size Rule of Urban Centres-1991**

| *City/Town* | *Rank* | *Estimated Population* | *Actual Population* | *Difference* | *Difference %* |
|---|---|---|---|---|---|
| *1* | *2* | *3* | *4* | *5* | *6* |
| Budge Budge | 1 | 1,47,682 | 77,575 | +70,107 | +47.47 |
| Panchur | 2 | 81,283 | 77,547 | + 3,736 | + 4.60 |
| Rajpur | 3 | 56,873 | 63,210 | - 6,337 | -11.14 |
| Nangi | 4 | 44,280 | 52,956 | - 8,676 | -19.59 |
| Baruipur | 5 | 36,467 | 37,659 | - 1,192 | - 3.27 |
| Canning | 6 | 31,118 | 33,904 | - 2,786 | - 8.95 |
| Diamond Harbour | 7 | 27,212 | 30,266 | - 3,054 | -11.22 |
| Batanagar | 8 | 24,228 | 27,421 | - 3,193 | -13.18 |
| Birlapur | 9 | 21,868 | 24,465 | - 2,597 | -11.88 |
| Jaynagar Mazilpur | 10 | 19,953 | 20,217 | - 264 | - 1.32 |
| Jagannathgarh | 11 | 18,365 | 18,310 | + 55 | + 0.30 |
| Uttar Raypur | 12 | 17,026 | 17,547 | - 521 | - 0.03 |
| Sonarpur | 13 | 15,881 | 16,672 | - 791 | - 4.98 |
| Gopalpur | 14 | 14,889 | 16,566 | - 1677 | -11.26 |
| Laskarpur | 15 | 14,022 | 16,304 | - 2282 | -16.27 |
| Chata Kalikapur | 16 | 13,256 | 16,247 | - 2991 | -22.56 |
| Barhans Fartabad | 17 | 12,575 | 14,669 | - 2094 | -16.65 |
| Bowali | 18 | 11,965 | 12,994 | - 1029 | - 8.60 |
| Sripur Bagherghol | 19 | 11,415 | 12,937 | - 1522 | -13.33 |
| Dakshin Raypur | 20 | 10,917 | 10,996 | - 79 | - 0.72 |
| Pujali | 21 | 10,463 | 10,112 | + 351 | + 3.35 |
| Noapara | 22 | 10,048 | 9,828 | + 224 | + 2.23 |
| Gobindopur | 23 | 9,667 | 9,480 | + 187 | + 1.93 |
| Kanyanagar | 24 | 9,316 | 9,262 | + 54 | + 0.58 |
| Krishnagar | 25 | 8,991 | 9,222 | - 231 | - 2.57 |
| Chak Alampur | 26 | 8,690 | 8,699 | - 9 | - 0.10 |
| Jalkhura | 27 | 8,408 | 8,531 | - 123 | - 1.46 |
| Chak Kasipur | 28 | 8,147 | 8,328 | - 181 | - 2.22 |
| Tentulberia | 29 | 7,902 | 8,162 | - 260 | - 3.29 |
| Maheshtala | 30 | 7,672 | 7,831 | - 159 | - 2.07 |
| Parui | 31 | 7,456 | 7,658 | - 202 | - 2.71 |
| Champahati | 32 | 7,253 | 7,180 | + 73 | + 1.01 |
| Memanpur | 33 | 7,061 | 7,002 | + 59 | + 0.84 |
| Chauhati | 34 | 6,880 | 6,569 | + 311 | + 4.52 |
| Chandannagar | 35 | 6,709 | 6,335 | + 374 | + 5.57 |
| Daulatpur | 36 | 6,547 | 6,132 | + 415 | + 6.34 |
| Amtala | 37 | 6,392 | 6,009 | + 383 | + 5.99 |
| Nischintapur | 38 | 6,246 | 5,764 | + 482 | + 7.12 |
| Raypur | 39 | 6,106 | 5,558 | + 548 | + 8.97 |
| Kumarakhali | 40 | 5,973 | 5,053 | + 920 | +15.40 |
| Bishnupur | 41 | 5,846 | 4,766 | + 1,080 | +18.47 |
| Joka | 42 | 5,725 | 4,438 | + 1,287 | +22.48 |

## REFERENCES

1. Gerasimov, I.P. *et al.*, (eds) (1975), *Man Society And Environment*, Progress Publishers Moscow, p. 234.

2. Daniel Peter, Michael Hopkinson (1986), *The Geography o, ettlement*, Oliver and Boyd, Edinburg, p.7.

3. Mitra Ashok (1954), *District Handbooks*, 24-Parganas West Bengal (Census of 1951), West Bengal Government Press Alipore, p. xvii,.

4. Hunter, W.W.(1875), *A Statistical Account of Bengal, 24 Parganas and Sundarbans*. Trubunor and Co. London p. 297.

5. Lots or Lats - The name give to a parcel of land freshly reclaimed in the Sundarbans, later they may grow into a village or a Mauza village.

6. Mukherjee, K.N. (1983), "History of Settlement in the Sundarban of West Bengal" *Indian Journal of Landscape Systems* 6 (pt.1,2) pp. 1-19.

7. Hunter, W.W. (1875) *op.cit.* p. 299.

8. Ahmad, Enayat (1987), "Indian Village Pattern" in *Contributions to Indian Geography: Rural Geography* Vol.9 ed. by H.N. Mishra, Heritage Publishers, New Delhi p. 83.

9. Hudson, F.S.(1976), *Geography of Settlements*, Mac Donald and Evans, UK (second edition) p. 35.

10. Nitz, H.J., (1987), "Objectives and Methods of Geographical Research in the Evolution of Rural Settlement Regions", Ref. 8 *op.cit.* p. 19.

11. Taffe (1970), *Geography*, Englewood Cliff: Prentice Hall pp. 5-6.

12. *Ibid.*

13. Hudson, J.C. and P.M. Fowler, (1972), "The Concept of Pattern in Geography", in *Man Space and Environment* ed P.W. English and R.C. Mayfield, London, Oxford University Press p. 545.

14. Doxiadis, C.A. (1968), *Ekistics, An Introduction to The Science of Settlements*, New York: Oxford University Press. pp 33.

15. Singh, Rana P.B. (1975), "Pattern Analysis of Rural Settlement Distribution and Their Types in Saran Plain: A Quantitative Approach" in *Readings in Rural Settlement Geography*, eds. R.L. Singh, K.N. Singh and Rana P.B. Singh, Varanasi N.G.S.I. p. 281.

16. Bunge, W. (1962) *Theoretical Geography: Lund Studies in Geography*, Series No. 1, Chap. 3.

17. The 'bigha system' or land measurement into square and rectangular blocks is comparable to that of the Japanese 'Jori System', Chinese 'Han-den' and 'Jugerui' system of Italy.

18. Singh, Kailash Nath, Rana P.B. Singh and Dinesh K Singh (1976), "Spatial - characteristics of Rural Settlements and Their Types in a part of Middle Ganga Valley" in *Geographic Dimensions of Rural Settlements*. (Proceeding

of I.G.U. Varanasi Symposium Dec. 1-7, 1975) Edited by R.L. Singh, K.N. Singh and Rana P.B. Singh, National Geographical Society of India, pp. 140-141.

19. Stone, K.H., (1968) 'Multiple Scale Classification for Rural Settlement Geography', *Acta Geographica* (Helsinki), Vol.20, No. 22 pp. 307-317, reprinted in '*Readings in Rural Settlement Geography*', ed. R.L. Singh, K.N. Singh and Rana P.B. Singh, Varanasi NGSI Res. Pub. No. 14(1975).

20. Robinson, A.H. and J.A. Barnes, (1940), 'A New Method for the Representation of Dispersed Rural Population', *Geographical Review* 30 pp. 134-137.

21. Singh, Rana P.B. (1975), "Pattern Analysis of Rural Settlement distribution and their types in Saran Plain. A Quantitative Approach" in *Readings in Rural Settlement Geography*, eds. R.L. Singh, K.N. Singh and Rana P.B. Singh, Varanasi N.G.S.I. p. 117.

22. Dacey, M.F. (1966), "A County Seat Model, for the Areal Pattern of an Urban System". *Geographical Review*, V 50 pp. 527-42.

23. The first approach towards disperson analysis has been initiated by Clark and Evans in their analysis of the distributional pattern of various species over a given space. Later Dacey followed this approach and tested it in geographic context in a series of papers and was able to enlarge the family of probability density functions describing point and central place pattern.

24. Clark P.J. and F.C. Evans (1954), 'Distance to Nearest Neighbour as a Relationship in Population', *Ecology* 35, pp. 445 - 453.

25. Dacey, M.F. and Tze-hsiung Tung (1962) 'Identification of Randomness in Point Pattern' *Journal of Regional Science* 4, pp. 83-96.

26. Pawlowski, S. (1938), 'Encore une Methode de Representation Cartographique Generale de l 'Habitat Rural', Comtes Rendus du Congres *Interntional de Geographic*, Amsterdam, vol.2 Sect. A, pp. 129 - 30 (Leiden, 1938).

27. Monkhouse F.J. and H.R. Wilkinson (1980), *Maps And Diagrams*, B I Publications, New Delhi, pp 429-433.

28. The Rank Size Rule is an empirical regularity found in the urban system of many countries in the world. According to the rule the population of a town is related with its rank in the following form of Pareto's distribution

$$Pr = KR^{-b},$$

where $Pr$ is the population of the town whose rank is $R$, $K$ and $b$ are the constants. The above relationship gets transformed into the following linear form after taking the logarithm of both the sides

$$Y = a - bx$$

$$\text{where } Y = \log Pr$$

$$X = \log R$$

$$\text{and } a = \log K$$

The regularity in the above relationship was originally observed by Zipf (1941) and later on Berry (1961) also showed that this regularity prevails in many part of the world. Statistically this regularity can be examined by fitting a regression line of log *Pr* on log *R*. The regression coefficient of this line reflects the degree of primacy in the entire urban system and the coefficient of determination may be taken as a measurement of its goodness of fit to the rank- size regularity.

# 5

# INTER-REGIONAL PATTERN OF POPULATION AND HUMAN SETTLEMENTS

## 5.1 INTRODUCTION

In order to portray the micro-regional patterns, field work was carried out in 200 villages (Appendix V.1) to analyse the settlement pattern and the rural to rural and rural to urban interaction within the region, to confirm the observations made in the earlier part of the study and to build up general hypothesis regarding the various aspects of settlements. The sample for field work (Map 5.1) includes a random sampling on the basis of 100 villages from the Stable Delta of the Hugli in the North and 100 villages from the Active Delta of the Sundarbans in the South. Within the Stable Delta again the break up of the sample of the three subregions are 34 villages each in the Western Hugli side Flats and Middle-Mature Delta of the Hugli, and 32 villages in the Piyali-Bidyadhari Plains.

In the Active Delta, 42 villages each has been covered in the Western and Eastern Sundarbans, while 16 villages have been selected for the Middle Sundarbans.

The area surveyed comprises of 749.39 sq.km covering a total population of 44,9229 (1992-93) i.e. 9 per cent of the total rural population of South 24-Parganas (1991 census). The various aspects of study include, age of the settlements, site, natural resource base, environmental constraints and land use; human resource base, housing, civic amenities and infrastructural facilities. Besides major trade connections, village arts and crafts, existing development plans are also discussed. Finally, through a composite index based on selected indicators, the surveyed villages have been grouped under different levels of development.

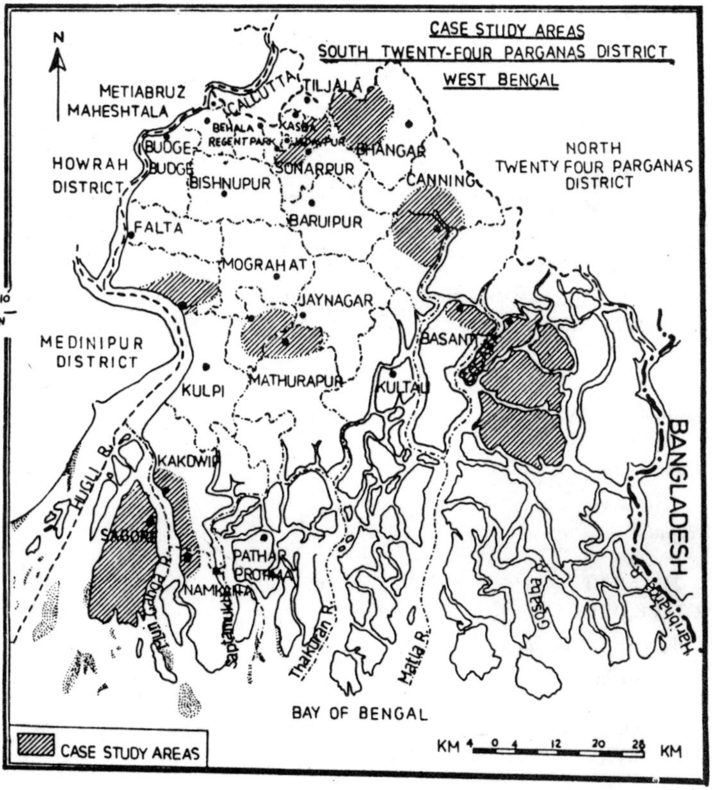


**MAP 5.1 :** Case Study Areas South Twenty-Four Parganas District West Bengal

## 5.2 AGE AND LOCATION PATTERN

### 5.2.1 Age

Most of the settlements here have *a recent origin*, their evolution being related to forest clearance, land reclamation and hence the

**TABLE 5.1 : Age and Location Pattern of Villalges—1992**

| *Geo ecological Regions/Blocks* | *Age of the Villages* | | | | *Origin of the Villages* | | |
|---|---|---|---|---|---|---|---|
| | *less than 50* | *50-100** | *100-150* | *More than 150* | *reclaim-ed land* | *around a temple* | *other histo-rical factors* |
| | *1* | *2* | *3* | *4* | *5* | *6* | *7* |
| **STABLE DELTA** | | | | | | | |
| *I. The Western Hugli Side Flats* | | | | | | | |
| Diamond Harbour | — | — | 34 | — | 34 | — | — |
| TOTAL I | | | | | | | |
| *II. The Middle Mature Hugli Delta* | | | | | | | |
| Sonarpur | (10) | (1) | (5) | — | (13) | — | — |
| Mandir Bazar | — | — | (18) | — | (18) | — | — |
| TOTAL II | 10 | 1 | 23 | — | 31 | 3 | — |
| *III. The Piyali Bidyadhari Plains—* | | | | | | | |
| Bhangar | | | | | | | |
| TOTAL III | — | — | 16 | 16 | 32 | 3 | — |
| **ACTIVE DELTA** | | | | | | | |
| *IV. Western Sundarbans* | | | | | | | |
| Sagar Island | — | (31) | (3) | — | 33 | — | 1 |
| Kakdwip | — | — | (2) | — | (2) | — | — |
| Namkhana | — | — | 6 | — | 6 | — | — |
| TOTAL IV | — | 31 | 11 | — | 41 | — | 1 |
| *V. Middle Sundarbans* | | | | | | | |
| Mathurapur | — | — | — | 16 | 16 | — | — |
| TOTAL V | | | | | | | |
| *VI. Eastern Sundarbans* | | | | | | | |
| Basanti | — | — | (14) | — | (14) | — | — |
| Gosaba | — | (27) | (1) | — | (21) | — | (7) |
| **TOTAL VI** | **—** | **27** | **15** | **—** | **35** | **—** | **7** |
| **TOTAL VILLAGES** | **10** | **59** | **99** | **32** | **189** | **3** | **8** |

* Figures in parenthesis include the blockwise information where more than one block has been selected for the region.

creation of 'abad' lands for cultivation during the British days.[1] The surveyed villages range in age from *less than 50 years to over 150 years*. Only 10 villages are under 50 years age (Table 5.1) and belong to Sonarpur in the Middle Mature Hugli Delta. These are very recent settlements near Calcutta, today marking the commuters zone previously being forested. 59 villages range in age between 50 to 100 years and of these 31 are located in the Western Sundarbans in Sagar, 27 in the Eastern Sundarbans in Gosaba and one only in the Middle Mature Delta in Sonarpur. Again 99 villages fall in the age group of 100 to 150 years, 34 being located in the Western Hugli Side Flats, 23 in the Middle Mature Hugli Delta, 16 in Piyali Bidyadhari Plains, 11 in Western Sundarbans and 15 in the Eastern Sundarbans. Finally 32 villages, 16 in the Piyali Bidhyadhari Plains and 16 in the Middle Sundarbans are more than 150 years in age. It is, therefore, evident that settlement evolution in the Active Delta specially in the fringe areas of Eastern and Western Sundarbans and also in Sonarpur near Calcutta in the Middle Mature Hugli Delta are of very recent origin.

Forest clearance and land reclamation resulted in the origin of 189 villages spread over all the six geo-ecological regions (Table 5.1). 3 villages in the Piyali Bidyadhari Plains have originated around temples in Bhangar. 8 settlements (one in Sagar and 7 in Gosaba) are of historical significance. Ganga Sagar in Sagar Island is famous for Kapil Muni's Ashram, one of the ancient pilgrimage centre's at the mouth of the Ganga. In the Eastern Sundarbans, 7 villages in Gosaba came up during the British period namely Gosaba, Rangabalia, Hamilton Abad, Annpur and Jamespur. Sir Daniel Hamilton converted the forest lands into abad lands in and around Gosaba; earlier being known as the Gosaba Estate. Annpur was named after his wife and Jamespur was named after his nephew, Sir James.

### 5.2.2 Site, Situation and Type

Table 5.1 shows the following broad physical sites identified for the villages : settlements on the *bank of a river* or a distributary with an embankment; on the *flood plain*; situated on the *coast*; or the settlement comprising an *island* by itself. Though broadly speaking, all the 200 settlements have a deltaic situation, 51 have riverine sites. River sites are discernable in the Stable Delta, whereas similar sites in the Active Delta, are along distributaries or 'Khals' with extensive

**TABLE 5.1 : (*Contd.*)**

| *Geo Ecological Regions/Blocks* | *Site and Situation* | | | | *Distance with the Nearest Urban Centre KILOMETERS* | | | | | |
|---|---|---|---|---|---|---|---|---|---|---|
| | *River or dis-tributory with embank-ment* | *Flood Plain* | *Coast* | *Island* | *1-15* | *16-30* | *31-45* | *46-60* | *61-75* | *76-90* |
| | *8* | *9* | *10* | *11* | *12* | *13* | *14* | *15* | *16* | *17* |
| **STABLE DELTA** | | | | | | | | | | |
| *I. The Western Hugli Side Flats* | | | | | | | | | | |
| Diamond Harbour | 10 | 24 | — | — | 34 | — | — | — | — | — |
| TOTAL I | | | | | | | | | | |
| *I. The Middle Mature Hugli Delta* | | | | | | | | | | |
| Sonarpur | — | (16) | — | — | (16) | — | — | — | — | — |
| Mandir Bazar | — | (18) | — | — | (17) | (1) | — | — | — | — |
| .TOTAL II | — | 34 | — | — | 33 | 1 | — | — | — | — |
| *III. The Piyali Bidyadhari Plains—* | | | | | | | | | | |
| Bhangar/ | | | | | | | | | | |
| TOTAL III | 7 | 25 | — | — | 2 | 14 | 11 | 5 | — | — |
| **ACTIVE DELTA** | | | | | | | | | | |
| *IV. Western Sundarbans* | | | | | | | | | | |
| Sagar Island | (15) | — | (15) | (4) | — | — | — | (1) | (17) | (16) |
| Kakdwip | (2) | — | — | — | — | — | — | (2) | — | — |
| Namkhana | — | — | (6) | — | — | — | — | — | (6) | — |
| TOTAL IV | 17 | — | 21 | 4 | — | — | — | 3 | 23 | 16 |
| *V. Middle Sundarbans* | | | | | | | | | | |
| Mathurapur | | | | | | | | | | |
| TOTAL V | 5 | 11 | — | — | 14 | 2 | — | — | | |
| *VI. Eastern Sundarbans* | | | | | | | | | | |
| Basanti | (10) | (4) | — | — | (12) | (2) | — | — | — | — |
| Gosaba | (2) | — | (15) | (11) | — | — | (3) | (13) | (4) | (8) |
| **TOTAL VI** | **12** | **4** | **15** | **11** | **12** | **2** | **3** | **13** | **4** | **8** |
| **TOTAL VILLAGES** | **51** | **98** | **36** | **15** | **95** | **19** | **14** | **21** | **27** | **24** |

stretches of embankments. Rivers sites are typical of 10 villages in the Western Hugli Side Flats, and 7 in the Piyali Bidyadhari Plains; whereas distributary with an embankment is a popular site in 17 villages in the Western sundarbans, 5 in the Middle and 12 in the Eastern Sundarbans.

98 villages in the Delta are situated away from river having a flood plain location mostly in the Stable Delta. Of these, 24 are in the Western Hugli Side Flats, 34 in the Middle Mature Delta, 25 in the Piyali Bidyadhari Plains, 11 in the Middle Sundarbans and 4 in the Eastern part.

Coastal and Island situation is typical of the villages of the Active Delta only. 36 villages have coastal boundary of which 21 are in the Western Sundarbans in Sagar and Namkhana associated with their sand dunes (Chapter 3) and 15 in the Eastern Sundarbans in Gosaba. 15 villages are islands by themselves, 4 being in the Sagar Block and 11 in Gosaba.

The location of the villages in respect to the nearest urban centre reveals 32 villages in Bhangar are situated near Calcutta, 42 villages near Port Canning, i.e., 14 in Basanti and 28 in Gosaba. 76 villages are situated near Diamond Harbour Town i.e., 34 in Diamond Harbour Block, 2 in Kakdwip and 6 in Namkhana. 34 villages are located near Jayanagar-Mazilpur of which 18 are in Mandir Bazar and 16 in Mathurapur. Again 14 villages of Sonarpur are situated near Sonarpur-Rajpur and 2 near Barhans Fartabad.

Their respective distances with these urban centres reveal that 95 villages are situated less than 15 km from the nearest urban centre. Of these, 34 are in the Western Hugli Side Flats, 33 in the Middle Mature Delta, 2 in the Piyali Bidyadhari Plains, 14 in the Middle Sundarbans and 12 in the Eastern Sundarbans. Again 19 villages lie in between 16 to 30 km from the urban centre, mostly in the Piyali Bidyadhari Plains. 14 villages lie within 31—45 km, again mostly in the Piyali Bidyadhari Plains. 21 villages mostly in the Eastern Sundarbans lie in between 46-60 km; 27 within 61-75 km mostly in the Western Sundarbans and finally 24 settlements of the Western (16 villages) and Eastern (8 villages) lie 76 to 90 km from the nearest urban centre. Thus the villages of the Active Delta specially in the Western Sundarbans followed by the Eastern Sundarbans are located at great distances from their nearest urban centres.

The settlements reveal 100 villages mostly in the Stable Delta are of *agglomerated* type; the highest of which being discernable in the Western Hugli Side Flats and in the Piyali-Bidyadhari Plains, i.e., 32 villages each, followed by the Middle Mature Delta with 26 settlements; and Middle Sundarbans exhibiting 10 settlements. *Semi-agglomerated* type characterise 58 villages in the transitional area in between complete agglomeration in the North to complete dispersion near the littoral. Finally 42 villages of the Sundarbans are of *dispersed* nature, the highest are in the Eastern Sundarbans in Gosaba, followed by the Western Sundarbans.

Of the external shapes and forms, 59 villages in general are of *rectangular* type common to the Stable Delta. Another 59 are linear in shape. *Linear* shapes are common along major national highways such as 12 villages in Bhangar, and also along extensive stretches of embankments bordering the Khals as in the Western Sundarbans in Sagar, Kakdwip, Namkhana and also in the Eastern Sundarbans in Basanti and Gosaba. Apart from this, 26 villages are *circular* in shape, 18 square shaped and 38 villages have no particular shape or are *amorphous*.

The distance of the surveyed villages with respect to Calcutta, can be grouped into four classes. The Middle Mature Delta in Sonarpur and the Piyali Bidyadhari Plains in Bhaugar are situated at a distance less than 40 km. There are 40 villages in this category all in the above mentioned subregions. 87 villages are located at a distance of 41 to 70 km mostly in the Stable Delta and also in the Middle and Eastern Sundarbans. Most of the Active Delta villages lie at a distance over 75 km from Calcutta. 25 fall in the size class of 71 to 100 km and 48 villages in more than 100 km. (Table 5.2)

## 5.3 NATURAL RESOURCE BASE AND ENVIRONMENTAL CONSTRAINTS

As discerned in the second chapter, being part of the Bengal Delta, the region comprises of extensive stretches of flat aggradational plain, ample supply of water, fertile soil cover, saline in the South and Tidal Mangrove Forests and Swamps in the Southern littoral, flourishing under a humid climatic cover of the Deltaic Type of Tropical Monsoons.

**TABLE 5.2 : Characteristics of Rural Settlements**

| *Geo Econogical Resions/Blocks* | *Distance From Calcutta* | | | | *Settlement Type* | | |
|---|---|---|---|---|---|---|---|
| | *Less than 40 km** | *40-70 km* | *70-100 km* | *More than 100 km* | *Agglomerated* | *Semi-Agglomerated* | *Dispersed* |
| | *1* | *2* | *3* | *4* | *5* | *6* | *7* |
| **STABLE DELTA** | | | | | | | |
| *I. The Western Hugli Side Flats* | | | | | | | |
| Diamond Harbour | — | 34 | — | — | 32 | 2 | — |
| *II. The Middle Mature Hugli Delta* | | | | | | | |
| Sonarpur | (16) | — | — | — | (16) | — | — |
| Mandir Bazar | — | (18) | — | — | (10) | (8) | — |
| TOTAL | 16 | 18 | — | — | 26 | 8 | — |
| *III. The Piyali Bidyadhari Plains—* | | | | | | | |
| Bhangar | 24 | 8 | — | — | 32 | — | — |
| **ACTIVE DELTA** | | | | | | | |
| *IV. Western Sundarbans* | | | | | | | |
| Sagar Island | — | — | — | (34) | — | (19) | (15) |
| Kakdwip | — | — | (2) | — | — | — | (2) |
| Namkhana | — | — | — | (6) | — | (3) | (3) |
| TOTAL | — | — | 2 | 40 | — | 22 | 20 |
| *V. Middle Sundarbans* | | | | | | | |
| Mathurapur | — | 13 | 3 | — | 10 | 6 | — |
| *VI. Eastern Sundarbans* | | | | | | | |
| Basanti | — | (14) | — | — | — | (6) | (8) |
| Gosaba | — | — | (20) | (8) | — | (14) | (14) |
| **TOTAL** | **—** | **(14)** | **(20)** | **(8)** | **—** | **(20)** | **(22)** |
| **TOTAL VILLAGES** | **40** | **87** | **25** | **48** | **100** | **58** | **42** |

* Figures within parenthesis refers to blockwise information where more than one block has been selected for the region.

The soil types Table 5.3 of the surveyed villages comprise of *clays, silts, sands* or a combination of these having *saline* and *non-saline phases*. Clayey loams characterise most of the Stable Delta villages and 111 villáges in general fall in this category. Silty clay loam with a saline phase, is a characteristic of 47 villages mostly in the Eastern Sundarbans and partly in the Western Sundarbans. Typical sandy clay loam occur only in a pocket covering 3 villages in Bhangar in the Piyali Bidyadhari Plains. However, such a soil having a saline phase covers 37 villages nearly all in the Western Sundarbans specially in Sagar. Finally only 2 villages in Bhangar have a combination of silty, sandy and clayey loams.

Natural drainage systems like the Muri Ganga, Sapta-Mukhi, Thakuran, Matla, Piyali and Bidyadhari, etc., provide good drainage to 102 or 51 per cent of the surveyed villages. These villages are also drained by an extensive network of distributaries or Khals, "do-aniya khals" and creeks; being mostly common in the Sundarban Region. Remaining 98 villages mostly in the Stable Delta lack natural drainage facilities.

Forested tracts are limited to the Sundarban Region to the South. Here, 36 villages are surrounded by tidal forests and mangrove swamps. 28 of these are located in Gosaba, 5 in Basanti and 3 in Mathurpur.

The surveyed villages are located mostly in the *environmental hazard prone* area comprising of tropical depressions, storms, cyclones, incessant rainfall, tidal bores and other related phenomena specially during the pre monsoon and the post monsoon period, thereby causing heavy damage.

134 villages were affected by storms, cyclones and related phenomena till the period of survey, mostly in the Active Delta regions, (Table 5.3). 66 villages were affected by storms only in the Stable Deltaic region demonstrating thereby that the fury of the Bay cyclones is greater towards the littoral. The frequency of these storms and cyclones range from 2 to 4 per year. Storms and cyclones accompanied by broken embankments and tidal insurgence lead to widespread destruction of crops, buildings and livestock. Damages caused during the past one year (Table 5.3) include crop destruction in 30 villages, crops and buildings (mostly *kutcha* homes) destroyed in 88 villages; crops, buildings destroyed together with broken embankments in 49 villages and in one village livestock was affected, along with the above mentioned destructions.

## 5.4 HUMAN RESOURCE BASE

In this section an inventory of human resources of the surveyed settlements has been made under the following heads; distribution and density of population; religion and caste composition; and finally the pattern of migration.

**TABLE 5.3 : Natural Resource Base And Environmental Constraints**

| *Geo-ecological Regions/Blocks* | *Nature of the Soil* | | | | | *Natural Drainage* | | *Natural Hazards* | |
|---|---|---|---|---|---|---|---|---|---|
| | *Clayey loam (Saline)* | *Silty clay loam* | *Sandy clay loam* | *Sandy clay loam (Saline)* | *Silty and Sandy clay loam* | *Existent* | *Non existent* | *Storms* | *Storm & cyclones and related phenomena* |
| | *1* | *2* | *3* | *4* | *5* | *6* | *7* | *8* | *9* |
| **STABLE DELTA** | | | | | | | | | |
| *I. The Western Hugli Side Flats* | | | | | | | | | |
| Diamond Harbour/ | 34 | — | — | — | — | 10 | 24 | — | 34 |
| TOTAL I | | | | | | | | | |
| *II. The Middle Mature Hugli Delta* | | | | | | | | | |
| Sonarpur | (16)* | — | — | — | — | — | (16) | (16) | — |
| Mandir Bazar | (18) | — | — | — | — | — | (18) | (18) | — |
| TOTAL II | 34 | — | — | — | — | — | 34 | 34 | — |
| *III. The Piyali Bidyadhari Plains—* | | | | | | | | | |
| Bhangar | | | | | | | | | |
| TOTAL III | 27 | — | 3 | — | 2 | 7 | 25 | 32 | — |

**TABLE 5.3 : (*Contd.*)**

| *Geo-ecological Regions/Blocks* | *Nature of the Soil* | | | | | *Natural Drainage* | | *Natural Hazards* | |
|---|---|---|---|---|---|---|---|---|---|
| | *Clayey loam (Saline)* | *Silty clay loam* | *Sandy clay loam* | *Sandy clay loam (Saline)* | *Silty and Sandy clay loam* | *Existent* | *Non existent* | *Storms* | *Storm & cyclones and rela-ted phenomena* |
| | *1* | *2* | *3* | *4* | *5* | *6* | *7* | *8* | *9* |
| **ACTIVE DELTA** | | | | | | | | | |
| *IV. Western Sundarbans* | | | | | | | | | |
| Sagar Island | — | — | — | (34) | — | (34) | — | — | (34) |
| Kakdwip | — | (2) | — | — | — | (2) | — | — | (2) |
| Namkhana | — | (4) | — | (2) | — | (6) | — | — | (6) |
| TOTAL IV | — | 6 | — | 36 | — | 42 | — | — | 42 |
| *V. Middle Sundarbans* | | | | | | | | | |
| Mathurapur/TOTAL V | 16 | — | — | — | — | 5 | 11 | — | 16 |
| *VI. Eastern Sundarbans* | | | | | | | | | |
| Basanti | — | (14) | — | — | — | (10) | (4) | — | (14) |
| Gosaba | — | (27) | — | (1) | — | (28) | — | — | (28) |
| TOTAL VI | — | 41 | — | 1 | — | 38 | 4 | — | 42 |
| **TOTAL VILLAGES** | **111** | **47** | **3** | **37** | **2** | **102** | **98** | **66** | **134** |

* Figures in parenthes include the blockwise information where more than one block has been selected for the region.

**TABLE 5.3 : (*Contd.*)**

| *Geo-ecological Regions/Blocks* | *Damages caused during the last one year* | | | | |
|---|---|---|---|---|---|
| | *Crops destroyed* | *Crops and buildings* | *Crops and buildings embankments* | *Crops buildings embankments livestock* | *Insignificant* |
| | *10* | *11* | *12* | *13* | *14* |
| **STABLE DELTA** | | | | | |
| *I. The Western Hugli Side Flats* | | | | | |
| Diamond Harbour/ Total I | — | 34 | — | — | — |
| *II. The Middle Mature Hugli Delta* | | | | | |
| Sonarpur | — | — | — | — | (16) |
| Mandir Bazar | (18) | — | — | — | — |
| Total II | 18 | — | — | — | 16 |
| *III. The Piyali Bidyadhari Plains—* | | | | | |
| Bhangar | | | | | |
| **TOTAL III** | **2** | **14** | — | — | **16** |

**TABLE 5.3 : (*Contd.*)**

| *Geo-ecological Regions/Blocks* | *Damages caused during the last one year* | | | | |
|---|---|---|---|---|---|
| | *Crops destroyed* | *Crops and buildings* | *Crops and buildings embankments* | *Crops buildings embankments livestock* | *Insignificant* |
| | *10* | *11* | *12* | *13* | *14* |
| **ACTIVE DELTA** | | | | | |
| *IV. Western Sundarbans* | | | | | |
| Sagar Island | — | (13) | (21) | — | — |
| Kakdwip | — | (2) | — | — | — |
| Namkhana | — | — | (6) | — | — |
| TOTAL IV | — | 15 | 27 | — | — |
| *V. Middle Sundarbans* | | | | | |
| Mathurapur/TOTAL V | 10 | 6 | — | — | — |
| *VI. Eastern Sundarbans* | | | | | |
| Basanti | — | (11) | (3) | — | — |
| Gosaba | — | (8) | (19) | (1) | — |
| TOTAL VI | — | 19 | 22 | 1 | — |
| **TOTAL VILLAGES** | **30** | **88** | **49** | **1** | **32** |

* Figures in parenthes include the blockwise information where more than one block has been selected for the region.

### 5.4.1 Distribution and Density of Population

The surveyed villages have an areal size ranging from 1.10 sq.km per village in the Western Hugli Side Flats to 6.96 sq.km per village in the Western sundarbans (Table 5.4). In general the Stable Delta have low areal sizes on an average being 1.46 sq. km in contrast to 6.03 sq. km of the Active Delta.

The average population size per village reveal low population size, 1153 persons in the Stable Delta and 2920 persons in the Active Delta. The lowest figure however occur in the Middle Mature Hugli Delta i.e., 1178 persons and the highest of 3369 persons in the Eastern Sundarbans.

Contrarily the density figures reveal higher densities in the villages of the Stable Delta on an average being 1073 persons per sq.km and a low density of 484 persons per sq. km in the Active Delta. The highest population density of the villages i.e., 556/sq. km occur in the Western Hugli Side Flats whereas the lowest of 427/ sq. km occur in the Western Sundarbans.

### 5.4.2 Caste and Religion

37.28 per cent of the total population of the surveyed settlements belong to the scheduled caste (Fig. 5.2) community and the respective figure of the scheduled tribes being 2.79 per cent only (Table 5.5). The highest proportion of scheduled caste is in the Eastern Sundarbans i.e., 58.59 per cent concentrated, mostly in Gosaba i.e., 64.75 per cent. Scheduled tribe population 0.92 per cent are found in the Western Sundarbans and 2.92 per cent in the Piyali Bidyadhari Plains. The tribals of Gosaba belong to the Mundari group who migrated from Chotanagpur are seen specially in the villages of Sadhupur forming the end limit of human habitation, and in Rajat Jubilee. Animism is widely practised here.

Hindus constitute the dominant religious group comprising of 83.25% of the total population of the surveyed villages. This is followed by the Muslims, the respective figure being 14.11per cent. Christians and tribal religions are noticeable in traces only in the Sundarbans, the figures here being 1.9 per cent and 0.75 per cent respectively.

**TABLE 5.4 : Population Characteristics of Surveyed Villages-1992**

| *Geo-Ecological Regions/Blocks* | *Number of villages* | *Total Area (sq.km)* | *Average Areal Size per Village* | *Total Popula-tion* | *Average Popula-tion* | *Density of popula-lation* | *Number of Occupied Residential Houses* | *Number of house-holds* |
|---|---|---|---|---|---|---|---|---|
| | *1* | *2* | *3* | *4* | *5* | *6* | *7* | *8* |
| **STABLE DELTA** | 100 | 146.51 | 1.46 | 157,275 | 1,573 | 1,073 | 27,288 | 27,369 |
| *I. The Western Hugli Side Flats* | | | | | | | | |
| Diamond Harbour | 34 | 37.39 | 1.10 | 58,177 | 1,711 | 1,556 | 10,201 | 10,186 |
| *II. The Middle Mature Hugli Delta* | | | | | | | | |
| Sonarpur | (16)* | (21.96) | (1.37) | (20,615) | (1,288) | (939) | (3,283) | (3,288) |
| Mandir Bazar | (18) | (14.89) | (0.83) | (19,455) | (1,081) | (1,307) | 3,588 | 3,600 |
| **TOTAL** | **34** | **36.85** | **1.08** | **40,070** | **1,179** | **1,087** | **6,871** | **6,888** |
| *III. The Piyali Bidyadhari Plains-* | | | | | | | | |
| Bhangar | 32 | 72.27 | 2.26 | 59,028 | 1,845 | 817 | 10,216 | 10,295 |

**TABLE 5.4** (*Contd.*)

| *Geo-Ecological Regions/Blocks* | *Number of villages* | *Total Area (Sq.Km)* | *Average Areal Size per Village* | *Total Popula-tion* | *Average Popula-tion* | *Density of popula-tion* | *Number of occupied Residential houses* | *Number of House-holds* |
|---|---|---|---|---|---|---|---|---|
| | *1* | *2* | *3* | *4* | *5* | *6* | *7* | *8* |
| **ACTIVE DELTA** | 100 | 602,88 | 6.03 | 291,954 | 2,920 | 484 | 52,663 | 52,752 |
| *IV. Western Sundarbans* | | | | | | | | |
| Sagar Island | (34) | (242.64) | (7.14) | (97,646) | (2,872) | (402) | (15,025) | (14,515) |
| Kakdwip | (2) | (15,72) | (7,86) | (8,507) | (4,254) | (541) | (1,382) | (1,398) |
| Namkhana | (6) | (33.92) | (5.65) | (18,598) | (3,100) | (548) | (2,723) | (3,120) |
| **TOTAL** | **42** | **292.28** | **6.96** | **125,751** | **2,970** | **427** | **19,130** | **19,033** |
| *V. Middle Sundarbans* | | | | | | | | |
| Mathurapur | 16 | 23,59 | 1,47 | 25,685 | 1,605 | 1,089 | 4,547 | 4,548 |
| *VI. Eastern Sundarbans* | | | | | | | | |
| Basanti | (14) | (71.61) | (5.12) | (38.741) | (2,767) | (541) | (6,798) | (6,853) |
| Gosaba | (28) | (215.40) | (7.69) | (102,777) | (3,671) | (477) | (22,188) | (22,318) |
| TOTAL | 42 | 287.01 | 6.83 | 141,518 | 3,369 | 493 | 28,986 | 29,171 |
| **TOTAL VILLAGES** | **200** | **749.39** | **3.75** | **449,229** | **2,246** | **599** | **79,951** | **80,121** |

* Data within parenthesis refers to blockwise breakup where more than one block has been selected for the region.

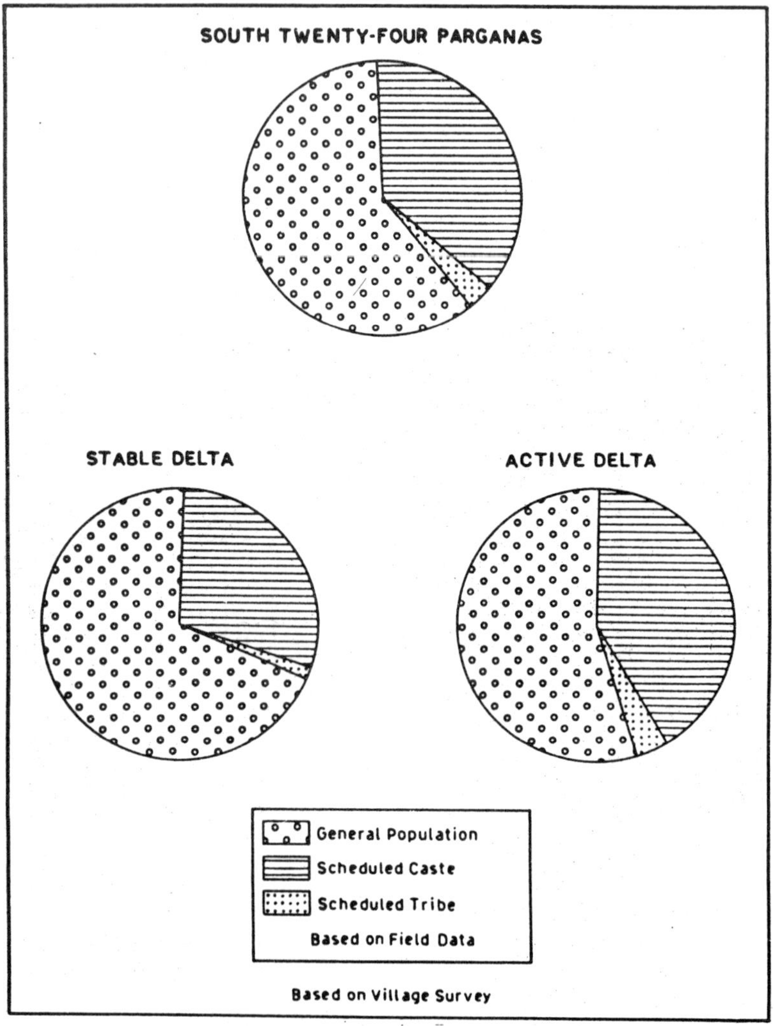


Fig 5.2 : South 24-Parganas : Proportion of Scheduled Caste & Tribe

### 5.4.3 Pattern of Migration

Land reclamation and forest clearance for the creation of "abads" have attracted streams of migrants in this region from the surrounding area specially in the South. In Sagar Island, migrants have come from the neighbouring Medinipur District as seen in the villages of Ganga-Sagar, Rudranagar etc. In Gosaba, migrants have infiltrated from the neighbouring Bangladesh as in Sadhupur, Annpur, Hamilton Abad, as well as traces of tribal Mundari population is seen here, who have migrated from Chotanagpur, Bihar some 100 years back. People from Bangladesh have also settled in Sonarpur near Calcutta some 75 years back.

The reasons behind immigration (Table 5.6.1) are economic or work, and 5 villages belong to this category. However, availability of 'abads' for settlement purpose and the system of land grants seem to be the most dominating reason in 112 (56%) villages mostly in the Active Delta in Eastern and Western Sundarbans. Other reasons such as marriage or political cause are insignificant being found only in 2 and 4 of the surveyed villages respectively.

The duration of immigration usually ranges from 20 years to over 75 years in these villages. In the Active Delta, people moved in more than 75 years ago. The place of origin of the immigrants include the same district in case of 11 villages in the Eastern Sundarbans, in Basanti; in 84 villages (located mostly in the Western and Eastern Sundarbans), migrants have come from the neighbouring districts like Medinipur, North Twenty-four Parganas, Hugli and Haora. In 5 villages (mostly in the Western Sundarbans), migrants arrived from the neighbouring states, Bihar and Orissa. In 17 villages, (mostly in the Middle Mature Hugli Delta in Sonarpur), migrants came from Bangladesh. Finally in 6 villages, (also in Sonarpur), people have moved in from Calcutta.

The surveyed villages also exhibit outmigration (Table 5.6.2). Of the reasons behind outmigration from the district, economic or for work seems to be the most dominating factor causing outmigration in 118 villages of the total, with the highest number of villages being in Sagar. The next important factor causing out migration is a combination of work, education and marriage as seen in 32 villages in the Piyali Bidyadhari Plains and in the Eastern Sundarbans.

**TABLE 5.5 : Caste and Religion (Proportion to Total Population)—1992**

| *Geo Ecological Resions/Blocks* | *Scheduled Caste** | *Scheduled Tribe* | *Hindu* | *Muslim* | *Christian* | *Others* |
|---|---|---|---|---|---|---|
| | *1* | *2* | *3* | *4* | *5* | *6* |
| **STABLE DELTA** | | | | | | |
| *I. The Western Hugli Side Flats* | — | — | — | — | — | — |
| Diamond Harbour | 17.71 | 0 | 82.50 | 17.50 | 0 | 0 |
| *II. The Middle Mature Hugli Delta* | | | | | | |
| Sonarpur | (28.26)* | (0) | (84.75) | (15.25) | (0) | (0) |
| Mandir Bazar | (32.73) | (0) | (91.21) | (8.79) | (0) | (0) |
| TOTAL | 30.43 | 0 | 87.96 | 12.00 | 0 | 0 |
| *III. The Piyali Bidyadhari Plains-* | | | | | | |
| Bhangar | 41.29 | 2.92 | 74.65 | 25.35 | 0 | 0 |
| **ACTIVE DELTA** | | | | | | |
| *IV. Western Sundarbans* | | | | | | |
| Sagar Island | (25.60) | (1.03) | (82.71) | (14.65) | (1.49) | (1.15) |
| Kakdwip | (28.49) | (0.52) | (96.25) | (3.75) | (0) | (0) |
| Namkhana | (17.23) | (0.54) | (95.61) | (4.390) | (0) | (0) |
| TOTAL | 24.55 | 0.92 | 91.50 | 7.60 | 1.49 | 1.15 |
| *V. Middle Sundarbans* | | | | | | |
| Mathurapur | 27.53 | 0 | 86.57 | 13.43 | 0 | 0 |
| *VI. Eastern Sundarbans* | | | | | | |
| Basanti | (42.24) | (2.64) | (78.56) | (18.31) | (2.15) | (0.98) |
| Gosaba | (64.75) | (8.42) | (73.21) | (19.20) | (5.21) | (2.38) |
| TOTAL | 58.59 | 6.84 | 75.81 | 18.72 | — | — |
| **Average of the surveyed settlements.** | **37.28** | **2.79** | **83.25** | **14.11** | **1.89** | **0.75** |

* Data within parenthesis refers to blockwise breakup where more than one block has been selected for the region.

The duration of out migration is much less, mostly in the range of 1 to 10 years as seen in 124 villages all over the Delta with a concentration in the Eastern and Western Sundarbans.

The destination of the out migrants are Calcutta from 74 villages (located mostly in the Stable Delta); and to the neighbouring district of Hugli, Haora and North Twenty Four Parganas in 77 villages—

**TABLE 5.6.1 : Migration Pattern of villages—Inmigration 1992**

| *Geo Ecological Resions/Blocks* | *REASONS FOR INMIGRATION* | | | | | *DURATION* | | | | | |
|---|---|---|---|---|---|---|---|---|---|---|---|
| | *Economic or work* | *Availab- ility of abad land* | *Marriage* | *Politi- cal* | *No Migra- tion* | *less than 1 yr.* | *1-10* | *11-20* | *20-75* | *More than 75* | *No inmi gra- tion* |
| | *1* | *2* | *3* | *4* | *5* | *6* | *7* | *8* | *9* | *10* | *11* |
| **STABLE DELTA** | | | | | | | | | | | |
| *I. The Western Hugli Side Flats* | | | | | | | | | | | |
| Diamond Harbour | — | — | — | 1 | 33 | — | — | 1 | — | | 33 |
| *II. The Middle Mature Hugli Delta* | | | | | | | | | | | |
| Sonarpur | — | (14)* | — | 2 | — | — | — | — | (16) | | |
| Mandir Bazar | — | (18) | — | — | — | — | — | — | | (18) | |
| TOTAL | — | 32 | — | 2 | — | — | — | — | 16 | 18 | |
| *III. The Piyali Bidyadhari Plains—* | | | | | | | | | | | |
| Bhangar | 2 | — | 2 | 1 | 27 | — | — | 1 | 4 | | 27 |

**TABLE 5.6.1 : (Contd.)**

| *Geo Ecological Resions/Blocks* | *REASONS FOR INMIGRATION* | | | | | *DURATION* | | | | | |
|---|---|---|---|---|---|---|---|---|---|---|---|
| | *Economic or work* | *Availability of abad land* | *Marriage* | *Political* | *No Migration* | *less than 1 yr.* | *1-10* | *11-20* | *20-75* | *More than 75* | *No immigration* |
| | *1* | *2* | *3* | *4* | *5* | *6* | *7* | *8* | *9* | *10* | *11* |
| **ACTIVE DELTA** | | | | | | | | | | | |
| *IV. Western Sundarbans* | | | | | | | | | | | |
| Sagar Island | — | (34) | — | — | — | — | — | — | — | (34) | |
| Kakdwip | — | — | — | — | (2) | — | — | — | — | — | (2) |
| Namkhana | — | (6) | — | — | — | — | — | — | — | (6) | |
| TOTAL | — | 40 | — | — | 2 | — | — | — | — | 40 | 2 |
| *V. Middle Sundarbans* | | | | | | | | | | | |
| Mathurapur | 1 | — | — | — | 15 | — | — | — | 1 | — | 15 |
| *VI. Eastern Sundarbans* | | | | | | | | | | | |
| Basanti | — | (14) | — | — | — | — | — | — | — | (14) | |
| Gosaba | (2) | (26) | — | — | — | (1) | (1) | — | — | (26) | |
| TOTAL | 2 | 40 | — | — | — | 1 | 1 | — | — | 40 | |
| **TOTAL VILLAGES** | **5** | **112** | **2** | **4** | **77** | **1** | **1** | **2** | **21** | **98** | **77** |
| %age | (2.5) | (56.0) | (1.0) | (2.0) | (38.5) | (0.5) | (0.5) | (1.00) | (10.5) | (49.0) | (38.9) |

* Figures within parenthesis refers to blockwise information where more than one block has been selected for the region.

**TABLE 5.6.1 : (*Contd..*)**

| *Geo ecological Regions/blocks* | *PLACE OF ORIGIN* | | | | | |
|---|---|---|---|---|---|---|
| | *Same District* | *Neighbouring District* | *Neighbouring State* | *Neighbouring Country* | *No inmigration* | *From Calcutta* |
| | *12* | *13* | *14* | *15* | *16* | *17* |
| **STABLE DELTA** | | | | | | |
| *I. The Western Hugli Side Flats* | | | | | | |
| Diamond Harbour | — | — | 1 | — | 33 | — |
| *II. The Middle Mature Hugli Delta* | | | | | | |
| Sonarpur | — | — | — | (10) | — | (6) |
| Mandir Bazar | — | (18) | — | — | — | — |
| TOTAL | — | 18 | — | 10 | — | 6 |
| *III. The Piyali Bidyadhari Plains—* | | | | | | |
| Bhangar | — | 2 | — | 3 | 27 | — |

**TABLE 5.6.1 : (*Contd.*)**

| *Geo Ecological Regions/Blocks* | *PLACE OF ORIGIN* | | | | | |
|---|---|---|---|---|---|---|
| | *Same District* | *Neighbouring District* | *Neighbouring State* | *Neighbouring Country* | *No inmigration* | *From Calcutta* |
| | *12* | *13* | *14* | *15* | *16* | *17* |
| **ACTIVE DELTA** | | | | | | |
| *IV. Western Sundarbans* | | | | | | |
| Sagar Island | — | (32) | (2) | — | — | — |
| Kakdwip | — | — | — | — | (2) | — |
| Namkhana | — | (5) | (1) | — | — | — |
| **TOTAL** | — | **37** | **3** | — | **2** | — |
| *V. Middle Sundarbans* | | | | | | |
| Mathurapur | — | 1 | — | — | 15 | — |
| *VI. Eastern Sundarbans* | | | | | | |
| Basanti | (11) | (3) | — | — | — | — |
| Gosaba | — | (23) | (1) | (4) | — | — |
| TOTAL | 11 | (26) | 1 | 4 | — | — |
| **TOTAL VILLAGES** | **11** | **84** | **5** | **17** | **77** | **6** |
| %age | (5.5) | (42.0) | (2.5) | (8.5) | (38.5) | (3.0) |

* Figures in parenthesis include the blockwise information where more than one block has been selected for the region.

**TABLE 5.6.2 : Migration Pattern of Villages Outmigration—1992**

| Geo Ecological Regions/Blocks | REASONS FOR OUTMIGRATION | | | | | DURATION | | | | | |
|---|---|---|---|---|---|---|---|---|---|---|---|
| | Economic or work | Education | Marriage | Work Educat-tion marriage | No out Migra-than | less than 1 yr. | 1-10 | 11-20 | 20-75 | More than 75 | No out migra-tion |
| | 1 | 2 | 3 | 4 | 5 | 6 | 7 | 8 | 9 | 10 | 11 |
| **STABLE DELTA** | | | | | | | | | | | |
| I. *The Western Hugli Side Flats* | | | | | | | | | | | |
| Diamond Harbour | 18 | — | — | — | 16 | 1 | 17 | — | — | | 16 |
| II. *The Middle Mature Hugli Delta* | | | | | | | | | | | |
| Sonarpur | — | — | — | — | (16) | — | — | — | — | | (16) |
| Mandir Bazar | (15)* | — | — | (3) | — | — | (13) | — | (1) | | (4) |
| **TOTAL** | **15** | — | — | **3** | **16** | — | **13** | — | **1** | — | **20** |
| III. *The Piyali Bidyadhari Plains—* | | | | | | | | | | | |
| Bhangar | 14 | — | 1 | 13 | 4 | 6 | 21 | — | 1 | 4 | |

**TABLE 5.6.2 :** (*Contd.*)

| Geo Ecological Regions/Blocks | REASONS FOR OUTMIGRATION | | | | | DURATION | | | | | |
|---|---|---|---|---|---|---|---|---|---|---|---|
| | Economic or work | Education | Marriage | Work Education marriage | No out Migration than | less than 1 yr. | 1-10 | 11-20 | 20-75 | More than 75 | No out migration |
| | 1 | 2 | 3 | 4 | 5 | 6 | 7 | 8 | 9 | 10 | 11 |
| **ACTIVE DELTA** | | | | | | | | | | | |
| IV. *Western Sundarbans* | | | | | | | | | | | |
| Sagar Island | (28) | — | — | (1) | (5) | — | (29) | — | | (5) | |
| Kakdwip | (2) | — | — | — | — | — | (2) | — | | | |
| Namkhana | (6) | — | — | — | — | (1) | (5) | — | | | |
| **TOTAL** | **36** | **—** | **—** | **1** | **5** | **1** | **36** | **—** | — | **5** | |
| V. *Middle Sundarbans* | | | | | | | | | | | |
| Mathurapur | 12 | — | — | 1 | 3 | 13 | — | — | | 3 | |
| VI. *Eastern Sundarbans* | | | | | | | | | | | |
| Basanti | (13) | — | — | — | (1) | — | (13) | — | | (1) | |
| Gosaba | (10) | (1) | — | (14) | (3) | (1) | (24) | — | | (3) | |
| TOTAL | 23 | 1 | — | 14 | 4 | 1 | 37 | — | | 4 | |
| **TOTAL VILLAGES** | **118** | **1** | **1** | **32** | **48** | **22** | **124** | **—** | **2** | **16** | **36** |
| %age | (59.0) | (0.5) | (0.5) | (16.0) | (24.0) | (11.0) | (62.0) | (1.0) | (8.0) | (18.0) | |

* Figures within parenthesis refers to blockwise information where more than one block has been selected for the region.

TABLE 5.6.2 : (Contd.)

| Geo Ecological Regions/Blocks | DESTINATION | | | |
|---|---|---|---|---|
| | To Calcutta | To Neighbouring District | To Neighbouring State | No Migration |
| | *12* | *13* | *14* | *15* |
| **STABLE DELTA** | | | | |
| I. *The Western Hugli Side Flats* | | | | |
| Diamond Harbour | 18 | — | — | 16 |
| II. *The Middle Mature Hugli Delta* | | | | |
| Sonarpur | — | — | — | (16) |
| Mandir Bazar | (12) | (6) | — | |
| **TOTAL** | **12** | **6** | **—** | **16** |
| III. *The Piyali Bidyadhari Plains—* | | | | |
| Bhangar | 28 | — | — | 4 |

**TABLE 5.6.2** (*Contd.*)

| *Geo Ecological Regions/Blocks* | *DESTINATION* | | | |
|---|---|---|---|---|
| | *To Calcutta* | *To Neighbouring District* | *To Neighbouring State* | *No Migration* |
| | *12* | *13* | *14* | *15* |
| **ACTIVE DELTA** | | | | |
| *IV. Western Sundarbans* | | | | |
| Sagar Island | — | (29) | — | (5) |
| Kakdwip | — | (2) | — | |
| Namkhana | — | (6) | — | |
| **TOTAL** | — | **37** | — | **5** |
| *V. Middle Sundarbans* | | | | |
| Mathurapur | 13 | — | — | 3 |
| *VI. Eastern Sundarbans* | | | | |
| Basanti | — | (13) | — | (1) |
| Gosaba | (3) | (21) | (1) | (3) |
| TOTAL | 3 | 34 | 1 | 4 |
| **TOTAL VILLAGES** | **74** | **77** | **1** | **48** |
| %age | (37.0) | (38.5) | (0.5) | (24.0) |

* Figures within parenthesis include the blockwise information where more than one block has been selected for the region.

(mostly in the Western and Eastern Sundarbans). Only one village in Gosaba exhibits outmigration to the neighbouring state.

It has been usually seen that the immigrants have migrated with their families but in case of the out-migrants of the district the case has been exactly opposite.

Daily commuting from home to work place is very common from the surveyed villages of the Stable Delta. Sixteen villages each of Diamond Harbour as well as Sonarpur and 4 villages of Mandir Bazar have also exhibited this trend. The magnetic pull of the Calcutta Metropolitan District is responsible for this long distance commuting.

## 5.5 LAND-USE

The five landuse categories identified in the 200 villages include forests, irrigated arable land, unirrigated arable land, culturable waste and area not available for cultivation (Table 5.7). 5.48 sq. km of the total area is under forests in the Active Delta. Here, 5.14 sq. km alone lies in the Eastern Sundarbans specially in Gosaba. The table also reveals that only 7.98 per cent of the total arable land is irrigated, the actual figure being 39.56 sq. km. The greatest share of irrigated arable land lies in the Stable Delta specially in the Piyali Bidyadhari Plains and in the Middle Mature Delta; and the greatest share of unirrigated arable land lie in the Sundarbans; specially the Eastern and Western Sundarbans. Only 7.89 sq. km comprise culturable wastes, the greater shares of which is noticeable in the Middle Mature Delta and in the Eastern Sundarbans. About 240 sq. km of land area is not available for cultivation. This area lies largely in Western Sundarbans, (118.64 sq.km); and Eastern Sundarbans (83.33 sq.kms.), (Fig. 5.3).

## 5.6 FUNCTIONAL CLASSIFICATION OF SETTLEMENTS

The people of South 24-Parganas pursue a *wide range of economic activities* that are mostly *primary* in nature. *Agriculture* and *fishing* comprise the most important economic activity of the region and is carried on in 129 villages (Table 5.8) i.e. 64.5 per cent of the villages of the region. 34 villages of the Western Hugli Side Flats in Diamond Harbour are primarily agricultural villages with secondary fishing activities. The examples are Bahadurpur, Bolsidhi, Durganagar, Badartala etc. 36 villages in the Western Sundarbans and 26 villages

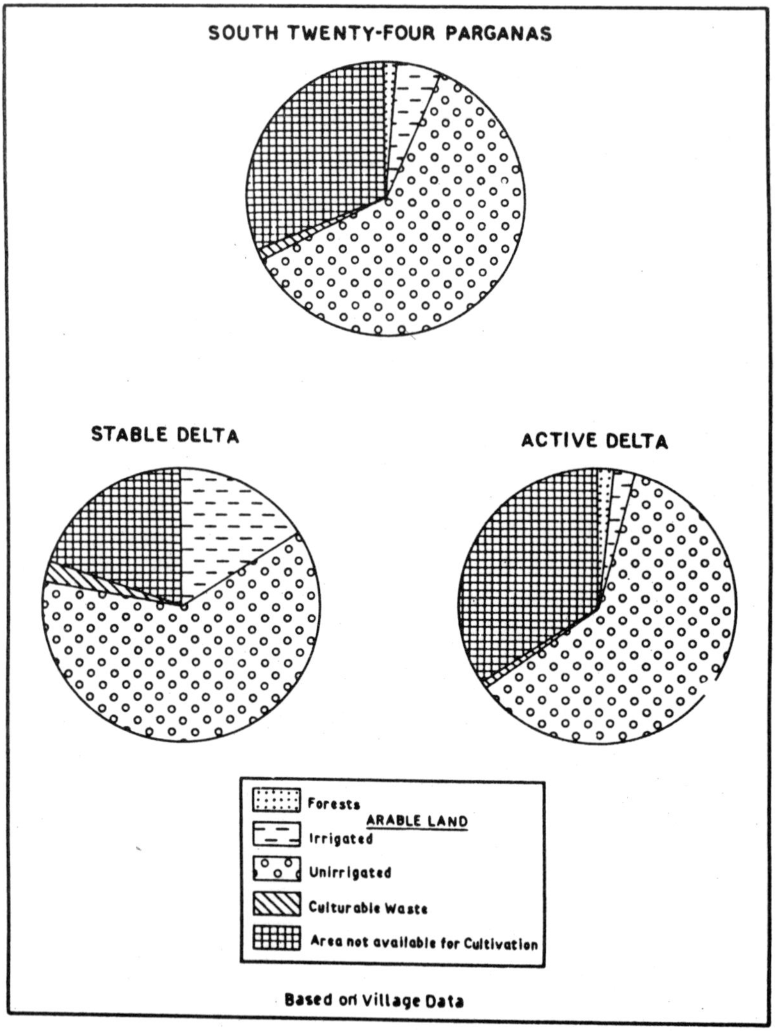


Fig. 5.3 : South 24-Parganas : Land use 1992

in Eastern Sundarbans fall in this category, examples, Manasdwip, Chemaguri, Rangabalia, Rajat Jubilee etc. In the Piyali Bidyadhari Plains, there are 19 such villages in Bhangar. Tardaha, Gadhuniriat, Karaidanga, Narayanpur etc. In only one village of Sagar i.e. Beguakhali, fishing comprises the most dominant activity followed by agriculture.

**TABLE 5.7 : Utilisation of Land in Square km.—1992**

| | | *ARABLE LAND* | | | |
|---|---|---|---|---|---|
| *Geo Ecological Regions/Blocks* | *Forests* | *Irrigated* | *Un-irrigated* | *Cultivable Waste* | *Area not avaiable for cultivation* |
| | *1* | *2* | *3* | *4* | *5* |
| **STABLE DELTA** | | | | | |
| *I. The Western Hugli Side Flats* | | | | | |
| Diamond Harbour | 0 | 5.95 | 24.55 | 0.14 | 6.75 |
| *II. The Middle Mature Hugli Delta* | | | | | |
| Sonarpur | (0) | (4.52) | (7.28) | (0) | (10.16) |
| Mandir Bazar | (0) | (2.27) | (5.84) | (2.97) | (3.81) |
| **TOTAL** | **0** | **6.79** | **13.12** | **2.97** | **13.97** |
| *III. The Piyali Bidyadhari Plains-* | | | | | |
| Bhangar | 0 | 11.30 | 46.33 | 0.63 | 14.01 |
| **ACTIVE DELTA** | | | | | |
| *IV. Western Sundarbans* | | | | | |
| Sagar Island | (0)* | (8.77) | (125.22) | (0.80) | (107.85) |
| Kakdwip | (0) | (0.17) | (13.08) | (0.16) | (2.31) |
| Namkhana | (0.34) | (0.51) | (24.18) | (0.41) | (8.48) |
| **TOTAL** | **0.34** | **9.45** | **162.48** | **1.37** | **118.64** |
| *V. Middle Sundarbans* | | | | | |
| Mathurapur | 0 | 0.97 | 18.96 | 0.11 | 3.55 |
| *VI. Eastern Sundarbans* | | | | | |
| Basanti | (0.22) | (0.77) | (39.95) | (2.34) | (28.33) |
| Gosaba | (4.92) | (4.33) | (150.82) | (0.33) | (55.00) |
| TOTAL | 5.14 | 5.10 | 190.77 | 2.67 | 83.33 |
| **TOTAL VILLAGES** | **5.48** | **39.56** | **456.21** | **7.89** | **240.29** |
| %age | 0.73% | 5.28% | 60.88% | 1.05% | 32.06% |

* Figures within parenthesis refers to blockwise information where more than one block has been selected for the region.

Of the total, in 30 villages of the total agriculture forms the only major activity. 16 such villages are in the Middle Sundarbans in Mathurapur like Gopinathpur, Raghabpur, Chak Madhu-Sudanpur 13 such villages are also noticed in the Piyali Bidyadhari Plains in Bhangar such as Ghatakpukur, Debipur, Dakshin Ghazipur, etc.

*Agriculture* together with *fishing* and *gathering* constitute the economic activity of 10 villages in Gosaba. In 2 villages of the same region agriculture and fishing is accompanied by *trade.* In 4 villages of the Western Sundarbans in Sagar Island and Kakdwip the combination is *agriculture*, *pastoral activities* and *fishing*. Similarly in another 4 villages of the Eastern Sundarbans in Gosaba the combination of agriculture, fishing, gathering of forest produce and *tourism* is observed. One village is Sagar Island depicts a combination of *tourism*, *agriculture*, *pastoral activities* and *fishing*. In the daily commuters zone in the Middle Mature Hugli Delta in Sonarpur and Mandir Bazar a combination of other services along with agriculture is seen in 19 villages and kitchen gardening in one village. Thus it is seen that fishing, tourism, pastoral activity and gathering of forest produce are important activities of the Active Delta. The following economic activities have been studied in a greater detail.

### 5.6.1 Agriculture

Though agriculture forms the backbone of the region, a *diversified cropping pattern* is seen in different parts of the Stable and the Active Delta. Rice is the dominant food crop of the region and is grown in association with a variety of other crops, vegetables and fruits. The greater part of the region is mono-cropped with only a negligible portion under the second crop. In the South, rice is cultivated mainly in the monsoon season known as 'aus' rice but summer and winter varieties i.e., 'aman' and 'boro' cultivation is done in the Northern part of the district.

Predominantly rice cultivation accompanied by potato cultivation is being carried on in 32 villages of the Active Delta mostly in the Eastern Sundarbans i.e., in 28 villages in Gosaba. A combination of vegetables and fruits occur in only one village in Sonarpur. 14 villages mostly in the Piyali-Bidyadhari Plains in Bhangar exhibit

**TABLE 5.8 : Functional Classification of Villages—1992**

| *Geo-Ecological Regions/Blocks* | | *Agriculture and fishing* | *Agriculture fishing gathering, tourism* | *Agriculture fishing gathering* | *Agriculture fishing, trade* | *Agriculture pastoral-fishing* | *Agriculture pastoral fishing* | *Agriculture commuting kitchen gardening* | *Agriculture & daily commuting* |
|---|---|---|---|---|---|---|---|---|---|
| | *1* | *2* | *3* | *4* | *5* | *6* | *7* | *8* | *9* |
| **STABLE DELTA** | | | | | | | | | |
| *I. The Western Hugli Side Flats* | | | | | | | | | |
| Diamond Harbour | — | 34 | — | — | — | — | — | — | |
| *II. The Middle Mature Hugli Delta* | | | | | | | | | |
| Sonarpur | — | — | — | — | — | — | — | (1) | (15) |
| Mandir Bazar | — | (14) | — | — | — | — | — | — | (4) |
| **TOTAL** | **—** | **14** | **—** | **—** | **—** | **—** | **—** | **1** | **19** |
| *III. The Piyali Bidyadhari Plains—* | | | | | | | | | |
| Bhangar | 13 | 18 | — | — | — | — | — | — | |

**TABLE 5.8** *(Conted.)*

| *Geo-Ecological regions blocks* | | *Agricul-ture and fishing* | *Agricul-ture fishing gather-ing, tourism* | *Agricul-ture fishing gather-ing* | *Agricul-ture fishing trade* | *Agricul-ture pasto-ral-fishing* | *Agricul-ture, pasto-ral fishing* | *Agriculture commu-ting kitchen garden-ing* | *Argriculture & daily commu-ting* |
|---|---|---|---|---|---|---|---|---|---|
| | *1* | *2* | *3* | *4* | *5* | *6* | *7* | *8* | *9* |
| **ACTIVE DELTA** | | | | | | | | | |
| *IV. Western Sundarbans* | | | | | | | | | |
| Sagar Island | (1)* | (30) | — | — | — | (2) | (1) | — | |
| Kakdwip | — | — | — | — | — | (2) | — | — | — |
| Namkhana | — | (6) | — | — | — | — | — | — | |
| TOTAL | 1 | 36 | — | — | — | 4 | 1 | — | — |
| *V. Middle Sundarbans* | | | | | | | | | |
| Mathurapur | 16 | — | — | — | — | — | — | — | — |
| *VI. Eastern Sundarbans* | | | | | | | | | |
| Basanti | — | (13) | — | — | (1) | — | — | — | |
| Gosaba | — | (13) | (4) | (10) | (1) | — | — | — | — |
| TOTAL | — | 26 | 4 | 10 | 2 | — | — | — | |
| **TOTAL VILLAGES** | | **30** | **129** | **4** | **10** | **2** | **4** | **1** | **119** |

* Figures within parenthesis refers to blockwise information where more than one block has been selected for the region.

a combination of rice, jute, wheat and oilseeds. Again 55 villages or 27.5 per cent of the villages all in the Stable Delta region with 32 villages in the Western Hugli Side Flats in Diamond Harbour, 11 in the Middle Mature Delta and 12 in the Piyali-Bidyadhari Plains grow rice, potato, wheat and fruits. In 9 villages mostly in the Piyali-Bidyadhari Plains, the crop combination is rice, potato, vegetables and mustard. 8 villages in Northern Middle Sundarbans in Mathurapur have a crop combination of rice, potato, khesari and mung. Twenty-Six villages mostly in Western and Middle Sundarbans grow rice together with potato, 'Khesari' and vegetables. Finally 55 villages in the Middle Mature Delta, Eastern and Western Sundarbans have a combination of rice, potato, vegetables and fruits.

Table 5.9 reveals that cereals, pulses, oilseeds, jute, mustard, fruits and vegetables characterise the Stable Delta whereas the Active Delta is characterised usually by a mono culture of paddy.

### 5.6.2 Fishing

A large part of the study area is interspread with innumerable tidal canals and creeks which form beautiful network of waterways, teeming with juvenile population of fish species. Since quality seeds, prawn and fish, particularly mullets abound in the region, many areas have been tapped for aquaculture and *inland fisheries* or 'bheries' have been created. The sources of fish catch are Khals and rivers in 63 villages (31.5%) all in the Active Delta, 35 villages in the Western Sundarbans and 28 villages in the Eastern Sundarbans (Table 5.10). Ponds in the Stable Delta provide fishing ground to 16 villages in Bhangar. Inland fisheries and bheries are typical of the Piyali Bidyadhari Plains in Bhangar (like the Gadhuniait bil) and also in the Eastern Sundarbans in Gosaba, famous for prawn culture. 16 villages thus have a fishing source of inland fisheries and 3 villages have fisheries together with ponds (Table 5.10). Khals and ponds are typical sources in the Active Delta covering 20 villages in Eastern and Western Sundarbans. Khals, ponds and bheries constitute the sources in 3 villages and finally khals and open seas in only one village in Beguakhali, Sagar Island.

The type of catches range from *fresh water, mixed to salt water* species. The fresh water supply comes mostly from the Stable Delta and 91 villages (45.5%) mostly in the Western Hugli Side Flats in

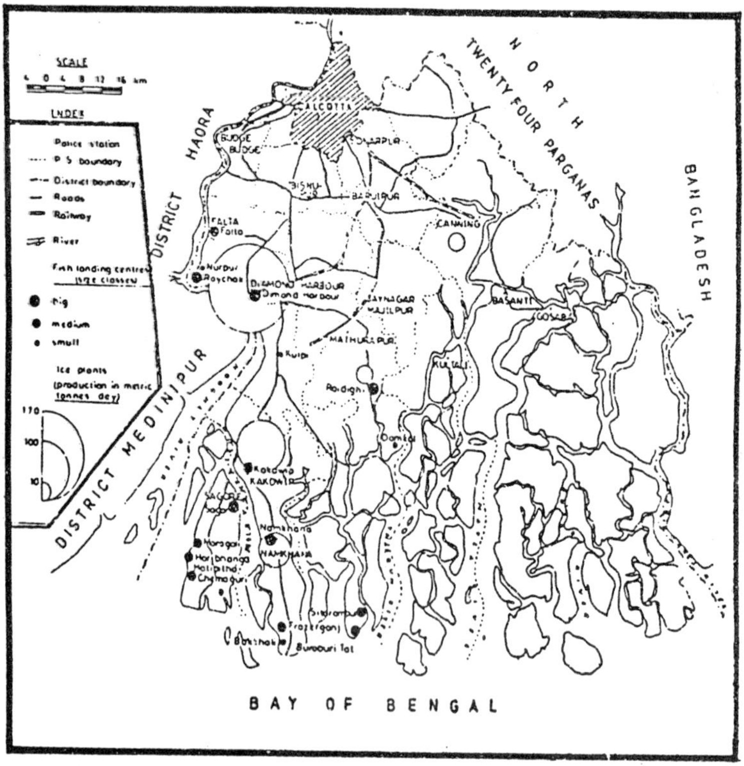


*Source* : Sharmila Das

**MAP 5.4 :** Fish Landing Centres and Ice Factories of South 24-Parganas

Diamond Harbour, the Middle Mature Delta in Mandir Bazar and the Piyali Bidyadhari Plains in Bhangar cater to this demand. The most common fresh water species include 'rohu', 'Katla', 'pona', 'Mrigal', 'Kalbose' and a variety of others. Salt water varieties of prawns, crabs, shrimps are the source in 60 villages and both salt water and fresh water form the fishing source in 22 villages. The time of fishing operation is throughout the year.

The most striking fact being the general absence of mechanised processing or preservation units, except for the provision of ice, (Table 5.11) through a few ice factories set up in certain blocks.[2] Thus 197 villages i.e., 98.5 per cent all over the Delta do not have access to proper preservation or processing facilities. Only in 3 villages in Sagar and Basanti have rudimentary fish drying mechanism.

The fish caught in the surveyed villages is sent to the Calcutta market and hence 4 places of dispatch can be discerned, (Map 5.4). The villages of Central and Eastern Sundarbans (mainly Basanti, Kultali and Gosaba) send their output to Canning. Hence Canning has emerged as a wholesale fish trading centre. Again the villages of the Western Sundarbans (in Sagar Island, Kakdwip and Namkhana) send their output to Calcutta via Diamond Harbour Town. The inland centres of the Stable Delta specially the fisheries of Bhangar send via Choubagha village that has developed as the *greatest wholesale fish trading centre* in the Northern part. Statistics reveal 41 villages send fish via Canning, 72 via Diamond Harbour 14 directly to Calcutta and 5 villages via Choubagha.

### 5.6.3 Animal Husbandry

Along with agriculture and fishing, animal husbandry is also practised in the villages. Besides domestic cattle, there are poultry farms, and piggeries developed by the Sundarban Development Board in recent years. In 135 villages the existing livestock includes cows, goat, sheep and poultry. In 6 villages poultry farming is important, while in 45 villages cows and poultry are the main stock. Cattle, piggery and poultry farms are seen in 13 villages of Eastern Sundarbans in Basanti and Gosaba. The animals are generally reared in the field and kept in the homestead, sometimes in specific enclosures like the cowshed as in case of Gosaba, to protect them from the tiger. The

**Plate 11 :** Betel Vine : Western Sundarbans (Sagar)

**Plate 12 :** Fishing by women : Eastern Sundarbans (Gosaba)

**TABLE 5.9 : Cropping Pattern of the Villages—1992**

| *Geo-ecological Regions/Blocks* | *Rice mainly Potato,* | *Rice Vegetables fruits* | *Rice, Jute, Wheat, oilseeds* | *Rice, potato, Wheat Fruits* | *Rice potato, Vegetables mustard* | *Rice potato, Khesari, mung* | *Rice, potato, Khesari, vegetables* | *Rice, potato vegetable fruits* |
|---|---|---|---|---|---|---|---|---|
| | *1* | *2* | *3* | *4* | *5* | *6* | *7* | *8* |
| **STABLE DELTA** | | | | | | | | |
| *I. The Western Hugli Side Flats* | | | | | | | | |
| Diamond Harbour | — | — | 1 | 32 | 1 | — | — | — |
| *II. The Middle Mature Hugli Delta* | | | | | | | | |
| Sonarpur | — | (1) | — | (8) | — | — | — | (7) |
| Mandir Bazar | — | — | — | (3) | (1) | — | (5) | (9) |
| TOTAL | — | 1 | — | 11 | 1 | — | 5 | 16 |
| *III. The Piyali Bidyadhari Plains—* | | | | | | | | |
| Bhangar | — | — | 13 | 12 | 7 | — | — | — |

TABLE 5.9 : (*Contd.*)

| *Geo-ecological Regions/Blocks* | *Rice mainly Potato,* | *Rice Vegetables fruits* | *Rice, Jute, Wheat, oilseeds* | *Rice, potato, Wheat Fruits* | *Rice potato, Vegetables mustard* | *Rice potato, Khesari, mung* | *Rice, potato, Khesari, vegetables* | *Rice, potato vegetable fruits* |
|---|---|---|---|---|---|---|---|---|
| | *1* | *2* | *3* | *4* | *5* | *6* | *7* | *8* |
| **ACTIVE DELTA** | | | | | | | | |
| *IV. Western Sundarbans* | | | | | | | | |
| Sagar Island | — | — | — | — | — | — | (14) | (20) |
| Kakdwip | (2) | — | — | — | — | — | — | — |
| Namkhana | — | — | — | — | — | — | — | (6) |
| TOTAL | 2 | — | — | — | — | — | 14 | 26 |
| *V. Middle Sundarbans* | | | | | | | | |
| Mathurapur | 1 | — | — | — | — | 8 | 7 | — |
| *VI. Eastern Sundarbans* | | | | | | | | |
| Basanti | (1) | — | — | — | — | — | — | (13) |
| Gosaba | (28) | — | — | — | — | — | — | — |
| TOTAL | 29 | — | — | — | — | — | — | 13 |
| **TOTAL VILLAGES** | **32** | **1** | **14** | **55** | **9** | **8** | **26** | **55** |

* Figures within parenthesis refers to blockwise information where more than one block has been selected for the region.

**TABLE 5.10 : Source and Type of Catch of fish in the Villages 1992**

| *Geo-ecological regions blocks* | *Khals and river* | *Ponds* | *Inland fisher-ies* | *Bheris and ponds* | *Khals and Bheris* | *Khals and Ponds* | *Khals ponds Bheris* | *Khals and Seas* |
|---|---|---|---|---|---|---|---|---|
| *1* | *2* | *3* | *4* | *5* | *6* | *7* | *8* | |
| **STABLE DELTA** | | | | | | | | |
| *I. The Western Hugli Side Flats* | | | | | | | | |
| Diamond Harbour | — | 29 | — | — | — | 5 | — | — |
| *II. The Middle Mature Hugli Delta* | | | | | | | | |
| Sonarpur | — | — | — | — | — | — | — | — |
| Mandir Bazar | — | (18) | — | — | — | — | — | — |
| TOTAL | — | 18 | — | — | — | — | — | — |
| *III. The Piyali Bidyadhari Plains—* | | | | | | | | |
| Bhangar | — | 3 | 16 | 3 | — | — | — | — |
| **ACTIVE DELTA** | | | | | | | | |
| *IV. Western Sundarbans* | | | | | | | | |
| Sagar Island | (32) | — | — | — | — | — | (1) | (1) |
| Kakdwip | — | — | — | — | — | (2) | — | — |
| Namkhana | (3) | — | — | — | — | (2) | (1) | — |
| TOTAL | 35 | — | — | — | — | 4 | 2 | 1 |
| *V. Middle Sundarbans* | | | | | | | | |
| Mathurapur | — | 16 | — | — | — | — | — | — |
| *VI. Eastern Sundarbans* | | | | | | | | |
| Basanti | (13) | — | — | — | — | (1) | — | — |
| Gosaba | (15) | — | — | — | (2) | (10) | (1) | |
| TOTAL | 28 | — | — | — | 2 | 11 | 1 | — |
| **TOTAL VILLAGES** | **63** | **66** | **16** | **3** | **2** | **20** | **3** | **1** |

**TABLE 5.10 : (*Contd.*)**

| *Geo-ecological Regions/Blocks* | *None* | *Fresh water river* | *Salt water* | *Mixed* | *None* |
|---|---|---|---|---|---|
| | *9* | *10* | *11* | *12* | *13* |
| **STABLE DELTA** | | | | | |
| *I. The Western Hugli Side Flats* | | | | | |
| Diamond Harbour | — | 29 | — | 5 | — |
| *II. The Middle Mature Hugli Delta* | | | | | |
| Sonarpur | (16) | — | — | (16) | |
| Mandir Bazar | — | (18) | — | — | |
| TOTAL | 16 | 18 | — | 16 | |
| *III. The Piyali Bidyadhari Plains—* | | | | | |
| Bhangar | 10 | 22 | — | — | 10 |
| **ACTIVE DELTA** | | | | | |
| *IV. Western Sundarbans* | | | | | |
| Sagar Island | — | (5) | (29) | — | — |
| Kakdwip | — | — | — | (2) | — |
| Namkhana | — | — | (3) | (3) | — |
| TOTAL | — | 5 | 32 | 5 | — |
| *V. Middle Sundarbans* | | | | | |
| Mathurapur | — | 16 | — | — | — |
| *VI. Eastern Sundarbans* | | | | | |
| Basanti | — | — | (13) | (1) | — |
| Gosaba | — | (1) | (17) | (10) | — |
| TOTAL | — | 1 | 30 | 11 | — |
| **TOTAL VILLAGES** | **26** | **91** | **62** | **21** | **26** |

products obtained from them are usually consumed locally or sold in local 'hats' by the villagers.

**TABLE 5.11 : Ice Factories of South 24-Parganas**

| *Name of the Company* | *Location (Blocks)* | *Regions* | *Installed capacity in tons/day* | *Private/ Public* |
|---|---|---|---|---|
| South 24-Parganas Central Fish | Diamond Harbour | I Western Hugli Side Flats | 10 | Public |
| Cooperative Society | | | | |
| Das Brothers Ice Factory | " | | 22 | Private |
| Katyani Ice Factory | " | | 10 | " |
| Purnalak Shmi Ice Factory | ' | | 44 | " |
| Narayani Ice Factory | " | | 40 | " |
| Ma Lakshmi Ice Factory | " | | 06 | " |
| Jafrani Ice Factory | " | | 34 | " |
| Sarda Ice Factory | Kakdwip | II The Western Sundarbans | 10 | " |
| Sarat Ice Factory | " | | 20 | " |
| Bindheswari Ice Factory | " | | 10 | " |
| Gobinda Ice Factory | " | | 10 | " |
| Lakshmi Narayani Ice Factory | " | | 20 | " |
| Bhagyalakshmi Ice Factory | Namkhana | | 10 | " |
| One | " | | 10 | " |
| One | " | | 10 | " |
| One | Canning | III The Piyali Bidyadhari Plains | 10 | " |

*Source* : D.F.O., Monetary Evaluation and Marketing Statistics, Directorate of Fisheries, Government of West Bengal.

### 5.6.4 Tourism

Of the total surveyed villages, 12 villages of the total are also places of tourist interest. There are 4 categories of tourist places in the district :

(a) *Places having Physical or Scenic Beauty* : 5 villages have picturesque spots as in Gosaba village and Hamilton Abad in Gosaba, Sonakhali on the Matla River in Basanti, (being also a halting ground), Bakkhali and Fraserganj in Namkhana famous for coastal scenery and sand dunes, and fianlly Beguakhali on the Western Coast of the Sagar Island. The attraction of Beguakhali lies in its non-electrified

85 feet high functioning light house established during the British regime, and its destructive advancing coast line.

(b) *Wild Life* : Wild life spots are 5 in number here, situated near Gosaba village in the Sundarban Reserved Forest Area. Sajnakhali is famous for Royal Bengal tigers, deers and birds; Pakhiralay has a bird sanctuary. Besides other villages of Gosaba likes Jamespur, Annpur, Dayapur and Rajat Jubilee also attract tourists interested to see the famous Sundarban settlements.

(c) *Pilgrimage* : Gangasagar at the Southern tip of the Sagar Island washed by the Bay currents is one of the oldest Pilgrimage centres due to the Sagar Mela held each year during 'Makar Sankranti' at Kapil Muni's Ashram here and attracts devotees across the length and breadth of the country.

(d) *Halting Ground* : Kachuberia at the Northern tip of the Sagar Island is the Gateway to the Island across the Hugli connecting it to the mainland through Lot No. 8, Hard Wood Point, (Kakdwip) on the mainland. Canning and Dock Ghat at Sonakhali, Basanti are also halting grounds catering to the whole of Eastern Interior Sundarbans.

Of the 12 resorts only 2 in Sagar Island originated during the pre-independence days. Except during the monsoons, the resorts are functional throughout the year, attracting both Indian and foreign tourists, but income from tourism is very nominal since the flow is restricted.

## 5.7 HOUSING AND BASIC AMENITIES

Rural housing forms a very important aspect since the littoral zone of the district is a disaster prone area and hence the housing needs are one of the most important pre-requisites of human settlements in these parts. In the Stable Delta the houses are ubiquitously distributed but in the Active Delta they are located at a distance from the 'Khals' or the littoral, protected by mud embankments of enormous stretches; affording protection from tidal incursions or wild animals. *Five aspects* of rural housing have been considered in this section and these include the materials of the walls, the materials of the roof, the material of the floor, sources of safe drinking water for the villages and the source of fuel materials.

**Plate 13 :** Kitchen Type : Gosaba

**Plate 14 :** Grain Storage : Piyali Bidyadhari Plain (Bhangar)

Most of the house types of the region are predominantly *kutcha*, though the structure of the house range from single to double storey. *Kutcha* double storey houses are found in the Sundarban area specially in the villages of Mandir Bazar, Gosaba (Pakhiralay village), whereas other houses of the area are single storied. By contrast, the houses of the Stable Delta are semi-kutcha by nature. Double storey frequents the richer sections of this area.

Data reveals that 111 villages in general (55.5%) are of *kutcha* type having mud walls and thatches, mud being plastered over bamboo framework. Mudwalls are a common feature of the Western Sundarbans specially in Sagar Island and in the Eastern Sundarbans specially in Gosaba. Only in 10 villages the predominant house type was *pucca*. 6 of them were in Sonarpur, 2 in Diamond Harbour of the Stable Delta and 2 in the Mathurapur block of the Active Delta. The rest of the houses of the area belong to semi *pucca* type.

The material of the roof exhibits that kutcha roofs made of thatch sometimes combined with tiles or tin predominate the area. The thatching materials are specially hay, leaves of the 'golpatta' and twigs in the Sundarban area. The roof types usually have four slopes on four sides with long eaves almost touching the ground. Thatched roofs are specially common in the Sundarban region of Sagar, Kakdwip, Namkhana, Basanti and Gosaba. Semi kutcha roofs are found mostly in the Stable Delta. Pucca or fully cemented roofs are unusual to the area. The material of the floor is usually mud. Mud floors are typical of the Sundarban region in Eastern and Western Sundarbans. Cemented or pucca floors occur in a few villages of the Stable Delta.

Along with house types and housing amenities, two basic rural amenities have been considered, these are source of safe drinking water and source of fuel. Though there are four sources of drinking water supply in the villages, tubewells are common in most of the villages. 184 villages (92%) have access to tubewells, spread all over the delta; 2 villages have tanks in addition to tubewells in Gosaba; in 5 villages in Sonarpur pumps and tubewells supply drinking water and in 8 villages spread over the Middle Mature Delta, Western and Eastern Sundarbans tubewells are supplemented by supply pipes.

The rural sources of fuel are mainly firewood, hay, dried leaves, cowdung and kerosene. The use of coal is conspicuously rare. In 160 villages the principal fuel materials used are firewood, hay, dried leaves, twigs and cowdung. Firewood, cowdung and kerosene are the fuel materials in 29 villages, whereas in 11 villages people use firewood, cowdung, kerosene and occasionally coal.

## 5.8 RURAL INFRASTRUCTURE

The infrastructural facilities of the surveyed villages have been discussed in this section under various heads to highlight the problems and prospects of this region.

### 5.8.1 Transport Services

Table 5.12 reveals that the road connections of the region range from metalled, unmetalled to footpaths and cart tracts. It is usually seen that metalled roadways are common along state highways in the blocks of Bhangar (State Highway No. 3), Sonarpur (State Highway No. 73), Diamond Harbour (State Highway No. 48). Unmetalled roads are characteristic of important villages, whereas the village interiors are characterised by footpaths and cart tracts and in the littoral fringes as in Gosaba, the uneven embankment top provides the footpaths. Metalled road (State Highway No. 3) is the characteristic of only one village in Bhangar, which is a well electrified large village having a large market and direct connectivity with Calcutta through the Eastern Metropolitan bypass. Unmetalled roadways characterise 11 villages in general mostly in the Piyali Bidyadhari Plains and Middle Sundarbans. 8 villages have a combination of both metalled and unmetalled roadways. 37 villages mostly in the Eastern Interior Sundarbans specially in Gosaba have only foot paths and cart tracts. During rains these get full of knee deep mud. A combination of all the types are seen in 103 (51.5%) villages spread all over the delta, mostly in the Stable Deltaic areas. Finally a combination of unmetalled roads together with foot paths and cart tracts are seen in 40 villages mostly in the Western Sundarbans in Sagar Island. Here long stretches of roads have been paved with bricks by the villagers themselves under the Jawahar Yojna Scheme. Thus road connections pose to be a problem that needs attention in the Eastern Interior Sundarbans.

**Plate 15 :** Footpaths on Embankments : Sagar

**Plate 16 :** Dinghy's as means of communication

The road connections of 3 villages in Gosaba get flooded during the rains, often the embankments are also broken and wiped off. 39 villages again mostly in the Eastern Sundarbans get flooded sometimes, whereas in 158 villages the roads do not get flooded at all, most of these villages belong to the Stable Delta.

**TABLE 5.12 : Connectivity and Mode of Conveyance 1992**

| | *I Road Connections* | | | | | |
|---|---|---|---|---|---|---|
| *Geo ecological Regions/blocks* | *Mettalled* | *Un-metalled* | *Both** | *Footpath and cartract* | *Metalled, unmetalled, foot path, cartract* | *Unmetalled footpoath, cartract* |
| | *1* | *2* | *3* | *4* | *5* | *6* |
| **STABLE DELTA** | | | | | | |
| *I. The Western Hugli Side Flats* | | | | | | |
| Diamond Harbour | — | — | — | — | 29 | 5 |
| *II. The Middle Mature Hugli Delta* | | | | | | |
| Sonarpur | — | — | — | — | (16) | — |
| Mandir Bazar | — | — | — | (1) | (9) | (8) |
| TOTAL | — | — | — | 1 | 25 | 8 |
| *III. The Piyali Bidyadhari Plains—* | | | | | | |
| Bhangar | 1 | 4 | 6 | — | 21 | — |
| **ACTIVE DELTA** | | | | | | |
| *IV. Western Sundarbans* | | | | | | |
| Sagar Island | — | — | — | (1) | (10) | (23) |
| Kakdwip | — | — | — | — | (2) | — |
| Namkhana | — | — | — | — | (2) | (4) |
| TOTAL | — | — | — | 1 | 14 | 27 |
| *V. Middle Sundarbans* | | | | | | |
| Mathurapur | — | 7 | 1 | — | 8 | — |
| *VI. Eastern Sundarbans* | | | | | | |
| Basanti | — | — | — | (11) | (3) | — |
| Gosaba | — | — | (1) | (24) | (3) | — |
| TOTAL | — | — | 1 | 35 | 6 | — |
| **TOTAL VILLAGES** | **1** | **11** | **8** | **37** | **103** | **40** |

* Figures within parenthesis refers to blockwise information where more than one block has been selected for the region.

**TABLE 5.12 :** (*Contd.*)

| *REGIONS/BLOCKS* | *II flooded or not* | | | *III Prevalent mode of Transport* | | | |
|---|---|---|---|---|---|---|---|
| | *Yes* | *Sometimes* | *No* | *Bus Rickshaw-van* | *Train Bus,* | *Boats and launches* | *Bus, boats launches, rickshaw-van* |
| | *7* | *8* | *9* | *10* | *11* | *12* | *13* |
| **STABLE DELTA** | | | | | | | |
| *I. The Western Hugli Side Flats* | | | | | | | |
| Diamond Harbour | — | — | 34 | 13 | 21 | — | — |
| *II. The Middle Mature Hugli Delta* | | | | | | | |
| Sonarpur | — | — | (16) | (16) | — | — | — |
| Mandir Bazar | — | — | (18) | (7) | (11) | — | — |
| TOTAL | — | — | 34 | 23 | 11 | — | — |
| *III. The Piyali Bidyadhari Plains—* | | | | | | | |
| Bhangar | — | — | 32 | 32 | — | — | — |
| **ACTIVE DELTA** | | | | | | | |
| *IV. Western Sundarbans* | | | | | | | |
| Sagar Island | — | — | (34) | — | — | (25) | (9) |
| Kakdwip | — | — | (2) | — | — | — | (2) |
| Namkhana | — | (3) | (3) | — | — | — | (6) |
| TOTAL | — | 3 | 39 | — | — | 25 | 17 |
| *V. Middle Sundarbans* | | | | | | | |
| Mathurapur | — | — | 16 | 12 | 4 | — | — |
| *VI. Eastern Sundarbans* | | | | | | | |
| Basanti | — | (11) | (3) | — | — | (12) | (2) |
| Gosaba | (3) | (25) | — | — | — | (28) | — |
| TOTAL | 3 | 36 | 3 | — | — | 40 | 2 |
| **TOTAL VILLAGES** | **3** | **39** | **158** | **80** | **36** | **65** | **19** |

*The prevalent mode of transport* displays a contrast between the Stable and the Active Deltas. In the Stable Delta, local train and bus constitute the most common mode of transport giving way to boats, launches and country boats or 'dinghy's' in the Sundarban region. Apart from the major bus routes, local trains have four different routes deviating from the Calcutta Region. One line goes to Budge Budge and one to Diamond Harbour Town both in the Western Hugli Side Flats. One line goes upto Lakshmikantapur of Mandir Bazar in the Middle Mature Delta and finally one line goes

**TABLE 5.12 (B) : Connectivity and Mode of Conveyance**

| Geo-ecological Regions/Blocks | IV NEAREST BUS STOP | | | | V FREQUENCY OF BUS SERVICE | | | |
|---|---|---|---|---|---|---|---|---|
| | *less than 1 km.* | *1-5 Km.* | *more than 5 km.* | *None service* | *1/2 hour* | *1 hour* | *more than 1 hour* | *No Service* |
| | *1* | *2* | *3* | *4* | *5* | *6* | *7* | *8* |
| **STABLE DELTA** | | | | | | | | |
| *I. The Western Hugli Side Flats* | | | | | | | | |
| Diamond Harbour | 6 | 28 | — | — | 17 | 17 | — | — |
| *II. The Middle Mature Hugli Delta* | | | | | | | | |
| Sonarpur | (5) | (11) | — | — | (10) | (6) | — | — |
| Mandir Bazar | (9) | (9) | — | — | (2) | (16) | — | — |
| TOTAL | 14 | 20 | — | — | 12 | 22 | — | — |
| *III. The Piyali Bidyadhari Plains—* | | | | | | | | |
| Bhangar | 22 | 9 | 1 | — | 32 | — | — | — |

**TABLE 5.12 (B) : (*Contd.*)**

| Geo-ecological Regions/Blocks | *IV NEAREST BUS STOP* | | | | *V FREQUENCY OF BUS SERVICE* | | | |
|---|---|---|---|---|---|---|---|---|
| | *less than 1 Km.* | *1-5 Km.* | *more than 5 km.* | *None* | *1/2 hour* | *1 hour* | *more than 1 hour* | *No Service* |
| | *1* | *2* | *3* | *4* | *5* | *6* | *7* | *8* |
| **ACTIVE DELTA** | | | | | | | | |
| *IV. Western Sundarbans* | | | | | | | | |
| Sagar Island | — | (4) | (5) | (25) | (4) | (5) | — | (25) |
| Kakdwip | — | (2) | — | — | (1) | (1) | — | — |
| Namkhana | (1) | (5) | — | — | — | (4) | (2) | — |
| TOTAL | 1 | 11 | 5 | 25 | 5 | 10 | 2 | 25 |
| *V. Middle Sundarbans* | | | | | | | | |
| Mathurapur | 9 | 6 | 1 | — | 7 | 6 | 3 | |
| *VI. Eastern Sundarbans* | | | | | | | | |
| Basanti | (2) | — | — | (12) | — | (2) | — | (12) |
| Gosaba | — | — | — | (28) | — | — | — | (28) |
| TOTAL | 2 | — | — | 40 | — | 2 | — | 40 |
| **TOTAL VILLAGES** | **54** | **74** | **7** | **65** | **73** | **57** | **5** | **65** |

* Figures within parenthesis refers to blockwise information where more than one block has been selected for the region.

TABLE 5.12 (B) : (*Contd.*)

| *Geo Ecological Regions/Blocks* | *VI NEAREST FERRY SERVICE CENTRE* | | | | | |
|---|---|---|---|---|---|---|
| | *Gosaba Ghat* | *Local Ghat* | *Sonakhali Dock Ghat* | *Kachuberia, Sagar* | *Namkhana* | *No ferry service* |
| | *9* | *10* | *11* | *12* | *13* | *14* |
| **STABLE DELTA** | | | | | | |
| *I. The Western Hugli Side Flats* | | | | | | |
| Diamond Harbour | — | — | — | — | — | 34 |
| *II. The Middle Mature Hugli Delta* | | | | | | |
| Sonarpur | — | — | — | — | — | (16) |
| Mandir Bazar | — | — | — | — | — | 34 |
| TOTAL | | | | | | |
| *III. The Piyali Bidyadhari Plains—* | | | | | | |
| Bhangar | — | — | — | — | — | 32 |

**TABLE 5.12 (B) : (*Contd.*)**

| *Geo Ecological Regions/Blocks* | *VI NEAREST FERRY SERVICE CENTRE* | | | | | |
|---|---|---|---|---|---|---|
| | *Gosaba Ghat* | *Local Ghat* | *Sonakhali Dock Ghat* | *Kachuberia Sagar* | *Namkahan* | *No ferry service* |
| | *9* | *10* | *11* | *12* | *13* | *14* |
| **ACTIVE DELTA** | | | | | | |
| *IV. Western Sundarbans* | | | | | | |
| Sagar Island | — | — | — | (34) | — | — |
| Kakdwip | — | — | — | — | (2) | — |
| Namkhana | — | — | — | — | (6) | — |
| TOTAL | — | — | — | 34 | 8 | — |
| *V. Middle Sundarbans* | | | | | | |
| Mathurapur | — | — | — | — | — | 16 |
| *VI. Eastern Sundarbans* | | | | | | |
| Basanti | — | — | (14) | — | — | — |
| Gosaba | (4) | (24) | — | — | — | — |
| TOTAL | 4 | 24 | 14 | — | — | — |
| **TOTAL VILLAGES** | **4** | **24** | **14** | **34** | **8** | **116** |

* Figures within parenthesis refers to blockwise information where more than one block has been selected for the region.

upto Port Canning in the Piyali Bidyadhari Plains and after this point water transport is the only means.

Bus accompanied by rickshaw-van constitute the familair mode of transport in 80 villages mostly in the Stable Delta (Table 5.12); the greatest number of villages i.e. 32 with this mode of communication being seen in Bhangar. 36 villages have access to train and bus mostly in the Stable Delta in Diamond Harbour and Mandir Bazar. 65 villages mostly in the Eastern and Western Sundarbans have boats and launches as the only mode of conveyance. Almost all the villages of Basanti, Gosaba and Sagar use boats and launches as means of transport. Finally a combination of bus, boats, launches and rickshaw-van in the village interiors is a characteristic of 19 villages mostly in the Western Sundarbans.

The nearest bus stop ranges from less than 1 km to over 5 km. 54 villages in all (27.0%) have bus stop within 1 km, most of these villages are seen in the Piyali Bidyadhari Plains in Bhangar, in the Western Hugli Side Flats in Diamond Harbour, in Middle Mature Delta in Mandir Bazar, and Basanti in Eastern Sundarbans. 74 villages have a bus stop within 5 kms., of which 28 villages are in Diamond Harbour, 7 villages have a bus stop over 5 kms. and 65 villages have no bus facilities in the neighbourhood. 28 of such villages are in Gosaba and 25 in Sagar. The frequency of bus service ranges from half an hour to over one hour. Seventeen-three villages have frequency of half an hour, (in Diamond Harbour 17 villages, 2 in Mandir Bazar, 32 in Bhangar etc). 57 villages have a frequency of one hour and 5 villages have a frequency over one hour. Rickshawvan provide conveyance within the villages.

The important ferry stations include Port Canning (on the Matla), Gosaba forming gateway to the Eastern interior Sundarbans, Lot No. 8 or Hardwood Point in Kakdwip, providing the only connecting point (on the mainland) with Sagar Island or Kachuberia (village) across the Ganga. Sonakhali across the Matla opposite Canning provide the gateway to the middle Sundarbans in Basanti and Kultali. Apart from these major centres, there are innumerable small local 'ferry ghats' of the individual villages as seen in Gosaba like Rajat Jubilee Ghat, Chota Mollakhali, Kumirmari, Jhaukhali etc. Of the surveyed villages, 116 villages have no ferry service in the Stable Delta, 84 villages have ferry service, out of which 4 villages have

**Plate 17 :** Inside Village Potter's Home: Diamond Harbour

**Plate 18 :** Local Train : Diamond Harbour to Calcutta

Gosaba as the Ghat. 14 villages have Sonakhali, Basanti as the nearest Ghat, 34 villages have Kachuberia the nearest point, 8 villages have Namkhana as the Ghat and 24 villages (16.5%) have local Ghats.

The important bus stations in the surveyed area include Ghatakpukur, Bhojherhat, Bhatipota, Bhangar in Bhangar Block; Rudranagar, Sridham Kali Bazar, Ganga Sagar in Sagar Island; Babuli Bazar in Mathurapur and Chouhati in Sonarpur.

### 5.8.2 Educational Institutions

Table 5.13 reveals that the surveyed villages face the problem of not only connectivity but also that of educational institutions. 167 villages in general (83.5%) have access to primary schools whether inside or just outside the village, 91 villages have secondary or middle schools; 30 villages have higher secondary schools. Thus there is a general *paucity of schools* at higher levels. There is a marked absence of colleges in the surveyed area.

Fighty-five villages (43.5%) have a single primary school (mostly in Sonarpur, Mandir Bazar, Sagar Island and in Basanti) 2 primary schools are characteristic of 49 villages in Diamond Harbour, Bhangar, Sagar and Gosaba, 17 villages in Sagar, Diamond Harbour and Gosaba have 3 primary schools. 4 primary schools are characteristic of only 9 villages.

Secondary schools range from 1 to a maximum of 2 per village. One school is noticed in 69 villages all over the Active and Stable Delta. Two middle schools are seen in 22 villages. 30 villages have only 1 higher secondary school.

Twenty-seven villages have educational institutions situated outside with distances ranging over 11 km to even 50 km. Colleges are markedly absent from the region. So for higher education one has to travel to either Calcutta (from Bhangar, Sonarpur areas), to Canning town from Eastern Sundarbans, to Diamond Harbour town from Western Sundarbans and to Jaynagar—Mazilpur town from Mathurapur and Mandir Bazar areas. 187 educational institutions (93.5%) make sure of the availability of teachers in 10 villages. 5 per cent make the complaint of non-availability and in 3 villages 1.5 per cent there are very few and inadequate teaching staff.

**Plate 19 :** Adult Education : Literacy Mission : (Sagar)

**Plate 20 :** Local Ferry Ghat in Sagar

TABLE [illegible]: Number of Villages having Educational Institutions 199[illegible]

| Geo-ecological Regions/Blocks | Number of Primary Schools | | | | | | Number of Secondary Schools (10th) | | | | Num. of Hr. sec. Schools (12th) | |
|---|---|---|---|---|---|---|---|---|---|---|---|---|
| | 0* | 1 | 2 | 3 | 4 | 5 | 0 | 1 | 2 | 3 | 0 | 1 |
| | 1 | 2 | 3 | 4 | 5 | 6 | 7 | 8 | 9 | 10 | 11 | 12 |
| **STABLE DELTA** | | | | | | | | | | | | |
| *I. The Western Hugli Side Flats* | | | | | | | | | | | | |
| Diamond Harbour | — | 15 | 17 | 2 | — | — | 19 | 15 | — | — | 32 | 2 |
| *II. The Middle Mature Hugli Delta* | | | | | | | | | | | | |
| Sonarpur | (6) | (5) | (5) | — | — | — | (9) | (7) | — | — | (15) | (1) |
| Mandir Bazar | (7) | (7) | (3) | (1) | — | — | (15) | (3) | — | — | (16) | (2) |
| TOTAL | 13 | 12 | 8 | 1 | — | — | 24 | 10 | — | — | 31 | 3 |
| *III. The Piyali Bidyadhari Plains—* | | | | | | | | | | | | |
| Bhangar | 4 | 27 | 1 | — | — | — | 27 | 3 | 2 | — | 26 | 6 |

**TABLE 5.13 :** *(Contd.)*

| *Geo-ecological Regions/Blocks* | *Number of Primary Schools* | | | | | | *Number of Secondary Schools (10th)* | | | | *Num. of Hr. sec. Schools (12th)* | |
|---|---|---|---|---|---|---|---|---|---|---|---|---|
| | *0** | *1* | *2* | *3* | *4* | *5* | *0* | *1* | *2* | *3* | *0* | *1* |
| | *1* | *2* | *3* | *4* | *5* | *6* | *7* | *8* | *9* | *10* | *11* | *12* |
| **ACTIVE DELTA** | | | | | | | | | | | | |
| *IV. Western Sundarbans* | | | | | | | | | | | | |
| Sagar Island | — | (5) | (8) | (10) | (7) | (4) | (8) | (16) | (10) | — | (26) | (8) |
| Kakdwip | — | — | — | — | (1) | (1) | — | (2) | — | — | (1) | (1) |
| Namkhana | (1) | (3) | (2) | — | — | — | (4) | (2) | — | — | (6) | — |
| TOTAL | 1 | 8 | 10 | 10 | 8 | 5 | 12 | 20 | 10 | — | 33 | 9 |
| *V. Middle Sundarbans* | | | | | | | | | | | | |
| Mathurapur | 5 | 6 | 3 | 2 | — | — | 13 | 2 | 1 | — | 15 | 1 |
| *VI. Eastern Sundarbans* | | | | | | | | | | | | |
| Basanti | (5) | (8) | (1) | — | — | — | (6) | (4) | (4) | — | (10) | (4) |
| Gosaba | (5) | (9) | (9) | (2) | (1) | (2) | (8) | (15) | (5) | — | (23) | (5) |
| TOTAL | 10 | 17 | 10 | 2 | 1 | 2 | 14 | 19 | 9 | — | 33 | 9 |
| **TOTAL VILLAGES** | **33** | **85** | **49** | **17** | **9** | **7** | **109** | **69** | **22** | — | **170** | **30** |

* Figures within parenthesis refers to blockwise information where more than one block has been selected for the region.

**Plate 21 :** Village School : Beguakhali, Sagar

**Plate 22 :** Solar Reactors : Ganga Sagar

### 5.8.3 Communication Facilities

Of the surveyed villages only 88 villages have the facility of Post Offices. Of these 87 villages have the Post Office within a radius of 1 km and in one village it is situated at 2 km. 112 villages spread all over the Delta do not have the facility of a Post Office within the village. This is also characteristic of small area villages of the Stable Delta. Ten villages in all, all in the Stable Delta have a facililty of a telegraph office. Most of these are located in the Middle Mature Delta. Telephone facility are available in only 14 villages mostly in the Stable Delta (Middle Mature Delta).

Combining all the communication facilities, 86 villages in all do have any such facility within the village. Seventy-four villages have access to communication at a distance ranging from 0.5 to 2 km, 20 villages have a distance range of 2.5 to 4 km., 15 have a distance of 4.5 to 6 and 5 have a distance range of 6.5 to 8 km. Table 5.14 depicts the regional breakup.

### 5.8.4 Health Services

In this section, both modern means of health services and the traditional methods have been taken into consideration. Among the modern means the number of Dispensaries, Public Health Centres, number of Government Hospitals and Family Planning Centres and number of Private Hospitals have been considered, and statistics reveal a dismal picture (Table 5.15).

Medical Facilities are available in a *few villages*. Only 40 villages have access to a medical institution. In Diamond Harbour the villagers go to Diamond Harbour town or to the sub-centre at Basuldanga village. In Sonarpur block, there is a general hospital at Subhasgram village, and other medial facilities at Chouhati. In Mandir Bazar villagers go to Mandir Bazar for medical purposes. In Bhangar block there are 3 centres, the most important being the primary health and family planning unit at Bhatipota. Besides there is another Primary Health Centre (PHC) at Panapukur village and a dispensary at the block headquarters at Bhangar. In Sagar block the major centre revolves round Rudranagar situated at the centre of the Island with subcentres at Kachuberia at the Northern tip of the Island

**TABLE 5.14 : Villages having Communication Facilities 1992**

| *Geo Ecological Regions/Blocks* | *Number of Villages having Post Office* | | | *Number of Villages having telegraph office* | | *Num. of Vill. having a Tele phone facility* | |
|---|---|---|---|---|---|---|---|
| | *0* | *1* | *2* | *0* | *1* | *0* | *1* |
| | *1* | *2* | *3* | *4* | *5* | *6* | *7* |
| **STABLE DELTA** | | | | | | | |
| *I. The Western Hugli Side Flats* | | | | | | | |
| Diamond Harbour | 30 | 4 | — | 33 | 1 | 31 | 3 |
| *II. The Middle Mature Hugli Delta* | | | | | | | |
| Sonarpur | (6) | (10) | — | (10) | (6) | (9) | (7) |
| Mandir Bazar | (11) | (7) | — | (17) | (1) | (18) | — |
| TOTAL | 17 | 17 | — | 27 | 7 | 27 | 7 |
| *III. The Piyali Bidyadhari Plains—* | | | | | | | |
| Bhangar | 26 | 6 | — | 30 | 2 | 32 | — |
| **ACTIVE DELTA** | | | | | | | |
| *IV. Western Sundarbans* | | | | | | | |
| Sagar Island | (10) | (24) | — | (34) | — | (34) | — |
| Kakdwip | — | (2) | — | (2) | — | (1) | (1) |
| Namkhana | (3) | (3) | — | (6) | — | (5) | (1) |
| TOTAL | 13 | 29 | — | 42 | — | 40 | 2 |
| *V. Middle Sundarbans* | | | | | | | |
| Mathurapur | 10 | 6 | — | 16 | — | 15 | 1 |
| *VI. Eastern Sundarbans* | | | | | | | |
| Basanti | (8) | (6) | — | (14) | — | (13) | (1) |
| Gosaba | (8) | (19) | (1) | (28) | — | (28) | — |
| TOTAL | 16 | 25 | 1 | 42 | — | 41 | 1 |
| **TOTAL VILLAGES** | **112** | **87** | **1** | **190** | **10** | **186** | **14** |

* Figures within parenthesis refers to blockwise information where more than one block has been selected for the region.

**TABLE 5.14 :** *(Contd..)*

| *Geo Ecological Regions/Blocks* | *Number of Villages and Distance of Communication Facility* | | | | |
|---|---|---|---|---|---|
| | *0 km* | *0.5 - 2 km* | *2.5 - 4 km* | *4.5 - 6 km* | *6.5 - 8 km* |
| | *8* | *9* | *10* | *11* | *12* |
| **STABLE DELTA** | | | | | |
| *I. The Western Hugli Side Flats* | | | | | |
| Diamond Harbour | 4 | 30 | — | — | — |
| *II. The Middle Mature Hugli Delta* | | | | | |
| Sonarpur | (10) | (6) | — | — | — |
| Mandir Bazar | (6) | (5) | (2) | (5) | — |
| TOTAL | 16 | 11 | 2 | 5 | — |
| *III. The Piyali Bidyadhari Plains—* | | | | | |
| Bhangar | 6 | 15 | 8 | 3 | — |
| **ACTIVE DELTA** | | | | | |
| *IV. Western Sundarbans* | | | | | |
| Sagar Island | (24) | (5) | (1) | (2) | (2) |
| Kakdwip | (2) | — | — | — | — |
| Namkhana | (3) | (2) | (1) | — | — |
| TOTAL | 29 | 7 | 2 | 2 | 2 |
| *V. Middle Sundarbans* | | | | | |
| Mathurapur | 6 | 3 | 3 | 3 | 1 |
| *VI. Eastern Sundarbans* | | | | | |
| Basanti | (6) | (4) | (2) | (1) | (1) |
| Gosaba | (19) | (4) | (3) | (1) | (1) |
| TOTAL | 25 | 8 | 5 | 2 | 2 |
| **TOTAL VILLAGES** | **86** | **74** | **20** | **15** | **5** |

and Ganga Sagar at the Southern tip. In Kakdwip and Namkhana villagers go to Kakdwip for medical requirements. Similarly medical facilities are available in Sonakhali in Basanti and for the whole of Gosaba, Gosaba village is the main centre. In most of the blocks there are revolving mobile primary health and family planning units. Such *mobile units* are typical of the Sundarban area that lack medical and communication facilities specially in Gosaba and Sagar blocks. Delivery cases still in most of the villages are conducted by local midwives or '*dhai's*'.

Forty villages only have the facility of a dispensary, the maximum of which being located in the Active Delta (16 in Western Sundarbans, 2 in Middle and 6 in Eastern Sundarbans). 6 villages

**TABLE 5.15 : Villages having Medical Facilities 1992**

| *Geo-ecological Regions/Blocks* | *Number of Villages having Dispensary* | | | *Number of Villages having Health Centres* | | *Number of Villages having Govt. and Family Palnning Centres* | | *Number of Private and Family Hospitals* | |
|---|---|---|---|---|---|---|---|---|---|
| | *0* | *1* | *2* | *0* | *1* | *0* | *1* | *0* | *1* |
| | *1* | *2* | *3* | *4* | *5* | *6* | *7* | *8* | *9* |
| **STABLE DELTA** | | | | | | | | | |
| *I. The Western Hugli Side Flats* | | | | | | | | | |
| Diamond Harbour | 26 | 6 | 2 | 30 | 5 | 33 | 1 | 34 | — |
| *II. The Middle Mature Hugli Delta* | | | | | | | | | |
| Sonarpur | (12) | (4) | — | (12) | (4) | (16) | — | (16) | |
| Mandir Bazar | (15) | (3) | — | (18) | — | (18) | — | (18) | |
| TOTAL | 27 | 7 | — | 30 | 4 | 34 | — | 34 | |
| *III. The Piyali Bidyadhari Plains—* | | | | | | | | | |
| Bhangar | 29 | 3 | — | 27 | 5 | 31 | 1 | 32 | — |

**TABLE 5.15 :** *(Contd.)*

| *Geo-ecological Regions/Blocks* | *Number of Villages having Dispensary* | | | *Number of Villages having Health Centres* | | *Number of Villages having Govt. and Family Planning Centres* | | *Number of Private Hospitals* | |
|---|---|---|---|---|---|---|---|---|---|
| | *0* | *1* | *2* | *0* | *1* | *0* | *1* | *0* | *1* |
| | *1* | *2* | *3* | *4* | *5* | *6* | *7* | *8* | *9* |
| **ACTIVE DELTA** | | | | | | | | | |
| *IV. Western Sundarbans* | | | | | | | | | |
| Sagar Island | (18) | (12) | (4) | (31) | (3) | (31) | — | (33) | (1) |
| Kakdwip | (2) | — | — | (2) | — | C(2) | — | (2) | |
| Namkhana | (2) | (4) | — | (4) | (2) | (6) | — | (6) | |
| TOTAL | 22 | 16 | 4 | 37 | 5 | 39 | 3 | 41 | 1 |
| *V. Middle Sundarbans* | | | | | | | | | |
| Mathurapur | 14 | 2 | — | 15 | 1 | 16 | — | 16 | |
| *VI. Eastern Sundarbans* | | | | | | | | | |
| Basanti | (12) | (2) | — | (14) | — | (14) | — | (14) | |
| Gosaba | (24) | (4) | — | 923) | (5) | (28) | — | (28) | |
| TOTAL | 36 | 6 | — | 37 | 5 | 42 | — | 42 | |
| **TOTAL VILLAGES** | **154** | **40** | **6** | **176** | **24** | **195** | **5** | **199** | **1** |

* Figures within parenthesis refers to blockwise information where more than one block has been selected for the region.

TABLE 5.15 : (*Contd..*)

| *Geo-ecological Regions/Blocks* | *Number of Villages with Private Practioners* | | | | | |
|---|---|---|---|---|---|---|
| | *0* | *1* | *2* | *3* | *4* | *5 or more* |
| | *10* | *11* | *12* | *13* | *14* | *15* |
| **STABLE DELTA** | | | | | | |
| *I. The Western Hugli Side Flats* | | | | | | |
| Diamond Harbour | 13 | 17 | 3 | 1 | — | — |
| *II. The Middle Mature Hugli Delta* | | | | | | |
| Sonarpur | (10) | (6) | — | — | — | — |
| Mandir Bazar | (12) | (5) | (1) | — | — | — |
| TOTAL | 22 | 11 | 1 | — | — | — |
| *III. The Piyali Bidyadhari Plains—* | | | | | | |
| Bhangar | 11 | 14 | 4 | — | — | — |

**TABLE 5.15 : (*Contd.*)**

| *Geo-ecological Regions/Blocks* | *Number of Villages with Private Practioners* | | | | | |
|---|---|---|---|---|---|---|
| | *0* | *1* | *2* | *3* | *4* | *5 or more* |
| | *10* | *11* | *12* | *13* | *14* | *15* |
| **ACTIVE DELTA** | | | | | | |
| *IV. Western Sundarbans* | | | | | | |
| Sagar Island | (3) | (17) | (15) | (2) | (1) | — |
| Kakdwip | — | (1) | — | (1) | — | — |
| Namkhana | (1) | (5) | — | — | — | — |
| TOTAL | 4 | 23 | 15 | 3 | 1 | — |
| *V. Middle Sundarbans* | | | | | | |
| Mathurapur | 3 | 10 | 1 | 1 | 1 | — |
| *VI. Eastern Sundarbans* | | | | | | |
| Basanti | (4) | (8) | (2) | — | — | — |
| Gosaba | (3) | (19) | (4) | (1) | — | — |
| TOTAL | 7 | 27 | 6 | 1 | — | — |
| **TOTAL VILLAGES** | **60** | **100** | **29** | **6** | **3** | **2** |

* Figures within parenthesis refers to blockwise information where more than one block has been selected for the region.

(2 in Diamond Harbour and 4 in Sagar) have the facility of 2 dispensaries. In total there are only 24 primary health centres and 176 surveyed villages do not have this facility. Again the maximum of these are seen in the Active Delta. There are only 5 Government Hospitals, 1 in Diamond Harbour town, 1 in Bhangar and 3 in Sagar. The number of Private Hospitals is only 1 (0.5%) in Kakdwip—Namkhana.

Only 41 villages have a single or more medical facility located within the village and in the rest, people have to travel a distance of 4 to 6 km and even 10 kms in case of Gosaba block. It was noticed that in 187 villages (93.5%), people buy medicines on their own from outside and only in 7 villages people buy at subsidized rates.

Besides these institutions it was noticed that in 140 villages private practioner's treat the local inhabitants. Many of them were unregistered practioners.

There are various *traditional methods* in the villages as well (Table 5.16). Of these 24 villages have traditional hakims and 4 villages have 2 each, mostly in the Stable Delta. There are single homeopaths in 94 villages, 2 homeopaths in 21 villages, all over the Delta. There are single ayurvaids in only 4 villages and 2 ayurvaids in a single village. The most common form of the traditional health workers are '*Ojhas*'. Ojhas are common to 69 villages, the highest number of whom are seen in the Active Delta in Gosaba, Sagar and Basanti. If located outside, 21 villages have traditional workers at a range of 0.5 to 2 km and in 193 villages; people go in for traditional treatment. Of the diseases treated, mild diseases like common cough and cold are usually being treated by the traditional methods in 132 villages, snake bites in 21 villages (of which 16 are in Gosaba, 4 in Basanti and only 1 in Sagar). Both mild diseases and snake bite treatment by traditional means is done in 44 villages, again in the Active Delta.

The availability of chemists shop within the village is also an important factor and 134 villages have a chemist shop located within the village, the highest number of which is seen in Bhangar (26 villages) followed by Diamond Harbour (25 villages). In the other 66 villages the chemist shop is located at a distance of 0.1 to 5 kms.

**TABLE 5.16 : Villages having Traditional Health Workers 1992**

| *Geo Ecological* | *Hakims* | | | *Homeopaths* | | | | *Ayurvaids* | | |
|---|---|---|---|---|---|---|---|---|---|---|
| *Regions/Blocks* | *0* | *1* | *2* | *0* | *1* | *2* | *3* | *0* | *1* | *2* |
| | *1* | *2* | *3* | *4* | *5* | *6* | *7* | *8* | *9* | *10* |
| **STABLE DELTA** | | | | | | | | | | |
| *I. The Western Hugli Side Flats* | | | | | | | | | | |
| Diamond Harbour | 11 | 19 | 4 | 5 | 24 | 5 | — | 34 | — | — |
| *II. The Middle Mature Hugli Delta* | | | | | | | | | | |
| Sonarpur | (16) | — | — | (8) | (6) | (2) | — | (16) | — | — |
| Mandir Bazar | (15) | (3) | — | (3) | (14) | (1) | — | (18) | — | — |
| TOTAL | 31 | 3 | — | 11 | 20 | 3 | — | 34 | — | — |
| *III. The Piyali Bidyadhari Plains—* | | | | | | | | | | |
| Bhangar | 30 | 2 | — | 30 | 2 | — | — | 30 | 2 | — |
| **ACTIVE DELTA** | | | | | | | | | | |
| *IV. Western Sundarbans* | | | | | | | | | | |
| Sagar Island | (34) | — | — | (9) | (17) | (8) | — | (32) | (2) | — |
| Kakdwip | (2) | — | — | (1) | (1) | — | — | (2) | — | — |
| Namkhana | (6) | — | — | (2) | (2) | (2) | — | (5) | — | (1) |
| TOTAL | '42 | — | — | 12 | 20 | 10 | — | 39 | 2 | 1 |
| *V. Middle Sundarbans* | | | | | | | | | | |
| Mathurapur | 16 | — | — | 5 | 7 | 2 | 2 | 16 | — | — |
| *VI. Eastern Sundarbans* | | | | | | | | | | |
| Basanti | (14) | — | — | (4) | (10) | — | — | (14) | — | — |
| Gosaba | (280 | — | — | (16) | (11) | (1) | — | (27) | 1 | — |
| TOTAL | 42 | — | — | 20 | 21 | 1 | — | 41 | 1 | — |
| **TOTAL VILLAGES** | **172** | **24** | **4** | **83** | **94** | **21** | **2** | **194** | **5** | **1** |

* Figures within parenthesis refers to blockwise information where more than one block has been selected for the region.

### 5.8.5 Credit Institutions

The various sources of credit (Table 5.17) in the surveyed area include money-lenders, cooperative and credit societies and commercial banks. It was noticed that 81 villages had no money lenders,

**TABLE 5.16 : (Contd.)**

| *Geo Ecological Regions/Blocks* | *Faqueer* | | *Ojhas* | | | |
|---|---|---|---|---|---|---|
| | *0* | *1* | *0* | *1* | *2* | *3* |
| | *11* | *12* | *13* | *14* | *15* | *16* |
| **STABLE DELTA** | | | | | | |
| *I. The Western Hugli Side Flats* | | | | | | |
| Diamond Harbour | 34 | — | 33 | 1 | — | — |
| *II. The Middle Mature Hugli Delta* | | | | | | |
| Sonarpur | (16) | — | (16) | — | — | — |
| Mandir Bazar | (180 | — | (18) | — | — | — |
| TOTAL | 34 | — | 34 | — | — | — |
| *III. The Piyali Bidyadhari Plains—* | | | | | | |
| Bhangar | 30 | 2 | 30 | 2 | — | — |
| **ACTIVE DELTA** | | | | | | |
| *IV. Western Sundarbans* | | | | | | |
| Sagar Island | (33) | (1) | (11) | (20) | (1) | (2) |
| Kakdwip | (2) | — | — | (2) | — | — |
| Namkhana | (6) | — | (4) | (2) | — | — |
| TOTAL | 41 | 1 | 15 | 24 | 1 | 2 |
| *V. Middle Sundarbans* | | | | | | |
| Mathurapur | 16 | — | 16 | — | — | — |
| *VI. Eastern Sundarbans* | | | | | | |
| Basanti | (14) | — | (1) | (11) | (2) | — |
| Gosaba | (28) | — | (2) | (22) | (4) | — |
| TOTAL | 42 | — | 3 | 33 | 6 | — |
| **TOTAL VILLAGES** | **197** | **3** | **131** | **60** | **7** | **2** |

* Figures within parenthesis refers to blockwise information where more than one block has been selected for the region.

in 47 villages there was only one money lender, in 58 villages there were 2 money lenders, in 3 villages there were 3 money lenders, 1 village with 4 and 10 villages with 5 money lenders, thus pointing to the fact that loopholes still exist in our credit system.

Only 21 villages had a cooperative and credit institution. The Sagar Gramin Bank is located at Sagar Island, another at Bhojherhat in Bhangar. Other credit societies were seen in Diamond Harbour, Sonarpur, Mandir Bazar and Mathurapur. Of the total surveyed villages only 18 have the facililty of a bank. In Bhangar, banks like

**TABLE 5.17: Number of Villages having Credit Facilities—1992**

| *Geo-ecological Regions/Blocks* | *(Money lenders)* | | | | | | *(cooperative and credit societies)* | | *(Banks)* | |
|---|---|---|---|---|---|---|---|---|---|---|
| | *0* | *1* | *2* | *3* | *4* | *5* | *0* | *1* | *0* | *1* |
| | *1* | *2* | *3* | *4* | *5* | *6* | *7* | *8* | *9* | *10* |
| **STABLE DELTA** | | | | | | | | | | |
| *I. The Western Hugli Side Flats* | | | | | | | | | | |
| Diamond Harbour | 4 | 5 | 20 | 2 | 1 | 2 | 32 | 2 | 32 | 2 |
| *II. The Middle Mature Hugli Delta* | | | | | | | | | | |
| Sonarpur | (15) | — | (1) | — | — | — | (16) | — | (13) | (3) |
| Mandir Bazar | (13) | (1) | (4) | — | — | — | (16) | (2) | (16) | (2) |
| TOTAL | 28 | 1 | 5 | — | — | — | 32 | 2 | 29 | 5 |
| *III. The Piyali Bidyadhari Plains—* | | | | | | | | | | |
| Bhangar | 11 | 16 | 4 | — | — | 1 | 30 | 2 | 28 | 4 |

TABLE 5.17 : (*Contd.*)

| *Geo-ecological Regions/Blocks* | *(Money lenders)* | | | | | | *(Cooperative and Credit Societies)* | | *(Banks)* | |
|---|---|---|---|---|---|---|---|---|---|---|
| | *0* | *1* | *2* | *3* | *4* | *5* | *0* | *1* | *0* | *1* |
| | *1* | *2* | *3* | *4* | *5* | *6* | *7* | *8* | *9* | *10* |
| **ACTIVE DELTA** | | | | | | | | | | |
| *IV. Western Sundarbans* | | | | | | | | | | |
| Sagar Island | (10) | (5) | (15) | — | — | (4) | (27) | (7) | (32) | (2) |
| Kakdwip | (1) | (1) | — | — | — | — | (1) | (1) | (1) | 1 |
| Namkhana | (1) | — | (4) | — | — | (1) | (4) | (2) | (6) | — |
| TOTAL | 12 | 6 | 19 | — | — | 5 | 32 | 10 | 39 | 3 |
| *V. Middle Sundarbans* | | | | | | | | | | |
| Mathurapur | 38 | 4 | — | — | 1 | 14 | 2 | 14 | 2 | |
| *VI. Eastern Sundarbans* | | | | | | | | | | |
| Basanti | (7) | (6) | (1) | — | — | — | (13) | (1) | (13) | (1) |
| Gosaba | (16) | (5) | (5) | (1) | — | (1) | (26) | (2) | (27) | (1) |
| TOTAL | 23 | 11 | 6 | 1 | — | 1 | 39 | 3 | 40 | 2 |
| **TOTAL VILLAGES** | **81** | **47** | **58** | **3** | **1** | **10** | **179** | **21** | **182** | **18** |

* Figures within parenthesis refers to blockwise information where more than one block has been selected for the region.

the Bank of India at Tardaha village and the Allahabad Bank are located at Narayanpur village. United Bank of India together with the State Bank are located at Rajpur near Sonarpur, the only bank in Gosaba is the State Bank of India; in Mathurapur the United Bank of India is located and the State Bank at Diamond Harbour. Considering all the credit institutions and facilities 80 villages (40%) do not have any facilities, the villagers here have to travel from 0.5 to over 20 km for credit. 44 villages have the facility of one credit instituion, 54 villages have 2, 12 villages have 3, 2 villages have 4 and 3 villages each have 5 and 6 credit institutions. A maximum number of 7 was seen in 2 villages. For 77 villages the availability of credit was claimed difficult to obtain.

### 5.8.6 Marketing Facilities

Maketing facilities (Table 5.18) existing in this area are (a) haats and bazaars, (b) Itenary traders and (c) fair price shops. It is noticed that weekly and biweekly haats are characteristic in many villages; but some market places acquire a permanent nature and become important interaction points in the commodities traded. Such important centres are Bhojherhat and greatest fish trading centre i.e. Choubagha in Bhangar, Paglahat near Narayanpur village also in Bhangar, Chouhati in Sonarpur, Babuli Bazar in Mathurapur, Rudranagar, Kali Bazar and Gangasagar in Sagar, Gosaba village in Gosaba and Port Canning.

98 villages do not have any haats and bazaars whereas 102 villages have the advantage of 1 haat or bazaar (of which 26 are located in Sagar, 13 in Gosaba, 19 in Diamond Harbour etc.). Of the 102 villages 15 villages have weekly markets mostly in the Eastern Sundarbans, 73 villages have biweekly markets, 23 villages have daily markets (mostly in Diamond Harbour, Sonarpur, Mandir Bazar).

Only 37 villages have the facility of roaming itenary traders mostly in the Sundarbans, usually trading consumer durables.

Again in 24 villages there are fair price shops, of which 17 villages have a single shop and 7 villages have 2 shops. In general 93 villages have marketing facilities located within the village and the villagers in the rest of the villages travel a distance of 5 km to over 10 km for the purchase of commodities.

**TABLE 5.18 : Number of Villages having Marketing Facility 1992**

| Geo Ecological Regions/Blocks | *Number of Haats and Bazar* | | | *Time of Operation* | | |
|---|---|---|---|---|---|---|
| | *0* | *1* | *Weekly* | *Biweekly* | *Daily* | *None* |
| | *1* | *2* | *3* | *4* | *5* | *6* |
| **STABLE DELTA** | | | | | | |
| *I. The Western Hugli Side Flats* | | | | | | |
| Diamond Harbour | 15 | 19 | — | 17 | 2 | 15 |
| *II. The Middle Mature Hugli Delta* | | | | | | |
| Sonarpur | (8) | (8) | — | (2) | (6) | (8) |
| Mandir Bazar | (12) | (6) | — | — | (6) | (12) |
| TOTAL | 20 | 14 | — | 2 | 12 | 20 |
| *III. The Piyali Bidyadhari Plains—* | | | | | | |
| Bhangar | 23 | 9 | — | 15 | 4 | 13 |
| **ACTIVE DELTA** | | | | | | |
| *IV. Western Sundarbans* | | | | | | |
| Sagar Island | (8) | (26) | — | (25) | (1) | (8) |
| Kakdwip | (1) | (1) | — | (1) | — | (1) |
| Namkhana | (1) | (5) | — | (4) | — | (2) |
| TOTAL | 10 | 32 | — | 30 | 1 | 11 |
| *V. Middle Sundarbans* | | | | | | |
| Mathurapur | 8 | 8 | — | 4 | 4 | 8 |
| *VI. Eastern Sundarbans* | | | | | | |
| Basanti | (7) | (7) | (3) | (4) | — | (7) |
| Gosaba | (15) | (13) | (12) | (1) | — | (15) |
| TOTAL | (22) | (20) | (15) | 73 | 23 | 89 |
| **TOTAL VILLAGES** | **98** | **102** | **15** | **73** | **23** | **89** |

* Figures within parenthesis refers to blockwise information where more than one block has been selected for the region.

TABLE 5.18 : (*Contd.*)

| *Geo Ecological Regions/Blocks* | *Number of Itenary Traders* 0 | 1 | 2 | 3 | 4 or more |
|---|---|---|---|---|---|
| | *1* | *2* | *3* | *4* | *5* |
| **STABLE DELTA** | | | | | |
| *I. The Western Hugli Side Flats* | | | | | |
| Diamond Harbour | 27 | 10 | 2 | 1 | — |
| *II. The Middle Mature Hugli Delta* | | | | | |
| Sonarpur | (16) | — | — | — | — |
| Mandir Bazar | 18 | — | — | — | — |
| TOTAL | 34 | — | — | — | — |
| *III. The Piyali Bidyadhari Plains-* | | | | | |
| Bhangar | 32 | — | — | — | — |
| **ACTIVE DELTA** | | | | | |
| *IV. Western Sundarbans* | | | | | |
| Sagar Island | (18) | (8) | (6) | (1) | (1) |
| Kakdwip | (2) | — | — | — | — |
| Namkhana | (4) | — | 2 | — | — |
| TOTAL | 24 | 8 | 8 | 1 | 1 |
| *V. Middle Sundarbans* | | | | | |
| Mathurapur | 15 | 1 | — | — | — |
| *VI. Eastern Sundarbans* | | | | | |
| Basanti | (12) | — | (2) | — | — |
| Gosaba | (25) | (1) | (1) | — | (1) |
| TOTAL | 37 | 1 | 3 | — | 1 |
| **TOTAL VILLAGES** | **163** | **20** | **13** | **2** | **2** |

* Figures within parenthesis refers to blockwise information where more than one block has been selected for the region.

**TABLE 5.18** (*Contd.*)

| *Geo Ecological Regions/Blocks* | *Number of Fair Price Shops* | | | *Distance* | | |
|---|---|---|---|---|---|---|
| | *0* | *1* | *2* | *0.1—5* | *5.1—10* | *more than 10* |
| | *1* | *2* | *3* | *4* | *5* | *6* |
| **STABLE DELTA** | | | | | | |
| *I. The Western Hugli Side Flats* | | | | | | |
| Diamond Harbour | 29 | 4 | 1 | 20 | 14 | — |
| *II. The Middle Mature Hugli Delta* | | | | | | |
| Sonarpur | (15) | (1) | — | (8) | (8) | — |
| Mandir Bazar | (18) | — | — | (6) | (12) | — |
| TOTAL | 33 | 1 | — | 14 | 20 | — |
| *III. The Piyali Bidyadhari Plains-* | | | | | | |
| Bhangar | 29 | 1 | 2 | 6 | 26 | — |
| **ACTIVE DELTA** | | | | | | |
| *IV. Western Sundarbans* | | | | | | |
| Sagar Island | (28) | (5) | (1) | (24) | (10) | — |
| Kakdwip | (1) | — | (1) | (1) | (1) | — |
| Namkhana | (5) | (1) | — | (4) | (2) | — |
| TOTAL | 34 | 6 | 2 | 29 | 13 | — |
| *V. Middle Sundarbans* | | | | | | |
| Mathurapur | 14 | 1 | 1 | 2 | 13 | 1 |
| *VI. Eastern Sundarbans* | | | | | | |
| Basanti | (13) | (1) | — | (7) | (7) | — |
| Gosaba | (24) | (3) | (1) | (15) | (11) | (2) |
| TOTAL | 37 | 4 | 1 | 22 | 18 | 2 |
| TOTAL VILLAGES | 176 | 17 | 7 | 93 | 104 | 3 |

* Figures within parenthesis refers to blockwise information where more than one block has been selected for the region.

## CORRELATION ANALYSIS

Certain amenities have been taken as indicators of development and have been correlated with the population size of the villages. 200 surveyed villages seem to be strongly and positively correlated with the following :

(i) Population and number of schools of village—correlation coefficient = 0.71
(ii) Population and total marketing facilities—correlation coefficient = 0.43
(iii) Population and total medical facilities correlation coefficient = 0.36
(iv) Population and total communication facility correlation coefficient = 0.42
(v) Population and total credit facilities correlation coefficient = 0.29

## 5.9 TRADE CONNECTION AND INTERACTION

This section deals with the tradable commodities of the area and the connection or interaction points. The commodities include agricultural products in 101 villages (50.5%), mostly in the Stable Delta in Diamond Harbour, (in 12 villages) 15 villages in Sonarpur and 18 villages in Mandir Bazar, 17 in Bhangar, 34 in Sagar and 5 in Mathurapur. Agriculture together with fish form the trading commodities of 72 villages mostly in the Active Delta in Gosaba and Basanti. Fish, vegetables, and poultry items form the base of 10 villages (5%), agriculture, fish, vegetables in 6 villages, fish and forest produce in 4 villages and fruits form the basis of 2 villages in Sonarpur.

The trade connections and interlinkages include at the preliminary level, various regional sub-centres and finally all trade flows to the Calcutta Metropolitan Region.

For the whole of the Sundarban Region, Canning forms the sub-centre of Central and Eastern Sundarbans, Kakdwip and Diamond Harbour form the centres for Western Sundarbans and Southern Western Hugli Flats; Jaynagar-Mazilpur forms the centre for Mathurapur and Mandir Bazar in the Middle Mature Delta. Ghatakpukur, Choubagha, Bhojherhat and Tardaha form the centres at Bhangar, Piyali Bidyadhari Plains. Some villages in Sonarpur near Calcutta send their products directly to the Calcutta market.

Diamond Harbour has emerged as the *most important centre* with 41 villages in Diamond Harbour and Sagar sending their products directly here, Canning ranks next with 41 villages in the Sundarbans (Gosaba and Basanti) under it. Jaynagar-Mazilpur has 34 villages

There are 23 villages under Ghatakpukur, Choubagha, Bhojherhat in Bhangar and finally, 18 villages come directly under Calcutta.

## 5.10 VILLAGE ARTS, CRAFTS

Certain village arts and crafts have been noticed in the surveyed villages. Apart from brick making, oil and rice milling is common in most villages of the Active Delta. In the Western Hugli Side Flats of Diamond Harbour certain village crafts have developed coming under the Integrated Rural Development Project (IRDP) (loan of Rs. 4500 every 3 years). These include 'Talgur' or molasse (gur) making, bamboo net weaving, fishing net weaving, and palm leaf handicrafts in Ramgobindapur such as hats, bags, and other luxury items. Besides there are other crafts here like paper cutting for making of envelopes etc. In the Active Delta too smaller crafts are carried on. One such centre is located in Rangabalia, near Gosaba that has involved the local females in the village in small tailoring units and small handicraft making, processing of honey etc. There is a patch of black soil in this village where cotton cultivation has been tried on an experimental basis. Again in Beguakhali village (South Western Sagar Island) weaving of fishing net, drying and processing of fish is noticeable.

In general 89 villages of the total have a single art and craft and 111 villages have two on the average. The number of females and children involved in these are very less. Only 14 villages have involved females and children in these works.

## 5.11 EXISTING PLANS AND PROPOSALS

In 1980, 124 villages came under the scheme of Marginal Farmers and Agriculture Labourers, and Integrated Rural Area Development, and 24 villages came under the self employed Jawahar Yojna Scheme and other such plans of the 1990's. Of the total, 145 villages (72.5%) have plans implemented, and in 3 villages planning is yet to be implemented and in 52 villages do not fall under any plans.

In the Active Delta, the Sundarban Development Board came into existence (together with the Government of West Bengal and Ministry of Agriculture and Irrigation, Government of India) in the 80's.

The Sundarban Development Board aims at :

(a) Improvement of drainage components and creation of irrigation facilities by constructing sluices, intermediate drains and contour bunds.

(b) By providing 50 per cent subsidy by way of inputs for raising selected rabi crops in order to enable small and marginal farmers to realise the benefits of extended irrigation and land improvement.

(c) To provide 'term credit' through PACS for agro-processing, animal husbandry, fisheries, village industry, transportation etc.

(d) Encouragement for raising crops for rabi cultivation like chillies, sesamum, wheat, water melon and mung.

(e) Next to crop production, the most promising developmental activity is brackishwater fisheries development and prawn larvae culture.

(f) Providing necessary infrastructure to dairy services and piggery and poultry units.

(g) Setting up of agro-processing units based on agricultural surpluses using indigenous technology. These units will undertake chilli grinding, pulses and cereals processing, water melon processing, and bee-keeping.

(h) To strengthen marketing facilities (at centres like Canning and Kakdwip).

(i) Development of social forestry to strengthen embankments.

(j) Finally for facilitating all the above mentioned aspects, proposal was made for strengthening of extension, technical and administrative set-up.

## 5.12 QUALITY OF HUMAN SETTLEMENTS

After studying the inter-regional settlement pattern and characteristics, it how becomes imperative to categorise the 200 villages into a *developmental scale* and to find out the hierarchy level resulting out of the developmental process. A composite index has been worked out considering some selected indicators of the villages. These are :

(i) Proportion of pucca houses.

(ii) Proportion villages having tubewells for safe drinking water.

(iii) Proportion of total irrigated agricultural land per village.

(iv) Proportion of the villages having access to a Metalled road.

(v) Proportion of villages having schools.
(vi) Proportion of villages having health institutions.
(vii) Proportion of villages having the facility of credit institutions.
(viii) Proportion of villages having communication facility.

After weighing the indicators by their respective scores, the individual values of all the villages was found ranging from 2 to 39. Five size classes (Table 5.19) were then worked out according to the range method viz. Very High Development, High Development, Moderate Development; Low and Very Low Development and the villages falling within each category was recorded (given in Appendix V.2).

(i) *A Comparatively Very High Quality* (Value Level 33 to 40) is discernable in the Western Hugli Side Flats in Diamond Harbour, in the Western Sundarbans in Sagar Island and in the Middle Sundarbans in Mathurapur, Kamarpol in Diamond Harbour, Rudranagar in Sagar and Uttar Kasinagar stands highest in the hierarchy of rural settlements of the area having nearly all facilities. 1.5 per cent of the total villages come under this category.
(ii) *A High Quality* (Value Level 25 to 32) is again observed in Western Sundarbans in Sagar, Hugli Side Flats in Diamond Harbour, and in the Middle Mature Delta in Sonarpur. The villages at the next hierarchic order are Beguakhali in Sagar, Sarisha in Diamond Harbour and Nischintapur in Sonarpur. Two per cent of the villages come under this category.
(iii) *A Moderate Quality* (Value Level 17 to 24) 24 villages stand in the next hierarchic level spread over the Piyali Bidyadhari Plains, Western Hugli Side Flats, Middle Mature Hugli Delta and Eastern Sundarbans; thus covering 17.5 per cent of the total villages.
(iv) *A Low Quality* (Value level 9 to 16)—In the low category fall 87 villages or (43.5%). These are located in the Piyali-Bidyadhari Plains, Eastern Sundarbans, Western Sundarbans, Western Hugli Side Flats and the Middle Mature Mugli Delta.

(v) *A very Low Quality* (Values 2 to 8)—is registered in 71 villages (35.5% of the total villages), mostly in the Piyali Bidyadhari Plains. The whole of Sundarbans, besides certain villages in the Western Hugli Side Plains and in the Middle Mature Delta also fall within this group.

**TABLE 5.19: Quality of Human Settlements 1992**

| *Geo Ecological Regions/Blocks* | *Very High* | *High* | *Moderate* | *Low* | *Very Low* |
|---|---|---|---|---|---|
| | *1* | *2* | *3* | *4* | *5* |
| *I. The Western Hugli Side Flats* | | | | | |
| Diamond Harbour | 1 | 1 | 7 | 21 | 4 |
| *II. The Middle Mature Hugli Delta* | | | | | |
| Sonarpur | — | (1) | (3) | (12) | — |
| Mandir Bazar | — | — | (1) | (10) | (7) |
| TOTAL | — | 1 | 4 | 22 | 7 |
| *III. The Piyali Bidyadhari Plains—* | | | | | |
| Bhangar | — | — | 8 | 12 | 12 |
| STABLE DELTA | | | | | |
| Number and | 1 | 2 | 19 | 55 | 23 |
| Percentage of village | 0.5% | 1.0% | 9.5% | 27.5% | 11.5% |
| *IV. Western Sundarbans* | | | | | |
| Sagar Island | (1) | (1) | (6) | (16) | (10) |
| Kakdwip | — | (1) | (1) | — | — |
| Namkhana | — | — | — | (4) | (2) |
| TOTAL | 1 | 2 | 7 | 20 | 12 |
| *V. Middle Sundarbans* | | | | | |
| Mathurapur | 1 | — | 1 | 1 | 13 |
| *VI. Eastern Sundarbans* | | | | | |
| Basanti | — | — | (2) | (1) | (11) |
| Gosaba | — | — | (6) | (10) | (12) |
| Total Villages | — | — | 8 | 11 | 23 |
| ACTIVE DELTA | | | | | |
| Number and ) of | 2 | 2 | 16 | 32 | 48 |
| Percentage ) villages | 1.0% | 1.0% | 8.0% | 16.0% | 24.0% |
| **South 24—Parganas** | **3** | **4** | **35** | **87** | **77** |
| **% age** | **1.5%** | **2.0%** | **17.5%** | **43.5%** | **35.0%** |

* Figures within parenthesis refers to blockwise information where more than one block has been selected for the region.

Table 5.19 shows that of the 200 villages, 1 village (0.5%) falls in the very high group, 2 (1.0%) in the high group, 19 (9.5%) in the moderate group, 55 (27.5%) in the low and 23 (11.5%) in the very low group, in the Stable Delta of the North. In the Active Delta of the South, these proportions are 2 or (1.0%) in very high, 2 villages in the high group (1.0%), 16 villages (8.0%) in the moderate group, 32 villages (16.0%) in the low and 48 (24.0%) in the very low group. Thus it is seen that even though the Stable Delta enjoys better connectivily and nearness to the Calcutta Metropolitan Region, in terms of village amenities, they have similar shortage as that among the villages of the Active Delta.

## 5.13 CONCLUSION

The Inter-Regional Pattern of Human settlements reveal a *striking contrast* between the Stable and Active Deltas. To summarize briefly some of these differences are : villages of the Active Delta are of a more recent origin mostly developed on reclaimed embanked land in Western, Middle and Eastern Sundarbans. Most of the Stable Delta villages are located on the flood plain near urban settlements while those of the Active Delta are either situated beside an embanked river or distributary or on the coast as in the Western Sundarbans or is an island by itself as in the Eastern Sundarbans; situated away from urban settlements. The natural resources also vary from non saline clays and silts in the Stable Delta to saline silty, clayey loams and sandy patches of the Active Delta. Natural drainage facility is greater in the Active Delta.

Population resources exhibit a similar pattern as revealed from the analysis of (Chapter 4). The Stable Delta villages have lesser areal sizes, greater human numbers and higher densities. The Active Delta villages have greater area sizes, greater human numbers but lower densities. The Active Delta exhibits a greater tribal concentration. Hindus form the dominant population group followed by the Muslims. Inmmigration has resulted more in the Active Delta due to land availability. Outmigration is noticeable due to economic pressures, but in this case the duration of migration is less. The settlement characteristics also conform to the secondary data base of Chapter 4. The landuse categories reveal more of forested land in the South and more of irrigated arable land in the Stable Delta.

The cropping pattern reveals a diversity of crops in the North replaced by mono culture of rice in the South. Fishing, forestry and pastoral activities are more important in the Active Delta.

Infrastructural facilities reveal bus, train connections dominant in the Stable Delta replaced by boats and launches in the South. Pucca and semi pucca houses are rare in the region. The number of schools, credit institutions, marketing facilities do not exhibit marked contrasts between the two deltas; since the Active Delta has to be self reliant because it is farthest away from the metropolitan influence. Hence the development level does not highlight any region in particular.

After analysing the problems and prospects of the study area certain points indicating bottlenecks and backwardness in the whole development process of the area has emerged. Inspite of SDB and other agencies enlightening proposals; apart from the introduction of a few new crops in the area and the functioning of certain brackish water fisheries for cultivating prawn larvaes; the organisational set up of the whole area is highly inadequate. Except for rice milling and local indigenous industries like handlooms, pottery and other handicrafts, the area lacks specially in the development of organised cottage and forest based industries.

The development bottlenecks are mainly due to the existence of several factors :

(i) There are major constraints in more intensive landuse like lack of irrigation facilities due to surface flows being saline and groundwater level too deep for economic exploitation;

(ii) Economy of the region is overwhelmingly dependent on agriculture. With gradual marginalisation more and more farmers are driven out from ownership of land to swell the ranks of landless cultivators, thereby adding to the incidence of large-scale unemployment;

(iii) Soils though productive are not managed properly and are not put under suitable cropping patterns;

(iv) The area is subject to natural hazards (storms and cyclones) occasionally breaking the embankments and inundating lowlying areas;

(v) Additional agricultural production obtained through development efforts including those of the SDB could not fetch fair returns to the producers due to lack of adequate marketing and processing facilities and insufficient economic demand; and

(vi) Insufficient power supply, lack of electrification and inadequate communication facilities have hindered development.

In a short-term perspective, the region has to depend more on modernisation of waterways, although overland market links should feed the river trade centres. Moreover electrification should be extended and roadways and village embankments strengthened, cyclone shelters costructed. Finally cottage industries and forest based industries should be developed in a properly organised fashion to benefit the whole area.

**REFERENCES**

1. K.N. Mukherjee, "History of Settlement In the Sundarban of West Bengal", '*Indian Journal of Landscape Systems*' January 1983 Vol. 6 No. 1 & 2, pp. 1-19.
2. Sharmila Das, "Development of Fisheries In South 24 Parganas District : Problems And Prospects", *Geographical Review of India*, June 1991, Vol. 53, No. 2, pp. 69-79.

# 6

# A MICRO LEVEL ANALYSIS OF POPULATION AND HUMAN SETTLEMENTS

## 6.1 INTRODUCTION

The present chapter contains the analysis of some aspects of Population and Human Settlements of Deltaic West Bengal at a micro-level through a detailed analysis of data collected through questionnaires from 400 households spread over 36 villages. Section I deals with the Population Characteristics of the households focussing on socio-economic aspects, mortality, diseases, health and family planning. Section II has a focus on certain aspects of Human Settlements such as quality of housing and basic amenities, environmental hazards and consequences, the social environment, pattern of interaction, commutation, its frequency, purpose and finally the quality of life. According to the Indian Census,"A household is a group of persons who commonly live together and would take their meals from a common kitchen unless the exigencies of work prevent any of them from doing so. There may be a household of persons related by blood or a household of unrelated persons or having a mix of both. Examples of unrelated households are boarding houses, messes, hostels, residential hotels, rescue houses, jails, ashrams etc. These are called institutional households. There may be one member household, two member households or multi member households. For census purpose each one of this type is regarded as a household.

The United Nations Definition of a private household stands as "persons who jointly occupy the whole or part of a housing unit, sharing the principal meals and having common provisions for basic living needs."[1] Within the households it is possible to identify families, who are persons related by blood, marriage or adoption, although in many cases the family and the household will be the same (John I Clarke, 1972)[2] .

The household samples have been selected with the population limits in mind. 60 per cent of the household samples are from the Stable Delta covering 59 per cent of the total surveyed population spread over 18 villages. 40 per cent of the households are from the Active Delta forming 41 per cent of the surveyed population, also spread over 18 villages. The regional breakup are as follows—23 per cent of household samples are from the Western Hugli Side Flats and the Middle Mature Hugli Delta, 14 per cent from the Piyali Bidyadhari Plains. 13 per cent of the samples approximately are from the Western, Middle and Eastern Sundarbans respectively. Table 6.1 gives the sample size of the six geo-ecological subregions.

SECTION-I POPULATION

## 6.2 POPULATION CHARACTERISTICS

In this section, size of the family, family types, Age- Sex Composition, Marital Status, Age at Marriage and Migration Pattern of the households have been discussed.

### 6.2.1 Size of the Families

The family size in the 400 sample households range from one person to 17 persons' family. Nuclear families consisting of parents and children are reported to comprise 105 households (26%) in the Stable Delta, mostly around Calcutta and Diamond Harbour. 295 households, or 74 per cent of the total samples presented joint family type comprising of parents, children, grand parents, brothers and sisters. 259 or 65 per cent of the total households had 5 to 10 members, 11 to 15 members were common to 29 households and only 7 households had more than 15 members. In 385 or in 96 per cent of the households, the head of the household is a male and in the rest the head is a female.

### 6.2.2 Age-Sex Pattern of Population

The Age-Sex pattern of households have been conducted in great detail in quinquinnial age groups starting from 0 years to over 75

**TABLE 6.1 : A Scheme of Household Survey of South 24-Parganas - 1992**

| *Geo—Ecological Resion* | *Blocks* | *Surveyed Villages Number** | *Villages Percentage* | *Surveyed Households Number* | *Households Percentage* | *Surveyed Population Number* | *Total Percentage* |
|---|---|---|---|---|---|---|---|
| **STABLE DELTA** | (Total of I,II,III) | 18 | 50.0 | 238 | 60.0 | 1493 | 59.0 |
| I. The Western Hugli Side Flats. | Diamond Harbour | 7 | 19.0 | 92 | 23.0 | 607 | 24.0 |
| II. The Middle Mature Delta | Sonarpur | (3) | — | (37) | — | (175) | — |
| | Mandir Bazar | (4) | — | (54) | — | (366) | — |
| **Total** | | **7** | **19.0** | **91** | **23.0** | **541** | **21.0** |
| III. The Piyali Bidyadhari Plains. | Bhangar | 4 | 11.0 | 55 | 14.0 | 345 | 14.0 |
| **ACTIVE DELTA** | (Total of IV,V,VI) | 18 | 50.0 | 162 | 40.0 | 1039 | 41.0 |
| IV. The Western Sundarbans | Sagar Island | (6) | (17.0) | (54) | (13.50) | (444) | (17.0) |
| V. The Middle Sundarbans | Mathurapur | 6 | 17.0 | 54 | 13.50 | 273 | 11.0 |
| VI. The Eastern Sundarbans | Gosaba | 6 | 17.0 | 54 | 13.50 | 322 | 13.0 |
| **TOTAL** | | **36** | **100** | **400** | **100** | **2532** | **100** |

* (Figure in paranthesis include regions with more than one sampled block)

years. The proportion of population is higher in the lower age groups and lower at higher levels, both in case of males and females. 0 to 4 age group reveals comparatively smaller proportion, this being due to the higher incidence of infant mortality, this proportion increases in the 5-9, 10-14 and 20-24 age groups. The falling proportions at higher level exhibit a greater incidence of deaths at higher ages conjointly with a greater incidence of births at lower ages. Table 6.2 gives an account of the detailed age-sex structure in both the deltas.

The three Age Sex pyramids for the district, Stable as well as Active Delta exhibit a broad base and relatively smaller proportion of population in the upper ages indicating that the sample belongs to *a high fertility population* (Figs. 6.1, 6.2)

### 6.2.3 Marital Status

The marital status of a population refers to the proportions of single, married, widowed and divorced persons. Both age structure and sex-ratio directly influence these proportions, so do social institutions and economic conditions. Therefore, the marital status of a population is never constant (1976, John I Clarke).[3] 40.6 per cent of the total household members are married, 56.3 per cent belong to the unmarried category, 2.96 per cent are widowed and 0.08 per cent are divorced, (Map 6.3). Sagar Island in Western Sundarbans represents the highest proportion of married i.e. 48.2 per cent followed by 41.2 per cent of the Middle Mature Delta. Higher proportions are due to the low age at marriage in the rural areas. The proportion of unmarried is highest in the Western Hugli Side Flats i.e. 59.5 per cent. 4.1 per cent of the members of the Piyali Bidyadhari Plains are widowed, exhibiting the highest proportion among the regions. Divorced population is also exhibited by the Piyali Bidyadhari Plains in Bhangar being 0.6 per cent (Table 6.3).

### 6.2.4 Age at Marriage

The age marriage is a very good indicator that brings out clearly the reasons behind a progressive or a regressive population.
From Table 6.4, it is clearly reflected that—

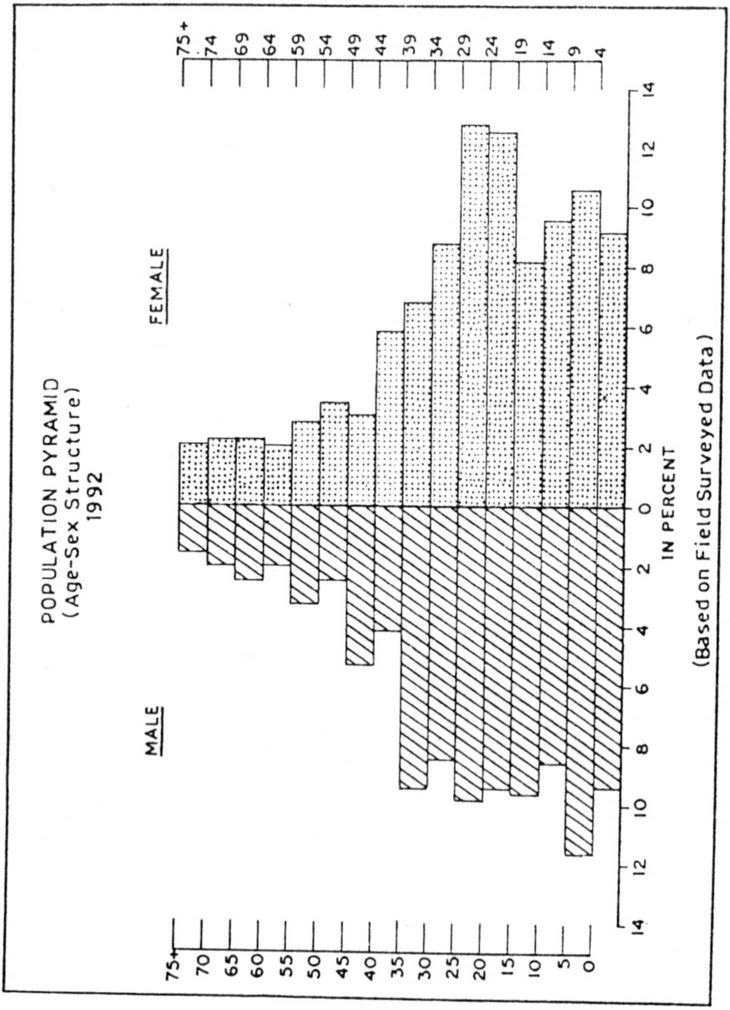


**Fig. 6.1 : South 24-Parganas**

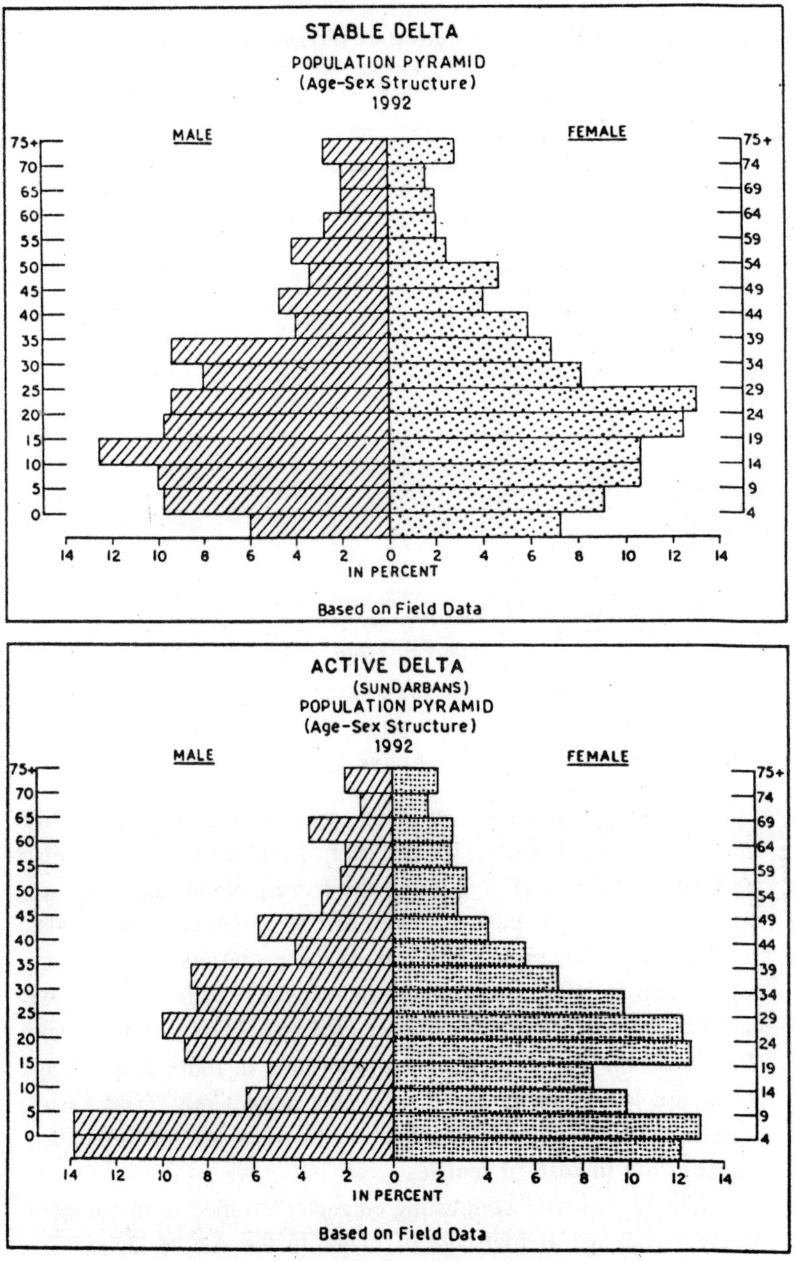


**Fig . 6.2 : South 24-Parganas**

**TABLE 6.2 : Age- Sex Structure (Proportions to Total) 1992**

| *Age Groups* | *South Twenty-Four Parganas* | | *Stable Delta* | | *Active Delta* | |
|---|---|---|---|---|---|---|
| | *Males* | *Females* | *Males* | *Females* | *Males* | *Females* |
| 0 - 4 | 9.4 | 9.1 | 6.1 | 7.2 | 13.9 | 12.1 |
| 5 - 9 | 11.6 | 10.6 | 9.8 | 9.1 | 13.9 | 12.9 |
| 10 - 14 | 8.5 | 9.5 | 10.1 | 10.5 | 6.4 | 7.9 |
| 15 - 19 | 9.6 | 8.1 | 12.6 | 10.6 | 5.4 | 4.2 |
| 20 - 24 | 9.5 | 12.5 | 9.8 | 12.5 | 9.0 | 12.5 |
| 25 - 29 | 9.8 | 12.8 | 9.5 | 13.0 | 10.1 | 12.3 |
| 30 - 34 | 8.2 | 8.7 | 8.0 | 8.1 | 8.5 | 9.7 |
| 35 - 39 | 9.2 | 6.8 | 9.5 | 6.8 | 8.7 | 6.9 |
| 40 - 44 | 4.1 | 5.8 | 4.0 | 5.9 | 4.2 | 5.6 |
| 45 - 49 | 5.3 | 2.9 | 4.9 | 2.2 | 5.9 | 4.0 |
| 50 - 54 | 2.4 | 3.4 | 2.1 | 4.6 | 3.0 | 1.6 |
| 55 - 59 | 3.3 | 2.7 | 4.2 | 2.4 | 2.1 | 3.0 |
| 60 - 64 | 2.0 | 1.6 | 2.6 | 0.9 | 2.0 | 2.6 |
| 65 - 69 | 2.6 | 2.2 | 2.0 | 1.9 | 3.0 | 2.6 |
| 70 - 74 | 2.0 | 1.4 | 2.1 | 1.5 | 1.2 | 1.6 |
| 75 + | 1.9 | 2.0 | 2.8 | 2.8 | 2.0 | 2.0 |

(a) There is a marked difference between the marriageable ages between the males and females,

(b) There is also a contrasting character between the regions of the Stable and Active Deltas.

In the age group less than 14 years only 1.1 per cent of the males are married while 31.8 per cent of the females are recorded married. In 15 to 19 age group the corresponding marriage proportions are 35.5 per cent for males and 58.15 per cent for females.

Again in the higher age groups the proportion of males are higher than females. For instance the respective male female values in 20 to 24 age group are 46.7 per cent and 9.5 per cent. Finally the corresponding male female proportions in more than 25 age group are 16.7 per cent and 0.5 per cent respectively. This clearly reflects the higher age at marriage in case of males, that are exceptionally low in case of females.

The region-wise contrasting character is reflected in comparatively lower age at marriage of males in the Active Delta. For instance the proportion of 51.3 and 50 per cent is characteristic of

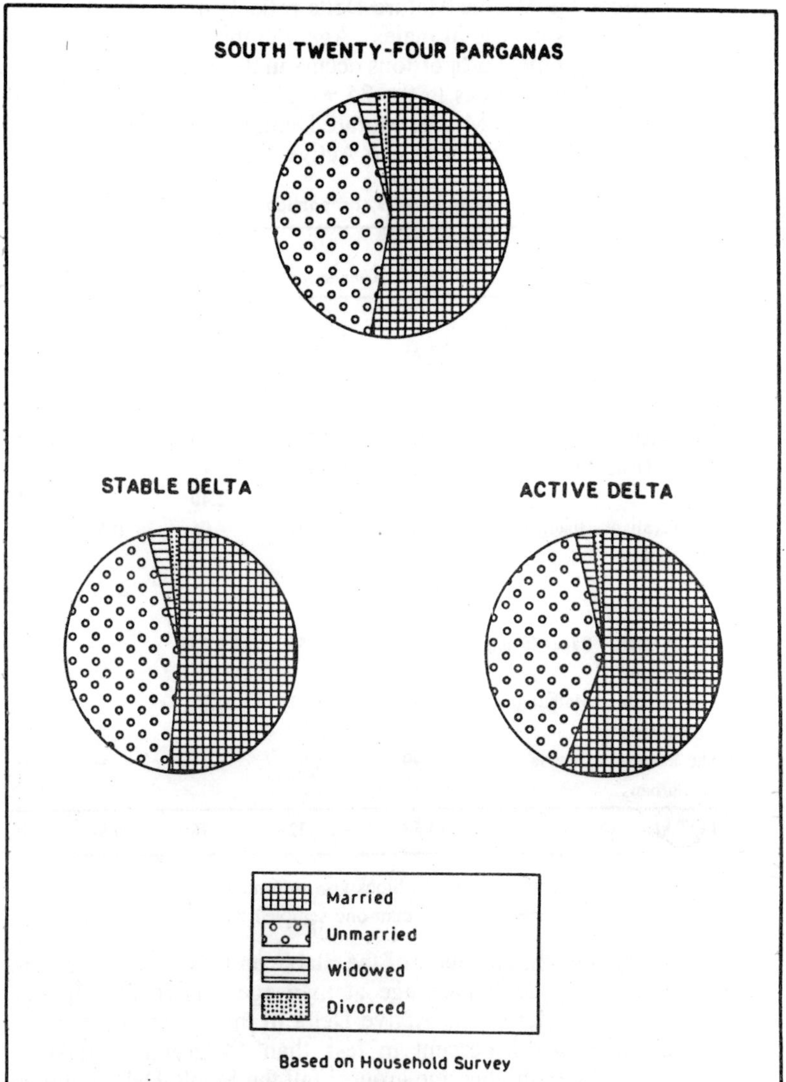


**Fig. 6.3 :** South 24-Parganas Marital Status 1992

*(As Proportion toTotal Population)*

the Eastern and Western Sundarbans in the age group of 15 to 19 years, whereas the Middle Mature Delta reflects only 18.7 per cent in this age groups in case of males. Again in the 20 to 24 years age group, the highest male proportions occurs in the Middle Sundarbans i.e. 67.5 per cent; whereas in the 25 + age group the highest male proportion occur in the Middle Mature Delta i.e. 36.5 per cent, and lower proportions characterize the Active Delta.

**TABLE 6.3 : Marital stauts (Proportions to Total) 1992**

| *Geo-Ecological Retion* | *Blocks* | *Married* | *Unmarried* | *Widowed* | *Divorced* | *Total* |
|---|---|---|---|---|---|---|
| **STABLE DELTA** | | | | | | |
| I. The Western Hugli Side Flats. | Diamond Harbour | 37.23 | 59.47 | 3.29 | — | 100 |
| II. The Middle Mature Delta | Sonarpur | (44.57)* | (54.29) | (1.14) | — | (100) |
| | Mandir Bazar | (39.62) | (57.38) | (3.00) | — | (100) |
| **Total** | | **41.22** | **56.38** | **2.40** | **—** | **100** |
| III. The Piyali Bidyadhari Plains. | Bhangar | 37.39 | 57.97 | 4.06 | 0.58 | 100 |
| **ACTIVE DELTA** | | | | | | |
| IV. The Western Sundarbans | Sagar Island | 48.20 | 49.55 | 2.25 | — | 100 |
| V. The Middle Sundarbans | Mathurapur | 38.46 | 58.61 | 2.93 | — | 100 |
| VI. The Eastern Sundarbans | Gosaba | 40.99 | 55.90 | 3.11 | — | 100 |
| **TOTAL** | | **40.64** | **56.32** | **2.96** | **0.08** | **100** |

* The figures in paranthesis refer to blockwise information where the region consist of more than one sampled block.

The contrasting character of the Stable and the Active Delta is also reflected in the female age at marriage. Here also higher proportions characterise the Active Delta in the lower age groups; being as high as 61 percent in less than 14 group in Eastern Sundarbans. In the higher age groups, fall the Stable Delta regions. However, in general, the lower age at marriage of females increase the reproductive span and hence result ultimately in a high fertility population as already exhibited by the population pyramids; the fact being more pronounced in the Sundarbans.

**TABLE 6.4 : Age At Marriage (Proportions to Total) - 1992**

| *Geo-Ecological Regions/Blocks* | | | *MALES Years* | | | | | *FEMALES Years* | | | | |
|---|---|---|---|---|---|---|---|---|---|---|---|---|
| | | | *Less than 14* | *15-19* | *20-24* | *25 +* | *Total* | *Less than 14* | *15-19* | *20-24* | *25 +* | *Total* |
| **STABLE DELTA** | | | | | | | | | | | | |
| I. | The Western Hugli Side Flats. | Diamond Harbour | 0.00 | 36.55 | 47.58 | 15.86 | 100 | 42.60 | 52.66 | 4.73 | 0.00 | 100 |
| II. | The Middle Mature Delta | Sonarpur | (0.00) | (7.14) | (42.86) | (50.00) | (100) | (8.70) | (52.17) | (39.13) | (0.00) | (100) |
| | | Mandir Bazar | (0.00) | (22.78) | (45.57) | (31.65) | (100) | (22.50) | (59.17) | (18.33) | (0.00) | 100) |
| | | Total | 0.00 | 18.69 | 44.86 | 36.45 | 100 | 18.67 | 57.23 | 24.10 | 0.00 | 100 |
| III. | The Piyali Bidyadhari Plains. | Bhangar | 2.22 | 34.44 | 52.22 | 11.11 | 100 | 15.46 | 71.13 | 12.37 | 1.03 | 100 |

TABLE 6.4 : (*Contd.*)

| *Geo-Ecological Regions/Blocks* | | *MALES Years* | | | | | *FEMALES Years* | | | | |
|---|---|---|---|---|---|---|---|---|---|---|---|
| | | *Less than 14* | *15-19* | *20-24* | *25 +* | *Total* | *Less than 14* | *15-19* | *20-24* | *25 +* | *Total* |
| **ACTIVE DELTA** | | | | | | | | | | | |
| IV. The Western Sundarbans | Sagar Island | 2.50 | 50.00 | 35.00 | 12.50 | 100 | 43.10 | 55.17 | 1.72 | 0.00 | 100 |
| V. The Middle Sundarbans | Mathurapur | 0.00 | 20.48 | 67.47 | 12.05 | 100 | 14.63 | 70.73 | 13.42 | 1.21 | 100 |
| VI. The Eastern Sundarbans | Gosaba | 2.56 | 51.28 | 37.18 | 8.97 | 100 | 60.95 | 39.05 | 0.00 | 0.00 | 100 |
| **TOTAL OF HOUSEHOLDS** | **South 24 Parganas** | **1.12** | **35.47** | **46.71** | **16.69** | **100** | **31.81** | **58.15** | **9.52** | **0.52** | **1 0 0** |

* The figures in paranthesis refer to blockwise information where the region consist of more than one sampled block.

### 6.2.5 Migration Pattern

Only 13.5 per cent of the total surveyed population is that of migrants. The recently settled Active Delta however has the greater share of the migrant population (Table 6.5). Within the Active Delta again the Eastern Sundarbans exhibit the highest proportion of 20.2%. Again the proportion of inmigrants is higher in the Eastern Sundarbans, with highest in Gosaba (9.28 per cent). The proportion of migrants is lowest in the Piyali Bidyadhari Plains, that has an early history of settlement.

**TABLE 6.5 : Proporation of Migrants to Total Population -1992**

| *Geo-Ecological Regions/Blocks* | | *Inmigrants* | *Out Migrants* | *Total Migrants* | *Total Non-Migrants* | *Total Population* |
|---|---|---|---|---|---|---|
| **STABLE DELTA** | | | | | | |
| I. The Western Hugli Side Flats. | Diamond Harbour | 11.04 | 2.80 | 13.84 | 86.16 | 100 |
| II. The Middle Mature Delta | Sonarpur | (18.29) | (1.14) | (19.43) | (80.57) | (100) |
| | Mandir Bazar | (6.56) | (3.82) | (10.38) | (89.62) | (100) |
| **Total** | | **10.54** | **2.96** | **13.50** | **86.50** | **100** |
| III. The Piyali Bidyadhari Plains. | Bhangar | 1.74 | 6.96 | 8.70 | 91.30 | 100 |
| **ACTIVE DELTA** | | | | | | |
| IV. The Western Sundarbans | Sagar Island | 7.43 | 4.95 | 12.38 | 87.62 | 100 |
| V. The Middle Sundarbans | Mathurapur | 8.79 | 3.66 | 12.45 | 87.55 | 100 |
| VI. The Eastern Sundarbans | Gosaba | 14.91 | 5.28 | 20.19 | 79.81 | 100 |
| **TOTAL OF Households** | **South 24-Parganas** | **9.28** | **4.19** | **13.47** | **86.53** | **100** |

* The figures in paranthesis refer to blockwise information where the region consist of more than one sampled block.

Table 6.6 exhibits the pattern of migration. Of all the factors, marriage oriented female migration is most pronounced in the rural areas constituting 64.7 per cent of the total migration. Availability of 'abad' land for settlement comprises the next highest proportion of 11.7 per cent, the trend still existing today. 10.9 per cent have migrated for employment purposes and 10.33 due to political cause from the erstwhile East Pakistan or Bangladesh, the majority of whom are settled in the Middle Mature Delta in Sonarpur near

**TABLE 6.6 : Pattern of Migration - 1992**

| *Geo-Ecological Regions/Blocks* | | *REASONS BEHIND MIGRATION (as proportion to Total Migrants)* 'abad' land | Employ-ment | Marri-age | Educa-tion | Poli-tical | Total | *DURATION OF MIGRATION (as proportion to Total Migrants)* 0-10 Year | 11-20 Year | 21 + Year | Total |
|---|---|---|---|---|---|---|---|---|---|---|---|
| | | 1 | 2 | 3 | 4 | 5 | 6 | 7 | 8 | 9 | 10 |
| **STABLE DELTA** | | | | | | | | | | | |
| I. The Western Hugli Side Flats. | Diamond Harbour | 0.00 | 2.25 | 93.26 | 0.00 | 4.49 | 100 | 69.51 | 25.61 | 4.88 | 100 |
| II. The Middle Mature Delta | Sonarpur | (18.75) | (0.00) | (6.25) | (0.00) | (75.00) | (100) | (47.83) | (20.29) | (31.88) | (100) |
| | Mandir Bazar | (2.56) | (5.13) | (89.75) | (2.56) | (0.00) | (100) | (69.23) | (30.77) | (0.00) | 100) |
| **Total** | | **9.86** | **2.82** | **52.11** | **1.41** | **33.80** | **100** | **47.83** | **20.29** | **31.88** | **100** |
| III. The Piyali Bidyadhari Plains. | Bhangar | 0.00 | 39.29 | 57.14 | 3.57 | 0.00 | 100 | 41.93 | 45.16 | 12.90 | 100 |
| **ACTIVE DELTA** | | | | | | | | | | | |
| IV. The Western Sundarbans | Sagar Island | 25.40 | 25.40 | 38.09 | 4.76 | 6.35 | 100 | 28.30 | 45.28 | 26.41 | 100 |
| V. The Middle Sundarbans | Mathurapur | 0.00 | 11.11 | 77.78 | 11.11 | 0.00 | 100 | 100.00 | 0.00 | 0.00 | 100 |
| VI. The Eastern Sundarbans | Gosaba | 25.00 | 6.25 | 60.00 | 1.25 | 7.50 | 100 | 31.58 | 40.79 | 27.63 | 100 |
| **TOTAL OF HOUSEHOLDS** | **South 24-Parganas** | **11.68** | **10.87** | **64.67** | **2.45** | **10.33** | **100** | **51.30** | **29.97** | **18.73** | **100** |

* The figures in paranthesis refer to blockwise information where the region consist of more than one sampled block.

**TABLE 6.6 : (*Contd.*)**

| *Geo-Ecological Regions/Blocks* | | *Proportion of Total Migrants* | | | *Occupation of Migrants at the Place of Origin (as proportion to total Migrants)* | | | | | | |
|---|---|---|---|---|---|---|---|---|---|---|---|
| | | *Migrated only once* | *Stayed in other places* | *Total* | *Farmers* | *Agricultural Labourers* | *Students* | *Teachers* | *Private Service* | *Public Service* | *Total* |
| | | *11* | *12* | *13* | *14* | *15* | *16* | *17* | *18* | *19* | *20* |
| **STABLE DELTA** | | | | | | | | | | | |
| I. The Western Hugli Side Flats. | Diamond Harbour | 93.18 | 6.82 | 100 | 12.19 | 0.00 | 82.93 | 0.00 | 4.88 | 0.00 | 100 |
| II. The Middle Mature Delta | Sonarpur | (57.14) | (42.86) | (100) | (23.08) | (0.00) | (57.69) | (0.00) | (11.54) | (7.69) | (100) |
| | Mandir B. | (97.44) | (2.56) | (100) | (0.00) | (16.68) | (83.32) | (0.00) | (0.00) | (0.00) | (100) |
| | Total | 78.38 | 21.62 | 100 | 9.68 | 9.68 | 72.58 | 0.00 | 4.84 | 3.23 | 100 |
| III. The Piyali Bidyadhari Plains. | Bhangar | 100 | 0.00 | 100 | 22.41 | 6.90 | 58.62 | 5.17 | 6.90 | 0.00 | 100 |
| **ACTIVE DELTA** | | | | | | | | | | | |
| IV. The Western Sundarbans | Sagar Island | 92.98 | 7.02 | 100 | 40.00 | 4.89 | 55.10 | 0.00 | 0.00 | 0.00 | 100 |
| V. The Middle Sundarbans | Mathurapur | 100 | 0.00 | 100 | 0.00 | 0.00 | 100 | 0.00 | 0.00 | 0.00 | 100 |
| VI. The Eastern Sundarbans | Gosaba | 84.42 | 15.58 | 100 | 34.29 | 0.00 | 62.86 | 0.00 | 0.00 | 2.86 | 100 |
| **TOTAL OF HOUSEHOLDS** | **South 24 Parganas** | **88.89** | **11.11** | **100** | **20.51** | **3.37** | **71.07** | **0.84** | **3.09** | **1.12** | **100** |

* The figures in paranthesis refer to blockwise information where the region consist of more than one sampled block.

**TABLE 6.6 : (*Contd.*)**

| *Geo-Ecological Regions/Blocks* | | CONTACT IN MIGRATION (as proportion to Total) *Friends* | *Relatives* | *None* | *Total* |
|---|---|---|---|---|---|
| | | *21* | *22* | *23* | *24* |
| **STABLE DELTA** | | | | | |
| I. The Western Hugli Side Flats. | Diamond Harbour | 0.00 | 48.28 | 51.72 | 100 |
| II. The Middle Mature Delta | Sonarpur | (0.00) | (43.75) | (56.25) | (100) |
| | Mandir Bazar | (0.00) | (60.00) | (40.00) | (100) |
| | Total | 0.00 | 53.66 | 46.34 | 100 |
| III. The Piyali Bidyadhari Plains. | Bhangar | 24.14 | 41.38 | 34.48 | 100 |
| **ACTIVE DELTA** | | | | | |
| IV. The Western Sundarbans | Sagar Island | 12.77 | 44.68 | 42.55 | 100 |
| V. The Middle Sundarbans | Mathurapur | 23.08 | 57.69 | 19.23 | 100 |
| VI. The Eastern Sundarbans | Gosaba | 7.02 | 57.89 | 35.09 | 100 |
| **TOTAL OF HOUSEHOLDS** | **South 24-Parganas** | **8.01** | **50.52** | **41.46** | **100** |

* The figures in paranthesis refer to blockwise information where the region consist of more than one sampled block.

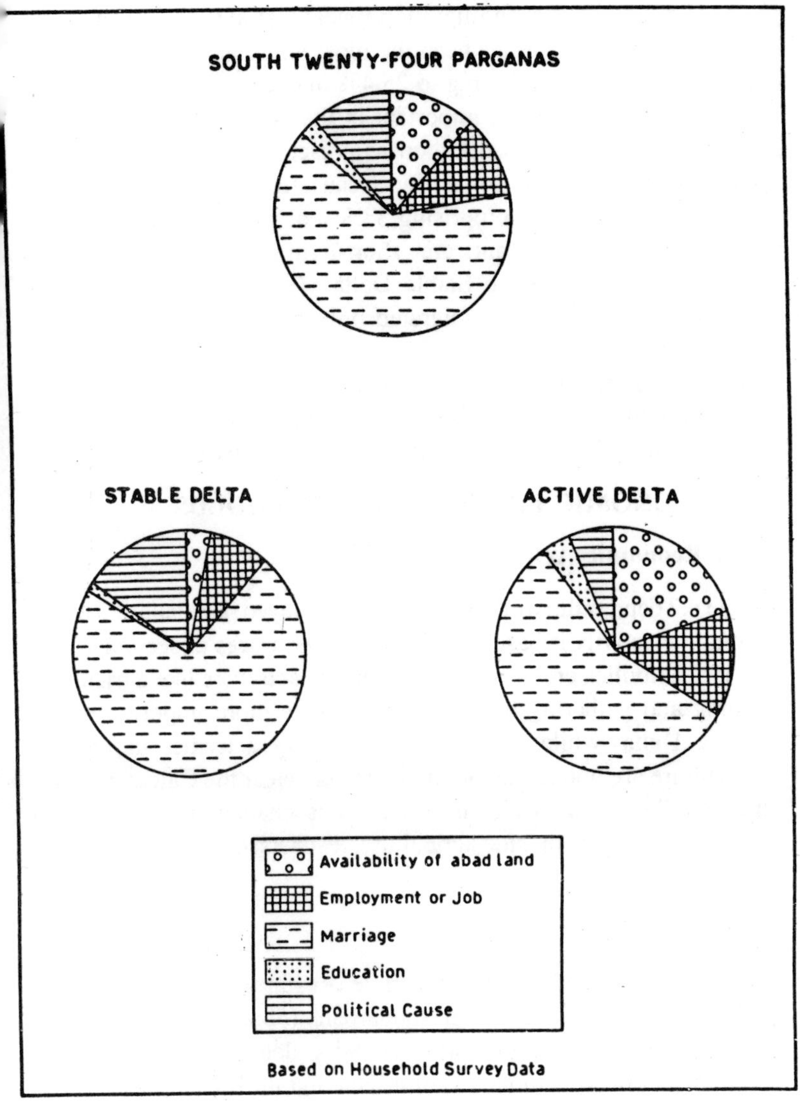


**Fig. 6.4 :** South 24-Parganas Reasons for Migration 1992
*(As proportion to Total Migrants)*

Calcutta; where refugee colonies have come up.(Fig. 6.4)

The reasons behind migration reveal that availability of 'abad' land and employment has been the most important factors in Western Sundarbans, contributing to 25.4% in each case here. Marriage migration has been most important in the Westen Hugli Side Flats contributing 93.3%. Education as a factor is of less importance whereas migration due to political cause is most important in the Middle Mature Delta comprising 33.8% of the total migrants here.

Most of the migrants are short-term migrants and their proportion is highest in the Stable Delta. The larger proportion of migrants i.e. 88.9% have migrated only once.

The occupation of the migrants in the place of origin exhibits that most of them (71.1%) were students. About 20.5% were farmers and 3.4% agricultural labourers. Nearly half the migrants reported that their contact in migration were relatives.

## 6.3 ECONOMIC PROFILE OF HOUSEHOLDS

### 6.3.1 Economic Activities

Table 6.7 depicts the work pattern of the surveyed population. Though economic activity is based on *primary work*, traces of secondary and tertiary activities are present too. Primary activities like agriculture, fishing and gathering of forest produce are more important in the Active Delta, while secondary and tertiary activities along with agriculture are noticed in the Stable Delta. Near the Calcutta region, the Middle Mature Delta in Sonarpur is characterised by factory workers, labourers outside agriculture, teachers, businessmen, traders etc.

#### Agriculture

32.5% of the workers in the sample are farmers their proportion being highest in the Western Sundarbans (52.2% in Gosaba), they being absent in Sonarpur area around Calcutta. In Sagar Island migrants from Medinipur (Kanthi, Nandigram Blocks) are cultivators with large land holdings but simultaneously pursue other services like school teaching etc. In many households a combination of occupations are reported. In the Piyali-Bidyadhari Plains in Bhangar for instance people occupied in agriculture were also seen to perform other duties like peons in Junior High School and thus it becomes

**TABLE 6.7 : Work Pattern**

*(As proportion to total population 1992)*

| Geo-Ecological Regions/Blocks | | Farmers | Agricultural labourer. | Fishing and forestry | Traders | Teachers | Small business-men | Government servants | Labourers(including factory, construction etc. | Unemployed | Total |
|---|---|---|---|---|---|---|---|---|---|---|---|
| | | 1 | 2 | 3 | 4 | 5 | 6 | 7 | 8 | 9 | 10 |
| **STABLE DELTA** | | | | | | | | | | | |
| I. The Western Hugli Side Flats. | Diamond Harbour | 10.55 | 6.42 | 0.92 | 12.84 | 3.67 | 17.89 | 22.94 | 11.93 | 12.84 | 100 |
| II. The Middle Mature Delta | Sonarpur | — | — | — | — | — | (38.60) | (33.33) | (22.81) | (5.26) | (100) |
| | Mandir Bazar | (29.17) | (4.17) | — | — | (5.83) | (13.33) | (28.33) | (16.67) | (2.50) | (100) |
| **Total** | | **19.77** | **2.82** | — | — | **3.95** | **21.47** | **29.94** | **18.64** | **3.39** | **100** |
| III. The Piyali Bidyadhari Plains. | Bhangar | 38.74 | 12.61 | 1.80 | 1.80 | 6.31 | 6.31 | 10.81 | 12.61 | 9.01 | 100 |

TABLE 3.7 : (*Contd.*)

| *Geo-Ecological Regions/Blocks* | | *Farmers* | *Agri-cul-tural labou-rer.* | *Fishing and forestry* | *Traders* | *Teachers* | *Small busi-ness-men* | *Govern-ment servants* | *Labour-ers(incl-uding fac tory construc-tion etc.* | *Unemp-loyed* | *Total* |
|---|---|---|---|---|---|---|---|---|---|---|---|
| | | *1* | *2* | *3* | *4* | *5* | *6* | *7* | *8* | *9* | *10* |
| **ACTIVE DELTA** | | | | | | | | | | | |
| IV. The Western Sundarbans | Sagar Island | 52.20 | 4.40 | 11.32 | 1.89 | 7.55 | 13.84 | 2.52 | 5.03 | 1.26 | 100 |
| V. The Middle Sundarbans | Mathurapur | 46.67 | 4.44 | 1.11 | 2.22 | 11.11 | 7.78 | 18.89 | 5.56 | 2.22 | 100 |
| VI. The Eastern Sundarbans | Gosaba | 40.30 | 11.94 | 32.84 | — | 3.73 | 5.97 | 0.75 | 2.24 | 2.24 | 100 |
| **TOTAL OF HOUSEHOLDS** | **South 24-Parganas** | **32.52** | **6.97** | **8.01** | **0.81** | **5.46** | **14.40** | **16.14** | **11.27** | **4.41** | **100** |

* The figures in paranthesis refer to blockwise information where the region consist of more than one sampled block.

difficult to categorise them into a particular class. However, the highest proportion of farmers had been reported from the Active Delta.

Agricultural labourers constitute 6.9% of the total population surveyed with highest proportion observed in the Piyali-Bidyadhari Plains (12.6%). The next highest proportion of agricultural labourers is seen in Eastern Sundarbans (11.9%).

About 8% of the total household members report other primary activities like fishing and collection of forest produce are seen mostly in the Active Delta of the Sundarbans. Within this area the highest proportion is seen in Eastern Sundarbans i.e. 32.8% in Gosaba followed by 11.3% in Western Sundarbans in Sagar. In Gosaba the household members engage in fishing in the Khals (distributaries) and collect forest produce illegally like honey, wax, twigs, golpatta (used as a roofing material etc.).

For the whole district the total area available for pisciculture is 31,864 hectares with 828 bheries (brackish water fisheries), 262 Government assisted coastal units, 634 Government assisted river units and 2716 hectares of vested impounded water areas, engaging 66,232 fishermen families. The fishermen's area in the district include (a) **Inland fisheries** with fresh water species such as Rohu, Katla, Mrigal, Kalbose etc. (b) **Estuarine fisheries** and brakish water fish culture locally called "Bhasa - bada" `nona'bheri' (nona-gheri) fisheries which may be again of (i) Nona-Gheri fish farm (ii) Nona-Gheri paddy cum fish culture farm and (iii) Nona-Gheri fish cum paddy culture farm and finally (c) **Offshore fisheries**. But unfortunately, inadequate and in some cases absence of proper infrastructural facilities such a quick transport and marketing facility, inadequate iceplants and cold storage facility, non-availability of loans through banks and cooperatives, lack of knowledge about modern scientific fishing technique, poor organisation among fishermen; all these stand in the way for the growth of fishing as an organised industry.

## Trade and Commerce

Only 0.8% of the total household members are engaged in trade. About 5.5% are teachers. Small business engage about 14.4% of the total population. Their highest proportion is seen in the Stable Delta. In the Middle Mature Delta 21.5% are businessmen and 17.9% of the population in Diamond Harbour in the Western Hugli Side Flats pursue the same. In the villages around Calcutta in Sonarpur and around Diamond Harbour Town, workers are engaged in small business like making of brass items, furniture, idol (in Diamond Harbour) and in tailoring and allied activities, largely catering to the urban markets of either Calcutta or Diamond Harbour. 16.1% of the household members are Government servants in the Western Hugli Side Flats, Middle Mature Delta, Piyali Bidyadhari Plains and in the Middle Sundarbans in Mathurapur, and they form the commuters area in these parts. 11.3% are non-agricultural labourers engaged in occupations as carpenters, service mechanics, raj mistry, bus conductors and drivers, daily workers in 'bidi' manufacturing units, construction workers and electric mistry. The phenomena of unemployment was reported among 4.4% of the household members in the Western Hugli Side Flats in Diamond Harbour.

### 6.3.2 Distance and Duration of Work

Table 6.8 reveals that 29.7% of the total workers do not have to travel far for work. They largely work within the village. Their highest proportion is in the Piyali- Bidyadhari Plains i.e. 59.3% and also in all the sub regions of the Active Delta. 46.9% of the workers in Mathurapur in Middle Sundarbans, 34.8% in Sagar or Western Sundarbans and 21.5% in Gosaba in Eastern Sundarbans do not travel for work.

The highest travel to work (for 59% of the total workers) upto 20 km is seen in the Eastern Sundarbans i.e. 70.1%. The reason for travelling upto 20 km in the Active Delta is due to the large areal spread of the villages here; whereas the phenomena of commuting for other services as well, may be the reason for travel in the Stable Delta.

Due to the presence of local railways connecting places like Diamond Harbour, Mathurapur, Mandir Bazar, and Sonarpur to Calcutta, the phenomena of daily commuting to the Calcutta District has resulted in people travelling upto 50 km or even more. About

**TABLE 6.8: Distance And Puration of work And Family Income 1992**

*(As proportion to total workers)*

| Geo-Ecological Regions/Blocks | | Distance of Work (km) | | | | | Duration of Work | | | | Income (Rs.) | | | |
|---|---|---|---|---|---|---|---|---|---|---|---|---|---|---|
| | | Less than 1 | 1-20 | 21-50 | More than 50 | Total | Full Time | Part Time | Seas-onal | Total | Less than 500 p.m. | 500-1000 p.m. | More than 1000 p.m. | Total |
| | | 1 | 2 | 3 | 4 | 5 | 6 | 7 | 8 | 9 | 10 | 11 | 12 | 13 |
| **STABLE DELTA** | | | | | | | | | | | | | | |
| I. The Western Hugli Side Flats. | Diamond Harbour | 17.56 | 68.70 | 2.29 | 11.45 | 100 | 97.25 | 2.65 | 00.00 | 100 | 30.20 | 44.97 | 24.83 | 100 |
| II. The Middle Mature Delta | Sonarpur | — | (96.23) | (3.77) | — | (100) | (100) | — | — | (100) | (22.64) | (35.85) | (41.51) | 100 |
| | Mandir Bazar | (18.63) | (51.96) | (27.45) | (1.96) | (100) | (96.40) | (1.80) | (1.80) | (100) | (16.35) | (54.81) | (28.85) | 100 |
| **Total** | | **12.26** | **67.10** | **19.35** | **1.29** | **100** | **97.47** | **1.27** | **1.27** | **100** | **18.47** | **48.41** | **33.12** | **100** |
| III. The Piyali Bidyadhari Plains. | Bhangar | 59.29 | 36.28 | 4.42 | — | 100 | 90.29 | 8.79 | 0.97 | 100 | 26.44 | 48.28 | 25.29 | 100 |

**TABLE 6.8 :** *(Contd.)*

| *Geo-Ecological Regions/Blocks* | | *Distance of Work (km)* | | | | | *Duration of Work* | | | | *Income (Rs.)* | | | |
|---|---|---|---|---|---|---|---|---|---|---|---|---|---|---|
| | | *Less than 1* | *1-20* | *21-50* | *More than 50* | *Total* | *Full Time* | *Part Time* | *Seas-onal* | *Total* | *Less than 500 P.M.* | *500-1000 P.M.* | *More than 1000 P.M.* | *Total* |
| | | *1* | *2* | *3* | *4* | *5* | *6* | *7* | *8* | *9* | *10* | *11* | *12* | *13* |
| **ACTIVE DELTA** | | | | | | | | | | | | | | |
| IV. The Western Sundarbans | Sagar Island | 34.78 | 56.52 | 8.70 | — | 100 | 92.13 | 7.87 | — | 100 | 35.46 | 44.68 | 19.86 | 100 |
| V. The Middle Sundarbans | Mathurapur | 46.88 | 46.88 | 6.25 | — | 100 | 80.23 | 19.77 | — | 100 | 22.22 | 41.57 | 38.20 | 100 |
| VI. The Eastern Sundarbans | Gosaba | 21.50 | 70.09 | 6.54 | 1.87 | 100 | 59.63 | 40.37 | — | 100 | 44.44 | 35.04 | 20.51 | 100 |
| **TOTAL OF HOUSEHOLDS** | **South 24-Parganas** | **29.66** | **59.04** | **8.61** | **2.68** | **100** | **87.87** | **11.72** | **0.41** | **100** | **29.32** | **44.05** | **26.62** | **100** |

* The figures in paranthesis refer to blockwise information where the region consist of more than one sampled block.

8.6% of the total workers travel upto 50 km, their highest proportion being reported from Diamond Harbour. Lastly 2.7% of the total, travel even beyond 51 km.

### 6.3.3 Household Income

The reported income of the household members has been categorised into 3 categories given in Table 6.8.

(a) Less than Rs.500 per month : About 29.3% of the total earn such an amount; their highest proportion occur in the Active Delta specially in Gosaba.

(b) Rs. 501 to Rs.1000 per month : The majority of the population i.e. 44.1% fall within this group specially in the Stable Delta. For instance about 48.4% of the workers in the Middle Mature Delta earn this amount.

(c) More than Rs.1001 per month characterise only 26.6% of the total; their greatest share occurring in the Stable Delta and in the Mathurapur. *The income level* of the rural folks are thus found to be *very low* in Deltaic West Bengal; the fact being more accentuated in the Western and Eastern Sundarbans.

## 6.4 SOCIAL PROFILE OF HOUSEHOLDS

The social profile of the household has been discussed under composition of religion of the households, caste composition, language and education level.

### 6.4.1 Religion

The surveyed population exhibit four different religious groups viz. Hindu, Muslim, Christian, and Tribal or Animistic. Of the 400 households 87% are Hindus, 8% Muslims and 21% are tribals practising animism. The Stable Delta has the highest proportion of Hindus i.e. 91% followed by 9% Muslims. The Active Delta has lower proportion of Hindus i.e. 79% of the households, 8% Muslims and 13% of tribal religious groups most pronounced among the Mundas of Gosaba. The regionwise break-up exhibits the highest proportion of Hindus in Mandir Bazar of Western Hugli Side Flats and the Muslims in the Piyali Plains in Bhangar. Tribals are found only in the Eastern Sundarbans in Gosaba constituting 40% of the households surveyed here.

### 6.4.2 Caste Composition

Of the total households surveyed, 59% belong to scheduled castes and 5% are scheduled tribes. The Stable Delta has the highest proportion of Scheduled Caste population i.e.62%. Within this delta the highest proportion of Scheduled Castes are concentrated in the Western Hugli Side Flats and in the Middle Mature Delta. About 55% of the households of the Active Delta belong to Scheduled Castes; the highest proportion being seen in Sagar Island of Western Sundarbans.

Scheduled Tribe population constitutes 13% of the total households of the Active Delta mainly concentrated in Gosaba where 40% of the surveyed population belong to this category.

### 6.4.3 Language

The major languages spoken in the area include Bengali, English, Hindi, Sanskrit, Urdu and Mundari. The proportion of households knowing Bengali are 51%, 21% of the households know Bengali and English, 9% Bengali and Hindi, 1% Bengali, Sanskrit and English, 16% Bengali, English and Hindi, 2% Bengali and Mundari and only 1% Bengali and Urdu.

The highest proportion of Bengali speaking households is seen in the Active Delta i.e. 53%; and 50% of the households of the Stable Delta belong to this category. Bilingualism with Bengali - English combination is seen in 21% of the households of the Stable Delta and 22% of the households in the Active Delta; here the highest proportion belongs to the Western Sundarbans. Bengali and English combination is observed in lesser proportions i.e.8% of the households of the Stable Delta and in 11% of the members in the Active Delta. Bengali and Mundari combination is seen only in 6% of the surveyed villages of the Active Delta in Gosaba, and Bengali - Urdu combination in only 4% of the households in the Stable Delta and 2% of the households of the Active Delta.

Multi-lingualism is seen in certain households. Bengali, English and Hindi combination is seen in 20% of the households in the

Stable Delta (highest proportion in the Middle Mature Delta); and only 9% of the villages in Active Delta.

A very small proportion of the households speak Bengali, Sanskrit, and English combination as seen in 1% of the households in the rural villages of the Stable Delta.

### 6.4.4 Literacy and Education

Table 6.9 exhibits the literacy level among the surveyed households. Only 56.9% of the reported are literates. The Stable Delta again registers the greatest proportion of literates specially in the Western Hugli Side Flats in Diamond Harbour where 64.1% of the population belong to this category. Within the Active Delta, the highest proportion of literates is in the Western and Middle Sundarbans. The highest proportion of illiterates (47%) is observed in the Eastern Sundarbans.

Educational attainment reveals that 41.7% of the literate population have attained primary education, 32.8% middle school education, 10.8% secondary or high School education, and 5.9% have attained intermediate level education. About 6.1% are pass graduates, the other categories being negligible. Among the regions the Eastern Sundarbans represent the highest proportion of primary educated persons, in this case being 47.6%, whereas the Piyali Bidyadhari Plains reports the highest proportion of middle school education i.e. 41% in Bhangar and the Western Hugli Side Flats reports the highest proportion of secondary education i.e. 14.1% of the population of Diamond Harbour belong to this category. The proportion of MA and MBBS are insignificant all over the delta. Of the total household members 24% have left education due to economic pressure, their proportion being 25% in the Active Delta and 24% in the Stable Delta. 12% of the household members have left education after marriage and this is specially in case of the females, their proportion being 14% in the Active Delta and 10% in the Stable Delta.

A negligible portion or 0.4% of the total household members have left education due to diseases and ailment.

## 6.5 FAMILY ASSETS

In this section the family assets of the households have been studied in detail. The household members dwelling in rural areas

**TABLE 6.9 : Educational Attainment 1992**

| Geo-ecological Regions/Blocks | | Proporation of Literate to Total Pupulation | | | Educational Attainment as Proportion to Total Population | | | | | | | | |
|---|---|---|---|---|---|---|---|---|---|---|---|---|---|
| | | liter-ates | Illi-trates | Total | Primary | Middle | Second-ary or High | Hr.Sec. or Inter-medi-ate | Pass Gradu-ates | Hon. Gradu-ates | Master of Arts | MBBS | Total Lite-rates |
| | | 1 | 2 | 3 | 4 | 5 | 6 | 7 | 8 | 9 | 10 | 11 | 12 |
| **STABLE DELTA** | | | | | | | | | | | | | |
| I. The Western Hugli Side Flats. | Diamond Harbour | 64.09 | 35.91 | 100 | 42.67 | 28.53 | 14.14 | 5.66 | 7.71 | 1.28 | — | — | 100 |
| II. The Middle Mature Delta | Sonarpur | (54.29) | (45.71) | (100) | (29.47) | (29.47) | (17.89) | (12.63) | (2.10) | (8.42) | — | — | 100 |
| | Mandir Baz. | (53.55) | (46.45) | (100) | (36.73) | (34.18) | (10.71) | (5.61) | (9.69) | (1.02) | (1.53) | (0.54) | 100 |
| | Total | 53.79 | 46.21 | 100 | 34.36 | 32.65 | 13.06 | 7.90 | 7.22 | 3.44 | 1.03 | 0.34 | 100 |
| III. The Piyali Bidyadhari Plains. | Bhangar | 56.52 | 43.48 | 100 | 43.59 | 41.02 | 6.15 | 3.59 | 3.59 | 0.51 | 1.03 | 0.51 | 100 |

TABLE 6.9 : (*Contd.*)

| *Geo-ecological Regions/Blocks* | | *Proporation of Literate to Total Pupulation* | | | *Educational Attainment as Proportion to Total Population* | | | | | | | | |
|---|---|---|---|---|---|---|---|---|---|---|---|---|---|
| | | *liter-ates* | *Illi-trates* | *Total* | *Primary* | *Middle* | *Second-ary or High* | *Hr.Sec. or Inter-medi-ate* | *Pass Gradu-ates* | *Hon. Gradu-ates* | *Master of Arts* | *MBBS* | *Total Lite-rates* |
| | | *1* | *2* | *3* | *4* | *5* | *6* | *7* | *8* | *9* | *10* | *11* | *12* |
| **ACTIVE DELTA** | | | | | | | | | | | | | |
| IV. The Western Sundarbans | Sagar Island | 55.18 | 44.82 | 100 | 45.71 | 35.51 | 7.76 | 4.90 | 4.90 | 0.41 | 0.82 | — | 100 |
| V. The Middle Sundarbans | Mathurapur | 55.20 | 44.80 | 100 | 37.50 | 33.75 | 9.38 | 7.50 | 6.25 | 3.12 | 1.88 | 0.62 | 100 |
| VI. The Eastern Sundarbans | Gosaba | 52.80 | 47.20 | 100 | 47.65 | 28.82 | 10.00 | 5.29 | 4.71 | 1.76 | 1.76 | — | 100 |
| **TOTAL OF HOUSEHOLDS** | **South 24 Parganas** | **56.93** | **43.07** | **100** | **41.66** | **32.83** | **10.76** | **5.86** | **6.07** | **1.72** | **0.90** | **0.20** | **100** |

* The figures in paranthesis refer to blockwise information where the region consist of more than one Sampled block.

have assets such as the stocks that are reared and kept, the products obtained, the total area under cultivation and crops grown, the amount of agricultural produce, value and amount, the items of possession, house owned, number of rooms shared and the use of rooms. This would give us an idea of the relative affluence of the household members in the different geoecological regions.

### 6.5.1 Stocks Raised and Products Obtained

Fifty-five per cent of the total household members rear only cows, the highest proportion of which is reported from the Middle Sundarbans or Mathurapur (49%). The proportion of cows reared is greater in the villages of the Sundarbans and the Active Delta; but surprisingly very few households (only 6%) of the urban fringe areas like Sonarpur villages rear cows.

Twenty-eight per cent of the total household members rear only poultry birds, the greatest proportion of birds being reared by the households in Sonarpur and near Diamond Harbour Town. fifteen per cent of the households rear both cows and poultry, the highest proportion of which is seen among the household members of the Active Delta specially in Gosaba i.e. 28%. Finally cows, poultry and pigs are reared by only 2% of the household members in the Active Delta.

Of the total stocks reared, 70% belong to the Active Delta and 30% to the Stable Delta. 69% of the household members rear and keep their stock in the homestead itself specially in the Active Delta; 25% have provisions for a cowshed specially in the Active Delta in the Sundarbans where there is fear of wild animals and snakes, 6% rear the stock in the farmland itself.

Twenty-six per cant of the households of the study area obtain milk, 6% have the facility of obtaining eggs, 2% meat, 42% milk and eggs and 24% milk, eggs and meat as products from the stocks they rear. 35% of the household incur income of Rs.500 annually, 33% earn a significant income of Rs.2500 annually and 33% do not earn anything. Income wise the Active Delta households i.e. 52% gain considerably through stocks.

### 6.5.2 Land under cultivation and crops grown

The total area under cultivation is 2222 Bighas of which 61% are in the Active Delta. Within this delta, the highest proportion of area under cultivation is in Mathurapur followed by Sagar and Gosaba. The Stable Delta has 39% of the total cultivated area under its domain, highest being in the Piyali Bidyadhari Plain.

Of the total number of households, 53% of the household members have the facility of irrigation, of which 71% are in the Stable Delta and 29% in the Active Delta, that lacks irrigation facilities; 47% of the total households do not share the benefit of irrigation and depend entirely on the vagaries of the monsoons.

The agricultural practice and products obtained by the households include a *monoculture* of Kharif or aman rice in many places to a *multiple crop* of rice, wheat, mustard, pulses etc. The cropping pattern of the household differ from region to region.

36% of the households mostly in the Active Delta depend entirely on rice, of which the highest proportion is seen in Mandir Bazar i.e. 43%, Gosaba i.e. 33% and Mathurapur 24%.

22% grow rice in combination with potato and vegetables, 40% in the Active Delta and 60% in the Stable Delta within this combination; highest proportion being observed in the Diamond Harbour Block i.e. 42% of the total.

Eighteen per cent of the households only in the Active Delta grow paddy as the major crop in combination with wheat, vegetables and mustard. Within this group, however the highest proportion occur in Piyali Bidyadhari Plains in Bhangar, 40 per cent of the total.

Three per cent of the total households in Sagar or Western Sundarbans grow paddy as a single crop in combination with chillies. Seven per cent again in Sagar grow rice in combination with chillies and water melon and 2% also in Sagar have paddy, chillies and betel vine as the combination. 4 per cent of the total households entirely in the urban fringe area in Sonarpur (Middle Mature Delta) practise *market gardening* growing fruits and vegetables only.

### 6.5.3 Items of Possession

With a bountiful of natural resources the surveyed region is *one of the poorest regions* of the country as demonstrated by the items of possession enjoyed by the households. 10% of the households have a bed only, thc highest proportion of which is in Gosaba followed by Diamond Harbour and Sagar, 2% of the households have bed as well as an almirah. 16% of the households own bed, almirah and books as items of possession. 47% have the facility of bed, almirah and transistor or a radio. In this group belong only 40% of the households of the Active Delta and 60% of the households of the Stable Delta. Again 26% of the households own bed, almirah, radio, television and cycle. 67% of the household members of the Stable Delta fall within this group mostly around urban areas, and 33% of the households members of the Active Delta fall within this category. Only 0.3% of the total households enjoy all the above facilities plus the additional advantage of a rifle, motor - boat, agricultural machinery etc. and this is marked among the households having large land holdings in Gosaba who obtained land through land grants during the British regime.

Ninety-eight per cent of the surveyed households have their own homes used only for residential purposes and 2% live in rented homes in Mandir Bazar and in Sonarpur (urban fringe area of Calcutta with rents varying between Rs. 90 to Rs.120 per month).

Ninety-four per cent of the household members live in single storey homes and 6% in double storeys, the number of rooms varying from one to three in most cases (87% of the household members) and 3 to 6 in the rest (13% of the households). The mud houses in the Sundarbans area specially is Gosaba are often double storeys with four slanting roofs and long eaves almost touching the ground. An outside mud wall is noticeable specially in Gosaba, where there is the fear of wild animals. It was noticed that 58% of the household members have a single bed room, 11% use the rooms as bed rooms cum kitchen cum drawing rooms, usually the balcony is made use of for that purpose.

## 6.6 MORTALITY, MORBIDITY AND HEALTH CARE

A detailed health survey has been conducted in the 400 sample households in which aspects like mortality and its causes, common diseases and treatment received, family planning and child and mother care has been taken into consideration, in order to probe into the health conditions of the study area.

### 6.6.1 Mortality and its Causes

Of the total samples surveyed, the number of persons who died in 1992 were 50 or 13% of the total households, of which 3% died of cardiac failure, 4% of the total households died due to old age, 2% died to tuberculosis (in the Active Delta), 1% due to cancer, 3% due to gastro-entrities and 0.8% (or 2 persons) has been killed by the Royal Bengal Tiger in Gosaba. The question of mortality does not arise in the remaining 87% of the households.

The age at which death occurred ranges from less than 14 to over 65 years. 0.3% of the deaths have occurred at an age less than 14 years. 6% have died in between 15 to 60 years and another 6% above 60 years. Of the total number of deaths 66% are males and the rest females. In case of deaths other than old age, are those killed by tiger in the Sundarbans. The duration of sickness range from less than one year in 2% of the households to over five years, in 4% of the households. The duration of treatment again range from less than one year in 4% of the households, 1-5 years in 4% of the households and only 0.5% have been treated more than five years. Considering all the causes of death, the Active Delta registers 56% of the total deaths followed by the 44% of the Stable Delta.

### 6.6.2 Morbidity

Of the total population of 2532 persons surveyed, 559 persons or 22% suffer from some or the other form of common diseases. Region-wise picture reveals 65% of the total sick households belong to the Stable Delta and 35% of the total sick households belong to the Active Delta.

Of the total diseases, 48% has been sick less than 15 years, 32% in between 16-60 years, 2.5% more than 61 years and in 17% of the rest, the year was unknown. The most common diseases of the district include asthma and gastro-stomach related diseases. Data reveals that of the common diseases like common cough and cold claims the highest percentage of 38% (highest number suffering from this disease is in the Stable Delta), followed by asthma, 24% (highest portion being in the Active Delta), the yearlong humid conditions of the Delta is the main reason behind such a disease. 15% of the total disease is attributable to gastro-stomach related diseases due to unhygienic sanitary and water conditions specially in the Active Delta and also due to the fact that rice is the main food of the area. Breakfast, lunch and dinner all comprise of rice or rice items and this *without hardly any supplement of protein intake* for thc poorer folks is responsible for gastric diseases. 14% suffer from fever associated with diarrhoea, 4% from rheumatism. The other insignificant proportions include heart diseases 0.25%, paralysis 1%, tuberculosis 0.75%, and high blood pressure 0.5%. Of the total households surveyed 11% of the households go to Calcutta for medical treatment purpose. Within this category 27% belong to the Active Delta and the rest 73% belong to the Stable Delta. The Stable Delta being nearer to the Calcutta Metropolitan District and having better connectively with it, is the main reason behind such a percentage distribution.

69% of the total households go to their respective local regions. In the Active Delta, 8% of the families of Gosaba Block go to Gosaba for treatment, 18% of Sagar's household go to Rudranagar, Gangasagar, and 12% of Mathurapur's household members go to the hospital at Mathurapur. In the Stable Delta, 15% of the Western Hugli Side Flats in Diamond Harbour go to the town itself, 14% of the Mandir Bazaar's household in the Middle Mature Delta go to the Public Health Centre at Nayerhat, and 14% of the sample households in the Piyali Bidyadhari Plains in Bhangar go to Bhatipota Primary Health Centre. Among the villages of the Stable Delta surrounding urban centres, 9% go to Diamond Harbour town and in Sonarpur, 9% go to the Rajpur and Chouhati here.

13% of the total households instead of going to Calcutta or attending local centres go to other places for treatment. For the Eastern and Central Sundarbans people travel to Port Canning, and to Kakdwip which is the major centre for Central and Western Sundarbans. People of the Stable Delta in Mandir Bazar also travel to Kakdwip or Kulpi. For the rest 7% of the households any specialised medical treatment is not taken help of but they may use certain traditional methods.

Of the total diseased household members treatment has been undertaken for less than one year in 15% of the cases, one to five years in 57% of the cases, more than 5 years in 11% of the cases and in 17% of the cases the question of treatment do not arise.

Again of the total diseased only 5% are given specific food and water, in 26% of the cases sometimes precaution is taken and in the rest 69% no precaution is taken at all. Certain family diseases are genetic and hereditary in character and prove to be dangerous in the long run. Such diseases of the delta include asthma, tuberculosis and certain skin diseases. 6% of the total household members have genetic asthma, 5% have genetic tuberculosis, 1% has skin diseases and the rest of 88% do not have any genetic diseases.

In general 34% members have genetic diseases of which 62% are males and 38% females. Most of these diseases are under treatment and are not cured.

### 6.6.3 Family Planning and Health Care

Of the total household members only 26% always use some form of family planning methods, 32% occasionally and 42% never. Though mobile famaily planning units have been introduced in many parts, people are not much interested in the fact. Of the families abiding by family planning 60% are in the Stable Delta and only 40% are in the Active Delta of the Sundarbans. Here again Mathurapur is much advanced than either Gosaba or Sagar.

In South Twenty Four Parganas the most common method that has been adopted is female sterilization. Among the total households surveyed 19% has taken help of sterilization, only 8% use condoms, 1% use oral pills, 21% believe in natural abstinence, 10% in coitus interruptus and 42% do not practise anything. The use of intra-uterine devices (IUD) was particularly insignificant. In general 93% of the families have some form of knowledge of delimitation of the family size, and the rest 7% are ignorant. Most of the development in family planning has been in the Stable Delta and that too among the urban fringe villages here specially near Calcutta.

The work status of female reveal that most of them, 96% are housewives all over the Delta, engaging full time to their infants apart from the other domestic chores. The rest 4% devote part time to their children. These include 2% of females engaged in farming (in Bhangar, Mathurapur and Sagar), 0.3% in Bhangar engaged in cottage industries and 1.7% (in Mandir Bazar, Diamond Harbour and Mathurapur) are engaged in teaching. Of the married females 90% do receive some form of pre-natal care and 10% do not. Again 91% receive postnatal care and 9% do not.

The common diseases of the child include common cough and cold in 65% of the cases, stomach disorder in 21% of the cases and fever in the rest 14% of the cases.

Again 83% go to the local doctors for treatment of the child and only 17% of the households to specialised doctors.

Of all the medical sources taken help of, for the treatment of the child, public health centres are the most important specially in the

Sundarbans (51% of the households here take the help of the PHC) and this is also true in the Stable Delta (49%).

Government Hospitals specially those at Gosaba, Kakdwip, Diamond Harbour and Calcutta constitute the next important source providing treatment. The PHC provide treatment to 64% of the households, Government hospital to 26% of the households, 5% get treatment from private sources, 2% from traditional sources and 3% get treated from the PHC as well as the hospital. In the urban fringe villages of Diamond Harbour most persons go to hospital in Diamond Harbour Town and in case of Sonarpur (urban fringe of Calcutta) people go to the hospital at Rajpur or to Calcutta.

The distance of the source of treatment ranges from less than 5 km to over 20 km. 59% of the households have to travel less than 5 km, 25% in between 5 to 10 km, 9%, 10 to 20 km and 7% more than 20 km. It is usually seen that in the remote areas such as the Sundarbans people have to travel as far as 15-20 km or more for medical treatment and specially in case of Gosaba which suffers severely from the facility of medical treatment.

It is noticed that 87% of the households have to buy medicine on their own and 13% of the rest have access to medicines that are partly subsidized. Again 50% of the households complain of difficulty in the availability of medical and paramedical staff, (specially in the Active Delta and in Mandir Bazar of the Stable Delta) and in the rest 50% there is no complaint.

## SECTION II

## HUMAN SETTLEMENTS

## 6.7 QUALITY OF HOUSING, BASIC AMENITIES AND PERSONAL HYGIENE

### 6.7.1 Housing Facilities

Table 6.10 depicts the housing quality and certain basic amenities in the different regions. Kutcha houses are dominant features of the area, the material used is mud plastered over a bamboo framework. Straw is the main item used for thatching purposes, whereas in semi pucca houses, tin, tiles comprise the roofing items.

Kutcha walls constitute 52% of the total houses, of the surveyed households, semi pucca 36% and 12% only have pucca walls mostly around Calcutta and Sonarpur. Kutcha walls, characterise the Active

**TABLE 6.10: Housing And Basic Amenties - 1992**

*(As proportion to total Households)*

| *Geo-Ecological Regions/Blocks* | | *Material of Wall* | | | | *Material of Floor* | | | | *Material of Roof* | | | |
|---|---|---|---|---|---|---|---|---|---|---|---|---|---|
| | | *Kutcha* | *Semi Kutcha* | *Pucca* | *Total* | *Kutcha* | *Semi Kutcha* | *Pucca* | *Total* | *Kutcha* | *Semi Kutcha* | *Pucca* | *Total* |
| | | *1* | *2* | *3* | *4* | *5* | *6* | *7* | *8* | *9* | *10* | *11* | *12* |
| **STABLE DELTA** | | | | | | | | | | | | | |
| I. The Western Hugli Side Flats | Diamond Harbour | 44.32 | 35.23 | 20.45 | 100 | 47.73 | 39.77 | 12.50 | 100 | 21.59 | 70.45 | 7.95 | 100 |
| II. The Middle Mature Delta | Sonarpur | (51.61) | (16.13) | (32.26) | (100) | (25.81) | (45.16) | (29.03) | (100) | — | (93.55) | (6.45) | 100 |
| | Mandir Baz. | (49.30) | (42.25) | (8.45) | (100) | (49.30) | (43.66) | (7.04) | (100) | (46.48) | (43.66) | (9.86) | 100 |
| | Total | 50.00 | 34.31 | 15.69 | 100 | 42.16 | 44.12 | 13.72 | 100 | 32.35 | 58.82 | 8.82 | 100 |
| III. The Piyali Bidyadhari Plains | Bhangar | 46.00 | 40.00 | 14.00 | 100 | 52.00 | 36.00 | 12.00 | 100 | 48.00 | 44.00 | 8.00 | 100 |
| **ACTIVE DELTA** | | | | | | | | | | | | | |
| IV. The Western Sundarbans | Sagar Island | 54.55 | 40.00 | 5.45 | 100 | 83.64 | 10.91 | 5.45 | 100 | 83.64 | 16.36 | — | 100 |
| V. The Middle Sundarbans | Mathurapur | 30.77 | 65.38 | 3.85 | 100 | 23.08 | 73.08 | 3.85 | 100 | 5.77 | 65.38 | 28.85 | 100 |
| VI. The Eastern Sundarbans | Gosaba | 94.34 | 5.66 | — | 100 | 92.45 | 7.55 | — | 100 | 94.34 | 3.77 | 1.89 | 100 |
| **TOTAL OF HOUSEHOLDS** | **South 24-Parganas** | **52.00** | **36.00** | **12.00** | **100** | **55.00** | **36.00** | **9.00** | **100** | **44.00** | **46.00** | **10.00** | **100** |

* The figures in paranthesis refer to blockwise information where the region consist of more than one sampled block.

**TABLE 6.10 : (*Contd.*)**

*(As proportion to total Households)*

| *Geo-Ecological Regions/Blocks* | | *Lighting* | | | | | *Sanitation* | | |
|---|---|---|---|---|---|---|---|---|---|
| | | *Electricity* | *Kerosene* | *Wood* | *Electricity and Kerosene* | *Total* | *Yes* | *No* | *Total* |
| | | *1* | *2* | *3* | *4* | *5* | *6* | *7* | *8* |
| STABLE DELTA | | | | | | | | | |
| I. The Western Hugli Side Flats | Diamond | 19.32 | 50.00 | 4.54 | 26.14 | 100 | 33.00 | 67.00 | 100 |
| II. The Middle Mature Delta | Sonarpur | (29.03) | (64.52) | — | (6.45) | (100) | (45.00) | (55.00) | (100) |
| | Mandir Bazar | (39.44) | (50.70) | — | (9.86) | (100) | (30.00) | (70.00) | (100) |
| | Total | 36.27 | 54.90 | — | 8.82 | 100 | 37.50 | 62.50 | 100 |
| III. The Piyali Bidyadhari Plains | Bhangar | 14.00 | 86.00 | — | — | 100 | 25.00 | 75.00 | 100 |
| **ACTIVE DELTA** | | | | | | | | | |
| IV. The Western Sundarbans | Sagar Island | — | 85.45 | 7.27 | 7.27 | 100 | 23.00 | 77.00 | 100 |
| V. The Middle Sundarbans | Mathurapur | 42.31 | 57.69 | — | — | 100 | 31.50 | 68.50 | 100 |
| VI. The Eastern Sundarbans | Gosaba | — | 96.23 | — | 3.77 | 100 | 24.00 | 76.00 | 100 |
| **TOTAL OF HOUSEHOLDS** | **South 24-Parganas** | **21.00** | **68.00** | **2.00** | **9.00** | **100** | **28.92** | **71.08** | **100** |

* The figures in paranthesis refer to blockwise information where the region consist of more than one sampled block.

Delta where about 94.3% of the houses in the Eastern Sundarbans belong to this category. Pucca walls on the other hand are mostly found in the Stable Delta.

55% of the households have mud floors. 9% only have plastered or pucca floors and the rest belong to the semi pucca category.

Again the roofing material is of the Kutcha type in 44% of the households, 10% have pucca roofs and the rest are semi pucca. Therefore, in general Kutcha houses dominate the rural scenario, their proportion being higher in the Active Delta, specially in the Eastern and Western Sundarbans.

### 6.7.2 Basic Amenities and Personal Hygiene

Certain basic amenities of the households have been studied in detail like source of lighting, fuel materials used, source of drinking water and its distance, drinking water as used and source of bathing water. The aspects considered are whether the ponds are chlorinated or not, handling of food items, source of cleaning utensils, existence of drainage, sanitation or latrine facility and method of disposing garbage. These facts help to gauge to some extent the *standard of living of the households* and their level of personal hygiene.

#### *Lighting*

The lighting materials used by households include electricity, in very few households i.e. 21% of the total; kerosene in 68% of the total households, wood, constituting only 2% of the households and a combination of electricity and kerosene in 9% of the total households. The highest usage of electricity occurs in the Stable Delta, specially in the Middle Mature Delta of the Hugli and in the Western Hugli Side Flats as well as in the fringe areas around Calcutta and Diamond Harbour. Most of the Active Delta villages are still to be electrified and here kerosene comprises the only medium. 47% of the households here use kerosene as the lighting material. A very few households of the Stable Delta use wood as lighting materials specially in winter to provide heat as well. 61% of the households near the urban areas of Calcutta and Diamond Harbour have a dual source of electricity and kerosene combine.

### *Fuel Materials*

The most common fuel material in both the Deltas include a combination of cowdung, firewood, gobar gas, hay and coal to a very limited extent. 66% of the total households members depend on some combination of this, mostly in the Active Delta. Only 3% of the households use kerosene as the fuel, coal is used only by 1.0%, 4% of the households depend entirely on hay and firewood, 13% depend on cowdung together with firewood, 11% have cowdung, coke, wood and kerosene and only 2% have the facility of cooking gas entirely in the urban fringe villages.

### *Drinking Water and its Use*

Most of the household members have the facility of a tubewell which is the most common source in South 24-Parganas. 61.27% of the household members have the benefit of a tubewell of which 15% have within their compounds and 85% have a tubewell within a distance of 250 yards. Most of the villages of the Stable Delta including the urban fringe areas use the tubewell. But in some villages the household members use the pond as well. Tubewells were installed in the remote Gosaba (interior Sundarbans) unit very recently and even today people here use boiled water from the freshwater ponds for drinking purposes. 38.73% of the households in general also use pond water for drinking purposes.

In general 89% of the families use water unboiled and keep covered, 8% use unboiled water and uncovered and only 3% use boiled and covered water and this low hygiene level is responsible for stomach disorders, gastro-enteritic diseases in these parts.

### *Bathing Water*

50% of the households members use pond water for bathing purposes in both the Deltas, only 9% specially in the urban fringes and in certain tourist spots like Gangasagar use tap water. 22% use both pond water and tubewell water for bathing purposes specially in the Stable Delta; 19% use only tubewell water and only a negligible proportion of household members use river water in Sagar Island for bathing purposes specially at the mouth of the Hugli.

The ponds owned by single household or jointly shared by a few households are hardly maintained in a hygienic condition because the villagers use the water for bathing, cleaning utensils, bathing animals all in the same pond which often leads to contamination and cause varied type of fish diseases. Only in 14% of the families the pond water is purified by adding lime regularly, in 51% of the households they are occasionally disinfected, and never in rest of the cases. The phenomena of adding lime is mostly seen in the Sundarbans area and also in the villages of the Stable Delta away from urban influence.

### *Drainage of Waste Waters and Sanitation*

In the surveyed villages, there is hardly any system of drainage facility that is typical of urban and semi urban areas. Yet the villages have a rudimentary way of draining the waste waters of the house into the fields. In 75% of the households such a system exists and in 25% there is no provision of drainage. Within the Stable Delta, some form of rudimentary drainage is seen. In Bhangar, for instance the waste waters of the village fall into the Calcutta Drainage Out Fall (which occupy the silted upper portion of the Bidyadhari River) and ultimately drains into the sea through the Bidyadhari River. In case of the Active Delta, the waste water usually find their way to some distributary and khal and ultimately drains into the sea. In the urban fringe areas near Calcutta there is no proper system of drainage, all waste finding their way to the unused ponds or fields.

In rural South Twenty Four Parganas certain facilities of sanitation are entirely lacking. Only 28.92% of the households have latrine facility including both pucca or sanitary type and the rudimentary type. It has been observed that 61% of the households scientifically dispose the child's excreta and 30% just throw it outside.

Personal hygiene is not paid much attention as in the urban areas. Here 94% of the household members wash their hands before eating and the rest occasionally. In 99% of the cases it was found that food is covered effectively. The source of cleaning utensils in most cases range from ash, sand, mud and water though the cleaning powder has infiltrated in some of the villages of the Stable Delta that constitute the daily commuters zone with persons commuting daily to Calcutta. 63% of the households members use ash, water and sand (their cases are higher in case of the Active Delta). 16% use mud and water, 11% use both, 9% use ash and cleaning power simultaneously and only just 0.7% use cleaning powder only.

## 6.8 IMPACT OF ENVIRONMENTAL HAZARDS ON HUMAN SETTLEMENTS

In a world where an exploding human population fights frantically for space and food, a disaster does introduce an element of probability in the very concept of survival. The deltaic region of the Sunderbans is *highly unstable* due to its geomorphic factors and exposition to natural disasters or calamities.

The littoral belt with approximately 60 odd islands, large and small, as well as recently grown 'Char' lands (or freshly evolved unvegetated islands)—often are victims of natural calamities. Out of them, the disaster inflicted by storms and cyclones are a regular feature. During pre as well as post-monsoon season 2 or 3 cyclonic storms (of stronger type) per year witness land-fall in this coastal belt. The fury of the associated wind force, high storm surge, tidal bores cause large scale disaster by the way of loss of human life, blown off or damaged dwellings, shelters, crop and forest destruction, washing away the long stretches of embankments (typical of the Sundarbans region), and consequent inundation of a sizeable tract by saline sea water. As a result, quality of drinking water and potentiality of agricultural land gets seriously impaired. Large number of fishermen and their boats never return as a result of such vagaries.

The onslaught of such disasters is obviously more so in the entirely rural settlements of the Active Delta and as one proceeds away from the coastal zone towards the interior the fury decreases.

Data reveals that storms and cyclones are the most common form of disaster of the area and 91% of the families surveyed in 1992 experienced it. 8% in the Northern Stable Delta experienced storms and the remaining 1% of households of the Eastern Sundarbans in Gosaba experienced flooding of the villages due to broken embankments. In 60% of the families, the storm and cyclone frequency ranges from 2 to 4 per cent, in 21% of the families in the Northern delta were affected by storms and in the rest 13% of the cases, families specially in the Eastern Sundarbans in Gosaba there were complaints of more than 4 storms or cyclones.

88% of the families were affected by recent calamities and 12% by recent as well as past calamities. Again 65% of the families complained that the recent one was worse than the previous one.

The damages that occurred during the year surveyed include damages to crops, kutcha buildings, embankments and roads, and to fishermen. 39% of the families complained of damage of crops only, mostly in the Sundarbans.

Again 11% of the families also in the Stable Delta complained of damages to kutcha buildings, 2% complained of damaged roads and 29% of the households entirely in the Sundarbans reported damages to crops, washed off embankments, destroyed houses and damage to the fisherman folk. The remaining 19% did not have any serious complaints.

The aftermath of such calamities affect the life of the individuals here. The availability of essential commodities is affected serially. 62% of the families report that essential commodities are difficult to obtain in such times in the Stable Delta. 27% mostly in the Active Delta report that non-availability of commodities and in 11% of the families near Calcutta Region report the effect not so serious.

The protection taken by individuals include staying indoors for 65% of the families, strengthening buildings and embankments for 3% of the families and both for 32% of the families.

The flow of tourists is highly restricted at such times specially in Sagar Island, Gosaba and Diamond Harbour.

Though there had been many proposals for mitigation of natural calamities like (i) Design for economic dwellings, shelters, for coastal inhabitants less prone to such disasters, (ii) Economic embankments having protective design (using lime fly ash and the like) capable of withstanding such outslaughts and adaptable to the local alluvial conditions; and (iii) and cyclone shelters; yet in actual terms nothing has been done till the year surveyed and Government's nominal relief measures in the form of providing tripol, foodstuff etc. is available to 89% of the families surveyed and 11% complain the non-availability of any such help.

## 6.9 SOCIAL ENVIRONMENT

The villages of South Twenty Four Parganas though may be economically and technologically backward but are picturesque self-contained units. The villagers have deep attachment to their own village for their own identity and their dialect depends on their origin. 97% of the families did respond that they like staying in their respective villages, and only 3% reported of their dislike due to poverty and lack of facilities. Again only 2% of the respondents protested against the village social environment, because of poverty, ignorance and theft.

Of the major problems faced by the villagers, 61% of the families complained of lack of amenities and proper infrastructural facilities, 10% of the households lack police protection, 8% suffer due to natural problems and 21% of the respondents complained of all the above mentioned categories. When asked about their demand from the Government, 75% asked for provision of more amenities and infrastructural facilities and the rest 25% demanded Government loan for work.

The households or migrants of South Twenty Four Parganas have contact with other places usually from which they have migrated. 55% of the households are from the same district, 24% from other districts of West Bengal, 8% from other States and 13% from Bangladesh (specially in Gosaba and Sonarpur). Again 14% of the migrants had contacts with friends and 35% with relatives.

Though the villagers are found to be less mobile than urban folk when entertainment is concerned, 86% expressed their desire to visit relatives and 10% desired to visit tourist places and the rest 4% wished to stay in the same place.

## 6.10 PATTERN OF INTERACTION, COMMUTATION, FREQUENCY AND PURPOSE

The 400 households in 36 villages have also been surveyed in the light of their interregional linkages and interaction for various goods and services. This section deals with (i) pattern of interaction and (ii) Frequency and purpose of interaction.

### 6.10.1 Pattern of Interaction

**Stable Delta**

***Employment***

Agriculture is the most important activity of the three subregions of the Stable Delta (Appendix V.I). In the Western Hugli Side Plains in Diamond Harbour, Banitala, Bolsidhi, Ramgobindapur, and Bahadurpur provide employment in agriculture to a considerable number of people. But people also pursue other functions of small business in the Diamond Harbour market like fruit and vegetable selling, idol making and selling, selling of village handicrafts as well certain shop owners own lottery shops, electric shops etc. A certain section of the employees constitute daily commuters to Calcutta (travelling over 40 km by train) and work in the Calcutta Metropolitan Region as construction workers, electric mistry etc.

The Middle Mature Delta, in Mandir Bazar the villages of Baidyapur, Ghateshwar, Nalpukur and Gabberia also represent that agriculture is the most important occupation here, but there are daily commuters to Calcutta (over 40 km by train) that comprise of service class in Government offices and certain sections of labour class.

Agriculture is markedly absent in the villages of Sonarpur near Calcutta, but around Diamond Harbour town it is noticed in Badartala and Gurudasnagar. For other occupations people in Diamond Harbour block travel to Diamond Harbour town, these include small businessmen, service people working in Municipal Corporation and other Government offices. Besides, there are the daily commuters (in various services) to Calcutta. In Sonarpur people travel to nearby towns of Rajpur, Sonarpur as well as to Calcutta and work as office peons, bearers, telecom factory workers, labourers and small businessmen, carpenters, and ONGC drivers, contractors, bidi manufacturers, tutors etc. People here do *long distance commuting* to Calcutta by cycles and buses.

In the Piyali Bidyadhari Plains, Bhangar, Tardaha, Debipur, Narayanpur and Krolberia are also agricultural villages but fishing (inland fisheries) comprise an important activity. Therefore, here arises the fishermen folk in addition to agriculturists who sell their products to local wholesale markets at Choubagha and even travel upto Sealdah (Calcutta) (25-30 km) to sell their products. One household member in village for instance functions as Secretary to the Gram - Panchayat.

### *Education*

For Primary Education, most of the students go to the schools in their own villages or to the neighbouring villages, but for Secondary and

Higher Secondary Education they travel longer distances. In Diamond Harbour, for Higher Secondary education, people travel to the town, in Mandir Bazar students travel over 12 km to Dakshin Barasat (Dhrubachand Haldar College) and in Bhangar locally educational facilities are obtainable at Tardaha only, that is a very important village in terms of amenities.

All the villages around Diamond Harbour Town send their children to the town itself for education, whereas in Sonarpur, the students travel to nearly Harinavi, Chouhati or Sonarpur for primary and secondary education and for higher studies students travel as far as Garia, (K.K. Das College), Calcutta.

***Health***

Medical facilities are studied in the form of access to Primary Health Centres and Government Hospitals, though there are local village doctors and persons practising other traditional methods. In Diamond Harbour the two villages of Basuldanga, Bolsidhi have PHC catering to over 80% of the population here. In Mandir Bazar, the PHC is at another village in Nayerhat and Bhatipota is the main centre at Bhangar catering to about 100% of the surveyed population here.

Around Diamond Harbour all medical facilities are provided by the town itself in 99% of the cases though in special cases people may travel to Calcutta. In Sonarpur the main centre is the hospital at Subhasgram for the surveyed villages and also Calcutta provides specialised medical facilities.

***Banking***

Though there are cooperatives, local money lenders, the commercial banking system has extended far and wide among the villages of South Twenty Four Parganas. In Diamond Harbour the town itself provides and functions as the main commercial centre for the surveyed surrounding villages. In Sonarpur the people travel to nearby Rajpur, Sonarpur, Calcutta for banking purposes. In Mandir Bazar the families go to Lakshmikantapur for banking facilities (United Bank of India) and in Bhangar there are two banks catering to the surveyed population, the Allahabad Bank at Narayanpur and the Bank of India at Tardaha. Inspite of banking facilities the households under survey do not frequent them much for the system of money lenders as an institution still stands strong in these villages.

***Marketing Facilities***

The marketing facilities for the households of the Stable Delta has been grouped into two, viz. general marketing for daily provisions etc., and special marketing or shopping for the purchase of cloth and special items etc. In Diamond Harbour the households buy their daily use food items etc. from local market or hats at Banitala, Bolsidhi or Diamond Harbour town. In Mandir Bazar the centres are at Baidyapur, Ghateshwar and Gabberia and the small hats and bazaars of Bhangar include Tardaha, Paglahat and Krolberia. But for specialized shopping the surveyed households prefer to travel further but occasionally. Diamond Harbour Town for instance provides special marketing facilities but people decide to travel even further to Calcutta in certain occasions. The people of Mandir Bazar prefer to travel to Calcutta and in certain cases to Diamond Harbour. In Bhangar, Ghatakpukur is the special market centre but people prefer to travel further over 15 km to Calcutta.

***Communication and Transport***

Post and Telegraph Offices are locted at Bahdurpur and Diamond Harbour town in case of Diamond Harbour, in all the surveyed villages of Mandir Bazar and Tardaha, Narayanpur and Krolberia in Bhangar.

Post and Telegraph facilities here are provided by Diamond Harbour Town and Chouhati. Train forms the major transport of Diamond Harbour whereas bus is more important around Calcutta.

Of the 3 regions of the Stable Delta, train is more important than bus in Diamond Harbour and Mandir Bazar being connected directly with Calcutta and hence serve a larger section of the surveyed population, the main stations being Diamond Harbour, Baidyapur and Lakshmikantapur (Mandir Bazar). In Bhangar bus is more important and the main stoppage is at Ghatakpur (State Highway No. 3).

**Active Delta**

The interaction pattern of the rural villages of the Active Delta of the Sundarbans (Appendix V.2) have been also studied in great detail. These villages being farthest from the Calcutta Region have developed *separate identity of their own*. The Western Sundarbans is represented by Sagar Island. The six villages include Gangasagar (at the Southern tip of the Island), Chemaguri, Beguakhali, Natendrapur and Dhoblat (also in the Southern portion of the island and Rudranagar (the heart throb of Sagar at the centre of the island). The Central Sundarbans is represented by Mathurapur and here the six villages are Mathurapur, Gopinathpur, Raghabpur, Khonjkhidir, Uttarkasinagar and Bade Barasi. Finally the Eastern interior Sunarbans is represented by Gosaba through the six villages of Gosaba, Rangabalia, Rajat Jubilee, Dayapur, Hamilton Abad and Pakhiralay.

### Employment

Over 80% of the villagers at Sagar Island are agriculturists. Besides there are professions other than cultivation including fishing and selling of local products. In Gangasagar there are a class of small businessmen like small shop owners, roadside hotel owners (found during the survey work) catering to the tourists, who come here. Beguakhali is a major fishing village, and here in addition to the fishing operations the surveyed households are engaged in weaving fishing nets as well. In Rudranagar there are small shop owners selling vegetables, groceries etc. The fishermen folk travel as far as Kakdwip (over 45 km) and Diamond Harbour (over 60 km) to sell their products.

In Mathurapur all the 6 villages surveyed are agricultural villages, and over 75% of the population here are engaged in agriculture locally but there are certain service class people also who take advantage of the direct train connection to Calcutta, and work in offices here. In two households, the heads were working in National Atlas and Thematic Mapping Organization (NATMO, Government of India). Other section comprise of small businessmen who travel as far as Mathurapur to sell their local products (mainly agricultural items).

In Gosaba, all the 6 villages are strictly agricultural, over 90% of the surveyed working population is engaged in primary activities mainly agriculture, fishing (very important here) and collection of forest products. The local products are sold in the Gosaba market by small businessmen who travel as far as Port Canning across the Matla River (over 45 km).

### *Education*

The Active Delta reveal a local set up for primary school students, who have to depend on their own village or the surrounding villages. The households in Gangasagar, neighbouring Chemaguri, send their children to Gangasagar that has a primary as well as secondary school. Beguakhali, Natendrapur and Dhoblat also have primary and secondary schools. But the main centre for education is Rudranagar at the heart of the Sagar Island and most of the families opting for high schools have to travel there and in case of specialised college education (that is very rare), people have to travel to Kakdwip or Diamond Harbour through launches and bus services.

In Mathurapur the students travel to either Mathurapur (Block headquarters) or to Uttarkasinagar that are the local centres for education, and in case of specialised education people travel as far as Dakshin Barasat or Jaynagar-Mazilpur.

In Gosaba, primary, secondary and high schools are located either at Gosaba, at Rangabalia and at Rajat Jubilee. Very few students opt for education beyond this level.

### *Medical facility*

In Sagar, the surveyed families travel to either the PHC at Gangasagar, Chemaguri or Rudranagar. Hospitals handle female sterilization cases. But most of the delivery cases are conducted mostly through midwives or 'dhai'. In case of specialised treatment the people are seriously handicapped and have to travel as far as Kakdwip Hospital or to Diamond Harbour Town. Among the 6 villages surveyed in Mathurapur all of the families have to travel to Uttarkashinagar that has a PHC. For specialised facilities people travel to either Mathurapur or Jayanagar-Mazilpur Town (5 to 10 km). The people of Gosaba have serious problem regarding medical facilities. Though there are mobile PHC units and staffs visiting the respective villages once a month, people have to travel far and that too through boats and launches to either the hospital at Gosaba or to Port Canning. In case of serious patients who need immediate help specially in cases of tiger attacks or snake bites, the problem is never ending.

### *Financial facility*

Cooperatives are more important in these parts than banks but in general few households take advantage of these facilities. In Sagar,

Gramin Bank (Cooperative) is in Gangasagar, Natendrapur and Rudranagar (State Cooperative Bank). In Mathurapur the cooperative is located at Mathurapur and banks at Bijoyganj and Joynagar. In Gosaba, the cooperative is located in Gosaba and the main and only Commercial Bank here is the State Bank of India, providing credit to few families who need it.

### *Marketing facility*

For general marketing the people in Sagar depend either on Rudranagar and Kalibazar for the southern villages of the island and for specialized shopping people have to travel as far as Kakdwip or Diamond Harbour. In Mathurapur, the main bazaars are located at Mathurapur, Babuli Bazar, Raghabpur, and Uttarkasinagar and for special marketing people travel as far as Jaynagar or Calcutta. In Gosaba local weekly hats are found at Rangabalia, Dayapur, Hamilton Abad, whereas Gosaba village has a special permanent market place. For specialised market people travel as far as Port Canning or even Calcutta (in very rare cases).

### *Communication and Transport*

Every village in the Active Delta do not have a Post Office and people sometimes have to travel as far as 5, 10 or even 15 km. In Sagar the P.O. is at Gangasagar, Kali Bazar, Rudranagar (main) and at Dhoblat. In Mathurapur Block, it is at Mathurapur and Uttarkasinagar; and in Gosaba Block it is at Gosaba, Rangabalia and Dayapur. Of the three forms of transport, train forms the most important medium of transport in Mathurapur having direct linkage with Calcutta.

In Sagar, people use bus as the conveyance when within the island connecting Kachuberia at the Northern tip of the island and passing through Rudranagar,.connecting Gangasagar at the Southern end of the island. But when travelling to the main land people have to board launches at Kachuberia to cross the Hugli and land at Lot No. 8 or Hardwood Point at Kakdwip. In Gosaba the only form of transport connecting sometimes different villages which are islands by themselves are launches, motor boats or 'dinghy's'. So every village has a local Ghat like that of Rajat Jubilee, Dayapur and

**TABLE 6.11 : Interaction Pattern 1992**
**Proportion of Families Moving to a Particular Distance for Goods and Services**

| *Regions* | *Emp-loy ment* | *Prim ary Edu.* | *Secon-dary Edu.* | *Hr. Sec. Edu.* | *Med.-cal faci.* | *Medi-cines* | *Buying of of Agri. inputs* | *Hat & Bazaars* | *Fair Price shops* | *Special Shopp-ing* | *Bank-ing* | *Post Offi-ce* |
|---|---|---|---|---|---|---|---|---|---|---|---|---|
| | *1* | *2* | *3* | *4* | *5* | *6* | *7* | *8* | *9* | *10* | *11* | *12* |
| **STABLE DELTA** | | | | | | | | | | | | |
| (i) Villages less than 10 km from urban centres | | | | | | | | | | | | |
| In the Village | 37 | 95 | 42 | 8 | 45 | 24 | 21 | 91 | 11 | 3 | 4 | 48 |
| 5-15 km | 40 | 5 | 33 | 35 | 34 | 68 | 65 | 9 | 84 | 20 | 71 | 52 |
| 16-30 km | 6 | 2 | 25 | 57 | 11 | 8 | — | — | 5 | 31 | 14 | |
| 31-45 km | 10 | — | — | — | 6 | — | 15 | — | — | 25 | 11 | |
| > 45 km | 7 | — | — | — | 4 | — | — | — | — | 21 | — | |

**TABLE 6.11 : (*Contd.*)**

| *Regions* | *Emp—loy ment* | *Prim ary Edu.* | *Secon—dary Edu.* | *Hr. Sec. Edu.* | *Med.—cal faci.* | *Medi—cines* | *Buying of of Agri. inputs* | *Hat & Bazaars* | *Fair Price shops* | *Special Shopp—ing* | *Bank—ing* | *Post Offi—ce* |
|---|---|---|---|---|---|---|---|---|---|---|---|---|
| | *1* | *2* | *3* | *4* | *5* | *6* | *7* | *8* | *9* | *10* | *11* | *12* |
| (ii) Villages within 10 km from urban centres. | | | | | | | | | | | | |
| In the village | 6 | 71 | 5 | 3 | 27 | 15 | 3 | 21 | 19 | 2 | 2 | 23 |
| 5 — 15 km | 10 | 29 | 88 | 65 | 35 | 85 | 78 | 79 | 81 | 89 | 98 | 77 |
| 16 — 30 km | 78 | — | 7 | 32 | 25 | — | 19 | — | — | — | — | |
| 31 — 45 km | 1 | — | — | — | 8 | — | — | — | — | — | — | |
| > 45 km | 5 | — | — | — | 5 | — | — | — | — | 9 | — | |
| **ACTIVE DELTA** (entirely rural) | | | | | | | | | | | | |
| In the village | 33 | 88 | 27 | 7 | 35 | 22 | 2 | 79 | 8 | 1 | 3 | 33 |
| 5 — 15 km | 59 | 10 | 63 | 8 | 47 | 48 | 72 | 21 | 75 | 8 | 34 | 67 |
| 16 — 30 km | 3 | 2 | 4 | 25 | 9 | 17 | 10 | — | 17 | 25 | 26 | |
| 31 — 45 km | 3 | — | 6 | 60 | 6 | 13 | 9 | — | — | 28 | 28 | |
| > 45 km | 3 | — | — | — | 3 | — | 7 | — | — | 38 | 9 | |

Hamilton Abad that ultimately connects to Gosaba Ghat which is the *Main Ferry Ghat* through different khals and the opposite point to mainland across the Matla is Port Canning, from which there is a direct local train line in Calcutta.

### 6.10.2 Commutation

After studying the interaction pattern for various goods and services between villages; and villages and urban centres it now becomes imperative to study the distance commuted by villagers in pursuit of various goods and services (Table 6.11).

Data reveals that commutation is greater in the Stable Delta than in the Active Delta specially around the urban centres regarding employment. Commutation is less regarding primary schooling, hats and bazars and post office facilities. But in certain services like higher education, medical facilities, special shopping and banking, commutation is greater even in the villages situated more than 10 km from the urban centre. The villages near cities have the easy advantage and access to every facility and also they have a better connectivity in terms of linkage with the city.

Active Delta or the littoral part is handicapped transportwise and here people have to travel even further for specialized services as exemplified specially by Gosaba village. Though the table reveals distances over 45 km, the Active Delta have households often travelling over 80 km in order to reach Calcutta and from Gosaba and Sagar it often takes a whole day.

### 6.10.3 Frequency and Purpose of Movements for Goods and Services

In this portion (Table 6.12) the frequency of trips made by households for purpose of purchasing provisions, medicines and special shopping is considered. By frequency, *the rate of movements* like daily, biweekly, weekly, fortnightly, monthly, twice per year, once per year, and occasionally is considered. The different types of trips by what percentage of families emphasizes the *intensity of commutation* to a particular place. For general provisions the frequency is more in all the distance zone since in these villages people do not have to concept of storing groceries, vegetables etc., they consume as and when purchased in rural Bengal. For medicines, the frequency is lesser specially in the rural villages and people travel only when absolutely necessary.

**TABLE 6.12 : Frequency and Purpose of Movement for Purchases 1992 (A Case Study of 400 Households)**

| *Frequency* | *Stable Delta* | | | | *Active Delta* | |
|---|---|---|---|---|---|---|
| | *Villages more than 10 km from urban centres* | *% of village* | *Villages less than 10 km from urban centres* | *% of village* | *No. of villages* | *% of village* |
| *1* | *2* | *3* | *4* | *5* | *6* | *7* |
| (PROVISION) DAILY | 88 | 54 | 50 | 67 | 48 | 30 |
| Biweekly | 40 | 25 | 13 | 17· | 55 | 34 |
| Weekly | 30 | 18 | 12 | 16 | 45 | 28 |
| Fortnightly | 5 | 3 | — | — | 14 | 8 |
| Monthly | — | — | — | — | — | — |
| MEDICINES | | | | | | |
| Weekly | 20 | 12 | 8 | 11 | 18 | 11 |
| Fortnightly | 35 | 21 | 12 | 16 | 32 | 20 |
| Monthly | 55 | 34 | 17 | 23 | 59 | 36 |
| Occasionally | 53 | 33 | 38 | 50 | 53 | 33 |
| SPECIAL SHOPPING | | | | | | |
| Monthly | 5 | 3 | 15 | 20 | 3 | 2 |
| Twice per year | 57 | 35 | 15 | 20 | 60 | 37 |
| Once per year | 75 | 46 | 26 | 35 | 75 | 46 |
| Rarely | 26 | 16 | 19 | 25 | 24 | 15 |
| **TOTAL** | **163** | **100%** | **75** | **100%** | **162** | **100%** |

Special shopping has low frequency portraying the poor standard of the rural folks here. The households buy cloths and luxury items on special occasions as during festivals (like Durga Puja) or at the time of marriages. Both in the Stable and Active Deltas frequency of special shopping is lower in case of villages located away from the urban centres.

## 6.11 Quality of Housing

Five indicators have been chosen in this section to portray the quality of housing in South 24 Parganas. These are (proportion of households having) pucca houses, safe drinking water, electrification, toilet facility and 3 rooms per family. Only 10.33% on the average have the facility of pucca houses, 61.27% have access to a tubewell, 21% have electric connection, 28.92% have toilet facilities and only 6.67% have the facility of 3 rooms to their family. This clearly reflects the rurality of the region and its backwardness. People in these parts are so poor that even 3 rooms per joint family are a myth.

**TABLE - 6.13 : Quality of Housing**
**(As Proportion to total Households)**

| Geo-Ecological Regions/Blocks | | Pucca Houses | Safe Drinking Water | Electricity | Toilet facility | 3 rooms per family | Composite score | Rank |
|---|---|---|---|---|---|---|---|---|
| | | 1 | 2 | 3 | 4 | 5 | 6 | 7 |
| **STABLE DELTA** | | | | | | | | |
| I. The Western Hugli Side Flats | Diamond Harbour | 13.63 | 95.00 | 19.32 | 33.0 | 5.5 | 72.94 | 2 |
| II. The Middle Mature Delta | Sonarpur | (22.81)* | (100) | (29.03) | (45.00) | (3.00) | — | — |
| | Mandir Bazar | (8.45) | (100) | (39.44) | (30.00) | (2.00) | — | — |
| | Total | 12.74 | 100 | 36.27 | 37.50 | 2.50 | 80.20 | 1 |
| III. The Piyali Bidyadhari Plains | Bhangar | 11.33 | 65.50 | 14.00 | 25.00 | 6.00 | 5139 | 3 |
| **ACTIVE DELTA** | | | | | | | | |
| IV. The Western Sundarbans | Sagar Island | 3.63 | 65.00 | — | 23.00 | 7.00 | 47.27 | 4 |
| V. The Middle Sundarbans | Mathurapur | 12.18 | 27.00 | 42.31 | 31.50 | 15.00 | 35.64 | 5 |
| VI. The Eastern Sundarbans | Gosaba | 0.63 | 15.10 | — | 24.00 | 4.00 | 16.51 | 6 |
| **TOTAL OF Households** | **South-24 Parganas** | **10.33** | **61.27** | **21.00** | **28.92** | **6.67** | — | — |

* Figures within paranthesis refers to separate blocks surveyed under one region.

The composite scores, calculated through standardisation of each indicator reflect the following ranks of the six sub-regions. The Stable Delta has better housing quality than the Sundarbans in general. Here the Middle Mature Delta ranks first followed by the Western Hugli Side Flats. These two regions are relatively more developed than the other regions. The main reason behind is proximity to the Calcutta Agglomeration, transport linkages and their inherent interior location and early settlement. The Piyali-Bidyadhari Plains rank third. This region lying further East is more rural in character. The fourth rank is ocupied by the Western Sundarbans within the Active Delta. The Middle and Eastern Sundarbans occupy fifth and sixth positions respectively. There is a marked break in scores of the Eastern Sundarbans that reflects the extreme backwardness and least development of the region.

## 6.12 CONCLUSION

The characteristics of population and settlements among the rural households have been summarised in this section. The region depicts bigger size families, high fertility population i.e., about 58% under 14 years age group, which clearly stands above the national average. The Marital Status reflects low age at marriage specially among the females and that too more accentuated in the Active Delta. Marriage migration and short term migration are more pronounced.

The economic activities reveal more of primary activities with movement for work mostly within the villages; reflecting the agrarian base of the region. The income levels of individuals are extremely low. Religious diversity, pockets of tribal communities, bilingualism are also characteristics of the area. Literacy levels also portray the need for more facilities in the area, inspite of the fact that Literacy Mission is quite active in certain parts specially oriented towards educating adult females.

Morbidity reflects the predominance of stomach related diseases and the low hygienic conditions. The settlement charateristics reflect low housing quality of the entire region specially the Sundarbans. Kutcha houses predominate the area, prone to natural calamities, they pose constant problem in the littoral. Electricity has not reached a greater part of the Sundarbans and here batteries and solar reactors (in Gangasagar) provide little break from the monotony of the kerosene lamp. The interaction pattern reflects mostly self contained villages in the Active Delta with a very low frequency of movements for goods and services. The Stable Delta reflects higher interaction and a higher frequency of movements. Finally, the composite scores clearly reflect higher positions of the Stable Delta with respect to the Sundarbans; but at the same time also reflecting the general backwardness, poverty, low development and low housing conditions of the entire district.

### REFERENCES

1. Census of India 1981, *Series 23, West Bengal, Part XIII-B.* Twenty Four Parganas, District Census Handbook, Village and Townwise Primary Census Abstract.
2. Clarke, John I. *"Population Geography"*, Second Edition, Pergamon Press, pp. 23-25.

# 7

# SUMMARY AND CONCLUSIONS

This chapter sums up the research findings of all the aspects of Human Settlements in the Sundarban Delta as presented in the foregoing chapters.

In this region of marginal littorals, where land formation is still continuing, coastal hazards and other vagaries of nature continue to hamper the development process; Human Settlements reflect a man's constant battle for survival as part of the man-environment interaction.

The peculiar components of the *Natural Environmment* (Chapter 2) have given this tract a regional distinction. The delatic estuaries, mangrove vegetation, coupled with the tidal complicacies further divide the region into distinct sub-regions. A marked distinction is observed between the Stable Delta in the North and the immediate littoral of the Active Delta where the land is still in the process of formation. This is exemplified through new evolution of mud-flats, shifting sand banks and shoals; complex dune ridges and mangrove swamps. The Stable Delta is further divided into the Western Hugli Side Flats, The Middle Mature Delta of the Hugli and the Piyali Bidyadhari Plains in the East. The store house of the Sundarbans, the Active Delta, can be further divided into the largely deforested Western Sundarbans, in comparison to the largely forested Middle and the Eastern Interior Sundarbans. The settlement types, forms and patterns are distinct in all the subregions.

Before a detailed settlement analysis, *a study of the population resources* of the area (Chapter 3) in addition to the physical environment was considered essential to understand the nature of the Human Settlements. The findings reveal that the hypothesis regarding population size, density, as well as changes in density have a tendency to increase from the littoral margin towards the interior, to hold good. Besides, there is a marked contrast between the Active and the Stable Delta.

Again, within the micro regions, the highest density in the Stable Delta were found to be in the Western Hugli Side Flats and in the Active Delta the same was true in case of the Western Sundarbans. It was also observed that strikingly high population densities occur in the 42 urban centres of the Stable Delta accompanied by a high rate of change during 1981 and 1991 (urban centres being conspicuously absent in the Active Delta). The other observations made regarding the population characteristics include a balanced and improving sex-ratio in the area, a higher male literacy and a much higher urban literacy. Again the scheduled caste population is much higher than the scheduled tribe population; the work participation rates being clearly in favour of males and highly unfavourable in case of females. The dependency rate is much higher in the urban areas as compared to the rural areas. The population growth rates are higher in the Stable Delta compared to the littoral area. As such, greater pressure of population is experienced on the resources of the interior land specially marked by the urban areas.

*The analysis of settlement characteristics* (Chapter 4) point out that the cultural landscape of the district began changing rapidly only in recent times. History of origin of settlements in this area reveal that the early settlements in this region date back to the Pre-Aryan age. The Sundarbans reclamation, however, dates back to the British regime, when large scale land survey and reclamation work started. Today, the littoral portion also is by and large settled. Initially, majority of the settlers came from landless families, apart from the tribal migrants (Chapters 5 and 6). Later, refugees from the erstwhile East Pakistan (Bangladesh) settled in the Northern part of the district as well as in the Eastern Sundarbans.

The settlements of Deltaic South 24-Parganas are associated closely with the regional personality of the area (Chapter 4) and vary in types from nucleated and agglomerated through semi-nucleated to dispersed and highly dispersed varieties. Nucleation reaches its fullest form towards the North (near Calcutta District), and within the Stable Delta as one proceeds towards the East; the nucleated type is replaced by the semi-nucleated ones. The transition is not only a West to East feature but also a North to South one. Thus in the Active Delta, semi-nucleated villages in the North and West are replaced by dispersed and highly dispersed villages towards the South and South East. The external forms too undergo changes from nucleated through semi-nucleated to loose-knit villages; apart from a wide variety of shapes and forms discernable in various parts of the Delta.

In the next section of the chapter, dispersion analysis of rural settlements indicates that the inter settlement distances fall as one moves from the littoral towards the interior. Again, the nearest neighbour analysis reveals that the trend in spatial distribution of settlements is more regular than random and shows a tendency to move towards uniformity in the Active Delta.

The urban settlements all located in the Stable Delta, reveal large spacings and point towards a near clustering phenomena quite different from that of the rural settlements. Their numbers also reveal a slow growth since 1901. Since 1951, however, the pace of growth has been faster, with a sudden spurt in growth in the decade 1981 and 91, when the urban settlements rose to 42 in number. But still Class I towns are conspicuously absent in the area due to the overshadowing influence of Calcutta Metropolis. The Rank-Size Rule reveals that Budge Budge is the first ranking town followed by Panchur, having nearly double the population of Panchur.

*A reconnaisance survey of 200 villages*, brings out further contrasts in the pattern of Human Settlements in the Active and Stable Delta. The settlements in the Stable Delta are much older than those in the Active Delta. The proportion of migrant population is higher in the Active Delta. Here the settlements show a dispersed pattern than that of a clustered one of the Stable Delta. The proportion of pucca houses is higher in the settlements of the Stable Delta indicating a better quality of housing than in the Active Delta. The economic activities of the villages also show a transition from a primary base (agriculture, forestry, fishing) in the southern littoral to a more specialized agriculture and market gardening in the Stable Delta, towards Calcutta metropolis. In amenities and transport, the Stable Delta exhibits better infrastructure and connectivity.

*The Quality of Human Settlements* has been represented by a composite index of seven development indicators. They are:

(i) Proportion of pucca houses,

(ii) Proportion of villages having tubewells for safe drinking water,
(iii) Proportion of total irrigated agricultural land per village,
(iv) Proportion of villages having access to a metalled road,
(v) Proportion of villages having schools,
(vi) Proportion of villages having health institutions, and lastly
(vii) Proportion of villages having the facility of credit institutions.

This exercise reveals that forty eight villages out of 100 in the Active Delta and are at the lowest level of development. Twenty-three villages out of 100 villages selected from the Stable Delta are also at the same development level.

Finally, Chapter 6 provides an insight into *the population and settlement characteristics of 400 surveyed households.* Here, the observations speak of bigger family sizes in the study area, a high fertility rate, with high percentages of child population, lower female age at marriage and high proportion of migration in the Sundarbans. Marked contrasts are seen not only between the Active and the Stable Deltas but also between the six subregions. Though 57 per cent of the reported population is literate, proportions attaining higher education levels are very few.

An insight into morbidity and mortality indicate that stomach related gastro enterities followed by asthma are serious diseases of the region even claiming human lives. Mortality is further aggravated due to the lower hygiene level of the families. Family planning manifests itself through only female sterilization for those few who have adopted it. Midwifery exists in a large number of delivery cases.

The next section highlights the environmental disasters and their consequences. It is observed that 88 per cent of the families were affected by recent calamities (during survey in 1992).

The following section highlights the findings of an in-depth study of the pattern of interaction, commutation, frequency and purpose of movements by families. For specialized functions, urban centres specially Calcutta have exerted a dominating influence across distance barriers. In certain pockets of the Stable Delta, straight away local train connectivity with Calcutta have sprung up the 'Commuters Zone'; surprisingly even extending as far as Diamond

Harbour, Mathurapur, Mandir Bazar; besides the nearby block of Sonarpur.

The distance range of commutation is observed to be high in case of employment, specialised medical facilities, and special shopping, whereas higher frequency of purchases is noticeable for daily necessities and provisions purchased by the families, rather than for medicines and special shopping.

*The physical quality of housing* is derived from a composite index of five indicators (viz percentage of pucca houses, households having electricity connection, safe drinking water supply, toilet facility and at least 3 rooms to a family). The physical quality of housing appeared to be the highest in the Middle Mature Delta, followed by the Western Hugli Side Flats, Piyali Bidyadhari Plains and the Western, Middle and Eastern Sundarbans in descending order.

## CONCLUSION

Today, when mankind is really concerned about sustainable Human Settlements and the World Summit has just been hosted at Instanbul, Turkey, (Habital II), 3-14th June 1996; the area under concern still dwells in the realm of backwardness and a poor quality of housing and settlements. The major objectives stated in the resolution reads as, "in long term, to arrest the deterioration of global human settlements conditions and ultimately create conditions for achieving improvements in the living conditions of all people on a sustainable basis, with special attention to the needs and contributions of women and vulnerable social groups whose quality of life and participation in development have been hampered by exclusion and inequality, which affect the poor in general . . . ."

Thus keeping in mind a sustainable development of human settlements in the Sundarban Delta, certain improvements can be suggested for the region based on the field experience.

1. Strengthening the lengthy stretches of the earthen embankments along the numerous waterways in the Southern part of the district. This can be done by using more resistant material like brick and mortar to stand the onslaught of cyclones and tidal bores.
2. Installation of cyclone warning system equipped by efficient staff and creation of cyclone shelters.

3. Provision of better, low cost housing facilities. Mud walls can be replaced by bricks that can be locally manufactured at the same time generating local employment.
4. Extension of safe drinking water through more tubewell installations.
5. Electric connections should be extended to both the Stable and the Active Deltas, specially in the remote Sundarbans which is virtually non-electrified as noticed during the period of survey.
6. The village roads of the Eastern Interior Sundarbans that get transformed into knee deep mud with each rain, should be paved by creating local village self employment schemes.
7. Provision of better education, health for all, and popularisation of family planning measures, so that dependency burden on workers can be lessened.
8. In areas of water transport, better facilities as well as mechanisation of boats should be done, in order to bring in a speedy communication system.
9. In order to eradicate poverty, farmers should have easy access to farming inputs, salt tolerating crops should be introduced; along with an extension of mechanisation to fishermen.
10. In the villages next to the tiger reserve, protection measure should be taken against encroachment of the wild life that often proves a threat to the villagers. Many of them die through tiger attacks while illegally gathering forest produce. Moreover, the dearth of medical facilities in these parts together with slow, irregular and ineffective water transport are the causes resulting in deaths of tiger attacked and emergency case victims. Such facts should not only be the Government's concern but also should invite a peoples participation, so that the government is made cautious of initiating development at these grassroots.
11. The illegal gathering of forest produce should be regulated by introducing social forestry, small scale industries or handicrafts; generating rural employment and income.
12. Tourism can be encouraged in this area, at the same time, efforts should be made to exercise control so that the environment, ecology and life-style of the coastal people are not adversely affected.
13. The Sundarbans do not lack in resources, but these should be converted into a resource base. This can be achieved by backing

up the centres that are already existing here, to serve as growth points and hence to serve the surrounding settlements and in turn usher in growth resulting in a system of Sustaining Human Settlements. Centres such as Gosaba, Basanti, Canning, Kakdwip, Mathurapur can perform this duty if properly geared.

14. Last but not the least, it can be strongly recommended that an in-depth survey of this maritime country is necessary to fill in the wide gap of knowledge that still exists in reality about the people, their settlements and human activities; and the results of such a survey may be utilized for any plan of action to be undertaken regarding the area. A proper historical link between the past and the present is necessary to implement any measures required for proper growth and development of the area.

# APPENDICES

## *APPENDIX TO : CHAPTER - II*

*APPENDIX-II-1*

### NATURAL CALAMITIES

Many scientists believe that the frequent subsidence of the littoral part of South 24 Parganas which resulted in the disappearance of great coastal forests, busy ancient ports of Bengal and other settlement areas are due to the "Swatch of No Ground" in the Bay. Hence the silts and terrestrial materials are either diverted to the South of the Sundarban or are being pushed forward further eastward and new islands are formed. The indented topography and unsettled nature of this deltaic district has been attributed to the submarine hollow or the `Swatch of No Ground'. Not only subsidence, cyclone and floods have changed the physiography of the region but earthquakes from time to time have also played havoc and have caused considerable damage to the region, causing submergence wiping out the entire coastal population and some of the once existing important ports of the region. A chronological list of natural disasters is given below.

| *Year* | *Nature of Calamities* | *Year* | *Nature of Calamities* |
|---|---|---|---|
| 1582 | Cyclone | 1688 | Cyclone |
| 1707 | Cyclone | 1737 | Cyclone & earthquake |
| 1742 | Cyclone | 1762 | Earthquake |
| 1770 | Famine | 1791 | Famine |
| 1823 | Flood | 1833 | Cyclone |
| 1838 | Severe Flood | 1842 | Earthquake |
| 1856 | Flood | 1862 | Cyclone |
| 1864 | Flood, Cyclone | 1865 | Famine |
| 1866 | Famine | 1867 | Cyclone |
| 1868 | Flood | 1871 | Flood |
| 1874 | Famine | 1876 | Cyclone & Flood |
| 1885 | Flood | 1890 | Flood |
| 1897 | Earthquake, | 1900 | Flood Famine |
| 1904 | Flood | 1907 | Flood |
| 1909 | Cyclone | 1921 | Famine |

| *Year* | *Nature of Calamities* | *Year* | *Nature of Calamities* |
|---|---|---|---|
| 1934 | Earthquake, | 1942 | Cyclone Famine |
| 1943 | Famine | 1961 | Cyclone |
| 1965 | Cyclone | 1964 | Flood |
| 1966 | Storm | 1970 | Cyclone & Flood |
| 1978 | Flood | 1979 | Famine |
| 1981 | Flood | | |

*APPENDIX-II-2*

## SUNDARBAN

The name 'Sundarban' is most likely to have been derived from the 'Sundari' tree. Several other hypotheses have also been proposed by various authors regarding its name. (a) 'Sundarban' is named for having beautiful forest plants, (b) 'Sundari bund' meaning beautiful embankment common in this area, (c) Sundarban indicates the sea facing forest, (d) 'Chandra bhanda' denoting the primitive tribe named 'Chandra Bhanda' ultimately got transformed to Sundarbans, (e) Sundarban or Sugandha (the river of Barisal - Bangladesh) and the name has been derived from this river, (f) Chandarban was pronounced by many French people as 'Sunderban'. During the British rule it gradually being spelt as the Sundarban, (g) Chandradwip, a kingdom at Bakhergunj (now in Barisal, Bangladesh) from where the Chandra dwipban arises and ultimately appears as the Sundarban, (h) Sunderban is a recent name, during the Muslim and early Hindu periods this area was known as 'Bhati' (tidal). In Kautilya's period this area has been referred as Kalikaban. Through various literature this name has been spelt as Soondariban, Soondarban, Sunderbans and finally the Sundarbans.

*APPENDIX-II-3*

## ORIGIN OF THE GANGA

Origin of the Ganga (previous course in the district), the present channel of the Hugli is different from that which the Ganga formerly followed. The original channel was identical with the Tolly's Nullah (13 km. to the South of Calcutta - from Khidirpur to Garia), from this point it ran to the sea in a south - easterly direction. Traditionally it is said that it emerged out of the Sundarbans at Kakdwip and then passed along the present Muri Ganga, after which it found a passage along a Creek between Dhoblat and Monosadip and then proceeded first in a westerly and then in a southerly direction until it fell into the Bay of Bengal at Ganga Sagar. It is still traceable as far south as Jaynagar Block being variously known as Adi Ganga (or the original Ganga), Burha Ganga (Old Ganga) and Ganga Nullah.

*APPENDIX-II-4*

## LOCAL SOIL TYPES

The local people of the district have categorised the soil types into 4 classes, particularly on the basis of colour and texture. These are (a) 'Dhal' or lowest land soil, which is reddish in colour, (b) 'Dhap' or 'Chura' lies at higher elevation and whitish in colour, (c) 'Matial' or lose in composition also whitish in colour, and (d) Baliara or Dorasa that remain moist for a longer period and is reddish in colour.

*APPENDIX-II-5*

## PHYSIO-CHEMICAL CHARACTERISTICS OF COASTAL SOILS

Some important physico-chemical characteristics of the coastal soil associations of tidal regions in the estuarine area of the Sundarbans are given below :

| *Characteristics Soils* | *Saline alkali-soils* | *Saline-alkali soils* | *Non-Saline Saline Soils* | *Degraded* |
|---|---|---|---|---|
| (a) Soil re-action (PH) | 6.5-7.8 | 7.4 -9.0 | 7.2-8.3 | 4.3-7.0 |
| (b) Salinity percentage | 0.2-1.8 | 0.38-1.2 | 0.1-0.9 | 0.6-1.2 |
| (c) Profile Development | Immature | Immature | Immature | Immature |
| (d) Clay percen-tage | Avg to high | High and uniform | Avg to high | Avg to high |
| (e) Sesquioxides | Immobile | Immobile | Immobile Mobile | Slight |

| *Characteristics Soils* | *Saline alkali-soils* | *Saline-alkali soils* | *Non-Saline Saline Soils* | *Degraded* |
|---|---|---|---|---|
| (f) Percentage Saturation of mono valents in exchangeable bases | 11 - 12 | 40-55 | 30-45 | 12-17.5 |
| (g) Presence of lime (as carbonate) | (A) No Lime | (A) No Lime | (A) No Lime | (A) No Lime |
| | (B) Presence in fine form | (B) Presence in fine form | | |
| | (C) Magnesite present | concretions | | |

Along with chemical constituents, the temperature of the soil at different depths is equally important and plays a very vital role and is intimately connected with the productivity. Recently Rao and Misra (1981) have studied the soil temperature upto the depth of 20 cm. at Sagar Island towards the coast and found that during summer (Premonsoon) it varies from 32°C - 40°C, in winter it is about 14°C.

*APPENDIX-II-6*

## ORIGIN OF THE MANGROVES

The Mangrove can be referred as the community of trees and shrubs, growing in the particular intertidal ecosystem of the topics. This can also be considered as a self-maintaining coastal, intertidal estuarine component which thrives under constant interaction with terrestrial and marine ecosystem. The word 'Mangrove' appears to have been derived from the Portuguese word 'Mangaue' meaning, individual mangrove tree or bush, 'grove' being English. The word 'Mangle' is also sometimes referred to or almost synonymised now a days with the mangrove association. Literally it means the community, and it is used to signify the mangrove community as a whole traced from the beginning of the Eocene.

*APPENDIX-II-7*

## TIGER PROJECT

The objectives of the tiger project in the Sundarbans has been accomplished by declaring the Sundarban forest as a National Forest and the objectives are not only to protect the tiger but to conserve its natural habitat with a view to maintain the natural balance in the particular ecosystem. It is interesting to note that just about a hundred years ago the policy of the Government was to encourage killing tiger indiscriminately, because they were thought to be a great menace against development work and settlement. In the year 1852 as a special incentive for killing a tiger the Government announced a reward of Rs.5 to Rs.10 increased to Rs.20 in 1960. But for the general awareness and timely intervention of ICUN (International Union for the Conservation of Nature) through Government, it can safely be predicted that the tiger, probably would have been extinct by the turn of this century in the Sundarbans. IUCN at its 9th meeting in December 1969, declared that the tiger as an endangered animal and in 1970 the killing of tiger was banned and the Wild Life Protection Act was implemented in 1972 and the export of the Tiger skin was completely prohibited. In 1973 the World Wild Life Fund came forward with Rs.75 lakh for implementing the Tiger Project in India for 9 areas of which Sundarban was one. In addition the "Crocodile Project" has been taken up to increase the number of Estuarine Crocodiles by raising and breeding inside the farms. The collection of eggs, hatching and rearing in the farms at Bhagobatpur, Lothian Island have been carried out successfully and a good number of saltwater crocodiles have been released in the river within the Sundarban Tiger Reserve.

## *APPENDIX : TO CHAPTER III*

*APPENDIX-III.1*

**LITERACY 1981 - 1991**
**Proportion of Literates to total literate Population**

| *Regions/Blocks* | *1981* | | | *1991* | | |
|---|---|---|---|---|---|---|
| | *Person* 2 | *Male* 3 | *Female* 4 | *Person* 5 | *Male* 6 | *Female* 7 |
| **STABLE DELTA** | | | | | | |
| *I. THE WESTERN HUGLI SIDE FLATS* | | | | | | |
| 1. Thakurpur - Metiaburuz | 4.72 | 4.31 | 5.62 | 3.80 | 4.41 | 4.51 |
| 2. Mahestala | 6.12 | 5.53 | 7.42 | 7.43 | 6.89 | 8.43 |
| 3. Budge Budge | 7.71 | 7.67 | 7.81 | 6.88 | 6.57 | 7.46 |
| 4. Falta | 4.17 | 4.15 | 4.24 | 3.80 | 3.75 | 3.90 |
| 5. Diamond Harbour | 5.89 | 5.73 | 6.25 | 5.35 | 5.16 | 5.70 |
| 6. Kulpi | 3.73 | 3.74 | 3.70 | 3.22 | 3.28 | 3.13 |
| **TOTAL** | **32.35** | **31.13** | **35.04** | **30.49** | **29.04** | **33.13** |
| *II. THE MIDDLE MATURE DELTA OF THE HUGLI* | | | | | | |
| 7. Sonarpur | 5.08 | 6.17 | 9.10 | 8.27 | 7.63 | 9.45 |
| 8. Bishnupur | 6.82 | 6.82 | 6.56 | 6.45 | 6.45 | 6.75 |
| 9. Baruipur | 5.64 | 5.46 | 6.04 | 6.08 | 6.08 | 6.10 |
| 10. Mograhat | 6.26 | 6.27 | 5.36 | 6.59 | 6.73 | 6.34 |
| 11. Mandir - Bazar | 2.62 | 2.81 | 2.21 | 2.55 | 2.70 | 2.27 |
| 12. Jaynagar | 5.04 | 5.38 | 4.29 | 5.64 | 6.07 | 4.87 |
| **TOTAL** | **33.47** | **33.30** | **33.83** | **35.70** | **35.65** | **35.79** |
| *III. THE PIYALI BIDYADHARI PLAINS IN THE EAST* | | | | | | |
| 13. Bhangar | 4.36 | 4.22 | 4.37 | 4.49 | 4.49 | 4.15 |
| 14. Canning | 3.98 | 4.35 | 3.14 | 4.33 | 4.75 | 3.56 |
| **TOTAL** | **8.33** | **8.57** | **7.81** | **8.69** | **9.23** | **7.72** |
| **ACTIVE DELTA** | | | | | | |
| *IV. THE WESTERN SUNDARBANS* | | | | | | |
| 15. Sagar Island | 2.83 | 2.87 | 2.73 | 1.95 | 1.78 | 2.26 |
| 16. Kakdwip | 3.62 | 3.72 | 3.42 | 3.82 | 3.91 | 3.69 |
| 17. Namkhana | 1.85 | 1.87 | 1.81 | 1.92 | 1.91 | 1.92 |
| **TOTAL** | **8.30** | **8.46** | **7.96** | **7.69** | **7.60** | **7.87** |
| *V. THE MIDDLE SUNDARBANS* | | | | | | |
| 18. Mathurapur | 5.05 | 5.38 | 4.32 | 5.09 | 5.42 | 4.50 |
| 19. Pathar Pratima | 4.53 | 4.69 | 4.18 | 4.16 | 4.27 | 3.96 |
| **TOTAL** | **9.58** | **10.07** | **8.50** | **9.25** | **9.69** | **8.46** |
| *VI. EASTERN SUNDARBANS* | | | | | | |
| 20. Kultali | 1.69 | 1.87 | 1.31 | 1.96 | 2.26 | 1.41 |
| 21. Basanti | 2.63 | 2.88 | 2.09 | 2.78 | 3.05 | 2.29 |
| 22. Gosaba | 3.64 | 3.72 | 3.46 | 3.43 | 3.49 | 3.34 |
| **TOTAL** | | | | | | |
| **DISTRICT TOTAL** | **7.97** | **8.47** | **6.86** | **8.17** | **8.79** | **7.04** |

*APPENDIX-III.1.(Contd.)*

**LITERACY 1981 - 1991**
**Proportion of Rural literates to total Rural Population**

| Regions/Blocks | 1981 | | | 1991 | | |
|---|---|---|---|---|---|---|
| | Person | Male | Female | Person | Male | Female |
| | 2 | 3 | 4 | 5 | 6 | 7 |
| **STABLE DELTA** | | | | | | |
| *I. THE WESTERN HUGLI SIDE FLATS* | | | | | | |
| 1. Thakurpur - Metiaburuz | 1,25 | 1.10 | 1.60 | 0.86 | 0.71 | 1.15 |
| 2. Mahestala | 1.82 | 1.67 | 3.98 | 1.92 | 1.76 | 2.24 |
| 3. Budge Budge | 4.50 | 4.47 | 4.58 | 3.83 | 3.53 | 4.41 |
| 4. Falta | 5.17 | 5.02 | 3.54 | 4.80 | 4.62 | 5.13 |
| 5. Diamond Harbour | 6.42 | 6.19 | 6.96 | 5.80 | 5.52 | 6.35 |
| 6. Kulpi | 4.62 | 4.53 | 4.83 | 4.06 | 4.04 | 4.11 |
| **TOTAL** | **23.78** | **22.98** | **25.68** | **21.27** | **20.18** | **23.38** |
| *II. THE MIDDLE MATURE DELTA OF THE HUGLI* | | | | | | |
| 7. Sonarpur | 4.73 | 4.15 | 6.13 | 5.17 | 4.93 | 5.64 |
| 8. Bishnupur | 7.92 | 7.78 | 8.24 | 7.78 | 7.56 | 8.20 |
| 9. Baruipur | 5.61 | 5.49 | 5.90 | 6.07 | 6.10 | 6.01 |
| 10. Mograhat | 7.76 | 8.08 | 7.01 | 8.31 | 8.29 | 8.34 |
| 11. Mandir - Bazar | 3.25 | 3.40 | 2.90 | 3.21 | 3.33 | 2.98 |
| 12. Jaynagar | 5.47 | 5.86 | 4.55 | 6.47 | 6.91 | 5.60 |
| **TOTAL** | **34.74** | **34.75** | **34.73** | **37.01** | **37.12** | **36.78** |
| *III. THE PIYALI BIDYADHARI PLAINS IN THE EAST* | | | | | | |
| 13. Bhangar | 5.40 | 5.11 | 6.10 | 5.50 | 5.53 | 5.46 |
| 14. Canning | 4.04 | 4.48 | 2.99 | 4.57 | 5.04 | 3.65 |
| **TOTAL** | **9.44** | **9.59** | **9.09** | **10.08** | **10.57** | **9.11** |
| **ACTIVE DELTA** | | | | | | |
| *IV. THE WESTERN SUNDARBANS* | | | | | | |
| 15. Sagar Island | 3.50 | 3.47 | 3.57 | 2.46 | 2.19 | 2.98 |
| 16. Kakdwip | 4.49 | 4.50 | 4.47 | 4.82 | 4.81 | 4.85 |
| 17. Namkhana | 2.30 | 2.27 | 2.37 | 2.41 | 2.36 | 2.52 |
| **TOTAL** | **10.29** | **10.24** | **10.41** | **9.70** | **9.36** | **10.35** |
| *V. THE MIDDLE SUNDARBANS* | | | | | | |
| 18. Mathurapur | 6.26 | 6.51 | 5.65 | 6.42 | 6.68 | 5.91 |
| 19. Pathar Pratima | 5.61 | 5.68 | 5.46 | 5.24 | 5.26 | 5.21 |
| **TOTAL** | **11.87** | **12.19** | **11.11** | **11.66** | **11.93** | **11.12** |
| *VI. EASTERN SUNDARBANS* | | | | | | |
| 20. Kultali | 2.10 | 2.26 | 1.71 | 2.47 | 2.78 | 1.86 |
| 21. Basanti | 3.26 | 3.49 | 2.73 | 3.50 | 3.76 | 3.00 |
| 22. Gosaba | 4.51 | 4.51 | 4.53 | 4.33 | 4.29 | 4.39 |
| **TOTAL** | **9.87** | **10.25** | **8.97** | **10.29** | **10.83** | **9.25** |
| **DISTRICT TOTAL** | **100** | **100** | **100** | **100** | **100** | **100** |

*APPENDIX-III.1(Contd.)*

**LITERACY 1981 - 1991**

**Proportion of Urban literates to total Urban Population**

| *Regions/Blocks* | *1981* | | | *1991* | | |
|---|---|---|---|---|---|---|
| | *Person* | *Male* | *Female* | *Person* | *Male* | *Female* |
| | *14* | *15* | *16* | *17* | *18* | *19* |
| **STABLE DELTA** | | | | | | |
| *I. THE WESTERN HUGLI SIDE FLATS* | | | | | | |
| 1. Thakurpur - Metiaburuz | 19.22 | 19.55 | 18.68 | 15.09 | 15.03 | 15.16 |
| 2. Mahestala | 24.08 | 23.85 | 9.30 | 28.61 | 28.98 | 28.09 |
| 3. Budge Budge | 21.13 | 22.85 | 18.34 | 18.62 | 19.66 | 17.15 |
| 4. Falta | | | | | | |
| 5. Diamond Harbour | 3.72 | 3.56 | 3.96 | 3.62 | 3.59 | 3.66 |
| 6. Kulpi | | | | | | |
| **TOTAL** | **68.14** | **69.80** | **65.43** | **65.94** | **67.26** | **64.06** |
| *II. THE MIDDLE MATURE DELTA OF THE HUGLI* | | | | | | |
| 7. Sonarpur | 16.90 | 15.77 | 18.73 | 20.20 | 19.26 | 21.55 |
| 8. Bishnupur | 2.23 | 2.23 | 2.22 | 1.85 | 1.64 | 2.15 |
| 9. Baruipur | 5.78 | 5.33 | 6.50 | 6.13 | 5.95 | 6.40 |
| 10. Mograhat | | | | | | |
| 11. Mandir - Bazar | | | | | | |
| 12. Jaynagar | 3.25 | 3.12 | 3.47 | 2.49 | 2.44 | 2.55 |
| **TOTAL** | **28.15** | **26.45** | **30.91** | **30.67** | **29.28** | **32.65** |
| *III. THE PIYALI BIDYADHARI PLAINS IN THE EAST* | | | | | | |
| 13. Bhangar | | | | | | |
| 14. Canning | 3.71 | 3.74 | 3.65 | 3.39 | 3.46 | 3.28 |
| **15. TOTAL** | **3.71** | **3.74** | **3.65** | **3.39** | **3.46** | **3.28** |
| **DISTRICT TOTAL** | **100** | **100** | **100** | **100** | **100** | **100** |

*APPENDIX-III.2*

**SCHEDULED CASTE POPULATION AMONG TOTAL SCHEDULED CASTE 1981 - 1991**

**Proportion of Scheduled Caste to total Schedule Caste Population**

| *Regions/Blocks* | *1981* | | | *1991* | | |
|---|---|---|---|---|---|---|
| | *Person* | *Male* | *Female* | *Person* | *Male* | *Female* |
| | *2* | *3* | *4* | *5* | *6* | *7* |
| **STABLE DELTA** | | | | | | |
| *I. THE WESTERN HUGLI SIDE FLATS* | | | | | | |
| 1. Thakurpur - Metiaburuz | 2.23 | 2.20 | 2.16 | 2.55 | 2.57 | 2.54 |
| 2. Mahestala | 2.99 | 2.94 | 2.89 | 3.31 | 3.31 | 3.32 |
| 3. Budge Budge | 4.41 | 4.19 | 4.44 | 3.28 | 3.27 | 3.30 |
| 4. Falta | 2.72 | 2.63 | 2.69 | 2.32 | 2.57 | 2.05 |
| 5. Diamond Harbour | 3.56 | 3.45 | 3.51 | 3.01 | 3.41 | 2.59 |
| 6. Kulpi | 4.39 | 4.68 | 3.86 | 3.49 | 3.24 | 3.77 |
| **TOTAL** | **19.82** | **20.09** | **19.54** | **17.96** | **18.37** | **17.47** |
| *II. THE MIDDLE MATURE DELTA OF THE HUGLI* | | | | | | |
| 7. Sonarpur | 6.28 | 6.14 | 6.11 | 6.71 | 6.71 | 6.73 |
| 8. Bishnupur | 6.93 | 6.71 | 6.84 | 6.48 | 6.47 | 6.52 |
| 9. Baruipur | 6.94 | 6.78 | 6.78 | 6.92 | 7.00 | 6.86 |
| 10. Mograhat | 6.51 | 6.81 | 5.86 | 6.88 | 6.91 | 6.88 |
| 11. Mandir - Bazar | 3.06 | 3.91 | 4.03 | 3.84 | 3.85 | 3.85 |
| 12. Jaynagar | 7.35 | 7.17 | 7.20 | 7.96 | 7.95 | 7.99 |
| **TOTAL** | **37.19** | **37.52** | **36.82** | **38.80** | **38.89** | **38.83** |
| *III. THE PIYALI BIDYADHARI PLAINS IN THE EAST* | | | | | | |
| 13. Bhangar | 4.52 | 4.31 | 4.54 | 4.18 | 4.11 | 4.26 |
| 14. Canning | 7.24 | 6.99 | 7.16 | 7.48 | 7.43 | 7.55 |
| **TOTAL** | **11.49** | **11.30** | **11.70** | **11.66** | **11.55** | **11.71** |
| **ACTIVE DELTA** | | | | | | |
| IV. THE WESTERN SUNDARBANS | | | | | | |
| 15. Sagar Island | 2.06 | 1.96 | 2.07 | 2.22 | 2.15 | 2.30 |
| 16. Kakdwip | 3.25 | 3.14 | 3.22 | 3.88 | 3.83 | 3.95 |
| 17. Namkhana | 1.25 | 1.20 | 1.25 | 1.29 | 1.31 | 1.26 |
| **TOTAL** | **6.41** | **6.31** | **6.53** | **7.38** | **7.29** | **7.51** |
| *V. THE MIDDLE SUNDARBANS* | | | | | | |
| 18. Mathurapur | 3.28 | 5.50 | 5.62 | 5.61 | 5.59 | 5.65 |
| 19. Pathar Pratima | 3.17 | 3.03 | 3.17 | 3.22 | 3.01 | 3.15 |
| **TOTAL** | **8.65** | **8.54** | **8.79** | **8.83** | **8.60** | **8.80** |
| *VI. EASTERN SUNDARBANS* | | | | | | |
| 20. Kultali | 4.78 | 4.60 | 4.76 | 3.98 | 3.95 | 4.01 |
| 21. Basanti | 4.79 | 4.63 | 4.74 | 4.79 | 4.79 | 4.81 |
| 22. Gosaba | 7.23 | 7.02 | 7.11 | 6.59 | 6.55 | 6.66 |
| **TOTAL** | **16.42** | **16.25** | **16.61** | **15.36** | **15.00** | **15.70** |
| **DISTRICT TOTAL** | **100** | **100** | **100** | **100** | **100** | **100** |

*APPENDIX-III.2. (Contd.)*

**SCHEDULED CASTE POPULATION AMONG TOTAL SCHEDULED CASTE 1981 - 1991**

**Proportion of Rural Scheduled Caste to total Rural Scheduled Caste Population**

| Regions/Blocks | 1981 | | | 1991 | | |
|---|---|---|---|---|---|---|
| | Person | Male | Female | Person | Male | Female |
| | 2 | 3 | 4 | 5 | 6 | 7 |
| **STABLE DELTA** | | | | | | |
| *I. THE WESTERN HUGLI SIDE FLATS* | | | | | | |
| 1. Thakurpur - Metiaburuz | 1.96 | 0.97 | 0.99 | 1.59 | 1.59 | 1.59 |
| 2. Mahestala | 1.95 | 1.89 | 1.62 | 1.86 | 1.85 | 1.87 |
| 3. Budge Budge | 3.44 | 2.87 | 3.89 | 3.37 | 2.32 | 2.43 |
| 4. Falta | 2.90 | 2.81 | 2.85 | 2.49 | 2.78 | 2.21 |
| 5. Diamond Harbour | 3.65 | 3.55 | 3.58 | 3.03 | 3.47 | 3.57 |
| 6. Kulpi | 4.68 | 5.01 | 4.09 | 3.76 | 3.49 | 4.05 |
| **TOTAL** | **17.18** | **17.10** | **17.31** | **15.10** | **15.48** | **14.73** |
| *II. THE MIDDLE MATURE DELTA OF THE HUGLI* | | | | | | |
| 7. Sonarpur | 5.81 | 5.71 | 5.62 | 5.72 | 5.72 | 5.73 |
| 8. Bishnupur | 7.33 | 7.13 | 7.19 | 6.85 | 6.82 | 6.89 |
| 9. Baruipur | 6.93 | 6.68 | 7.25 | 6.78 | 6.86 | 6.71 |
| 10. Mograhat | 6.93 | 7.29 | 6.20 | 7.41 | 7.44 | 7.40 |
| 11. Mandir - Bazar | 4.33 | 4.18 | 4.27 | 4.41 | 4.15 | 4.14 |
| 12. Jaynagar | 7.63 | 7.40 | 7.50 | 8.40 | 8.39 | 8.43 |
| **TOTAL** | **37.99** | **38.39** | **37.65** | **39.29** | **39.40** | **39.31** |
| *III. THE PIYALI BIDYADHARI PLAINS IN THE EAST* | | | | | | |
| 13. Bhangar | 4.82 | 4.61 | 4.81 | 4.50 | 4.44 | 4.58 |
| 14. Canning | 6.82 | 6.62 | 6.23 | 7.10 | 7.07 | 7.18 |
| **TOTAL** | **11.35** | **11.23** | **11.50** | **11.61** | **11.51** | **11.76** |
| **ACTIVE DELTA** | | | | | | |
| *IV. THE WESTERN SUNDARBANS* | | | | | | |
| 15. Sagar Island | 2.19 | 2.09 | 0.73 | 2.39 | 2.32 | 2.47 |
| 16. Kakdwip | 3.47 | 3.36 | 1.14 | 4.18 | 4.13 | 4.24 |
| 17. Namkhana | 1.34 | 1.29 | 0.44 | 1.38 | 1.41 | 1.36 |
| **TOTAL** | **6.82** | **6.75** | **6.92** | **7.95** | **7.86** | **8.00** |
| *V. THE MIDDLE SUNDARBANS* | | | | | | |
| 18. Mathurapur | 3.49 | 5.89 | 1.98 | 6.04 | 6.03 | 6.08 |
| 19. Pathar Pratima | 3.38 | 3.25 | 1.12 | 3.47 | 3.24 | 3.39 |
| **TOTAL** | **9.21** | **9.14** | **9.31** | **9.51** | **9.27** | **9.64** |
| *VI. EASTERN SUNDARBANS* | | | | | | |
| 20. Kultali | 5.09 | 4.92 | 1.68 | 4.28 | 4.26 | 4.32 |
| 21. Basanti | 5.10 | 4.96 | 1.67 | 5.16 | 5.16 | 5.17 |
| 22. Gosaba | 7.10 | 7.51 | 2.51 | 7.09 | 7.06 | 7.17 |
| **TOTAL** | **17.46** | **17.39** | **17.31** | **16.54** | **16.17** | **16.56** |
| **DISTRICT TOTAL** | **100** | **100** | **100** | **100** | **100** | **100** |

*APPENDIX-III.2 (Contd.)*

**SCHEDULED CASTE POPULATION AMONG TOTAL SCHEDULE CASTE 1981 - 1991**

**Proportion of Urban Scheduled Caste to total Urban Schedule Caste Population**

| *Regions/Blocks* | *1981* | | | *1991* | | |
|---|---|---|---|---|---|---|
| | *Person* | *Male* | *Female* | *Person* | *Male* | *Female* |
| | *14* | *15* | *16* | *17* | *18* | *19* |
| **STABLE DELTA** | | | | | | |
| *I. THE WESTERN HUGLI SIDE FLATS* | | | | | | |
| 1. Thakurpur - Metiaburuz | 21.21 | 19.82 | 17.11 | 15.09 | 15.20 | 14.98 |
| 2. Mahestala | 18.98 | 17.97 | 18.92 | 22.21 | 22.08 | 22.37 |
| 3. Budge Budge | 19.34 | 23.03 | 10.65 | 15.13 | 15.51 | 14.72 |
| 4. Falta | | | | | | |
| 5. Diamond Harbour | 2.15 | 1.93 | 1.81 | 2.76 | 2.67 | 2.87 |
| 6. Kulpi | | | | | | |
| **TOTAL** | **61.68** | **62.76** | **60.23** | **55.21** | **55.46** | **54.94** |
| *II. THE MIDDLE MATURE DELTA OF THE HUGLI* | | | | | | |
| 7. Sonarpur | 13.52 | 12.31 | 11.23 | 19.65 | 19.49 | 19.82 |
| 8. Bishnupur | 0.81 | 0.70 | 0.71 | 1.75 | 1.93 | 1.55 |
| 9. Baruipur | 7.10 | 8.21 | 4.15 | 8.83 | 8.73 | 8.93 |
| 10. Mograhat | | | | | | |
| 11. Mandir - Bazar | | | | | | |
| 12. Jaynagar | 3.13 | 3.79 | 1.66 | 2.25 | 2.30 | 2.19 |
| **TOTAL** | **24.55** | **25.01** | **23.94** | **32.48** | **32.46** | **32.51** |
| *III. THE PIYALI BIDYADHARI PLAINS IN THE EAST* | | | | | | |
| 13. Bhangar | | | | | | |
| 14. Canning | 13.76 | 12.23 | 15.82 | 12.31 | 12.08 | 12.55 |
| **TOTAL** | **13.76** | **12.23** | **15.82** | **12.31** | **12.08** | **12.55** |
| **DISTRICT TOTAL** | **100** | **100** | **100** | **100** | **100** | **100** |

*APPENDIX-III.3*

**PROPORTION OF SCHEDULED TRIBE TO TOTAL SCHEDULED TRIBE POPULATION 1981-91**

**(Proportion of Scheduled Tribe to total population)**

| *Resions/Blocks* | *1981* | | | *1991* | | |
|---|---|---|---|---|---|---|
| | *Person* | *Male* | *Female* | *Person* | *Male* | *Female* |
| | *2* | *3* | *4* | *5* | *6* | *7* |
| **STABLE DELTA** | | | | | | |
| *I. THE WESTERN HUGLI SIDE FLATS* | | | | | | |
| 1. Thakurpur - Metiaburuz | 1.22 | 1.29 | 1.15 | 0.60 | 0.63 | 0.57 |
| 2. Mahestala | 0.78 | 0.78 | 0.77 | 1.56 | 1.71 | 1.41 |
| 3. Budge Budge | 2.01 | 1.85 | 2.18 | 1.70 | 1.54 | 1.86 |
| 4. Falta | 0.00 | 0.00 | 0.00 | 0.00 | 0.00 | 0.00 |
| 5. Diamond Harbour | 0.00 | 0.00 | 0.00 | 0.04 | 0.03 | 0.04 |
| 6. Kulpi | 0.00 | 0.00 | 0.00 | 0.00 | 0.00 | 0.00 |
| **TOTAL** | **4.02** | **3.93** | **4.11** | **3.90** | **3.95** | **3.85** |
| *II. THE MIDDLE MATURE DELTA OF THE HUGLI* | | | | | | |
| 7. Sonarpur | 4.09 | 4.40 | 3.77 | 4.61 | 4.98 | 4.24 |
| 8. Bishnupur | 0.17 | 0.23 | 0.11 | 0.05 | 0.06 | 0.04 |
| 9. Baruipur | 1.32 | 1.34 | 1.31 | 1.51 | 1.55 | 1.46 |
| 10. Mograhat | 0.04 | 0.03 | 0.04 | 0.00 | 0.00 | 0.00 |
| 11. Mandir - Bazar | 0.00 | 0.00 | 0.00 | 0.00 | 0.00 | 0.00 |
| 12. Jaynagar | 0.16 | 0.17 | 0.15 | 1.26 | 1.25 | 1.26 |
| **TOTAL** | **5.78** | **6.16** | **5.38** | **7.44** | **7.86** | **7.00** |
| III. THE PIYALI BIDYADHARI PLAINS IN THE EAST | | | | | | |
| 13. Bhangar | 7.68 | 7.71 | 7.65 | 5.78 | 5.68 | 5.89 |
| 14. Canning | 17.38 | 17.13 | 17.64 | 19.36 | 19.04 | 19.68 |
| **TOTAL** | **25.07** | **24.85** | **25.29** | **25.14** | **24.73** | **25.57** |
| **ACTIVE DELTA** | | | | | | |
| *IV. THE WESTERN SUNDARBANS* | | | | | | |
| 15. Sagar Island | 0.73 | 0.75 | 0.72 | 0.77 | 0.76 | 0.79 |
| 16. Kakdwip | 2.00 | 2.02 | 1.98 | 1.58 | 1.59 | 1.57 |
| 17. Namkhana | 0.61 | 0.66 | 0.55 | 0.75 | 0.76 | 0.75 |
| **TOTAL** | **3.34** | **3.42** | **3.25** | **3.11** | **3.12** | **3.10** |
| *V. THE MIDDLE SUNDARBANS* | | | | | | |
| 18. Mathurapur | 4.53 | 4.57 | 4.49 | 4.45 | 4.51 | 4.39 |
| 19. Pathar Pratima | 2.70 | 2.61 | 2.80 | 2.61 | 2.58 | 2.63 |
| **TOTAL** | **7.23** | **7.18** | **7.29** | **7.05** | **7.09** | **7.01** |
| *VI. EASTERN SUNDARBANS* | | | | | | |
| 20. Kultali | 6.94 | 6.82 | 7.05 | 6.23 | 6.29 | 6.16 |
| 21. Basanti | 18.94 | 18.94 | 18.94 | 19.28 | 19.34 | 19.22 |
| 22. Gosaba | 28.69 | 28.70 | 28.68 | 27.85 | 27.64 | 28.07 |
| **TOTAL** | **54.57** | **54.47** | **54.67** | **53.36** | **53.26** | **53.45** |
| **DISTRICT TOTAL** | **100** | **100** | **100** | **100** | **100** | **100** |

*APPENDIX-III.3 (Contd.)*

**PROPORTION OF SCHEDULED TRIBE TO TOTAL SCHEDULED TRIBE POPULATION 1981-91**

**(Proportion of Scheduled Tribe to total Rural Scheduled Tribe population)**

| Regions/Blocks | *1981* | | | *1991* | | |
|---|---|---|---|---|---|---|
| | *Person* | *Male* | *Female* | *Person* | *Male* | *Female* |
| | *8* | *9* | *10* | *11* | *12* | *13* |
| **STABLE DELTA** | | | | | | |
| *I. THE WESTERN HUGLI SIDE FLATS* | | | | | | |
| 1. Thakurpur - Metiaburuz | 0.46 | 0.50 | 0.42 | 0.19 | 0.20 | 0.19 |
| 2. Mahestala | 0.05 | 0.09 | 0.01 | 0.07 | 0.08 | 0.05 |
| 3. Budge Budge | 1.94 | 1.76 | 2.13 | 0.33 | 0.31 | 0.34 |
| 4. Falta | 0.00 | 0.00 | 0.00 | 0.00 | 0.00 | 0.00 |
| 5. Diamond Harbour | 0.00 | 0.00 | 0.00 | 0.00 | 0.00 | 0.00 |
| 6. Kulpi | 0.00 | 0.00 | 0.00 | 0.00 | 0.00 | 0.00 |
| **TOTAL** | **2.47** | **2.36** | **2.58** | **0.59** | **0.60** | **0.59** |
| *II. THE MIDDLE MATURE DELTA OF THE HUGLI* | | | | | | |
| 7. Sonarpur | 3.59 | 1.88 | 3.42 | 4.47 | 4.81 | 4.11 |
| 8. Bishnupur | 0.17 | 0.11 | 0.11 | 0.05 | 0.06 | 0.04 |
| 9. Baruipur | 1.20 | 0.62 | 1.16 | 1.27 | 1.33 | 1.21 |
| 10. Mograhat | 0.04 | 0.01 | 0.04 | 0.00 | 0.00 | 0.00 |
| 11. Mandir - Bazar | 0.00 | 0.00 | 0.00 | 0.00 | 0.00 | 0.00 |
| 12. Jaynagar | 0.16 | 0.09 | 0.15 | 1.29 | 1.29 | 1.29 |
| **TOTAL** | **5.16** | **5.43** | **4.88** | **7.09** | **7.51** | **6.66** |
| *III. THE PIYALI BIDYADHARI PLAINS IN THE EAST* | | | | | | |
| 13. Bhangar | 7.89 | 7.93 | 7.85 | 6.04 | 5.93 | 6.14 |
| 14. Canning | 17.61 | 17.40 | 17.83 | 20.00 | 19.70 | 20.31 |
| **TOTAL** | **25.50** | **25.32** | **25.67** | **26.04** | **25.63** | **26.45** |
| **ACTIVE DELTA** | | | | | | |
| *IV. THE WESTERN SUNDARBANS* | | | | | | |
| 15. Sagar Island | 0.75 | 0.78 | 0.74 | 0.81 | 0.79 | 0.82 |
| 16. Kakdwip | 2.05 | 2.08 | 2.03 | 1.65 | 1.66 | 1.64 |
| 17. Namkhana | 0.62 | 0.67 | 0.57 | 0.79 | 0.80 | 0.78 |
| **TOTAL** | **3.43** | **3.52** | **3.34** | **3.24** | **3.25** | **3.23** |
| *V. THE MIDDLE SUNDARBANS* | | | | | | |
| 18. Mathurapur | 4.65 | 4.70 | 4.60 | 4.64 | 4.70 | 4.57 |
| 19. Pathar Pratima | 2.77 | 2.68 | 2.87 | 2.72 | 2.70 | 2.74 |
| **TOTAL** | **7.42** | **7.38** | **7.47** | **7.36** | **7.40** | **7.31** |
| *VI. EASTERN SUNDARBANS* | | | | | | |
| 20. Kultali | 7.12 | 7.01 | 7.23 | 6.50 | 6.56 | 6.43 |
| 21. Basanti | 19.44 | 19.47 | 19.42 | 20.12 | 20.19 | 20.05 |
| 22. Gosaba | 29.46 | 29.51 | 29.40 | 29.06 | 28.84 | 29.28 |
| **TOTAL** | **56.02** | **55.99** | **56.05** | **55.67** | **55.60** | **55.75** |
| **DISTRICT TOTAL** | **100** | **100** | **100** | **100** | **100** | **100** |

*APPENDIX-III.3 (Contd.)*

**PROPORTION OF SCHEDULED TRIBE TO TOTAL SCHEDULED TRIBE POPULATION 1981-91**

**(Proportion of Urban Schedule Tribe to total Urban Scheduled Tribe population)**

| *Regions/Blocks* | *1981* | | | *1991* | | |
|---|---|---|---|---|---|---|
| | *Person* | *Male* | *Female* | *Person* | *Male* | *Female* |
| | *2* | *3* | *4* | *5* | *6* | *7* |
| **STABLE DELTA** | | | | | | |
| *I. THE WESTERN HUGLI SIDE FLATS* | | | | | | |
| 1. Thakurpur - Metiaburuz | 29.87 | 29.68 | 29.70 | 10.21 | 10.82 | 9.57 |
| 2. Mahestala | 28.03 | 25.35 | 30.70 | 35.93 | 39.0 | 32.73 |
| 3. Budge Budge | 4.62 | 4.97 | 4.16 | 33.24 | 29.73 | 36.89 |
| 4. Falta | 0.00 | 0.00 | 0.00 | 0.00 | 0.00 | 0.00 |
| 5. Diamond Harbour | 0.00 | 0.00 | 0.00 | 0.71 | 0.76 | 0.00 |
| 6. Kulpi | 0.00 | 0.00 | 0.00 | 0.00 | 0.00 | 0.00 |
| **TOTAL** | **62.00** | **60.00** | **64.42** | **80.09** | **80.76** | **79.50** |
| *II. THE MIDDLE MATURE DELTA OF THE HUGLI* | | | | | | |
| 7. Sonarpur | 22.81 | 27.13 | 17.65 | 7.96 | 8.75 | 7.14 |
| 8. Bishnupur | 0.27 | 0.25 | 0.29 | 0.00 | 0.00 | 0.00 |
| 9. Baruipur | 5.43 | 4.84 | 7.32 | 6.94 | 6.61 | 7.28 |
| 10. Mograhat | 0.00 | 0.00 | 0.00 | 0.00 | 0.00 | 0.00 |
| 11. Mandir - Bazar | 0.00 | 0.00 | 0.00 | 0.00 | 0.00 | 0.00 |
| 12. Jaynagar | 0.00 | 0.00 | 0.00 | 0.00 | 0.00 | 0.00 |
| **TOTAL** | **29.12** | **32.23** | **25.25** | **15.41** | **15.39** | **14.97** |
| *III. THE PIYALI BIDYADHARI PLAINS IN THE EAST* | | | | | | |
| 13. Bhangar | 0.00 | 0.00 | 0.00 | 0.00 | 0.00 | 0.00 |
| 14. Canning | 8.90 | 7.77 | 10.19 | 4.49 | 3.87 | 5.13 |
| **TOTAL** | **8.90** | **7.77** | **10.19** | **4.49** | **3.87** | **5.13** |
| **DISTRICT TOTAL** | **100** | **100** | **100** | **100** | **100** | **100** |

*APPENDIX-III.4*

**Proportion of Total Workers to Total Working Population 1981-1991**

| *Regions/Blocks* | *1981* | | | *1991* | | |
|---|---|---|---|---|---|---|
| | *Person* | *Male* | *Female* | *Person* | *Male* | *Female* |
| | *2* | *3* | *4* | *5* | *6* | *7* |
| **STABLE DELTA** | | | | | | |
| *I. THE WESTERN HUGLI SIDE FLATS* | | | | | | |
| 1. Thakurpur - Metiaburuz | 3.21 | 2.17 | 19.38 | 5.43 | 4.76 | 8.16 |
| 2. Mahestala | 4.18 | 4.24 | 3.23 | 5.45 | 5.72 | 3.63 |
| 3. Budge Budge | 6.79 | 6.90 | 5.07 | 5.49 | 5.88 | 2.83 |
| 4. Falta | 3.37 | 3.46 | 2.02 | 3.73 | 3.73 | 3.74 |
| 5. Diamond Harbour | 5.13 | 5.12 | 5.49 | 4.69 | 4.92 | 3.16 |
| 6. Kulpi | 3.64 | 3.74 | 2.03 | 3.41 | 3.16 | 5.05 |
| **TOTAL** | **26.31** | **25.63** | **36.71** | **27.09** | **27.18** | **26.50** |
| *II. THE MIDDLE MATURE DELTA OF THE HUGLI* | | | | | | |
| 7. Sonarpur | 5.37 | 5.27 | 6.96 | 5.62 | 5.82 | 4.32 |
| 8. Bishnupur | 6.51 | 6.48 | 5.66 | 5.37 | 5.83 | 5.89 |
| 9. Baruipur | 5.14 | 5.11 | 5.70 | 4.93 | 5.16 | 3.40 |
| 10. Mograhat | 6.80 | 7.05 | 3.11 | 6.63 | 6.91 | 4.76 |
| 11. Mandir - Bazar | 2.68 | 2.75 | 1.68 | 2.36 | 2.59 | 0.83 |
| 12. Jaynagar | 5.57 | 5.71 | 3.42 | 5.85 | 6.30 | 2.84 |
| **TOTAL** | **32.07** | **32.37** | **27.55** | **31.26** | **32.60** | **22.24** |
| *III. THE PIYALI BIDYADHARI PLAINS IN THE EAST* | | | | | | |
| 13. Bhangar | 5.87 | 6.03 | 3.40 | 5.31 | 5.73 | 2.44 |
| 14. Canning | 5.73 | 5.80 | 4.73 | 5.65 | 5.98 | 3.40 |
| **TOTAL** | **11.60** | **11.83** | **8.02** | **10.96** | **11.72** | **5.82** |
| **ACTIVE DELTA** | | | | | | |
| *IV. THE WESTERN SUNDARBANS* | | | | | | |
| 15. Sagar Island | 2.64 | 2.62 | 3.06 | 2.51 | 2.61 | 1.86 |
| 16. Kakdwip | 3.89 | 3.92 | 3.48 | 4.26 | 3.75 | 7.66 |
| 17. Namkhana | 1.73 | 1.71 | 2.14 | 2.63 | 1.88 | 7.69 |
| **TOTAL** | **8.27** | **8.25** | **8.37** | **9.40** | **8.24** | **17.18** |
| *V. THE MIDDLE SUNDARBANS* | | | | | | |
| 18. Mathurapur | 5.58 | 5.67 | 4.31 | 5.78 | 5.49 | 7.74 |
| 19. Pathar Pratima | 4.62 | 4.56 | 5.47 | 4.77 | 4.41 | 7.23 |
| **TOTAL** | **10.20** | **10.23** | **9.65** | **10.54** | **9.89** | **14.93** |
| *VI. EASTERN SUNDARBANS* | | | | | | |
| 20. Kultali | 3.44 | 3.50 | 2.45 | 2.44 | 2.61 | 1.31 |
| 21. Basanti | 3.99 | 4.09 | 2.47 | 4.03 | 4.00 | 4.22 |
| 22. Gosaba | 4.13 | 4.10 | 4.72 | 4.28 | 3.76 | 7.83 |
| **TOTAL** | **11.56** | **11.69** | **9.51** | **10.75** | **10.37** | **13.33** |
| **DISTRICT TOTAL** | **100** | **100** | **100** | **100** | **100** | **100** |

*APPENDIX-III.4 (Contd.)*

**Proportion of Total Workers to Total Working Population 1981-1991**

| Regions/Blocks | 1981 | | | 1991 | | |
|---|---|---|---|---|---|---|
| | *Person* | *Male* | *Female* | *Person* | *Male* | *Female* |
| | *2* | *3* | *4* | *5* | *6* | *7* |
| **STABLE DELTA** | | | | | | |
| *I. THE WESTERN HUGLI SIDE FLATS* | | | | | | |
| 1. Thakurpur - Metiaburuz | 1.70 | 1.02 | 13.00 | 2.83 | 2.01 | 8.02 |
| 2. Mahestala | 1.33 | 1.35 | 1.01 | 1.32 | 1.41 | 0.73 |
| 3. Budge Budge | 3.89 | 3.86 | 4.45 | 2.92 | 3.08 | 1.89 |
| 4. Falta | 3.83 | 3.91 | 2.47 | 4.33 | 4.37 | 4.08 |
| 5. Diamond Harbour | 5.32 | 5.29 | 5.78 | 4.84 | 5.15 | 2.95 |
| 6. Kulpi | 4.13 | 4.24 | 2.48 | 3.95 | 3.71 | 5.51 |
| **TOTAL** | **20.20** | **19.68** | **28.70** | **20.19** | **19.72** | **23.14** |
| *II. THE MIDDLE MATURE DELTA OF THE HUGLI* | | | | | | |
| 7. Sonarpur | 4.09 | 4.00 | 5.65 | 3.84 | 4.00 | 2.82 |
| 8. Bishnupur | 7.11 | 7.05 | 6.55 | 6.52 | 6.54 | 6.16 |
| 9. Baruipur | 5.23 | 5.18 | 6.05 | 4.93 | 5.20 | 3.23 |
| 10. Mograhat | 7.73 | 7.98 | 3.79 | 7.69 | 8.09 | 5.19 |
| 11. Mandir - Bazar | 3.05 | 3.11 | 2.05 | 2.73 | 3.03 | 0.90 |
| 12. Jaynagar | 5.94 | 6.08 | 3.70 | 6.42 | 6.99 | 2.84 |
| **TOTAL** | **33.14** | **33.40** | **29.00** | **32.13** | **33.85** | **21.36** |
| *III. THE PIYALI BIDYADHARI PLAINS IN THE EAST* | | | | | | |
| 13. Bhangar | 6.67 | 6.83 | 4.15 | 6.16 | 6.72 | 2.67 |
| 14. Canning | 5.86 | 5.95 | 4.59 | 5.91 | 6.34 | 3.25 |
| **TOTAL** | **12.53** | **12.83** | **8.58** | **12.07** | **13.06** | **5.90** |
| **ACTIVE DELTA** | | | | | | |
| *IV. THE WESTERN SUNDARBANS* | | | | | | |
| 15. Sagar Island | 3.00 | 2.96 | 3.74 | 2.91 | 13.05 | 2.04 |
| 16. Kakdwip | 4.42 | 4.44 | 4.25 | 4.94 | 4.39 | 8.37 |
| 17. Namkhana | 1.97 | 1.93 | 2.61 | 3.05 | 2.20 | 8.40 |
| **TOTAL** | **9.40** | **9.33** | **10.42** | **10.90** | **9.65** | **18.75** |
| *V. THE MIDDLE SUNDARBANS* | | | | | | |
| 18. Mathurapur | C.34 | 6.41 | 5.26 | 6.70 | 6.43 | 8.45 |
| 19. Pathar Pratima | 5.25 | 5.17 | 6.67 | 5.53 | 5.16 | 7.89 |
| **TOTAL** | **11.59** | **11.58** | **11.73** | **12.23** | **11.58** | **16.30** |
| *VI. EASTERN SUNDARBANS* | | | | | | |
| 20. Kultali | 3.91 | 3.96 | 2.99 | 2.84 | 3.06 | 1.43 |
| 21. Basanti | 4.53 | 4.63 | 3.01 | 4.67 | 4.69 | 4.61 |
| 22. Gosaba | 4.70 | 4.64 | 5.75 | 4.97 | 4.40 | 8.55 |
| **TOTAL** | **13.14** | **13.23** | **11.56** | **12.47** | **12.14** | **14.55** |
| **DISTRICT TOTAL** | **100** | **100** | **100** | **100** | **100** | **100** |

*APPENDIX-III.4 (Contd.)*

**Proportion of Total Workers to Total Working Population 1981-1991**

| Regions/Blocks | *1981* | | | *1991* | | |
|---|---|---|---|---|---|---|
| | *Person* | *Male* | *Female* | *Person* | *Male* | *Female* |
| | *2* | *3* | *4* | *5* | *6* | *7* |
| **STABLE DELTA** | | | | | | |
| *I. THE WESTERN HUGLI SIDE FLATS* | | | | | | |
| 1. Thakurpur - Metiaburuz | 14.28 | 10.85 | 48.48 | 13.64 | 13.98 | 9.58 |
| 2. Mahestala | 24.95 | 26.11 | 13.31 | 31.28 | 30.94 | 35.14 |
| 3. Budge Budge | 27.95 | 29.96 | 7.87 | 21.55 | 22.28 | 13.02 |
| 4. Falta | | | | | | |
| 5. Diamond Harbour | 3.81 | 3.78 | 4.15 | 3.72 | 3.58 | 5.44 |
| 6. Kulpi | | | | | | |
| **TOTAL** | **70.99** | **70.71** | **73.81** | **70.18** | **70.78** | **63.18** |
| *II. THE MIDDLE MATURE DELTA OF THE HUGLI* | | | | | | |
| 7. Sonarpur | 14.69 | 14.87 | 12.93 | 16.77 | 16.43 | 20.66 |
| 8. Bishnupur | 2.17 | 2.22 | 1.63 | 1.82 | 1.72 | 3.03 |
| 9. Baruipur | 4.53 | 4.57 | 4.09 | 4.96 | 4.93 | 5.29 |
| 10. Mograhat | | | | | | |
| 11. Mandir - Bazar | | | | | | |
| 12. Jaynagar | 2.88 | 2.95 | 2.14 | 2.29 | 2.24 | 2.83 |
| **TOTAL** | **24.26** | **24.61** | **20.80** | **25.83** | **25.32** | **31.81** |
| *III. THE PIYALI BIDYADHARI PLAINS IN THE EAST* | | | | | | |
| 13. Bhangar | | | | | | |
| 14. Canning | 4.75 | 4.68 | 5.39 | 3.99 | 3.90 | 5.01 |
| **TOTAL** | **4.75** | **4.68** | **5.39** | **3.99** | **3.90** | **5.01** |
| **DISTRICT TOTAL** | **100** | **100** | **100** | **100** | **100** | **100** |

# *APPENDIX TO : CHAPTER IV*

*APPENDIX-IV-1*

## Mahals of Todarmall as in Ain-i-Akbari (Vide Hunter, 1873) and Parganas as in 24 Parganas Dt. Gazetteer (O'Malley 1914)

| *Subeh Bengal's (incl Orissa) Satgaon Sirkar (No.18) (Mahals* | *Parganas (Nos.) as in Hunter/O'Malley* |
|---|---|
| 1. Mukowra | Magna (No. 15) |
| 2. Baleya | Balia (5) |
| 3. Bermudhutty | Baridhati (Burjhutty/6) |
| 4. Havelly Shehr | Havelishahar (Uttar Pargana/24) |
| 5. Calcutta, Mekonnek and Barbukpoor | Kalkatta (Calcutta/1) |
| 6. Anwarpoor | Anwarpur (Amarabad/3) |
| 7. Akbarpoor | Akbarpur (2) |
| 8. Balinda | Balinda |
| 9. Kharer | Khari (Kharijuri/12) |
| 10. Miduymull | Medinimal (14) |
| 11. Moondagatcha | Munragachha (18) |
| 12. Hayagarh | Hatigarhy (10) |
| 13. Bowdhen | Buran |
| 14. Poorah | Baduria |
| 15. Dhalypoor | Dhuliapur |
| 16. Mayhatty | Maihatty |
| 17. Jangal Mahal | Sundarban Forest |

Other Parganas: Azimabad (4), Basundha (7), Dakhin Sagar (8), Ghor (9), Iktierpur (11), Khuspur (13), Manpur (16), Mayda (17), Paikan (19), Pechkuli (20), Satal (21), Shahnagar (22), Shahpur (23).

# *APPENDIX TO : CHAPTER V*

*APPENDIX-V-1*

## SURVEYED VILLAGES

| Sl.No. | Name of Village | Sl.No. | Name of Village |
|---|---|---|---|
| | **STABLE DELTA** | | |
| **1.** | **THE WESTERN HUGLI SIDE FLATS P.S. OR BLOCK DIAMOND HARBOUR** | | |
| 1. | Bahadurpur | 2. | Banitala |
| 3. | Parbatipur | 4. | Mohanpur |
| 5. | Bolsidhi | 6. | Ramgobindopur |
| 7. | Durganagar | 8. | Gurudasnagar |
| 9. | Badarlata | 10. | Hanskhali |
| 11. | Gobindopur | 12. | Boria |
| 13. | Satminsha | 14. | Purbagobindopur |
| 15. | Banbahadurpur | 16. | Harindanga |
| 17. | Narayanpur | 18 | Dogarhia |
| 19. | Baradon | 20. | Parulia |
| 21. | Palia | 22. | Chanda |
| 23. | Ambalhanra | 24. | Panchgan Singbir |
| 25. | Lakshmipur | 26. | Kanpur |
| 27. | Kamarpal | 28. | Kalishankarpur |
| 29. | Kalagachi | 30. | Sarisha |
| 31. | Purba Bhabanipur | 32. | Marigachi |
| 33. | Paschim Durgapur | 34. | Mollapukur |
| **2.** | **THE MIDDLE MATURE DELTA P.S. or BLOCK SONARPUR.** | | |
| 35. | Chauhati | 36. | Sarmastapur |
| 37. | Raghabpur | 38. | Palghat |
| 39. | Bade Hugli | 40. | Gobindopur |
| 41. | Jaynagar | 42. | Sri Rampur |
| 43. | Kusumba | 44. | Jagannathpur |
| 45. | Nischintapur | 46. | Ukhila Paikpara |

47. Ramchandrapur
48. Raghunathpur
49. Dingalpota
50. Baragachi.

**P.S. OR BLOCK MANDIR BAZAR**

51. Nalpukur Mirpur
52. Durgapur
53. Gopalpur
54. Dhopahat
55. Baidyopur
56. Lakshmi Kantapur
57. Ramjeevanpur
58. Inyatpur
59. Ghateshwar
60. Madhusudanpur
61. Krishna Nagar
62. Krishna Rampur
63. Gabberia
64. Uttarkhraberia
65. Muraripur
66. Madhabpur
67. Khelarampur
68. Uttar Sultanpur.

**3. PIYALI BIDYADHARI PLAINS P.S. OR BLOCK-BHANGAR**

69. Chatakpukur
70. Narayanpur
71. Dhara
72. Debipur
73. Chandipur
74. Tardaha
75. Karaidanga
76. Gangapur
77. Ushpara
78. Bhatipota
79. Monsal
80. Andulgari
81. Gadhunirait
82. Rangsara
83. Karamba
84. Ghunimeghi
85. Dakshin Gazipur
86. Bairampur
87. Phulbari Bamunia
88. Gobindapur
89. Amreshwar
90. Sukhpukuria
91. Krolbaria
92. Chaltabaria
93. Bhangar
94. Bhangar
95. Maricha
96. Panapukur
97. Kantaba
98. Jagulgacchi
99. Nalmuri
100. Sainhati

**ACTIVE DELTA**

**4. WESTERN SUNDARBANS P.S. OR BLOCK SAGAR**

101. Rudranagar
102. Bagreakhali
103. Kirtankhali
104. Mansadwip

105. Kamalpur
106. Sumalinagar
107. Chemagudi
108. Krishnanagar
109. Harimbari
110. Natendrapur
111. Chandipur
112. Mahishamarhi
113. Radhakrishnapur
114. Purushottampur
115. Khansaheb Abad
116. Mandirtala
117. Ghoramarha
118. Bamunkhali
119. Dhaspara
120. Company's Char
121. Naraharipur
122. Bishnupur
123. Rashpur Dhablat
124. Gangasagar
125. Shibpur
126. Gobindapur
127. Muriganga
128. Banstala Mahendraganj.
129. Kachuberia
130. Chakphuldubi
131. Khasramkar
132. Dhablat
133. Prasadpur
134. Jewantala.

**P.S. OR BLOCK NAMKHANA**

135. Namkhana
136. Shibnagar
137. Narayanganj
138. Debnagar
139. Radhanagar
140. Dakshin Durgapur

**P.S. OR BLOCK KAKDWIP**

141. Durganagar (Narayanpur)
142. Ganesh Nagar (Narayanpur)

**5. MIDDLE SUNDARBANS**
**P.S. OR BLOCK MATHURAPUR**

143. Mathurapur
144. Gopinathpur
145. Raghabpur
146. Chawk Madhusudanpur
147. Barasi
148. Khonjkhidir
149. Bade Barasi
150. Tentul Baria
151. Barar
152. Sidheshwar
153. Shitalgachi
154. Mirzapur
155. Uttarshibpur
156. Ramjibanpur
157. Uttar Kasinagar
158. Naranipur

## 6. EASTERN SUNDARBANS
## P.S. OR BLOCK GOSABA

159. Gosaba
160. Atampur
161. Rangabalia
162. Rajat Jubilee
163. Dayapur
164. Amlermethi
165. Satjalia Bazar
166. Annpur,
167. Harishpur
168. Bipradaspur
169. Pathankhali
170. Chandipur
171. Gopalkata
172. Lahiripur
173. Mathurakhanda
174. Bara Mollakhali
175. Sonagaon
176. Sudhangshupur
177. Chota Mollakhali
178. Pakhiralay
179. Bali
180. Dulki
181. Lux Bagan
182. Kumirmari
183. Jhaukhali
184. Manmathanagar
185. Hamilton Abad
186. Kachukhali

## P.S. OR BLOCK BASANTI

187. Basanti
188. Nafarganj
189. Garanbos
190. Maheshpur
191. Sonakhali
192. Chandrakona
193. Sajinatala
194. Radhaballabhpur
195. Purandar
196. Dakshin-Mokamberia
197. Ramkrishnapur
198. Jyotishpur
199. Ramchandrakhali
200. Hogalduri.

*APPENDIX-V-2*

## LIST OF VILLAGES AND QUALITY OF HUMAN SETTLEMENTS - 1992

(i) *A Very High Quality* - Uttar Kasinagar (Mathurapur), Rudranagar (Sagar Island), and Kamarpal (Diamond Harbour).

(ii) *A High Quality* - Begukhali (Sagar Island), Ganeshnagar (Kakdwip), Sarisha (Diamond Harbour) and Nischintapur (Sonarpur).

(iii) *A Moderate Quality* - Ghatakpukur,Narayanapur, Tardaha, Krolbaria, Bhangar, Panapukur, Kantalia (Bhangar block); Mathurapur, (Mathurapur); Gosaba, Atampur, Rangabalia, Satjalia Bazar, Chottamollakhali, Kumirmari, (Gosaba block); Basanti, Sonakhali (Basanti block); Mansadwip, Chemagudi, Harinbari, GangaSagar, Muriganga, Kachuberia, (Sagar Island); Namkhana, Durganagar, (Kakdwip); Bolsidhi, Durganagar, Baradon, Patra, Panchgan, Singber, Marigachi, (Diamond Harbour); Chouhati, Gobindapur, Kusumba (Sonarpur); and Gabberia, (Mandir Bazar).

(iv) *A Low Quality* - Karaidanga, Gangapur, Ushpara, Bhatipota, Mousal, Andulgari, Kharamba, Gobindapur, Amreshwar, Chottabaria, Jagulgachi, (Bhangar Block); Uttar Sibpur, (Mathurapur); Amlermethi, Annpur, Harishpur, Bipradaspur, Lahiripur, Bara Mollakhali, Sudhansupur, Bali, Manmathanagar, Kachukhali, (Gosaba Block); Jyotishpur, (Basanti); Sumatingar, Krishnanagar, Purushottampur, Khansaheb Abad, Mandirtala, Ghoramarha, Bamunkhali, Dhaspara, Comapny's Char, Naraharipur, Bishnupur, Shibpur, Chakphuldubi, Khasramkar, Dhablat, Prasadpur (Sagar Island block); Shibnagar, Debnagar, Radhanagar, Dakshin Durgapur (Namkhana block); Bahadurpur, Banitali, Parbatipur, Ramgobindopur, Gurudasnagar, Badartala, Hanskhali, Gobindapur, Boria, Satminsha,

Purbagobindapur, Banbahadurpur, Harindanga, Narayanpur, Dogarhia, Parulia, Chanda, Kanpur, Kalishankarpur, Purbabvhabanipur, PaschimDurgapur, Mollapukur, (Diamond Harbour block); Sarmastapur, Raghabpur, Palghat, BadeHugli, Jaynagar, Srirampur, Jagannathpur, Ukhilapaikpara, Ramchandrapur, Raghunathpur, Dingalpota, Baragachhi, (Sonarpur block); and Nalpukur - Mirpur, Durgapur, Baidyapur, Lakshmikantapur, Ghateshwar, Krishnarampur, Uttarkhraberia, Madhabpur, Khelarampur, and Uttarsultanpur, (Mandir Bazar block).

(v) *A Very low Quality* - Dhara, Chandipur, Gadhunirait, Rangsara, Ghunimeghi, Dakshin-Gazipur, Bairampur, Phulbari Bamunia, Baghbari, Shukpukuria, Nalmuri, Sainhati (Bhangar block); Gopinathpur, Raghabpur, Chak-Madhusudanpur, Barasi, Khonjkhidir, Badebarasi, Tentulbaria, Barar, Siddheswar Mirzapur, Shitalgachi, Ramjibanpur, Naranipur (Mathurapur block); Rajat Jubilee, Dayapur, Pathankhali, Chandipur, Gopalkata, Mathurakhanda, Sonagaon, Pakhiralay, Dulki, Lux Bagan, Jhaukhali, Hamilton Abad (Gosaba); Nafarganj, Garanbos, Maheshpur, Chandrakhona, Sajinatala, Radhaballabhpur, Purandar, Dakshin Mokamberia, Ramkrishnapur, Ramchandrakhali, Hogalduri( Basanti); Kirtankhali, Kamalpur, Natendrapur, Chandipur, Mahishamarhi, Radhakrishnapur, Rashpur, Dhablat, Gobindapur, Jeevantala (Sagar block); Narayanganj (Namkhana); Mohanpur, Ambalhanra, Lakshmipur, Kalagachi (Diamond Harbour); Gopalpur, Dhopahat, Ramjeevanpur, Inyatpur, Madhusudanpur, Krishnanagar, Muraripur (Mandir Bazar).

# APPENDIX TO : CHAPTER VI

*APPENDIX-VI-1*

**INTERACTION PATTERN OF STABLE DELTA, SOUTH TWENTY FOUR PARGANAS**
**(A Case Study of 400 Households) 1992**

| | Agriculture | *Percentage of Families Moving to Different Places for various Goods and Services* | | | | | |
|---|---|---|---|---|---|---|---|
| | | *Other than Agriculture* | *Primary Schooling* | *Secondary Schooling* | *Higher Sec. Schooling* | *PHC* | *Hospital* |
| *1* | *2* | *3* | *4* | *5* | *6* | *7* | *8* |
| **STABLE DELTA** | | | | | | | |
| (i) The Western Hugli Side Flats. Diamond Harbour | | | | | | | |
| 1. Banitala | Banitala (57) | Diamond Har.(21) Calcutta (9) | Banitala (98) | Diamond Har.(71) | Diamond Har.(27) | Basuldanga(97) | Diamond Har.(100) |
| 2. Bolsidhi | Bolsidhi (86) | Diamond Har.(27) Calcutta (7) | Bolsidhi (97) | Bolasidhi(77) | Diamond Har.(25) | Bolsidhi(98) | Diamond Har.(100) |
| 3. Ramgo-bindapur | Ramgobinda-(77) | Diamond Har.(27) Calcutta (5) | Bolsidhi(91) | Bolsidhi (75) | Diamond Har.(22) | Bolsidhi (87) | Diamond Har.(100) |
| 4. Bahadurpur | Bahadurpur(81) | Diamond Har.(21) Calcutta (7) | Bahadurpur(99) | Diamond Har.(17) | Diamond Har.(68) | Basuldanga(81) | Diamond Har.(100) |
| Village near DH Town | | | | | | | |
| 1. Badartala | Badartala (61) | Diamond Har.(67) Calcutta (27) | Durganagar(98) | Diamond Har.(67) | Diamond Har.(21) | — | Diamond Har.(98) |
| 2. Ramrampur | — | D.H. Town(55) | Diamond Har.(89) | Diamond Har.(66) | Diamond Har.(21) | — — | Diamond Har.(100) |

APPENDIX-VI-I (Contd.)

| | Agriculture | Percentage of Families Moving to Different Places for various Goods and Services | | | | | |
|---|---|---|---|---|---|---|---|
| | | *Other than Agriculture* | *Primary Schooling* | *Secondary Schooling* | *Higher Sec. Schooling* | *PHC* | *Hospital* |
| *1* | *2* | *3* | *4* | *5* | *6* | *7* | *8* |
| 3. Gurudas-nagar | Gurudas- (57) nagar<br>Calcutta (7) | Diamond Har.(29) | Diamond Har.(91) | Diamond Har.(62) | Diamond Har.(19) | —<br>— | Diamond Har.(97) |
| Villages near Calcutta in Sonarpur Block. | | | | | | | |
| 1. Chouhati | — | Chouhati (5)<br>Raipur (17) | Harinavi (55)<br>Chouhati (12) | Sonarpur(22) | Sonarpur(55) | — | Subhasgram.(65)<br>Calcutta (15) |
| 2. Chouhati Local | — | Sonarpur(39)<br>Calcutta(15)<br>Chouhati ( 8) | Chouhati (5) | Rajpur (15) | Rajpur (20) | — | Subhasgram (71)<br>Calcutta (17) |
| 3. Promodnagar | — | Rajpur (21)<br>Sonarpur (41)<br>Chouhati (6)<br>Rajpur (15)<br>Sonarpur(18)<br>Calcutta (21) | Harinavi (17)<br>Sonarpur (21)<br>Chouhati (6)<br>Harinavi (5)<br>Sonarpur (22) | Calcutta (25) | Calcutta (17) | — | Subhasgram (15)<br>Calcutta (21) |
| (ii) The Middle Mature Delta | | | | | | | |
| MANDIR BAZAR | | | | | | | |
| 1. Baidyapur | Baidyapur(71) | Calcutta (7) | Baidyapur(98) | Dakshin(75)<br>Barasat | Dakshini(17) | Nayerhat(100) | Kulpi (99) |

*APPENDIX-VI-I (Contd.)*

| | *Agriculture* | *Percentage of Families Moving to Different Places for various Goods and Services* — *Other than Agriculture* | *Primary Schooling* | *Secondary Schooling* | *Higher Sec. Schooling* | *PHC* | *Hospital* |
|---|---|---|---|---|---|---|---|
| *1* | *2* | *3* | *4* | *5* | *6* | *7* | *8* |
| 2. Ghateshwar | Ghateshwar(77) | Calcutta (5) | Ghateshwar(97) Barasat | Dakshin (66) | Barasat(21) | Nayerhat(97) | Jaynagar(71) Mazilpur |
| 3. Nalpukur | Nalpukur(65) | Calcutta (3) D.H. (7) | Gabberia (87) | Dakshin - Jaynagar- Mazipur 36, 36 17, 22 | Barasat | Nayerhat(99) | Jaynagar(71) |
| 4. Gabberia | Gabberia(71) | Calcutta (5) Diamond Har.(11) | Gabberia(91) | Gabberia(71) | Dakshin Barasat(21) | Nayerhat(99) | Jaynagar(38), Kulpi (21) |
| (iii) The Piyali Bidyadhari Plains. | | | | | | | |
| BHANGAR | | | | | | | |
| 1. Tardaha | Tardaha(87) | Choubagha (27) Sealdah Calcutta)(19) | Tardaha(91) | Tardaha(75) | Tardaha(21) | Bhatipota(100) | Calcutta(57) |
| 2. Debipur | Debipur(91) | Choubagha(21) Sealdah (27) | Tardaha(87) | Tardaha(71) | Tardaha(19) | Bhatipota(100) | Calcutta(65) |
| 3. Narayanpur | Narayanpur(88) | Ghatakpukur(11) Calcutta (27) | Narayanpur(91) | Tardaha(67) | Tardaha(18) | Bhatipota(100) | Calcutta(67) |
| 4. Krolberia | Krolberia(75) | Bhojherhat(5) Choubagha(11) Sealdah (55) | Tardaha(79) | Tardaha(56) | Bhangar(17) | Bhatipota(100) | Calcutta(45) |

**APPENDIX•VI•(Contd.)**

| | Percentage of Families Moving to Different Places for various Goods and Services | | | | | |
|---|---|---|---|---|---|---|
| | *Banking* | *General Marketing* | *Special Marketing* | *P. O.* | *Train Station* | *Bus Stop* |
| | 8 | 9 | 10 | 11 | 12 | 13 |
| **STABLE DELTA** | | | | | | |
| (i) The Western Hugli Side Flats. Diamond Harbour | | | | | | |
| 1. Banitala | Diamond Har.(51) | Banitala(100) | Diamond Har.(71) Calcutta (29) | Diamond Har.(95) | Diamond Har.(9) | Diamond Har.(22) |
| 2. Bolsidhi | Diamond Har.(58) | Bolsidhi(100) | Diamond Har.(77) Calcutta (29) | Diamond Har.(99) | Diamond Har.(27) | Diamond Har.(27) |
| 3. Ramgo-bindapur | Diamond Har.(48) | Diamond Har.(100) | Diamond Har.(75) | Diamond Har.(91) Calcutta (17) | Diamond Har.(21) | Diamond Har.(31) |
| 4. Bahadurpur | Diamond Har.(51) | Bolsidhi (100) | Diamond Har.(91) Calcutta (7) | Bahadurpur(95) | Diamond Har.(12) | — |

APPENDIX-VI (Contd.)

| | Percentage of Families Moving to Different Places for various Goods and Services | | | | | |
|---|---|---|---|---|---|---|
| | Banking | General Marketing | Special Marketing | P. O. | Train Station | Bus Stop |
| | 8 | 9 | 10 | 11 | 12 | 13 |
| Villages near DH Town | | | | | | |
| 1. Badartala | Diamond Har.(98) | Badartala(100) | Diamond Har.(29) Calcutta (31) | Diamond Har.(71) | Diamond Har.(62) | Diamond Har.(21) |
| 2. Ramrampur | Diamond Har.(100) Calcutta (19) | Diamond Har.(31) Calcutta 65) | Diamond Har.(71) Calcutta (55) | Diamond Har.(71) Calcutta(17) | — — | — |
| 3. Gurudas-nagar | Diamond Har.(97) | Diamond Har.(100) | Diamond Har.(25) Calcutta (15) | Calcutta(77) | Calcutta(45) | Calcutta(16) |
| Villages near Calcutta in Sonarpur Block. | | | | | | |
| 1. Chouhati | Rajpur(57) Calcutta (21) | Chouhati(100) | Sonarpur(25) Calcutta (66) | Chouhati(79) | — | Chouhati (85) |
| 2. Chouhati Local | Rajpur (65) | Chouhati(100) | Sonarpur(19) | Chouhati(59) | — | Chouhati (71) |
| 3. Promodnagar | Calcutta(19) Rajpur (19) Sonarpur (20) Calcutta (15) | Chouhati(100) | Calcutta (71) Sonarpur (16) Calcutta (56) | Chouhati(81) | — | Chouhati (89) |

*APPENDIX-VI (Contd.)*

| | *Percentage of Families Moving to Different Places for various Goods and Services* | | | | | |
|---|---|---|---|---|---|---|
| | *Banking* | *General Marketing* | *Special Marketing* | *P. O.* | *Train Station* | *Bus Stop* |
| | 8 | 9 | 10 | 11 | 12 | 13 |
| (ii) The Middle Mature Delta | | | | | | |
| MANDIR BAZAR | | | | | | |
| 1. Baidyapur | Laksmikantapur(57) | Baidyapur(100) | Calcutta(21)<br>D.H. (25) | Baidyapur(87) | Baidyapur (11) | — |
| 2. Ghateshwar | Laksmikantapur(51) | Ghateshwar(100) | Calcutta(22)<br>D.H. (35) | Ghateshwar(71) | Baidyapur (21) | — |
| 3. Nalpukur | Laksmikantapur(57) | Gabberia (100) | Calcutta (21)<br>D.H. (35) | Nalpukur (66) | Baidyapur & Lakshmikantpur(31) | — |
| 4. Gabberia | Laksmikantpur(78) | Gabberia(100) | D.H. (67)<br>Calcutta (21) | Gabberia (57) | Baidyapur (21) | — |
| (iii) The Piyali Bidyadhari Plains. | | | | | | |
| BHANGAR | | | | | | |
| 1. Tardaha | Tardaha(55) | Tardaha (100) | Ghatakpukur(21)<br>Calcutta (47) | Tardaha(71) | — | Ghatakpukur(47) |
| 2. Debipur | Tardaha (47) | Paglahat (100) | Ghatakpukur(11)<br>Calcutta (27) | Tardaha(65) | | Ghatakpukur(55) |
| 3. Narayanpur | Narayanpur(51) | Paglahat (100) | Calcutta (51) | Narayanpur(71) | — | Ghatakpukur(2[illegible]) |
| 4. Krolberia | Narayanpur(47) | Krolberia(100) | Ghatakpukur(21)<br>Calcutta (55) | Krolberia(58) | — | Ghatakpukur(3[illegible]) |

## *APPENDIX : VI. 2*
**Interaction Pattern of Active Delta S. 24 Parganas 1992**

| | *Agriculture* | *Other than Agriculture* | *Primary Schooling* | *Secondary Schooling* | *Higher Sec. Schooling* | *PHC* | *Hospital* |
|---|---|---|---|---|---|---|---|
| | *1* | *2* | *3* | *4* | *5* | *6* | *7* |
| I. The Western Sundarbans Active Delta (SAGAR ISLAND) | | | | | | | |
| 1. Gangasagar | Gangasagar(71) | Gangasagar(21) Rudranagar (15) | Gangasagar(98) | Gangasagar(45) | Rudranagar(21) | Gangasagar(100 | Kakdwip(35) Diamond Har.(17) |
| 2. Chemaguri | Chemaguri(91) | Rudranagar(17) | Gangasagar(89) | Gangasagar(31) | Rudranagar(17) | Chemaguri(91) | Kakdwip(45) Diamond Har.(19) |
| 3. Beguakhali | Beguakhali(85) | Beguakhali(19) Kachuberia (7) | Beguakhali(100) | Beguakhali(57) | Rudranagar(11) | Gangasagar(78) | Kakdwip(35) Diamond Har.(21) |
| 4. Natendrapur | Natendrapur(95) | Rudranagar(18) | Natendrapur(98) | Natendrapur(29) | Natendrapur(21) | Gangasagar(71) | Kakdwip(51) Diamond Har.(16) |
| 5. Rudranagar | Rudranagar(89) | Kachuberia(5) Kakdwip (8) | Rudranagar(100) | Rudranagar(35) | Rudranagar(35) | Rudranagar(61) | Kakdwip(17) Diamond Har.(18) |
| 6. Dhoblat | Dhoblat(89) | Rudranagar(17) | Dhoblat(97) | Dhoblat(21) | Rudranagar(15) | Gangasagar(61) | Kakdwip(25) Diamond Har.(18) |

APPENDIX-VI.2 (*Contd.*)

| | *Agriculture* | *Other than Agriculture* | *Primary Schooling* | *Secondary Schooling* | *Higher Sec. Schooling* | *PHC* | *Hospital* |
|---|---|---|---|---|---|---|---|
| | *1* | *2* | *3* | *4* | *5* | *6* | *7* |
| H Middle Sundarbans (MATHURAPUR) | | | | | | | |
| 1. Mathurapur | Mathurapur(76) | Mathurapur(15)<br>Calcutta (5) | Mathurapur(41) | Mathurapur(21) | Uttar Kashi-nagar (59) | | Mathurapur(45)<br>Jaynagar (21) |
| 2. Gopinathpur | Gopinathpur(81) | Mathurapur(21)<br>Calcutta (7) | Mathurapur(97) | Mathurapur(47) | Mathurapur(17) | Uttarkashi-nagar (61) | Mathurapur(51)<br>Jaynagar (17) |
| 3. Raghabpur | Raghabpur(80) | Mathurapur(16)<br>Calcutta (2 ) | Mathurapur(95) | Mathurapur(35) | Mathurapur(12) | Uttarkashi-nagar (71) | Mathurapur(47)<br>Jaynagar(*) |
| 4. Khonjkhidir | Khonjkhidir(77) | Mathurapur(18)<br>Calcutta (9) | Mathurapur(87) | Mathurapur(51) | Mathurapur(11) | Uttarkashi-nagar (71) | Mathurapur(66)<br>Jaynagar (19) |
| 5. Uttarkashi-nagar | Uttarkashi-nagar (75) | Mathurapur(9)<br>nagar (99)<br>Calcutta (1) | Uttarkashi-nagar | Uttarkashi-nagar (57) | Uttarkashi-nagar (25) | Uttarkashi-nagar (85) | Mathurapur(59)<br>Jaynagar (12) |
| 6. Bade-Barasi | BadeBarasi(87) | Mathurapur(20)<br>Calcutta (3) | Uttarkashi-nagar (81) | Uttarkashi-nagar (30) | Uttarkashi-nagar (15) | Uttarkashi-nagar (15) | Mathurapur(45)<br>Jaynagar (7) |

***APPENDIX-VI.2** (Contd.)*

| | *Agriculture* | *Other than Agriculture* | *Primary Schooling* | *Secondary Schooling* | *Higher Sec. Schooling* | *PHC* | *Hospital* |
|---|---|---|---|---|---|---|---|
| | *1* | *2* | *3* | *4* | *5* | *6* | *7* |
| III. Eastern Sundarbans (GOSABA) | | | | | | | |
| 1. Gosaba | Gosaba (89) | Gosaba (21)<br>Canning (17) | Gosaba (98) | Gosaba (35) | Gosaba (21) | Mobile —PHC's | Gosaba (78)<br>Canning (22) |
| 2. Ranga-Baila | Rangabalia(91) | — (22)<br>(8) | Rangabalia(97) | Rangabalia(39) | Rangabalia(25) | — | — (71)<br>(20) |
| 3. Rajat Jubilee | Rajat Jubilee (97) | — (9)<br>(2) | Rajat - Jubilee (100) | Rajat - Jubilee (45) | Rajat - Jubilee (31) | — | — (65)<br>(15) |
| 4. Dayapur | Dayapur (98) | — (8)<br>(5) | Rajat- Jubilee(91) | Rajat- Jubilee (41) | Rajat- Jubilee(22) | — | — (71)<br>(18) |
| 5. Hamilton Abad | H.Abad (89) | — (11)<br>(2) | Rajat- Jubilee(89) | Rajat- Jubilee(39) | Rajat- Jubilee (21) | — | — (66)<br>(17) |
| 6. Pakhiralay | Pakhiralay (91) | — (12)<br>(8) | Gosaba (92) | Gosaba (40) | Gosaba (15) | — | — (59)<br>(11) |

(Contd.)

| Cooperative | Banking | General Marketing | Special Marketing | P. O. | Train | Bus | Bus Ferry Ghat |
|---|---|---|---|---|---|---|---|
| 8 | 9 | 10 | 11 | 12 | 13 | 14 | 15 |
| Gangasagar(81) | Gangasagar(45) | Kalibazar(2)<br>Gangasagar(98) | Kakdwip (55)<br>D.H. (21) | Gangasagar(78) | — | Gangasagar(75) | Kachuberia(100) |
| Gangasagar(78) | Gangasagar(35) | Kalibazar(99) | — (51)<br>(25) | Gangasagar(80) | — | Kalibazar(65) | Kachuberia(93) |
| Gangasagar(61) | Gangasagar(21) | Kalibazar(99) | — (66)<br>(21) | Kalibazar(69) | — | Kalibazar(71) | Kachuberia(83) |
| Natendrapur(56) | Rudranagar(67) | Rudranagar(91) | — (51)<br>(29) | Natendrapur(61) | — | Natendrapur(67) | Kachuberia(83) |
| Rudranagar(71) | Rudranagar(21) | Rudranagar(85) | — (60)<br>(17) | Rudranagar(89) | — | Rudranagar(91) | Kachuberia(91) |
| Gangasagar(51) | Rudranagar(35) | Rudranagar(96) | — (21) | Dhoblat(71) | — | Gangasagar(79) | Kachuberia(79) |

(Contd.)

| Cooperative | Banking Marketing | General Marketing | Special | P. O. | Train | Bus Ghat | Bus Ferry |
|---|---|---|---|---|---|---|---|
| 8 | 9 | 10 | 11 | 12 | 13 | 14 | 15 |
| II. Middle Sundarbans | | | | | | | |
| Mathurapur(51) | Bijoyganj(35) Jaynagar (7) | Mathurapur(100) | Jaynagar(51) Calcutta(25) | Mathurapur(59) | Baidyapur(69) | Mathurapur(67) | — |
| Mathurapur(65) | — (25) (2) | Babulibazar(98) | — (62) (31) | Mathurapur(45) | Baidyapur(56) | Mathurapur(59) | — |
| Mathurapur(49) | — (31) (7) | Raghabpur (91) | — (70) (36) | Mathurapur(51) | Baidyapur(47) | Mathurapur(51) | — |
| Mathurapur(57) | — (26) (11) | Uttarkashi-nagar (96) | — (66) (24) | Mathurapur(62) | Baidyapur(51) | Mathurapur(51) | — |
| Mathurapur(52) | — (31) (16) | Uttarkashi-nagar (93) | — (70) (15) | Uttarkashi-nagar (71) | Baidyapur (48) | Uttarkashi nagar(48) | — |
| Mathurapur(49) | — | Uttarkashi-nagar (99) | — (45) (20) | Mathurapur(49) | Baidyapur(37) | Mathurapur(56) | — |

(Contd.)

| Cooperative | Banking Marketing | General Marketing | Special | P. O. | Train | Bus Ghat | | Bus Ferry |
|---|---|---|---|---|---|---|---|---|
| 8 | 9 | 10 | 11 | 12 | 13 | 14 | | 15 |
| III. Eastern Sundarbans | | | | | | | | |
| Gosaba(59) | Gosaba(28) | Gosaba (100) | Canning (57) | Gosaba (58) | — | — | | Gosaba(100) |
| Gosaba(41) | Gosaba(15) | Rangabalia(98) | Canning (61) | Rangabalia(45) | — | — | | Gosaba(100) |
| Gosaba(47) | Gosaba(11) | Rangabalia(87) | Canning (49) | Rangabalia(47) | — | — | | RajatJubilee(100) |
| Gosaba(38) | Gosaba(7) | Dayapur (91) | Canning (57) | Dayapur (38) | — | — | | Dayapur (100) |
| Gosaba(29) | Gosaba(8) | Hamilton-Abad (91) | Canning (42) | Dayapur (29) | — | — | | Hamiltton Abad (100) |
| Gosaba(41) | Gosaba(5) | Gosaba(89) | Canning (58) | Gosaba(51) | — | — | | Gosaba(100) |

# LOCAL TERMINOLOGIES

1. *Haats* and *bazaars*—Periodic local market places.
2. Parganas—Mahals of Todarmall as in Ain-i-Akbari and revenue with a Parganas is 24 Parganas, Dt. Gazetteer (O'Malley 1914).
3. *Lot* or *Lat*—Estates under settlement in reclaimed Sundarbans.
4. *Aman*, *Aus*, *Boro rice*—Summer, Monsoon and Winter varieties of paddy.
5. *Khals*—distributaries.
6. *Do-aniya Khals*—interconnecting distributaries.
7. *Kapil Muni*—Purana Saint.
8. *Dinghy*—Small country boad.
9. *Dhai*—Midwife.
10. *Mundari*—Language of the Munda group of tribals.
11. *abad*—Land cleared for agriculture/settlements.
12. *Rohu*, *Katla*, *Pona*—Fresh water fish species.
13. *Bheries* or *Gheries*—fisheries.
14. *Ghat*, *ferry ghat*—Halting ground for boats and passenger.
15. Ojhas, *hakims*—traditional health workers.
16. *Gur*—Molasse.
17. *Khesari*—a variety of pulse.
18. *P.H.C.*—Primary Health Centre.
19. *SBI*—State Bank of India.
20. *SDB*—Sundarban Development Board.
21. *Dhapa*—Waste heap near Bhangar Block.
22. *Bhati*—Tidal.

# BIBLIOGRAPHY

## BOOKS AND ARTICLES


Ackerman, Edward A, 1958, "Geography as a Fundamental Research Discipline," Department of Geography, *Research Paper No. 53,* Chicago, Illinois.

Adhikary, P.K. (1987), "The History of Growth And Methodology For Mapping of Setttlement Pattern In 24-Parganas District, West Bengal", Mapping of Settlement Systems, NATMO Monograph No. 6 Government of India.

Ahmed, Enayat, 1962, "Indian Village Pattern," *Geographical Outlook,* University Department of Geography, Vol. 3, No. 1. Ranchi.

——, 1980, Regional Planning with Particular Reference to India, Oriental Publishers and Distributors.

——, 1952, Rural Settlement types in Uttar Pradesh, *Annals of the Association of American Geographers,* Vol. 42, No. 3.

Anas, Mohammad, 1954, "The Pattern of Rural Settlement in the Sub-Himalayan Region (East)". The Geographer, Vol. 6, No.2, pp. 23-24, *Journal of the Muslim University Geographical Society, Aligarh.*

Asthana, V.K., 1976, "Study of Rural Settlements around Almora and Environs," Geographic Dimensions of Rural Settlement by Prof. R.L. Singh, Dr. Kashi N. Singh, Dr. Rana, P.B. Singh, *National Geographic Society of India,* B.H.U. Varanasi.

Bagchi, Jahnabi and H.R. Betal (1977), "Population and Migration in West Bengal" (Geographical Note) *Geographical Review of India*, Geographical Society of India, Vol. 39, No. 3, September.

Bagchi, K.G. (1978), "Diagnostic Survey of Deltaic West Bengal", Department of Geography, Calcutta University, Calcutta.

——(1960), "Drainage Pattern in Ganga Delta", *Geographical Review of India*, Vol. 22, No. 4, December.

——, (1944), "The Ganges Delta", University of Calcutta Publication, Calcutta.

Banerjee, K and B. Kar, (1987) "Urbanisation And Evolution of A City with Special Reference to Calcutta", Mapping of Settlement Systems, NATMO Monograph No. 6, Government of India.

Bala, N.C. and Karabi Chanda (1990), "Growth of Population and its Impact on the Socio-Economic Pattern of West Bengal". Cartography for Development of Outlying States and Islands of India, Part-II, NATMO Monograph No. 10, Government of India.

Bandyopadhyay, K.K. (1989), Cyclone Disaster Management of West Bengal Coastal Zone : Some Aspects, Coastal Zone Management of West Bengal, Sea Explorer's Institute, Calcutta.

Bandyopadhyay, Sunando (1990), "Evolution of the Sagar Island Coast Line, West Bengal, between 1923 and 1990", Cartography for Development of Outlying states and Islands of India Part-I, NATMO Monograph No. 10, Govt. of India.

Banerjee, Anuradha (1985), "Migration Pattern in India" Population Mapping, National Atlas and Thematic Mapping Organisation, Calcutta.

——, (1989), "The Coastal Districts of India: `An Attempt Towards Building up of a Human Resource Inventory'". S.P. Chatterjee, *Commemorative Volume*, NATMO, Calcutta.

Banerjee, Maya (1977), "The Pattern of Sex Ratio in Singhbhum District, Bihar" *Geographical Review of India*, Geographical Society of India, Vol. 39. No. 1, March.

——, (1985), Age Structure of the Population of Singhbhum District of Bihar, India and its Cartographic Representation", Population Mapping, National Atlas and Thematic Mapping Organisation, Calcutta. Govt. of India.

Banerjee, S.P., Jayashree Banerjee, B.B. Bandyopadhyay, N.E. Kabir (1989), "Some Problems of Improvement in Vegetable in Coastal Plain", Coastal Zone Management of West Bengal, Sea Explorer's Insitute, Calcutta.

Banerjee, U. (1989), "Social Forestry in Sundarban" A Tool for Rural Development". *Ibid.*

Barclay, George W. (1958), *Techniques of Population Analysis*, J. Willey and Sons, New York.

Basak, Tarak Nath (1985), "*Trend of Urban Population Growth of West Bengal 1971 to 1981*", Population Mapping, NATMO, Calcutta.

Baskin, C.W. (Translaltion of W. Christaller), 1933, "*Central Places in Southern Germany*", Englewood Cliffs, N.J. Pentince Hall.

Basu, D. (1987), "*The Settlement Pattern In The Sundarban Region,*" Mapping of Settlement Systems, NATMO Monograph No. 6, Govt. of India.

Berry, Brian J.L. (1960), "The Impact of Expanding Metropolitan Communities Upon Central Place Hierarchy", *Annals of The Association of American Geographers*, Vol. 50, No. 2.

Berry, Brian J.L. and Frank. E. Horton (1970), *Geographic Perspectives on Urban System with Integrated Readings*, Prentice Halll Inc, Englewood Cliffs, New Jersey.

Betal, H.R. (1985), "*Cartographic Techniques for the Comparison and Mapping of Different Population Characteristics of West Bengal", Population Mapping,* NATMO, Calcutta.

Bhattacharyya, Amitabha (1974), "West Bengal Needs an Integrated Urban Development Policy", in Conference on Urban Development: Problems and Issues, Institute of Management Calcutta, Centre for Management of Urban Systems, September 27-28.

Bhattacharyya, Asok Kumar (1989), "Coastal Geomorphology, Process and Hazards". A note on management measures", Coastal Zone Management of West Bengal, Sea Explorers's Institute, Calcutta.

Bhattacharya, A.N. and L.N. Verma (1957), Rural Settlement forms in the Son Valley (Rewa, M.P.). *The Indian Geographer*, Vol. 29, No. 12.

Bhattacharya, R. (December 1975), "Settlement Pattern in Deltaic West Bengal", *Geographical Review of India*, Vol. 37. No. 4.

Biswas, S.R. and Smt. Alpana Chatterjee (1985), "Statistical Techniques in Cartographic Representation of Population Characteristics" Population Mapping, NATMO, Calcutta.

Bogue, D.J. (1959), "*The Structure of the Metropolitan Community*", Ann Arbor, Michigan.

——, (1969), *Principles of Demography*, John Wiley and Sons, Inc. New York, London, Sidney, Toronto.

Bose, Ashish (1988), *From Population to People* Vol. 11, B.R. Publishing Corporation, Delhi. Ibid, Vol. 1,

Bose, Ashish and P.B. Desai (edited, 1989), "*Population Planning in India : Policy Issues and Research Priorities*", B.R. Publishing Corporation, Delhi.

Bose, A.N. (1989), "Fisheries Development in Coastal West Bengal: Socio-Economic Implications" in *Coastal Zone Management of West Bengal*, Sea Explorer's Institute, Calcutta.

Bose, Sriparna (1988), "Growth of Urban Centres and Urban Population of West Bengal", *Indian Journal of Landscape systems and Ecological Studies*. Vol. 11, No. 1 June.

Bourne, L.S, Sinclair, K. Dziewonski (edited, 1984), *Urbanisation and Settlement Systems: International Perspectives*. Oxford University Press.

Bowman, J. and J.E. Brush (1926), "The Scientific Study of Settlement", *Geographical Review of India*, Vol. 16.

Broek, Jan. O.M. (1965), "Geography Its Scope and Spirit", Columbus C.E. Merril Books,

Brush, John E. (1968), "Spatial Pattern of Population in Indian Cities", *Geographical Review*, Vol. 58. No. 4.

Burman, B.K. Roy (1985), "Distribution of the Scheduled Tribes of India, an Exploratory Geocultural Appraisal", in *Contribution to Indian Geography, Population Geography*. Vol. 6. Edited by Sundaram and Nangia.

Camm, J.C.R. and P.G. Irwin (1985), *Space, People, Place, Economic and Settlement Geography*, Longman Group (FE) Ltd.

Carter, Harold (1975), *The Study of Urban Geography*, Edward Arnold (Publishers) Ltd., London.

Chakraborti, Kalyan (1989), "Development Perspective of Coastal Eco system of Sundarban Forest", Coastal Zone Management of West Bengal, Sea Explorers Insitute, Calcutta.

Chakraborti, Swapna (1993), "Landuse in Gangetic West Bengal", *Indian Journal of Landscape System and Ecological Studies*, Vol. 16, No. 1. June, Institute of Landscape Ecology, and Ekistics.

Chakraborty, S.C. (1978), "*Development and Primate Metropolis Some Value Questions*", Socio Economic Development Problems in South and South East Asia, Popular Prakashan, Bombay.

Chandrashekhar, S. (1957), "Population Trends and Housing Needs in India", *Population Review*, Vol. 1, No. 1.

Chatterjee, Nandini (1986), "Impact of Irrigation on Agriculture in Southern West Bengal", *Geographical Review of India*, Vol. 48, No. 1. March, Geographical Society of India, Calcutta.

Chatterjee, S. and K.G. Bagchi, "Analytical Study of the Transport System of the Sundarban Region", *Geographical Review of India*, Vol. 41.

Chatterjee, S.P. and K.G. Bagchi (1960), "Hydrographic Features of the Adi Ganga Bhumi", Vol. 22. No. 1, *Geographical Society of India*, Calcutta.

Chatterjee S.P. (1962), "Regional Patterns of the Density and Distribution of Population in India", *Geographical Review of India*, Vol. XXIV: 2. June, Geographical Society of India.

——, (1945), Land Utilization in the District of 24 Parganas, West Bengal", B.C. Law, Vol. Part II, Calcutta.

Chattopadhyay, S. (1980), "Hydrology and Landuse in the Littoral Tract of Deltaic West Bengal", *Geographical Review of India*, Vol. 42.

Chattopadhyay, K. and S. Bandyopadhyay (1963) "Some Consider ations on the Human Factors in Urban Geography" *Geographical Review Of India*, Vol.25 No. 2, June, Geographical Society Of India.

Chowdhuri, M.R. (1971), "The Industrial Landscape Of West Bengal", Oxford and I.B.H. Publishing Co.

Chisholm, Michael (1962) "Rural Settlement and Landuse An Essay in Location", London , Hutchinson University Library.

Chorley, R.J. and P. Haggett (1967), *Models in Geography*, Metheun and Co. Ltd. pp-816.

Clarke, John I (1976), *Population Geography*, Second Edition, Pergamon Press Ltd.

Clark, P.J. and F.C. Evans (1954), Distance to NND as a Measure Of Spatial Relationship in Population, *Ecology*, Vol.35, pp 445-453.

Clawson, Marion (1966), "Factors and forces Affecting the Optimum Future of Rural Settlement Pattern in the U.S." *Economic Geogrphy* Vol. 42, No.4.

Dacey, M.F., "Analysis of Central Places and Point Pattern by a N.N.D. Method", *Land Studies in Geography*, Series B, Human Geography,

Dasgupta, K.K. (1989), "Disaster Mitigation in Coastal areas of West Bengal", in *Coastal Zone Management of W. Bengal*, Sea Explorers Institute, Calcutta.

Das Gupta, S.P. and S.M. Mishra (1976), "An analytical approach to the methodology of mapping rural settlements in India", *Geographic Dimensions of Rural Settlement* by Prof. R.L. Singh, Dr. Kashi N. Singh, National Geographic Society of India, B.H.U., Varanasi.

Das, Indira (1985), "*On Demographic Change Along the Lower Gangetic Delta Through Maps*", Population Mapping NATMO Calcutta. Govt. of India.

Das, Mira and Ranjana Ray (1989), "Role of Ecology in Adoption of Family Planning Practices : A case study from Lower Bengal", in *Coastal Zone Management of West Bengal*, Sea Explorer's Institute, Calcutta.

Das, P.K. (1968), *The Monsoon*, National Book Trust, India.

Das, P.K. (1987), "*Cartographic Analysis of Rural Settlement System of Mathurapur Police Station*", Mapping of Settlement Systems, NATMO Monograph No. 6, Govt. of India.

Das, Sharmila (1991), "Development of Fisheries in South 24 Parganas District :Problems & Prospects", *Geographical Review of India*, Vol. 53. No. 2, June, Geographical Society of India.

——, (1990), "Human Interference on the Ecology of Sundarban, West Bengal", *Indian Journal of Landscape System and Ecological Studies*, Vol. 13, No.2, December.

——, (1992), "Mangrove Forests of the Ganga Delta - A Geo Economic Appraisal", *Indian Journal of Landscape Systems and Ecological Studies"*, Vol. 15, No. 1, June.

——, (1990), "Scope for Scientific Development of Resources in Sundarbans", in *Cartography for Development of Outlying States and Islands of India*, Part II, NATMO. Monograph No. 10, Govt. of India.

Dutta, Gupta J. (1971), "Immigration into Calcutta" Proceedings of Symposium on Population Geography, National Committee for Geography, Calcutta.

Dayal, P. (1959) "Population and Rural Urban Migration in India", *The National Geographical Journal of India*, Vol. 5, Part-4.

De, Barun (1974) "The Roots of Urban Crisis in Bengal: The Historical Relationship between Metropolis and Market Periphery from 1756 to 1974", Conference on Urban Development : Problems and Issues, Indian Institute of Management Calcutta, Centre for Management of Urban Systems, Sept. 27-28.

Debnath, Shyamal (1990) "Sundarbans, West Bengal - its Problems and Prospects" *Cartogrophy for Devzlopment of Outlying States and Islands of India*, Part - II, NATMO, Monograph No. 10, Govt. of India.

Demangeon, Albert (1961), "The Origins and Causes of Settlment Types", *Readings in Cultural Geography* by Wagner and Minshull. The University of Chicago Press,

De, Rathindranath (1990) *The Sundarbans*, Oxford University Press, Calcutta.

Dickinson, Robert E. (1964), *City and Region: A Geographical Interpretation*, Routledge and Kegan Paul Ltd., London.

——, (1960), *City, Region and Regionalism : A Geographical Contribution to Human Ecology*, Routledge and Kegan Paul Ltd.

Dutta, Gouri (1982), "Analysis of Literacy Rates in Southern District of West Bengal", *The Geographical Review of India*, Vol. 44, No. 2, June, Geographical Society of India.

Fowcett, C.W. (1939), "Distribution of Rural Settlements", *Geographical Journal*, Vol. XCIII, No. 2.

Fergusson, J. (1963), "Delta of the Ganges" *Quarterly Journal of the Geological Society of India*, Vol. XIII, Part-1.

——, (1963), *Regional Development Policy : A Case Study of Venezuela*, M.I.T. Press, Massachussets.

Freidman, John R.P. (1956), "The Concept of Planning Region", *Land Economics*, Vol. 32, No. 1.

Gananthan, V.S. (1959), "Some aspects of Rural Urban Relationships in India," *The Indian Geographers* Vol. 4, No. 2.

Ganguly, Maya (1967), "The Nature of Fringe Areas of Calcutta", *Geographical Review of India*, Vol. 27(1). Geographical Society of India, Calcutta.

Garnier, B. (1970), *Geography of Population*, translated by S.H. Beaver Longman, U.K.

Ghosh, A.K. (1989), "Ecological Profile of W. Bengal Coastal Area", in *Coastal Zone Management of West Bengal*, Sea Explorer's Institute, Calcutta.

Ghosh, Ashok Kumar, Achintya Kumar Das, P.G. Chatterjee (1989), "Man Power and Resource Management of West Bengal. A Pilot Study in Sundarban Area", *ibid.*

Ghosh, Basabdatta and Bakul Rani Ghosh (1989), "Geography of Sundarbans - A Unique Part of the Biggest Delta in The World" Applied Geography S.P. Chatterjee Commemorative Volume, NATMO Monograph No. 9, Calcutta.

Ghosh, Chaitali (1989), "Application of Sattelite Imagery in Monitoring and Mapping the Forest Resource of the Sundarbans" *Applied Geography*, S.P.Chatterjee, Commemorative Volume, NATMO Monograph No. 9, Calcutta

Ghosh, Mira and Ruma Mitra (1989), "Regional Planning in Sundarbans" *ibid.*

Gibbs, Jack P. (1961), *Urban Research Methods*, N.J. Van Nostrand, Princeton.

Gosal, G.S. (1956), "The Regionalisation of Sex Composition of India's Population", *Rural Sociology*,. Vol. 26.

——, (1985), "Spatial Perspective on Literacy in India" *ibid.*

Gottman, J. and R.A. Harper (1967), *Metropolis on The Move*, John Wiley and Sons Inc.

Gowda, K.S. Rama (1972), *Landuse Pattern in Urban Areas*, 'Proceedings of Symposium on Urban Landuse', National Committee for Geography.

Guha, Meera (1972), "Aspects of Ecological Organisation in Calcutta". *ibid.*

——, (1955), "Transportation In and Around Calcutta : An Analysis of Traffic Condition", *Geographical Review of India*, Vol. 17, No.2, June.

Guha, M.K. and S.G. Bhattacharya (1989), "Cyclone Disaster and Preventive Measure in West Bengal Coast", *Coastal Zone Management of West Bengal*, Sea Explorar's Institute, Calcutta.

Gyanchand (1972), *Population in Perspective*, Orient Longman Ltd. India.

Habeeb, Atiya (1985), "Disparities in the levels of Regional Development and Spatial Differentiation in India in Historical

Context", U.G.C. Workshop on Research Methods in Regional and Urban Planning, 25th March to 13th April, CSRD, JNU, New Delhi-67.

Harris, Chauncy D. and Nelson H.J. (1967), *Classification of Cities*, Central Book Depot, Allahabad.

Hunter, N.W. (1868), *Annals of Rural Bengal*, Vol. 1, Smith, Elder & Co., London.

Jana, D.B. and O.G. Seal, *A Study of the Rural Settlement Types in the Sagar Police Station, District, 24-Parganas (South), Some Consideration for Mapping*, NATMO, Monograph No. 6.

Jana, D.B. and R.N. Datta (1990), "Assessment and Mapping of the Orchard areas of Baruipur Block - District 24-Parganas (South) - A Case Study in Mapping of Agri-horticultural Resources", in *Cartography for Development of outlying States and Islands of India*, Part - 1, NATMO. Monograph No. 10, Govt. of India.

Jana, Dibyendu Biswas and Rabindra Nath Dutta (1985), "Growth of Population in West Bengal and its Cartographic Representation, in *Population Mapping*, NATMO, Govt. of India.

Jhingran, Arun G. and Y.S. Yadav, (1989), "Coastal Eco System Management in West Bengal Fisheries : A Perspective in Contribution to Indian Geography", *Population Geography*, Vol. 6, Edited by Sundaram & Nangia.

Johnson, James H. (1967), *Urban Geography: An Introductory Analysis*, Pergamon Press Publication.

Jordon, Terry G. (1960), "On the Nature of Settlement Geography", *Professional Geographer*, Vol. XVIII, No. 1.

Kar, N.R. (1963), "Economic Character of Metropolitan Sphere of Influence of Calcutta", *The Geographical Review of India*, GSI, Calcutta, Vol. 25, No. 2.

——, (1962), "Pattern of Urban Growth in Lower West Bengal", *Geographical Review of India*, Vol. 22, No.1.

——, (1960), "Urban Hierarchy and Central Functions Around the City of Calcutta, and its Significance", Proceedings of IGU Symposium in Urban Geography.

Krishan, Gopal and Madhav Shyam (1977), "Literacy in India" *Geographical Review of India*, Geographical Society of India, Vol. 39, No. 2, June.

Lahiri, K.L. (1989), "Coast Zone Management of West Bengal" in *Coastal Zone Management of West Bengal*, Sea Explorers Institute, Calcutta.

Mahanta, H.B. (1990), "Dynamics of Urban Fringe : A Case Study of Mawsbiut Village near Shillong Urban Agglomeration", *Hill Geographer*, Vol. V, Nos. 1 and 2, 1986.

Mahmood, Aslam (1986), *Statistical Methods in Geographical Studies*, Rajesh Publications, New Delhi.

Mamoria, C.B. (1981), *India's Population Problem*, Kitab Mahal, India.

Mandal, A.K., R.K. Ghosh (1989), *Sundarban - A Socio Bio Ecological Study*, Bookland Pvt. Ltd., Calcutta.

Mondal, R.B., Joseph Uyanga and Hanuman Prasad (1989), *Introductory Method in Population Analysis*, Concept Publishing Company, New Delhi.

Mayer, Harold M and Clyde F. Konn. (Editors) (1967), *Readings in Urban Geography*, Central Book Depot, Allahabad.

Mayer, Harold and Dukinson Robert E (1967), *Approaches to the Study of Urban Geography, ibid.*

Minshull, Roger (1967), *Regional Geography Theory and Practice*, London, Hutchinson University Library.

Mitra, Ashok (1985), "Implications of Sex Ratio in India's Population", *Contributiuon to Indian Geography,* Vol. 6, Edited by Sundarm and Nangia.

Mondal, Deepak Kumar (1962), "Soil Salinity - A Hinderance of Double Cropping in Ichhamati - Bidyadhari Interfluve, West Bengal", *Indian Journal of Landscape Systems & Ecological Studies*, Vol. 15, No. 1, Geographical Society of India.

Mondal, U., S. Sen Roy, B.C. Majumdar (1962), " A Recently developed Agro-Industry in the Southern Suburb of Calcutta City, Utilising a Bramble Fruit", *Indian Journal of Landscape Systems and Ecological Studies*, Vol. 15, No.1, June, Calcutta.

Monkhouse, F. J. and H.R. Wilkinson (1964), *Maps and Diagrams*, University Paperbacks, Metheun, London.

Morrill, Richard L. (1964), "Expansion of the Urban Fringe: A Simulation Experiment" Papers and Proceedings, Regional Science Association, India.

Mukherjee, A.B. (1985), "Regional Contrasts in Distribution, Density and Relative Strength of Scheduled Caste Population in Andhra Pradesh", *Contribution to Indian Geography*, Vol. 6, edited by Sundaram and Nangia.

Mukherjee, D, V.S. Phadke and K. Sita (1983), "A Comparative Study of Settlements in the Metropolitan Regions of the Three Port Cities of India", *The Geographical Review of India, Geographical Society of India*, Vol. 45, Dec.

Mukherjee, K.N. (1969), "Nature and Problems of New Reclamation in the Sundarbans", *Geographical Review of India*, G.S,I., Calcutta, Vol. 31, No.2.

——, (1983), "History of Settlement In The Sundarban of West Bengal", *Indian Journal of Landscape Systems and Ecological Studies*, Vol. 6, Nos. 1 & 2, Jan.-Dec.

—————, (1976), "Harmonious Solution Of The Basic Problem of Sundarban Reclamation", *Geographical Review of India*, G.S.I.,Calcutta, Vol. 38, No.3.

Mukhopadhyay, Madhuri (1980), "Denisity of Population in West Bengal (1981), a Cartographic Approach", *Cartography for Development of Outlying States and Islands of India,* Part-1, NATMO, Monograph No. 10, Govt. of India.

Nag, Prithvish, (1990), *Population, Settlement And Development in Zambia*, Concept Publishing Company, New Delhi.

Nagabhushanam, N. (1986), "Identification of Central Places and Their Hinterlands", *Indian Journal of Landscape Systems and Ecological Studies*, Vol. 9, No. 11, December.

Nangia, Sudesh (1985), "A Demographic Profile of Metro Hinterlands in India", *Contribution to Indian Geography, Population Geography*, Vol. 6, edited by Sundaram & Nangia.

——, (1976), *Delhi Metropolitan Region, A Study in Settlement Geography*, K.B. Publications, New Delhi.

——, " Gradient Analysis In Delhi Metropolitan Region", *Analytical Geography*, Deptt. of Human Geography, Delhi School of Economics, University of Delhi, Vol. 71(Dec.) No.1.

Naskar, Kumudranjan and D.N. Guha Bakshi (1989), "Distribution of Mangroves in India and Assess Their Role in the Estuarine Eco Systems", *Applied Geography*, S.P. Chatterjee, Commemorative Volume, NATMO Monograph No. 9, Govt. of India.

Naskar, Kumudranjan and Apurba Ghosh (1989), "Mangrove Forests of Sundarban, Its Impact on Estuarine Fisheries", in *Coastal Zone Management of West Bengal*, Sea Explorer's Institute, Calcutta.

Naskar, Kumudranjan (1985), "Population Pressure in the Tidal Mangrove Swamps of Sundarbans in India: Its Causes and Problems", in *Population Mapping*, NATMO, Govt. of India.

Okafor, Francis. C. (1977), "Changing Pattern of Rural Settlement in Density Settled Region of Qgboland, Nigeria", *Geographical Review of India*, Geographical Society of India, Vol. 39, No: 2, June.

Oldham, R.D. (1917), "Structure of the Gangetic Plains", *Memoirs of the Geological Society of India*, Volume III, Part-1.

Pakrasi, Sraboni (1990), "Impact of Cyclonic Disaster On The Development of the Coastal Area of West Bengal", *Cartography for Development of Outlying States & Islands of India*, Part: II, NATMO. Monograph No. 10, Govt. of India.

Pathak, C.R. and R.K. Dhabai (1976), "Rural Settlement Structure of Mewar, Rajasthan", in *Geographic Dimensions of Rural Settlements* by Prof. R.L. Singh, Dr. Kashi N. Singh, Dr. Rana, P.B. Singh, National Geographic Society of India,BHU, Varanasi.

Paul, A.K. (1986), "Accumulation and Erosion in Coastal tracts of Balasore, Midnapur and 24-Parganas", *Indian Journal of Landscape Systems and Ecological Studies*, Vol. 9. No. 1, June.

Paul, Asish Kumar (1988), "Coastal Dune Sytems of the Sundarbans", *Geographical Review of India*, Vol. 5, No. 1, March, Geographical Society of India, Calcutta.

Paul, A.K., M.K. Bandyopadhyay and A.Chowdhury, "Morpho Ecological Variations in the Sundarban Mudflats", *Geographical Review of India*, Vol. 49, No. 1, March, Geographical Society of India, Calcutta

Paul, A.K. (1988), " Coastal Ecosystem and Its Conservation in West Bengal", *Indian Journal of Landscape Systems and Ecological Studies*, Vol. II, No. 2, December.

Phednekar, M.M. and K. Sita (1951 and 1971), "Spatial Patterns of Sex Ratio in South Konkan (Maharashtra)", *Contribution to Indian Geography, Popuation Geography*, Vol. 6, edited by Sundarban and Nangia.

Piow Zygmont (1966), "An Ecological Interpretation of Settlement Systems", *International Social Science Journal*, Vol. XVIII, No. 4.

Premi, M.K. and R.P. Tyagi (1985), "Distribution And Growth of Population in India", Population Geography, *Contribution to Indian Geography*, Vol. 6, edited by Sundaram and Nangia.

Ray, S. and Chitralekha Mondal (1989), "Flora, Fauna and Natural Resources of Mangroves Forest Region of Sundarbans (West Bengal)". *Applied Geography* S.P. Chatterjee Commenorative Volume, NATMO, Govt. of India.

Report on "Sundarban Survey", (1960) *Geographical Review of India*, Geographical Society of India, Calcutta. Vol. 22, No. 2. June.

Sadhu, M.K. Lily Saha (Mitra), Mahuya Pal Chowdhury, Gita Chattopadhyay, Kishor Kumar Patnaik (1989), *Possibilities of Growing Vegetables In Saline Soils*, Coastal Zone Management of West Bengal, Sea Explorers Institute, Calcutta.

Saha, Durgadas (1989), "Identification of Growth Centres by means of Hierarchy of Settlements As a Base for Developmental Planning : A Case Study", in *Applied Geography* by S.P. Chatterjee, Commemorative Volume, NATMO. Govt. of India.

Saha, Nirmal Kanti and Halder Kr. Samaresh, "Technology Adopter In Agriculture In Coastal West Bengal", in *Coastal Zone Management of West Bengal*, Sea Explorer's Institute, Calcutta.

Saigal, B.N. and Babu Lal (1989), "Physical and Biological Factors Affecting Fisheries In Estuarine and Coastal Ecosystems of West Bengal". *ibid.*

Sardar, Bishwanath (1990), "Planning Philosophy for the Development of Sundarbans", *Cartography For Development of Outlying States & Islands of India*, Part-1, NATMO, Monograph No. 10, Govt. of India.

Sarkar, Asish (1988), "Growth Size and Distribution of Urban Settlements in West Bengal", *Geographical Review of India*, Vol. 5, No. 1, March, Geographical Society of India, Calcutta.

Sen, A.K. and S. Chakraborty (1989), "Coastal Management: Balanced Landuse Planning For Sundarban Delta", *Coastal Zone Management of West Bengal*, Sea Explorer's Institute, Cal.

Sen, Aparajita (1992), "Mangrove Ecosystem in India (with special reference to the Sundarbans)" *The Observer* Vol. 32, A Student's Geographical Association Publication, University of Calcutta.

Sen, Gupta Anil (1989), "Agriculture in Coastal area of West Bengal'', *Coastal Zone Management of West Bengal*, Sea Explorer's Institute, Calcutta.

Sen Gupta, J.C. (1974), "Problems of Urbanisation in West Bengal", Conference on Urban Development: Problems & Issues, Indian Institute of Management Calcutta, Centre for Management of Urban System, September 27-28.

Sen Gupta R., C.S. Murty and P.M.A. Bhattathiri (1989), "Environmental Characteristics of the Ganga Estuary", in *Coastal Zone Management of West Bengal*, Sea Explorer's Institute, Calcutta.

Sen, J. and R. Bhattacharyya (1977), "A Study of Settlements along the Ajay Valley", *Geographical Review of India, Geographical Society of India*, Calcutta, Vol. 39, No. 2, June.

Sharma, B.L. (1990), "Rural Development: An Integrated Approach of Development,'' *Indian Journal of Regional Science*, Vol. XVII, No. 1, 1985.

Sharma H.N. and D.K. Singh (1971), "Nearest Neighbour Statistics As A Measure Of Spatial Relationship", Proceedings of Symposium of Quantitative Methods in Geography', National Committee for Geography, India.

Siddique, Giyasuddin and Arabinda Biswas (1989), "Resource Appraisal : Forests of West Bengal", in *Applied Geography* S.P. Chatterjee, Commemorative Volume, NATMO, Govt. of India.

Singh, B.B. (1976), "Spatial Organisation Of Settlement In Some North Indian Villages", *Geographic Dimensions of Rural Settlement* by Prof. R.L. Singh, Dr. Kashi N. Singh, Dr. Rana P.B. Singh, National Geographic Society of India, BHU, Varanasi.

Singh, D.K.B. Routray and S. Jena (1976), "Spatial Analysis of Rural Settlement Pattern In Orissa". *ibid.*

Singh, H.H., P. Nag and S.K. Singh (1976), "A Study of Settlement Distribution Indices In Rewa-Panna Plateau", *ibid.*

Singh, Jagadish (1988), "Upper Damodar Valley A Study in Settlement Geography", *Indian Journal of Landscape Systems and Ecological Studies*, Vol. 11, No. 1, June.

Singh, Jhujhar and R.P.S. Gosal (1986), "Density of Rural Population in An Indian Situation : A Contemporary Approach", *Population Geography*, Vol. VIII, Nos. 1 & 2, June-December.

Singh, Kailash Nath, Rana P.B. Singh and Dinesh Pratap Singh (1976), "Spatial Characteristics of Rural Settlements and Their Types In A Part Of Middle Ganga Valley", *Geographic Dimensions of Rural Settlements* by Prof. R.L. Singh, Dr. Kashi N. Singh, Dr. Rana P.B. Singh, National Geographic Society of India, BHU, Varanasi.

Singh, R.B. (1988), "Geography of Rural Development", *Geographical Review of India*, Vol. 50, No. 4, December. The Geographical Society of India, Calcutta.

Singh, R.L. (1955), "Evolution of Rural Settlement in Middle Ganga Valley", *The National Geographical Journal of India*, Vol. 1, Part - 5.

——, (1961), "Meaning, Objectives and Scope of Settlement Geography", *National Geographical Journal of India*, Vol. VII, Part-1.

——, (1971), "*India : A Regional Geography*" National Geographical Society of India, Varanasi.

Singh, R.N. and D.N. Singh (1990), "Rural Development in India: Problems, Strategies & Approaches", *National Geogaphical Society of India*, Varanasi.

Singh, R.Y. (1976), "Hierarchy of Rural Settlements and Identification of Locational Functional Gaps in Upper Charmanvati Basin", *Geographic Dimensions of Rural Settlements* by Prof. R.L. Singh, Dr. Kashi N. Singh, Dr. Rana P.B. Singh, National Geographic Society of India, BHU, Varanasi.

Sinha, U.P. (1985), *Planned Development of Resources in Developing Region: An Ecological and Geographical Analysis*, Inter India Publications, New Delhi.

Som, Pijush Kanti (1984), "*Problems of Human Settlement*", *Geographical Review of India*, Geographical Society of India, Calcutta. Vol. 46, No. 1, March.

Spate, O.H.K. and A. I.A Learmouth (1957), *India and Pakistan - A General & Regional Geography*. Methuen and Co. Ltd., (U.K.).

Stone, Kirk H. (1966), "Further Development of a Focus For The Geography Of Settlment", *The Professional Geographer*, Vol. 18, No. 4.

——, (1965), "The Development of a Focus For The Geography of Settlement":, *Economic Geography*, Vol. 41, No. 4.

Taylor, Griffith (1966), *Urban Geography : A Study of Site, Evolution, Pattern and Classification Of Villages, Towns And Cities*, Metheun & Co.Ltd., London.

Thompson, H.R. (1965), "Distribution of Population to Nearest Neighbour In a Population of Randomly Distributed Individuals",*Ecology* Vol. 37.

Tiwari, R.C. and N.U. Khan (1990), "Spatial Organisation of Rural Service Centres in Pratapgarh District", *National Geographer*, Vol. XIX. No. 2, December.

Trewartha, Glenn T. (1969), *A Geography of Population World Patterns*, John Coley and Sons, Inc., New York, London, Sydney, Toronto.

Venugopal, B. (1958), "Application of the Techniques of Near Neighbourhood Distance", Paper read at Symposium 18, Regional Planning in November, 1958 at Delhi.

Wadia, D.N. (1973), *Geography of India*, Tata McGraw Hill Publishing Company, New Delhi, pp. 370-371.

Wehrwein, George S. Harris, Mayer, and Clyde F. Kohn (1967), "The Urban Fringe", *Readings in Urban Geogrnphy*, edited by Mayer and Clyde F. Kohn, Central Book Dept., Allahabad.

Zelinsky, Wilbur (1968), *A Prologue to Population Geography*, Prentice Hall Inc., Englewood Cliffs, New Jersey.

——, (1962), Changes in The Geographical Pattern of Rural Population In The United States", *The Geographical Review*, G.S.I. Vol. 52, No. 4.

## GOVERNMENT PUBLICATIONS

*District Census Handbook*, Village and Town Directory', Series 23, Part XIII A, West Bengal, Census of India, 1981.

*District Census Handbook*, Village and Townwise Primary Census Abstract, Series 23, Part XIII B: West Bengal, Census of India, 1981.

Food and Agricultural Organisation of the U.N. (1976), Rural Settlments and Developing Countries, Trends and Issues From Selected Experiences In Improving Their Hamlet, A Contribution To The Habitat : U.N. Conference on Human Settlements held at Vancouver, Canada, May-June.

Mitra Asok (1951), Census of India, District Census Handbook, 24 Parganas, West Bengal, Govt. Press Alipore.

——, (1953), An Account Of Land Management In West Bengal, 1870-1890, Census of India 1951, West Bengal, Govt. Press, Alipur.

——, (1953), Tribes and Castes of West Bengal", Census, 1957, West Bengal, Govt. of West Bengal, Calcutta. p-18. Primary Census Abstract, General Population India Part -IIB,

(i), Census of India, 1981.

Project Report on Sundarban Development (SDB) (July 1979),

Sundarban Development Board and Working Group, Govt. of West Bengal in Collaboration with Central Project Preparation and Monitoring Cell, Ministry of Agriculture and Irrigation, Govt. of India.

Regional Division of India - *A Cartographic analysis*, Series 1, Vol. XXIII, West Bengal, Census of India 1981.

Ray B.K., Vijay S. Verma (1989), *Regional Divisions of India, A Cartographic Analysis*, Series Vol. XXII, West Bengal, Census of India.

Statistical Abstract, West Bengal 1976 and 1977 (combined), New Series 2 & 3, *Bureau of Applied Economics and Statistics*, Govt. of West Bengal.

Urban Growth of India 1951-81, A Statistical Analysis, Census Monograph No. 1, Census of India, 1981.

## TOPOGRAPHICAL SHEETS

| | |
|---|---|
| West Bengal (24-Parganas) | 79 B/7 |
| West Bengal (Mekdinipur and 24-Parganas) | 79 C/1 |
| West Bengal (24-Parganas) | 79 C/6 |
| West Bengal (24-Parganas) | 79 C/10 |
| West Bengal (24-Parganas) | 79 C/9 |
| West Bengal (24-Parganas) | 79 B/10 |
| West Bengal (Haora 24-Parganas) | 79 B/3 |
| West Bengal (Medinipur, Haora, 24-Parganas) | 79 B/4 |
| West Bengal (24-Parganas) | 79 B/8 |
| West Bengal (24-Parganas) | 79 B/12 |
| West Bengal (24-Parganas) | 79 B/16 |
| West Bengal (24-Parganas) | 79 B/11 |

| | |
|---|---|
| West Bengal (Haora, Hugli, 24-Parganas, Calcutta Presidency Town) | 79 B/16 |
| West Bengal (24-Parganas) | 79 C/13 |
| West Bengal (Hugli, Haora,24 Parganas) | 79 B/2 |
| West Bengal (24-Parganas) | 79 C/14 |
| Bangladesh, West Bengal, Khulna, 24-Parganas. | 79 C/1 |
| West Bengal (24-Parganas) | 79 C/5 |

# Index